TIBCO Spotfire: A Comprehensive Primer
Second Edition

Building enterprise-grade data analytics and visualization solutions

Andrew Berridge
Michael Phillips

BIRMINGHAM - MUMBAI

TIBCO Spotfire: A Comprehensive Primer
Second Edition

Commissioning Editor: Amey Varangaonkar
Acquisition Editor: Meeta Rajani
Content Development Editor: Princia Dsouza
Technical Editor: Sayali Thanekar
Copy Editor: Safis Editing
Project Coordinator: Nusaiba Ansari
Proofreader: Safis Editing
Indexer: Manju Arasan
Graphics: Jisha Chirayil
Production Coordinator: Arvindkumar Gupta

First published: February 2015
Second edition: April 2019

Production reference: 1300419

Published by Packt Publishing Ltd.
Livery Place
35 Livery Street
Birmingham
B3 2PB, UK.

ISBN 978-1-78712-132-4

www.packtpub.com

To my wife, Jenna, and my three children for their undying love and their support for my career.
To my father, John, for teaching me so many life lessons and being the inspiration for my career.
To my managers at TIBCO for enabling and encouraging me to write this book.

To Michael Phillips—the author of the first edition of this book, thank you for letting me carry the torch in this edition!

– Andrew Berridge

mapt.io

Mapt is an online digital library that gives you full access to over 5,000 books and videos, as well as industry leading tools to help you plan your personal development and advance your career. For more information, please visit our website.

Why subscribe?

- Spend less time learning and more time coding with practical eBooks and Videos from over 4,000 industry professionals

- Improve your learning with Skill Plans built especially for you

- Get a free eBook or video every month

- Mapt is fully searchable

- Copy and paste, print, and bookmark content

Packt.com

Did you know that Packt offers eBook versions of every book published, with PDF and ePub files available? You can upgrade to the eBook version at www.packt.com and as a print book customer, you are entitled to a discount on the eBook copy. Get in touch with us at customercare@packtpub.com for more details.

At www.packt.com, you can also read a collection of free technical articles, sign up for a range of free newsletters, and receive exclusive discounts and offers on Packt books and eBooks.

Contributors

About the authors

Andrew Berridge is a data scientist at TIBCO Software Ltd. He has 10 years' experience with TIBCO Spotfire—first as an end user and latterly (for nearly 8 years) as a TIBCO employee. He is a world-renowned Spotfire expert and has assisted with selling Spotfire and implementing it for many customers. He has also developed parts of the latest versions of Spotfire, being on the team that implemented the AI-Driven Recommendations feature in Spotfire X. Prior to his role at TIBCO, Andrew was an internal consultant at one of the world's largest pharmaceutical companies.

In his spare time, Andrew restores classic cars. He is also an orchestral horn player. He is dedicated to his family and enjoys spending time with his wife and children.

*Andrew would like to thank **Peter Shaw**, PhD., staff data scientist at TIBCO Software for additionally reviewing Chapter 9. He would also like to thank **Thomas Blomberg**, product manager at TIBCO Software for reviewing Chapter 10.*
Andrew is very grateful to Michael Phillips, who was the original author of the first edition of this book. He acknowledges the amazing contribution and the legacy of the first edition and thanks Michael for handing the project over to him and for his advice and council during the authoring process.

Michael Phillips is the original author of the first edition of *TIBCO Spotfire: A Comprehensive Primer*. He is an eClinical product innovator specializing in informatics solutions that support the drug development process generally, and clinical risk management in particular. He is a creative analyst with over 14 years' experience in IT and business intelligence and 5 years' experience in clinical informatics. He has a background in medicine and general science publishing, and a PhD in biochemistry (drug metabolism).

About the reviewer

Colin Gray has worked in industries such as pharmaceuticals, environmental, and IT, and has over 15 years of experience in data analysis and informatics. Throughout this time, he has led data analysis and informatics projects, has worked on developing methods to make better use of data, and has had a key focus on how to communicate data better to others. To this aim, he has heavily employed web-based technologies and statistical packages. Having worked with TIBCO Spotfire for many years, he is a keen enthusiast in using Spotfire to further data science in all areas of business.

Packt is searching for authors like you

If you're interested in becoming an author for Packt, please visit `authors.packtpub.com` and apply today. We have worked with thousands of developers and tech professionals, just like you, to help them share their insight with the global tech community. You can make a general application, apply for a specific hot topic that we are recruiting an author for, or submit your own idea.

Table of Contents

Preface

*Welcome to TIBCO Spotfire: A Comprehensive Primer—Second Edition—*Building enterprise-grade data analytics and visualization solutions. This book will introduce you to Spotfire and how to build analysis and visualization solutions using Spotfire. You'll learn how to determine what is going on in your data and then how to drill into it to determine why something is happening! You'll find out how to get to data-driven insights fast, with the help of real-world examples and visualizations. The book doesn't just cover the basics—if you're a seasoned user of Spotfire, there are many advanced topics that will extend and enhance your knowledge.

Who this book is for

This book is for those who wish to learn about how to use Spotfire and how to work with analytics in general. It is also for those who would like to evaluate Spotfire to help determine whether it's suitable for their own or their organization's analytics needs. Finally, advanced users will benefit from reading the book—there are many topics, technical hints, and tips that experienced Spotfire users will find very useful. You don't need any prior experience of Spotfire or analytics to get the best out of the book, although some background in how to work with data will be helpful.

What this book covers

Chapter 1, *Welcome to Spotfire*, introduces Spotfire, showing the different Spotfire clients and how to get started with them. It jumps right into analytics with a real-world example of analyzing data from the Titanic disaster.

Chapter 2, *It's All About the Data*, covers how to work with data in Spotfire by way of building a scatter plot showing world population growth. Along the way, the chapter discusses how to build detailed visualizations to gain additional insights.

Chapter 3, *Impactful Dashboards!*, shows how to construct attention-grabbing dashboards using KPI charts.

Chapter 4, *Sharing Insights and Collaborating with Others*, discusses how to share insights with others and how to use Spotfire's collaboration features.

Chapter 5, *Practical Applications of Spotfire Visualizations*, is a tour through some of the most frequently used visualizations in Spotfire's toolbox. It gives useful hints and tips as to how to use visualizations to their best effect and details common pitfalls to avoid.

Chapter 6, *The Big Wide World of Spotfire*, introduces the Spotfire platform. It covers scaling in brief and shows some of Spotfire's administration tools. It also introduces Automation Services.

Chapter 7, *Source Data is Never Enough*, covers data manipulation in Spotfire—creating calculated columns, working with custom expressions, and transforming data.

Chapter 8, *The World is Your Visualization*, rounds off what has been learned so far. It covers data relationships, adding smoothing and forecasting lines, error bars, and working with Spotfire's subsets and show/hide features. It finishes off by covering the final two visualization types that haven't yet been discussed.

Chapter 9, *What's Your Location?*, covers map charts and geo-analytics in Spotfire. It also introduces the concept of data functions and TIBCO Enterprise Runtime for R.

Chapter 10, *Information Links and Data Connectors*, shows you how to work with information links and data connectors in Spotfire. These features are important if you're working with anything other than flat files. In-database versus in-memory data is discussed, along with all the tools you'll need to work with both. The chapter also covers streaming (live) data.

Chapter 11, *Scripting, Advanced Analytics, and Extensions*, introduces how to work with IronPython and JavaScript in Spotfire. It covers how to work with the many and varied data science platforms that integrate with Spotfire and explains how to get started with developing custom extensions.

Chapter 12, *Scaling the Infrastructure; Keeping Data up to Date*, is designed primarily for Spotfire administrators. It shows how to scale up the Spotfire infrastructure to support as many users as you need. It also details the various mechanisms for keeping data in Spotfire files up to date, showcasing schedules and rules.

Chapter 13, *Beyond the Horizon*, covers searching in Spotfire, styling and theming, exporting, conditional alerting, JavaScript visualizations, and some additional products that work nicely with Spotfire.

To get the most out of this book

You can follow a large number of the examples in this book by just using a web browser, since you can sign up for a trial account for TIBCO Cloud Spotfire and use Spotfire in the cloud. However, the more in-depth examples require you to use Spotfire Analyst (more on this in Chapter 1, *Welcome to Spotfire*). You can download a version of Spotfire Analyst once you have signed up for a Cloud account. You'll need a reasonably modern PC running Microsoft Windows 7 or later. It should be a 64-bit computer system, as 32-bit systems are only suitable for analyzing small datasets or working with in-database analytics.

You can use Spotfire on a Mac computer too, but the Mac client isn't as fully-featured as the PC-based clients.

This book is specifically targeted toward Spotfire version 10.0.0 and later. You can still take advantage of the book, even if you're using Spotfire version 7, but just be aware that the menu selections won't correspond exactly, and some new functionality was released with Spotfire X (Spotfire 10) that wasn't available in previous versions. Specifically, AI-driven recommendations, natural language search, and streaming data are all new to Spotfire X.

If you're a new user to Spotfire, I recommend you start at the beginning of the book and work your way through it, sequentially, to Chapter 4, *Sharing Insights and Collaborating with Others*, or Chapter 5, *Practical Applications of Spotfire Visualizations*. Then, you should dip in and out of the rest of the book as you see fit. Chapter 10, *Information Links and Data Connectors*, is a must-read for when you want to connect Spotfire up to any data source other than flat files. Chapter 9, *What's your Location?*, is essential reading if you want to perform any kind of geoanalytics or other location-based analytics. Chapter 13, *Beyond the Horizon*, covers several interesting topics, from theming, through to export, search, and more.

A lot of the URLs provided in the book are quite long, so I used `https://bitly.com/` for link shortening (in most cases). `https://bitly.com/` does track how many clicks each of the links has received, but not who clicked them. Of course, you can always just use a search engine to find each of the references, but I have included the links so you know you're always looking at exactly the right topic on the web!

Although the author, Andrew Berridge, works for TIBCO Software Ltd., it must be stressed that any views or opinions expressed within the book are solely Andrew's. They are not sanctioned in any way by TIBCO Software Ltd. and do not represent the views or opinions of TIBCO Software. Any apparently forward-facing statements or opinions should not be used for purchasing decisions for Spotfire or any other TIBCO product.

All product names, trademarks, and registered trademarks are property of their respective owners. All company, product and service names used in this book are for identification purposes only. Use of these names and trademarks does not imply endorsement.

Download the color images

We also provide a PDF file that has color images of the screenshots/diagrams used in this book. You can download it here: `https://www.packtpub.com/sites/default/files/downloads/9781787121324_ColorImages.pdf`.

Conventions used

There are a number of text conventions used throughout this book.

`CodeInText`: Indicates code words in text, database table names, folder names, filenames, file extensions, pathnames, dummy URLs, user input, and Twitter handles. Here is an example: "Also, try changing the left-hand line chart to show `Avg(Volume)` rather than `Avg(Close)`."

A block of code is set as follows:

```
if (Document.Properties['SelectedMetrics'] ==
'Descriptions' ):
```

Bold: Indicates a new term, an important word, or words that you see onscreen. For example, words in menus or dialog boxes appear in the text like this. Here is an example: "Spotfire automatically recognizes that we have a zip-code column and so will load the **USA Zip Codes** geocoding table."

Warnings or important notes appear like this.

Tips and tricks appear like this.

Get in touch

Feedback from our readers is always welcome.

General feedback: If you have questions about any aspect of this book, mention the book title in the subject of your message and email us at customercare@packtpub.com.

Errata: Although we have taken every care to ensure the accuracy of our content, mistakes do happen. If you have found a mistake in this book, we would be grateful if you would report this to us. Please visit www.packt.com/submit-errata, selecting your book, clicking on the Errata Submission Form link, and entering the details.

Piracy: If you come across any illegal copies of our works in any form on the Internet, we would be grateful if you would provide us with the location address or website name. Please contact us at copyright@packt.com with a link to the material.

If you are interested in becoming an author: If there is a topic that you have expertise in and you are interested in either writing or contributing to a book, please visit authors.packtpub.com.

Reviews

Please leave a review. Once you have read and used this book, why not leave a review on the site that you purchased it from? Potential readers can then see and use your unbiased opinion to make purchase decisions, we at Packt can understand what you think about our products, and our authors can see your feedback on their book. Thank you!

For more information about Packt, please visit packt.com.

Section 1: Introducing Spotfire

The first section of this book is a general introduction to Spotfire—it shows how to load data and how to get started with Spotfire visualizations. Here, you will see how quick and easy it is to get started with producing insightful and impactful visualizations and how you can use Spotfire to collaborate with others.

In this section, the following chapters will be covered:

- Chapter 1, *Welcome to Spotfire*
- Chapter 2, *It's All About the Data*
- Chapter 3, *Impactful Dashboards!*
- Chapter 4, *Sharing Insights and Collaborating with Others*

Welcome to Spotfire 1

Welcome to the world of TIBCO Spotfire®! This book will take you on a journey through data discovery and visualization, advanced analysis, and beyond. It will show you how to get started really easily, then how to progress on to more advanced topics.

When you start Spotfire for the first time, your first task is to load some data. This data can be loaded from a wide variety of sources, from files through to database and big data repositories. It's then really easy to visualize and explore the data, gaining fresh insight and understanding all the time.

The following topics are covered in this chapter:

- Introduction to TIBCO Spotfire
- Getting started with TIBCO Spotfire
- The different Spotfire clients
- Importing and loading data into Spotfire
- The Spotfire recommendations engine
- Simple visualization types
- Building useful visualizations
- Details visualizations
- Introduction to marking and filtering
- Gaining insights from your data

Getting started with TIBCO Spotfire

In this section, we are going to explore loading and visualizing data using the Spotfire rich desktop client and the Spotfire web authoring clients.

There are a few different Spotfire client applications. As of Version X (pronounced 10), these are as follows:

1. Desktop clients (rich, installed):
   - **Spotfire Analyst**: This fully featured application connects to an on-premises Spotfire server that's installed at your organization and is sometimes called Spotfire professional.
   - **Spotfire Cloud Analyst**: A fully featured desktop application that connects to a cloud-based Spotfire server, you can download it from your Spotfire Cloud account if you have one.
   - **Spotfire for macOS**: This is a hybrid application—it's essentially a wrapper around the Spotfire web clients (detailed later), but it is installed on desktop machines.

2. Web clients (thin, accessible via a web browser):
   - **Spotfire Consumer**: This is a standard, read-only Spotfire web client, usually available on-premises. You can consume existing visualizations and data. You cannot create new visualizations, load data, or change the configuration of visualizations (unless explicitly enabled by the author of a Spotfire file).
   - **Spotfire Business Author**: This is an advanced web client. In addition to the features of consumer, it allows loading of data, configuration of visualizations, and many other Spotfire authoring capabilities. You can check if it's available to you by logging in to Spotfire web (Consumer) and checking if there's an option to edit or create an existing analysis—more on this later.
   - **TIBCO Cloud Spotfire**: This has all the features of Business Author and is accessible via `https://cloud.tibco.com/`. You can even sign up for a free trial account—I recommend you do this if you just want to explore Spotfire before you purchase it.

3. Mobile clients:
   - **Spotfire Analytics for iOS**: Provides Spotfire Consumer-type functionality for iPhone® and iPad® devices.
   - **Spotfire Analytics for Android**: Provides Spotfire Consumer-type functionality for Android phones and tablet computers.
   - **Important**: You cannot create new analyses or modify existing analysis files using the mobile clients.

Launching Spotfire Analyst

Spotfire Analyst is a rich desktop client and can be launched like any other Windows application. There are usually two shortcuts to Spotfire once it's installed. The first is as follows:

The other is as follows:

The first shortcut is the one you will use the most often. The **(show login dialog)** shortcut is useful if you've previously asked Spotfire to remember your server details and login information and you want to update these for any reason. By clicking on **Manage servers...**, you will be able to select which server to connect to (or, potentially, work offline, by selecting the corresponding option at the bottom-left of the page):

When you launch the Spotfire client, you will be presented with a home page that has shortcuts to various frequently used features, such as loading recently used analyses, loading recently used data, or looking at sample Spotfire files. This is the **Files and Data...** view, which can be shown or hidden by pressing the + sign on the top-left of the page. This page is the starting point for connecting to data and analyses, whether this be on the local system or in the Spotfire library:

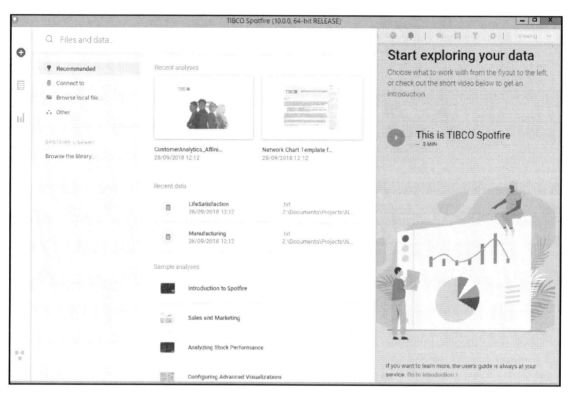

Feel free to explore some of the sample analysis files. I hope they inspire you to see what you can do with visualizations in Spotfire. Of course, you can always use the search box—it's really useful for finding files or connections to databases, and so on.

If you're interested, view the sample video! The link opens a YouTube video—while you're there, there are lots of other Spotfire videos that you can browse. Many of them cover some advanced topics, but hopefully they will inspire you to learn more and you'll come back repeatedly as there is always new content being published.

Logging in to TIBCO Cloud Spotfire

Visit `https://cloud.tibco.com/` and sign up for an account, if you don't have one already. Once you have an account, you can log in the usual way:

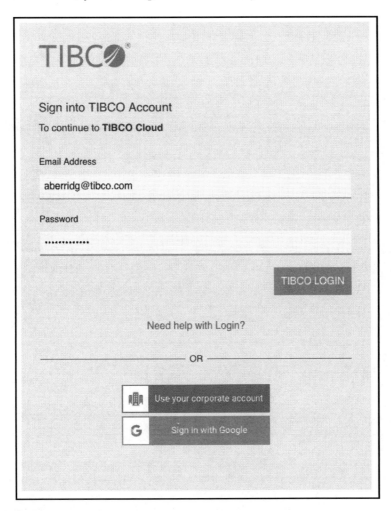

You will now be able to select which application(s) you would like to work with. In this case, choose **Analytics**:

Click **Spotfire**:

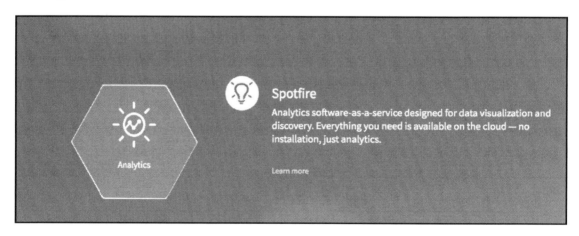

Spotfire will open and be shown to you. The web-based client looks very similar to the desktop (analyst) client, but has less functionality when it comes to building data workflows and various other authoring functions:

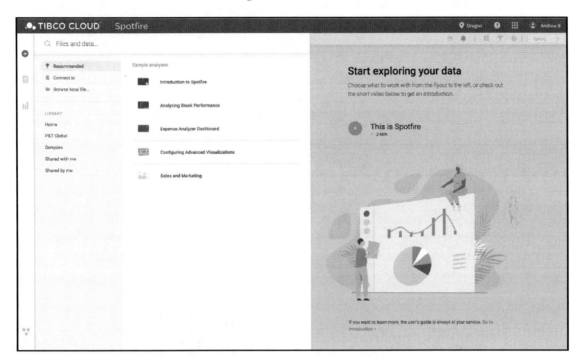

Downloading Spotfire Cloud Analyst

If you have a Spotfire Cloud account you can download Spotfire Cloud Analyst—this is a full-featured version of Spotfire that works on your desktop. I recommend that you download it as soon as you can—it's more powerful than the web-based clients, and some of the exercises in this book can only be performed using an analyst client.

To download and install Spotfire Cloud Analyst, follow these steps:

1. Make sure you're logged in to your TIBCO Cloud account and Spotfire has been launched (like we did previously).
2. Dismiss the left-hand panel by clicking anywhere on the right-hand side of the window.
3. You should be left with a blank Spotfire screen—from the **File** menu, choose **View library**:

Hint: If the menu bar is not visible, click the three vertical dots in order to expand it!

4. Click **Downloads** under **Resources**:

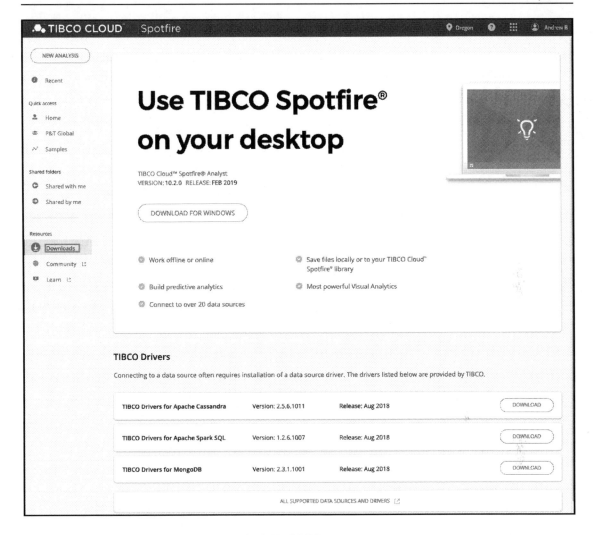

5. Click **DOWNLOAD FOR WINDOWS**.
6. Once the download has finished, install the application as you would do so with any other Windows application.

Installing the mobile apps and logging in to TIBCO Cloud

The Spotfire Analytics app is available for Android and iOS phones and tablets from the Google Play Store and the iTunes App Store, respectively.

Just search for Spotfire Analytics and install the app!

I have an Android phone, so I am going to use that to demonstrate this functionality. iOS is broadly similar.

Once you have opened the app, you should get something that looks a bit like this:

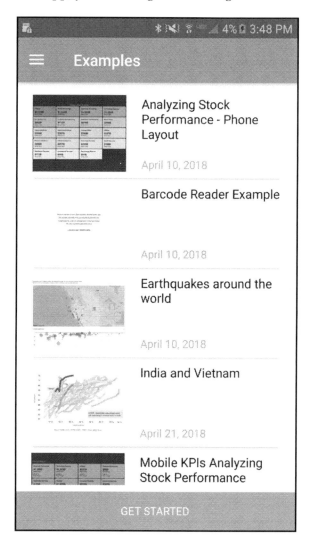

You can start off by looking at some of the examples—in fact, it's a great way to get started without even needing to log in anywhere!

However, let's get started by logging in to a Cloud account:

1. Tap the **Get Started** button.
2. Tap the **TIBCO Cloud** button (or **Sign up here** if you don't have an account yet):

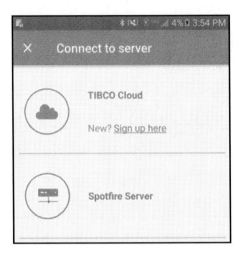

3. Log in to your TIBCO Cloud account:

4. Once you have logged in, you should be able to see Spotfire's library browser. This is what I get:

5. Feel free to browse the existing analyses. It's important to remember that you cannot create new analysis files or edit existing ones using the mobile apps.

You can also log in to your on-site Spotfire server if you have the requisite login and permissions (and potentially VPN access).

TIBCO Spotfire for macOS

As we mentioned previously, this is a lightweight wrapper around Spotfire's web clients, so you will need access to a Spotfire web server. This can either be in the cloud or on-premises.

Install Spotfire for macOS by searching for it on the App store. Once the application is installed, the following window is shown:

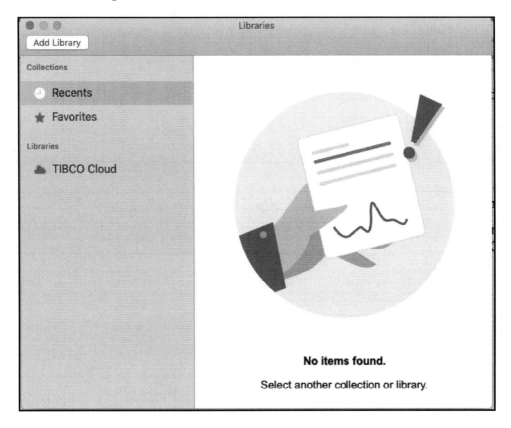

You can sign into your organization's Spotfire web server by clicking **Add Library** or log in to your Cloud account by clicking on **TIBCO Cloud**. In my case, I have logged in to my TIBCO Cloud account. If I select **Samples**, this is what I see:

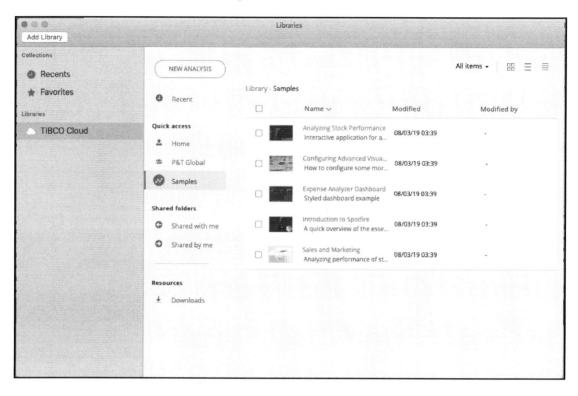

Logging in to the Spotfire web clients (on-premises)

Logging in to the Spotfire web clients is straightforward. Just navigate to the URL provided by your server administrator. Once you are logged in, you will be presented with a blank Spotfire client, a view of the Spotfire library, or with a blank analysis, depending on your access levels.

If you are using Spotfire Consumer, the ability to create a new analysis will not be available to you. You'll need to get access to Spotfire Business Author or one of the analyst clients (for example, Cloud Analyst) in order to be able to author Spotfire analyses, as per most of the examples in this book.

Spotfire licenses

Before we get started with loading data and doing some analysis, I'd just like to briefly cover the very important topic of Spotfire licenses. Spotfire licenses are not software licenses in the normal sense (where you have to buy a license in order to use the software). You can think of Spotfire licenses as permissions to perform certain functions in the application. Almost every function in Spotfire has an associated license. Licenses are assigned via user groups. Assigning licenses is an administrative function and, as such, will be controlled via your Spotfire administrator.

A TIBCO Cloud account will probably have the most licenses assigned to it, so you should be able to do most things with Cloud Analyst or the web (business) author.

However, if you struggle to follow along with the examples in this book—the options don't seem to be there, or you just can't even get started–it's possible that you don't have the required license(s) to perform the functions that are suggested. Please contact your Spotfire administrator to get this fixed.

 To emphasise: Licenses grant permissions to perform functions in TIBCO Spotfire. If you don't seem to be able to do what you want or cannot even get started, please contact your Spotfire administrator!

Getting started with loading data

The simplest way to get started with loading data into Spotfire is to import some data from a file such as an Excel spreadsheet, so that's what this tutorial will cover.

 Important! Before you start, you must be in **Editing** mode. I will periodically remind you of this throughout this book. The analyst client defaults to **Editing** mode—other clients, such as the web client, may not. So, beware!

To switch to **Editing** mode, follow these steps:

1. In the top right-hand corner of the application, click the dropdown.
2. Choose **Editing**:

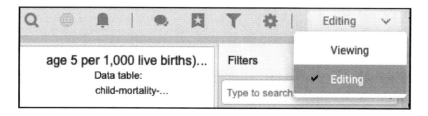

3. If **Editing** mode is not available to you, it means that you do not have the correct permissions (license) for editing, or that the Spotfire client itself does not support it (for example, the Android or IOS clients).

Importing Excel spreadsheets into Spotfire

The procedures for importing **comma-separated values** (**CSV**) files or Microsoft Excel spreadsheets in Spotfire are essentially identical:

1. From the Spotfire home page (shown initially when launching the Analyst or web clients), select **Browse local file...**:

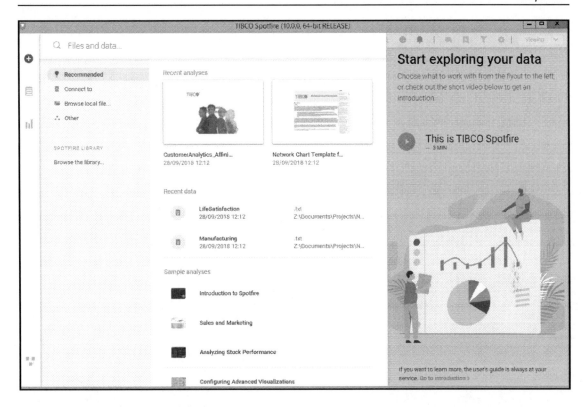

2. You will be presented with a standard **Open File** dialog, allowing you to navigate to the file that you want to load. For this example, let's use some publicly available data on the Titanic disaster—it can be downloaded from the following link:
   `http://biostat.mc.vanderbilt.edu/wiki/pub/Main/DataSets/titanic3.xls`
   or: `http://bit.ly/2HStQ7R`.

3. In the Analyst client, Spotfire will open a dialog, which will allow you to define the import settings:

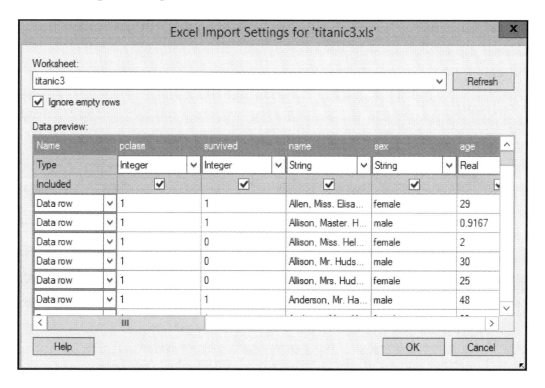

4. The first thing to notice is the **Worksheet** selection dropdown at the very top of the dialog window. Spotfire can only import one worksheet at a time. There is only one sheet in our file, so we don't need to do anything with this option.

5. The next thing to notice is the preview of the data and its structure. Spotfire will automatically detect and assign column headers and data types, but you can change any of these settings. You can also tell Spotfire not to import specific columns or rows.

6. We want to open the file with all defaults, so we're just going to click **OK**, but please do explore the drop-down options for columns and rows and experiment with the settings. The core philosophy of Spotfire is discovery, so start as you mean to continue and explore some of the options.

7. Once you click **OK**, Spotfire will show the **Add data to analysis** display:

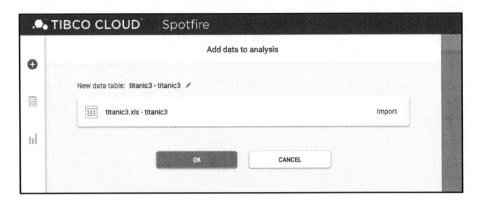

8. Click **OK** to load the data.

Introduction to the data panel

You'll find that a lot of work is done in Spotfire via the data panel. You can show the data panel by clicking on the big icon in the middle of the Spotfire window, or by pulling it out by clicking on the data icon on the left-hand side of Spotfire:

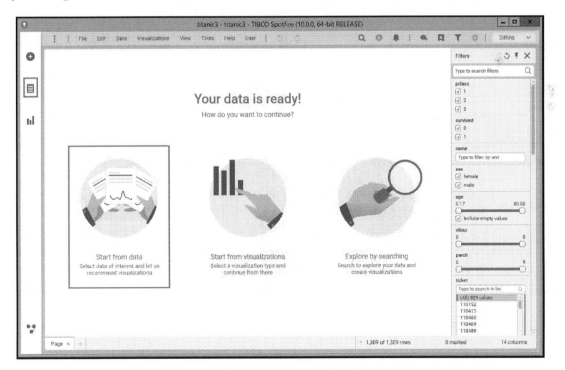

The data panel shows all the data tables and columns that are available in the analysis. Spotfire has already classified the columns into different groups of numerical and categorical columns:

In this particular dataset, some categorical columns have been loaded as numeric columns. It's not Spotfire's fault—it's just that some of the data columns are integers in the data, and represent categories. Think of the column called **survived**. This is a 1 or 0, indicating whether the passenger, died or survived. Similarly, passenger class (**pclass**), the class of passenger should be categorical since it is either 1, 2, or 3, and taking any kind of aggregation of this (average, max, and so on) probably doesn't make much sense. You can read more about the dataset and its data dictionary here:

`http://biostat.mc.vanderbilt.edu/wiki/pub/Main/DataSets/titanic3info.txt`

Or:

`http://bit.ly/2uDg6oX`

Next, we are going to use Spotfire's recommendations engine to build a visualization, but in order to get the best results from it, it can sometimes be a good idea to change the categorization of columns in order to give Spotfire some hints about how to display or analyse the data. So, let's do this first:

1. Right-click the **pclass** column and change its categorization to **Categories**:

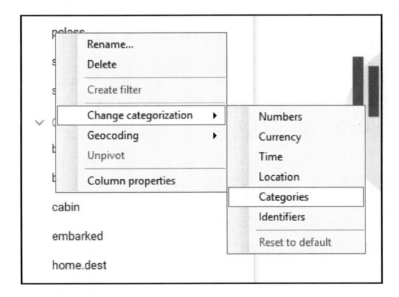

2. Do the same with the **survived** column.
3. Now, we can get started with building visualizations!

The Spotfire recommendations engine

The recommendations engine gives you instant insight into your data and some suggestions of which visualizations to use. Spotfire's analyst clients have an advanced feature called **AI-Powered Suggestions**. This is Spotfire's new way of helping make sense of any type of data, regardless of its size or shape. The basic premise is that you should select a "target" column in the data panel and Spotfire will do the rest. Spotfire runs a specialized algorithm over all the columns in the data and selects those that most strongly drive or influence the target. Those columns are called "predictors." It then produces suggested visualizations for the target and selected predictors.

The recommender is available in the web clients too, but (at the time of writing) the web clients do not have the AI element, where predictor columns are automatically selected. I hope that the feature will be made available at some point. In the meantime, if you're using the web clients, you can follow a slightly different path to create visualizations. I'll point out how to do that along the way.

Let's get started! In the case of the Titanic data, the most obvious target column is **survived**. In other words, we'd like to know which columns best predict, influence, or explain whether passengers survived the Titanic disaster or not:

1. In the data panel, select the **survived** column. In analyst clients, Spotfire will produce something that looks like this:

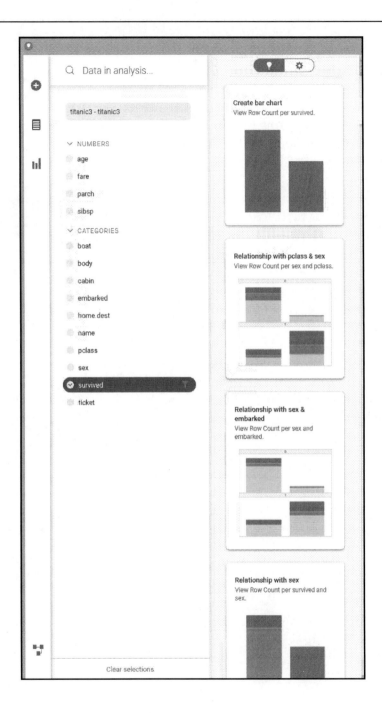

Interesting! Immediately, we can see that the strongest predictors of survival are **pclass** and **sex**. The very first visualization is always just the row count of each of the values in the target column, so the second visualization is the one that begins to explain the target.

2. To add the visualization to your analysis, just click on the visualization that shows the relationship with **pclass** and **sex**. Your Spotfire session should now look something like the following screenshot:

3. You can produce the same effect in Spotfire web clients by selecting the **survived** column, the **pclass** column, and the **sex** column. Hold down the *Ctrl* key while clicking to select multiple columns:

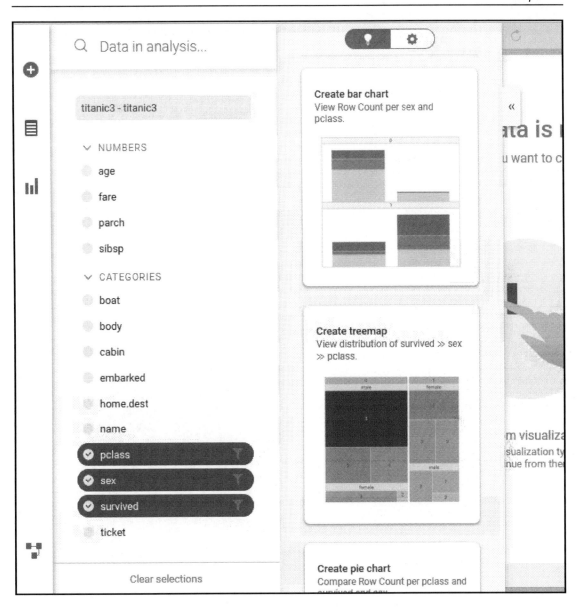

4. I think it's also interesting to explore the male/female ratio on board the Titanic, so we need to add a bar chart visualization that shows just **survived** and **sex**. The AI recommender will choose these columns—just scroll down the panel a bit to find the visualization that shows this relationship, or manually select the columns in the web clients, then click the visualization to add it to your analysis. Now, let's pause and look at what we've created. In a few clicks, we have loaded some data and created two visualizations that really explains a lot of findings (insights) all in one go! Here is the analysis without the data panel (collapse it by clicking the double arrow toward the top-right corner of the panel):

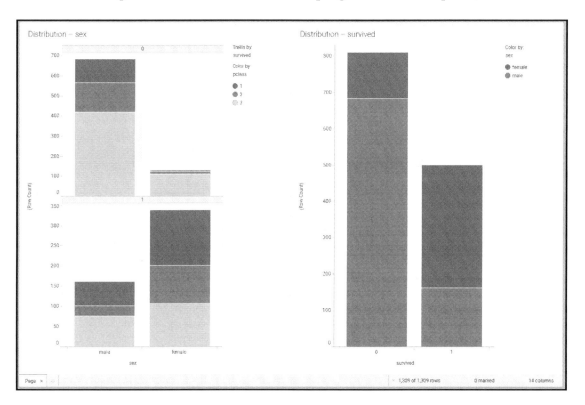

Here are my notes on interpreting these visualizations. Of course, what I say is only a matter of opinion, so feel free to draw your own conclusions:

1. Notice how many more men there were on board than women?
2. Look at how many more men died than survived! The survival rate of women was much higher—this would be borne by the "women and children first" policy of filling the lifeboats.

3. Look at the left-hand visualization. It is trellised by **survived**—this means that Spotfire has split it into panels, one for each data value.

4. First-class female passengers had the greatest chance of survival—suggesting that class and socioeconomic factors played a role in the survival rates.

5. More third-class males survived than first- or second-class ones. Might they have had stronger fighting instincts or been pushier? Were they more willing to cram into overcrowded lifeboats? All are potential explanations.

Saving Spotfire files

It's a good idea to get into the habit of saving your Spotfire analysis files. There's no auto-save capability at the time of writing, so save regularly!

Saving a file in analyst clients

When saving a file in Spotire Analyst, you have a lot more options than in web-clients. Here's how to save a file in Spotfire Analyst, with a couple of tips along the way:

1. You'll notice that when you save the file (**File** | **Save as** | **File**) for the first time, Spotfire will show this prompt:

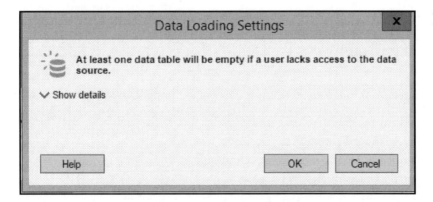

2. This is an important dialog to discuss. If you want to share your Spotfire file with another user, they will not be able to view it if they don't have access to the original data file. We can fix this now.

3. Click **Show details**. You'll see a dialog that allows you to choose what happens with the data. In this case, it's most appropriate to select **New data when possible**. This means that Spotfire will load new data if it's available (for example, if you updated the original Titanic data file), otherwise it will use data stored (embedded) in the Spotfire file:

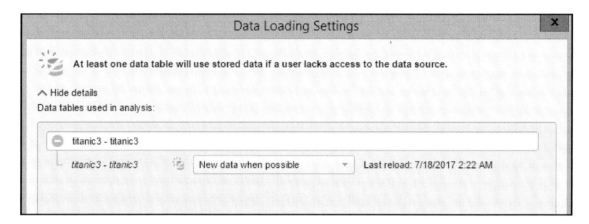

Saving a file in Spotfire Cloud or Business Author

Saving a file in Spotfire Cloud or Business Author is really straightforward. Saving a file will save it into the Spotfire library, where you and others can access the file (if folder permissions are set correctly—there is more on this later in this book):

1. Click the **Save** menu at the top of the screen and select **Save As | Library item...**:

2. The Spotfire web client will prompt you to choose the destination folder in the Spotfire library:

3. You can create a new folder using the + icon if you want.
4. Name the file as you see fit. Spotfire won't prompt you for the data saving settings (as it did in the analyst client) because the data is always embedded in the analysis.
5. When you're finished, click **Save**.

Producing a useful interactive dashboard

Now that we have produced some visualizations from the data, let's turn them into a useful interactive dashboard that we can use to gain more insight from the data.

Coloring

In our example, the right-hand bar chart is colored by **sex**. The colors assigned by Spotfire are not immediately indicative of the sex of a Titanic passenger, so let's fix that:

1. Locate the legend for the bar chart.
2. Click on the dot for the **female** data and choose a more appropriate color. I suggest a pale pink or similar:

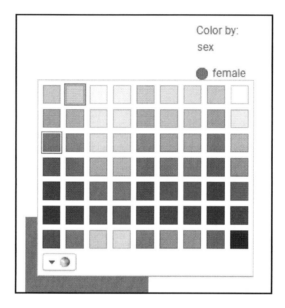

3. Do the same for male—click on the dot and choose a color suitable for **male**—I suggest a pale blue. For those viewing this in black and white, I apologize—you'll have to take my word for it...

Proportionality with bar charts and pie charts

It's all very well looking at the absolute numbers of female and male survivors, but this doesn't tell us the relative proportion of female and male passengers that survived.

Let's compare the use of bar charts and pie charts:

1. Open the data panel again by clicking the **Data** button on the left-hand side of the Spotfire window.
2. If the recommendations panel isn't shown, click the double arrow (>>) to display it. Now let's select the **sex** column as the target and scroll to see the relationship between **sex** and **survived** (analyst client). Choose the bar chart and add it to the analysis:

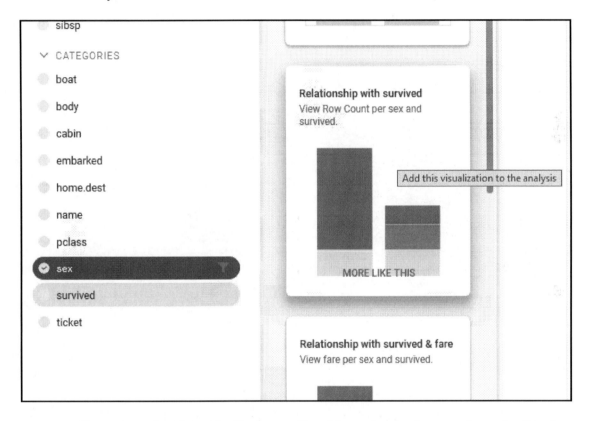

If you are using the web clients, you'll need to select both **sex** and **survived** and click **MORE LIKE THIS** on the bar chart for **survived** and **sex** to get to the bar chart for **sex** and **survived**. Note that the order is important here, as it determines which column goes on each axis of the bar chart. We need the **sex** column to be on the *x* (categorical) axis.

3. Now, apply some coloring to the resultant bar chart to indicate that surviving is good and not surviving is bad! You should end up with something that looks roughly like this:

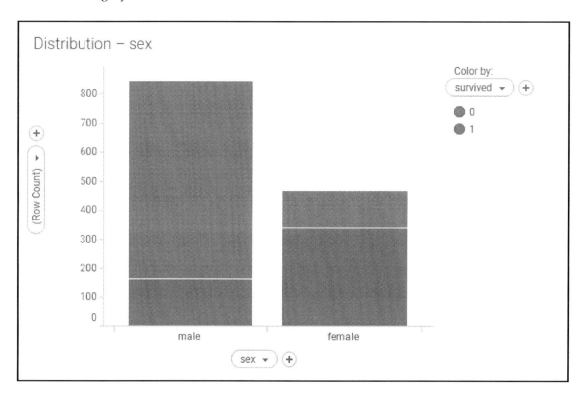

4. That visual tells us the exact numbers of males and females that survived. How about proportionality? Right-click the visual and select **100% Stacked Bars** (or in web clients, right-click to get access to the visualization **Properties** dialog and change the setting there):

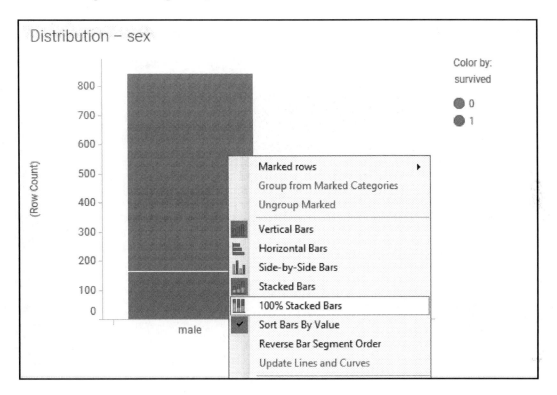

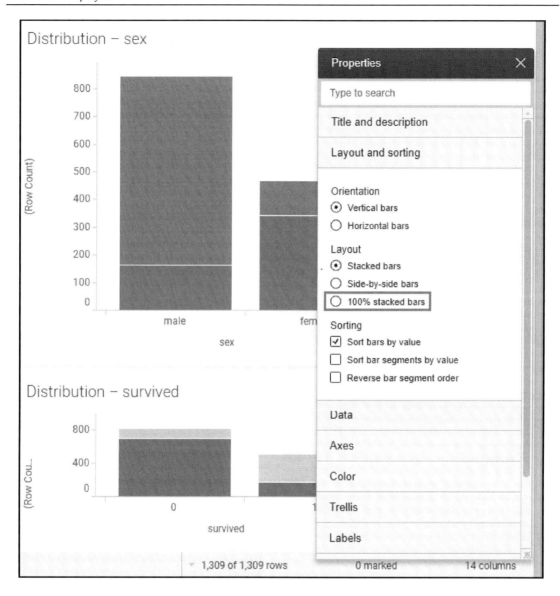

5. Let's return to the data panel once more in order to add a pie chart by showing the data panel and finding a pie chart that shows the same. In analyst clients, click **MORE LIKE THIS** to get to other representations of the relationship between **sex** and **survived**. In web clients, make sure **sex** and **survived** are selected in the data panel:

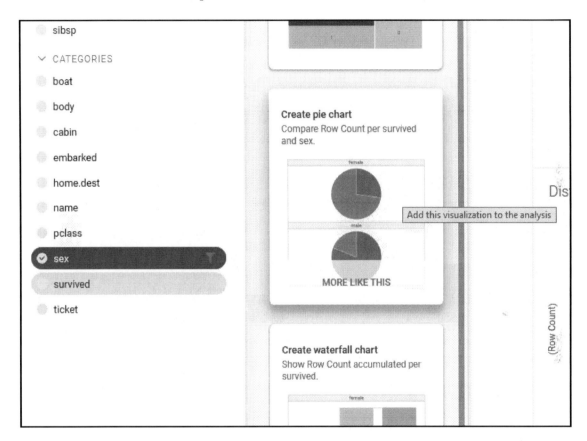

6. Color the pie chart using the same color scheme as the last bar chart—doing that ties the visualizations nicely and visually.

7. Your analysis should now look something like this. I have moved my visualizations around a bit by dragging their title bars:

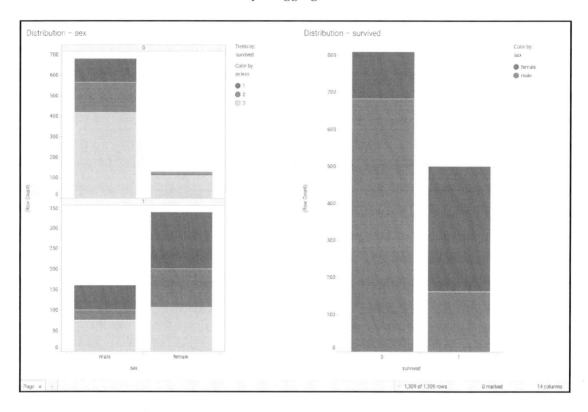

 A quick note on pie charts. There's a long-standing joke in the analytics community that the world's most accurate pie chart is this one:

The truth of the matter is that pie charts are not a good way of representing many categories of information—the human brain cannot easily interpret the chart if many slices of the pie are shown. The brain cannot distinguish between the different amounts of the area of the circle. So, in general, I would discourage you from using pie charts, or at least to think very carefully before doing so!

8. The bar chart tells us a lot more than the pie chart and is indicative of several dimensions of data. You can see the total number of passengers of each sex and the proportion of each that survived at a glance.

9. Experiment with the settings of the bar chart by right-clicking on it and selecting the various options. For example:
    - Change the bars to horizontal, stacked bars (the default), 100% stacked bars (as we just did), or side-by-side bars
    - Change the **Sort bars by value** setting of the bar chart

Bar chart modes
There's no right or wrong way to represent the bars—each setting is useful in different circumstances.
Stacked bars are useful if you want to represent the absolute numbers and proportions, or have a large number of values on the categorical (x) axis.
100% is useful if you want to represent the proportions in a similar fashion to (but better than) pie charts.
Side-by-side gives a clearer view of the absolute numbers in each category of data.

Drilling in to the data – details visualizations

The visualizations we've explored so far allows us to understand **what** is happening—in our case, we've understood the proportions of male and female survivors. That's great, but what about drilling into the details of the data? Drilling in can help us explore **why** something is happening in the main dataset.

Spotfire makes it really easy to drill in to the data:

1. Right-click on any of the visualizations you created earlier and highlight **Create Details Visualization**. A second menu will pop up:

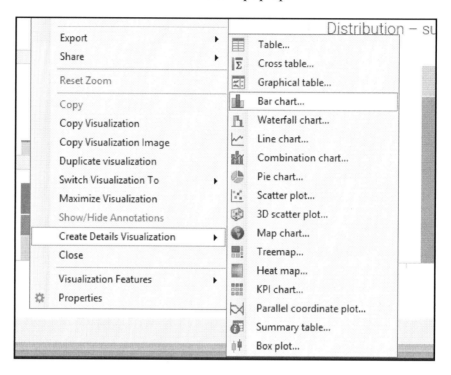

2. For the purposes of this exercise, let's use a bar chart (again!), so click **Bar chart...**. Bar charts are some of the most often used visualizations in Spotfire as they can represent data in so many different ways. I find them to be very useful!

3. Spotfire will create an auto-configured visualization that in itself isn't useful. It's also empty:

4. Never fear—we can fix both these issues with a few clicks! Note that a new item has been added to the legend **Data limiting: Marking**. This means that, by default, no data will be shown on the visualization unless some data is marked in another visualization. In order to show some data, hover the mouse over some data in another visualization, click and drag it to create a rectangle, and select some data:

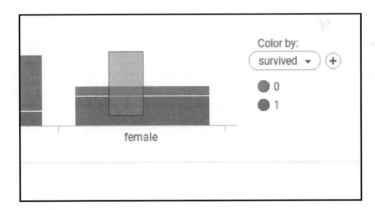

5. The details bar chart will now update to show the selected data. It's still not terribly useful as it's currently just showing the same as the original visualization chart. To configure the *x*-axis (the bottom one), hover over the visualization, then click the down arrow on the *x*-axis selector (it appears when you hover over the visualization):

6. From the resultant dropdown, choose **age**. That's more like it!

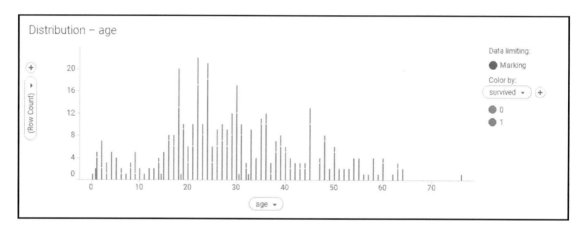

7. However, it's not yet quite as useful as it should be—notice that the overall shape of the graph is indicative of a distribution of the data (move on to see more), but the tall bars are often interspersed with very short bars between them. This is an example of a real-world data issue that prevents us from visualizing the trend in the data properly. The cause is that some people have been recorded with fractional ages. Babies under one year old have ages recorded as a fraction of a year; there are also some adults recorded as being x.5 years old. Why? I don't know, but let's fix it!

8. If you're using an analyst client, right-click on the *x*-axis selector (showing **age**) and choose **Auto-bin Column**:

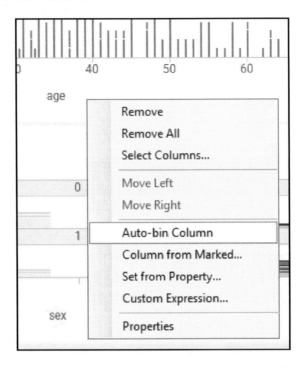

9. In a web-based client, follow these steps:
    1. Right-click on the *x*-axis column selector and choose **Custom Expression...**.
    2. Enter the following custom expression:

```
AutoBinNumeric([age],80)
```

10. You'll notice that the visualization will change to look more **blocky**. What's happening is that Spotfire is **binning** the data, or grouping close values together to reduce the number of categories on the *x*-axis. In analyst clients, you can slide the little slider up and down on the axis slider to change the number of bins (this affects the granularity of the *x*-axis), or you can edit the custom expression, just like we did on the web clients. I surmise that 80 bins is a good number because that gives one bin per year of age in our data:

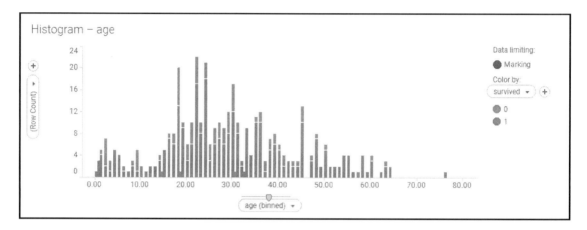

11. I have also rearranged the visualizations on the page slightly in order to give more room to this bar chart—you can do that by dragging the title bars of the visualizations and dragging the dividing lines between them.

12. Experiment with marking (selecting) different parts of the rest of the visualizations on the page in order to drill in to different parts of the data. Try selecting all male passengers, all female passengers, all females that survived, and so on.

13. As we described previously, the default behavior of a details visualization is for it to be empty if no data is marked elsewhere. That might not be what you want—you might want all data to be shown if nothing is selected. You can't change this behavior in the Spotfire web clients, but you can do it using Analyst. Right-click on the visualization and choose **Properties**, or click the cog wheel in the top right-hand corner of the visualization. The cog wheel isn't shown by default, so you'll need to hover over the corner of the visualization to make it visible.

14. Select the **Data** property page and open the setting under **If no items are marked in the master visualizations, show**:

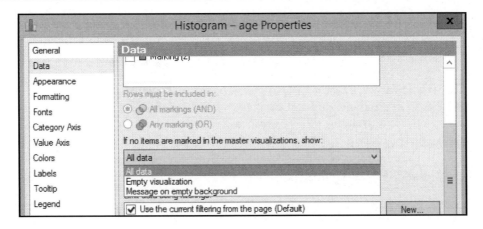

15. Change the setting to **All data**.
16. Now, if you go back to the analysis and unmark any marked data by clicking outside of the marked items, you'll see that all data will be shown on the details visualization.

Insights from details visualizations

Now that we have created a useful details visualization, what conclusions, insights, and findings can be drawn from it? I'll share some of mine with you—see if you can find more of your own:

1. Here, I have selected all the data. The age of the passengers is mostly normally distributed, but with a peak at the lower age range (there seemed to be a lot of babies on board):

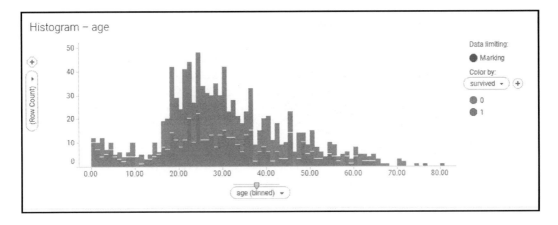

Normal distribution

A lot of data is normally distributed, particularly measured data—that is, data that has been recorded as a result of measured observation of real-world events or phenomena. Measuring the age of a population will nearly always result in some form of normal distribution. Blood pressure data in a patient population is usually normally distributed. I'm sure you can think of many other examples.

The normal distribution has informally been called the **bell curve**. This is because the curve looks like it's bell-shaped, with an enlarged middle, tailing off at each end.

2. Very young babies stood a good chance of survival, as did most young children, with the exception of about 3-year-old children.

3. Children from about 9 years old to 14 years old didn't fare too well, sadly.

4. There were very few passengers aged 60-80, but most of them did not survive. There is a lone exception—an 80-year-old male that did survive—good for him!

5. Compare the visualization for males versus females by selecting all the males, and then selecting the females.

This visualization shows the female passengers:

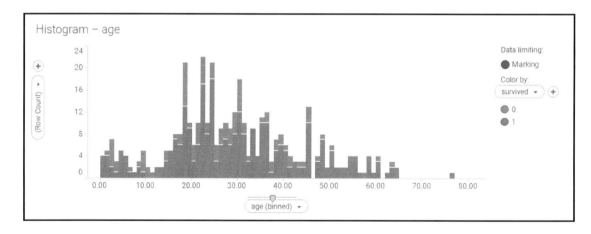

This histogram shows the survival rates of the male passengers only:

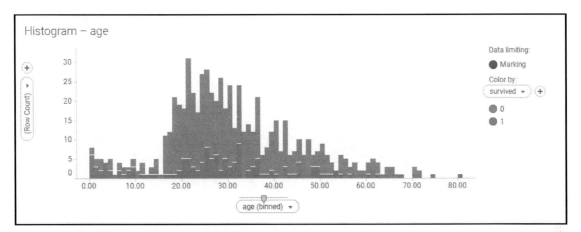

6. How much more depressing is the male survival histogram than the female? We already know that a much higher proportion of men didn't survive the disaster, but this visualization is very telling. With the exception of a few peaks at various age ranges, your chances of survival as an adult male were very slim.

Feel free to experiment by selecting other parts of the data in the original bar chart and seeing how it affects the histogram—see if you can gain any additional insights—I have just named a few!

Using filters

Spotfire's inbuilt **filters** offer a very powerful and immediate way to start analyzing your data. Every time you add a data table to an analysis file, Spotfire creates a filter for each column. Just reflect on this for a minute: if we are going to try to filter or screen our data in some way, we have to do so on the basis of the values in one or more of the data table's columns. That is why a filter always corresponds to a table column and its values to whatever data currently populates that column through the rows in the table.

You can access filters from the data panel (by clicking the button on the left-hand side of the Spotfire window) or the filters panel. The filters panel shows all current filters and their current settings. You can show and hide the filters panel from the **View** menu (**View** | **Filters**) or by clicking on the filtering icon on the toolbar. The following example will use the data panel, but it's just as valid to use the filter panel:

1. As we mentioned previously, the data panel is divided into numbers and categories. If we had date or time columns, location, identity, or other types of columns, these would be categorized as such.

2. Let's filter to first-class passengers only. Locate the **pclass** column and click on it to highlight it. You'll notice that a funnel icon will be shown:

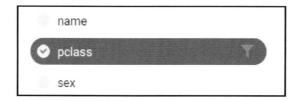

3. Click the funnel—you'll see a pop-out filter appear, so unselect **pclass 2** and **3**. Watch how the visualizations change as you do this—they'll all update together as they are showing the same data:

4. Let's look at how this leads to fresh insights. Select all the females in a main visualization chart—the histogram should look like this:

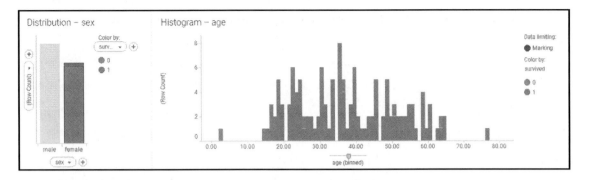

5. Look at that! If you were a first-class female passenger, you were almost guaranteed to survive.

6. Reset the filters by clicking the **Reset all filters** button at the bottom of the data panel. Feel free to play with the other filters in the meantime to see how they affect the data:

An important point to stress at this juncture is that we haven't removed any data from the underlying table. Our visualizations have changed and "lost" some rows, but as you saw, when you reset the filtering, the visualizations adjusted dynamically and displayed all the data.

Trellising

Filtering is very powerful as it allows you to filter out values from the dataset so that you can focus on what's important at any particular point. However, it's not very useful for comparing different subsets of the data. In the preceding example, we were comparing histograms by marking (selecting) different parts of the data and filtering out various rows of data. We can look at much more at a single glance by using **trellising**. Trellising splits visualizations into panels so that you can see subsets of the data all at the same time.

I suggest trellising by **pclass**—this is so that we can compare the survival rates of passengers in the various classes on board the Titanic:

1. Reset the filters as described in *Step 6* in the *Using filters* section.
2. From the data panel, click the **pclass** column and drag it onto the **age** histogram. You'll see a pop-up panel appear:

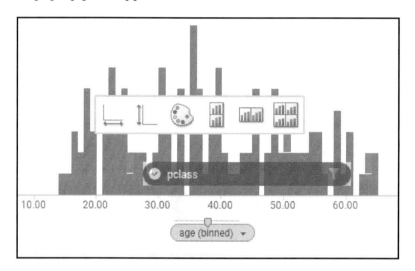

3. Drop **pclass** onto **Use 'pclass' on the vertical trellis axis.**:

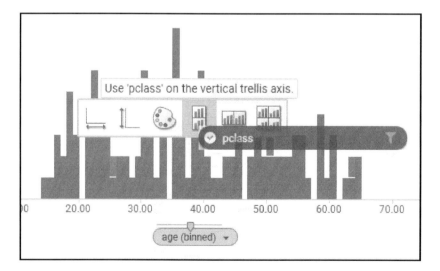

4. Notice what happens to the visualization (presuming we have selected all the data in the main bar chart):

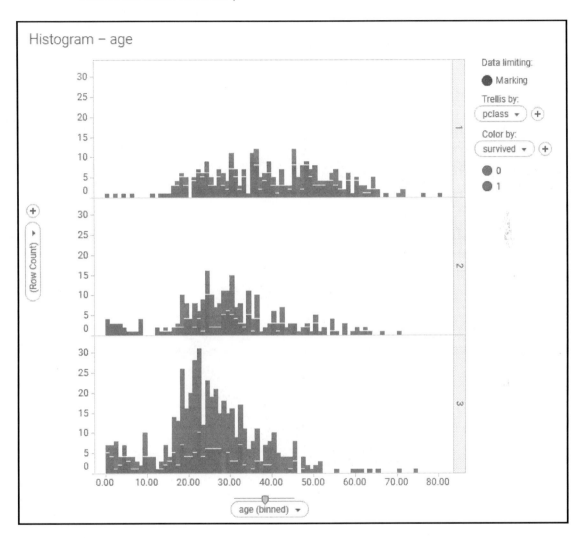

5. We have some fresh insights!
    - Unsurprisingly, but rather unfortunately, your chance of survival was much better as a first-class passenger than if you were from any other class. Notice the 80-year-old first-class passenger all on his own.
    - Third-class passengers were much more numerous than second-class ones, but their survival rate was much, much worse than the other classes'.
    - All second-class children survived.

6. Experiment with marking different subsets of the data in the main bar chart and observe how the trellised histogram behaves - see if you can gain additional insights!

Summary

In this chapter, we've dived right in to data analysis. We've seen how easy it is to load new data, to configure visualizations, and to use the various drill-down, filtering, and trellising features to gain fresh insights from any dataset. We've also experienced (and solved) some real-world data issues along the way.

I have also explained the different types of Spotfire client and used examples from web-based and desktop clients. Spotfire is hugely capable on any platform—I'm looking forward to showing you many more exciting and useful things you can do with it!

This chapter was an introduction to visual analytics in Spotfire. Let's build on that foundation in the next chapter to gain an understanding of how data underpins all analytics.

It's All About the Data

2

Now that we've had the chance to visualize some data and gain some interesting insights into it, it's time to delve more deeply into the data. Spotfire is all about visualizing data of all different shapes, sizes, and types, so this chapter will provide some background as to how data is managed in Spotfire and, by way of an example, show how you can work with Spotfire data in more detail.

In this chapter, you will learn how to visualize real-world data using a scatter plot. You will follow along as we use Spotfire to reconstruct a very famous visualization that shows world population growth and child mortality rates. You'll learn how to combine multiple datasets in order to add additional value to your data. Along the way, you'll also learn about working with hierarchical data in Spotfire and pick up some hints and tips for producing best-practice visualizations and analyses, and how to get the best out of them.

We'll be covering the following topics in this chapter:

- Understanding the basic row/column structure of a data table
- Exploring key data types
- Building a scatter plot with real-world data:
    - Combining data
    - What is a scatter plot?
    - Building the scatter plot using population growth versus child mortality
    - Working with natural hierarchies in data
    - Getting insight from the scatter plot
- Displaying information quickly in tabular form
- Enriching visualizations with color categorization
- Visualizing hierarchical data using treemaps

Technical requirements

For this chapter, we will be working with data on world population growth—the example data comes from the following page:

`https://ourworldindata.org/world-population-growth/`.

It can also be found by using the following shortened link:

`http://bit.ly/2FF09DU`.

Understanding the basic row/column structure of a data table

Before we get started with some examples, a basic understanding of the row/column structure of a Spotfire data table is essential for data analysis and report authoring.

The columns in the dataset represent how the information has been categorized. They exist even if there is no data. Most people these days are familiar with Microsoft Excel. When you start a new spreadsheet, one of the first things I suspect you to do is decide what types of information you are going to add; for example, using `First Name`, `Last Name`, and `Department` in column headings in a simple human resources spreadsheet.

Once you have structured your spreadsheet with column headings, you begin to add the actual information, row by row. Your columns don't usually change in number or description, but your rows grow and shrink in number, and corrections might be made to the information at any time.

One important distinction between Spotfire data tables and spreadsheet worksheets is the way in which the visual layout of the rows in a spreadsheet is represented. You might, for instance, not repeat a department value on a spreadsheet until it changes; you might merge cells to improve the look and feel. You cannot do that with Spotfire data tables. If the department column value for the first three rows is `Marketing`, then `Marketing` must be repeated in each row.

The following diagram shows the structures of Excel and Spotfire data together. On the left is how you might represent data in Excel—with merged row headers. On the right is how data must be structured in Spotfire:

Excel				Spotfire		
	A	B	C		A	B	C
1	Department	First Name	Last Name	1	Department	First Name	Last Name
2		John	Brown	2	Marketing	John	Brown
3	Marketing	Amit	Singh	3	Marketing	Amit	Singh
4		Sofia	Garcia	4	Marketing	Sofia	Garcia
5	Finance	Hina	Sato	5	Finance	Hina	Sato
6		Marie	Schmidt	6	Finance	Marie	Schmidt

If a data cell is not defined in the underlying data, Spotfire regards it as `(Empty)` and represents this fact within the data table. `(Empty)` and null are different ways of representing the same concept in Spotfire.

In Spotfire, data is filtered and selected through references to column names. For example, you could filter the **Department** column to show all the records for **Marketing**. The answer might be zero rows or several million rows, depending on how many records have `Marketing` in the `Department` column.

If you want to make a calculation in a data table, such as `sale amount minus cost amount`, Spotfire will apply the calculation across all rows. It's not possible (like in Excel) to have a per-row calculation or formula. However, it is possible to group values and perform calculations between rows using Spotfire's `OVER` calculation functions, which are explained in detail in `Chapter 7`, *Source Data is Never Enough*.

The fact that the calculation is applied over the entire column is a key distinction between data tables and spreadsheets. It might seem like a limitation in a data table, but the discipline of that structural integrity ultimately allows you to create very powerful analyses. There are ways to change the structure of a data table into new forms to support a particular calculation requirement. These are also covered in `Chapter 7`, *Source Data is Never Enough*.

Reports and visualizations are built around column names. For example, you might want to create a simple **sales by region** visualization. What you are doing is putting the `sales` column against the `region` column and asking Spotfire's visualization engine to populate the chart or graph with whatever row values are present beneath those columns at any given time.

This section was a very brief introduction to the way that data is structured in Spotfire. We have covered how data is stored in rows and columns and that each row and column must have a value so that Spotfire can work with it. As a reminder, we cannot reference individual "cells" within a Spotfire data table, at least not in the way that we can in Excel and other similar tools.

Exploring key data types

Another key data concept that is important to mention at this point is that of **data types.** This concept is equally important in spreadsheets, it's just that spreadsheets don't generally force you to declare the data type, and they allow you to mix and match data types in individual columns. In data tables, each column must have a single data type for all values in all rows.

So, what is meant by data type? There are (in essence) five types of data:

- Numbers
- Text
- Dates/times
- Boolean
- Binary

They are defined as such because they have distinct properties. Numbers can be used in calculations, and the vast array of mathematical functions and operators can be brought to bear on them. Text can be parsed, concatenated, counted, and arranged into categorical hierarchies. Dates have special meanings and can be used in time calculations and hierarchies (`year->month->day`, for example). Boolean values are one of either true or false. Binary data is machine-readable. Examples of binary data are images such as JPEG or PNG files, or map geometries.

However, life is never simple, and there are several subtypes of the five data categories and a few other special data types that you need to understand.

Spotfire uses 12 data types, and all data columns that are imported into Spotfire must be put into one of these type categories, unlike in Excel. The data in Spotfire is **strongly typed**. Strongly typing the data forces it to be structured by type and is much more robust for analysis than weakly typed data (as in Excel). The following table describes the data types you will use the most:

Please consult the TIBCO Spotfire documentation for a more technical description of the data types it uses:
`https://docs.tibco.com/pub/sfire-analyst/10.2.0/doc/html/en-US/`
`TIB_sfire-analyst_UsersGuide/ncfe/ncfe_data_types.htm.`
`Alternatively, you can use the following shortened link:`
`http://bit.ly/2Dk9YH0.`

Date type	Definition
Integer	Whole numbers (no decimal places)
Real	Numbers with decimal places
Date	Date with no time element
DateTime	Date and time combined
String	Text
Boolean	Logical True or False
Binary	Machine-readable data, for example, images, map shapes, or similar

Building a scatter plot with real-world data

Before we can begin building the scatter plot, we need to collect the data that we will use to build it. We need two datasets, one with population information and another with country and region information.

Gathering population data

As we stated previously in the *Technical requirements* section, the population data for this chapter is available at the Our World In Data website. The data that we will be using pertains to two specific topics: fertility and population growth and child mortality and population growth. Let's look at how to gather this data:

1. Visit the World Population Growth page at the Our World In Data website—`https://ourworldindata.org/world-population-growth/` Or (shortened link)—`http://bit.ly/2FF09DU.`

2. Navigate to the **Child mortality and population growth** graph:

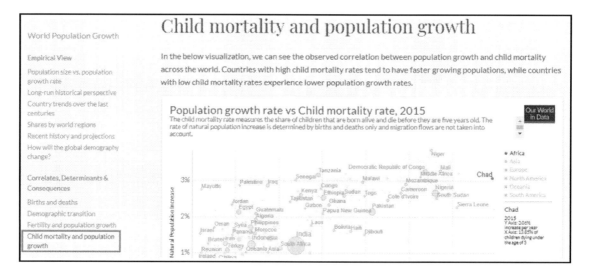

3. Download the data by clicking the **Data** tab on the chart and clicking on the file.
4. You should end up with a file called `child-mortality-vs-population-growth.csv`.

Gathering country and region data

You'll need to download a list of countries and their corresponding regions as well. To gather this data, follow these steps:

1. Navigate to the GitHub repository at `https://github.com/lukes/ISO-3166-Countries-with-Regional-Codes/blob/master/all/all.csv`, or use the following shortened link: `http://bit.ly/2Zo401p`
2. Click the **Raw** button
3. Copy all the text on the screen and paste it into an empty Notepad file
4. Save this file as `Countries and Regions.csv`

Combining the data

During the import process, we will combine the data in the `Countries and Regions` file with the `Child mortality and population growth` file into a single data table.

The process is pretty much identical for the Analyst and web clients:

1. Click the + icon on the left-hand side of the application and click **Browse local file...**:

2. Navigate to where you downloaded the data files.
3. Select the `Child-mortality-and-population-growth` and `Countries and Regions` data files and open them.
4. Accept the default column types for both files (Analyst clients only).

5. Expand the import panel for the `Countries and Regions` file (by clicking **Countries and Regions.csv**) and select **Add as columns to:**

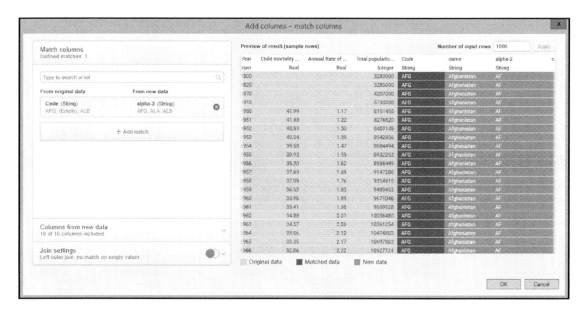

You will notice a red warning—that is because there isn't an obvious match between the column names in the two columns:

6. To fix this, click the cog wheel icon to open the match columns dialog.
7. Click the **Add match** button.
8. Select the **Code (String)** and **alpha-3 (String)** columns in each data table, respectively. Notice how Spotfire gives a helpful preview of the values in each of the columns to give a hint as to which columns you should choose to match on:

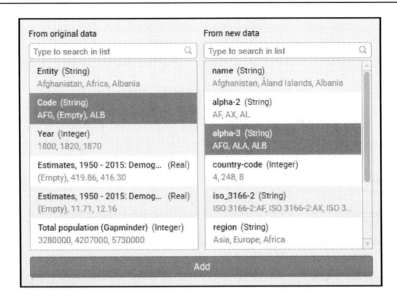

9. Click the **Add** button.

10. Now, look at the resulting preview—you can see how the columns have been matched and the resultant structure of the data that will be brought into Spotfire:

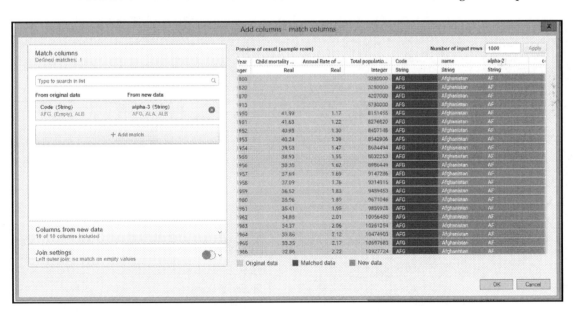

11. Click **OK** to accept the settings and then **OK** again to load the data.

Notice that we used the default join settings—this is for a left-outer join. Spotfire explains the join types nicely if we were to open the join settings and explore them further. In most cases, however, a left-outer join is what's required—it's absolutely ideal for adding columns to one data table from another data file.

So far in this example, we have learned how to load two data files and combine, or join, them into a single data table. The original population growth versus child mortality data did not contain any information about regions, so we have added columns from the countries and regions data to augment it. We can now go ahead and build a visualization that shows the combined data.

What is a scatter plot?

A scatter plot is quite recognizable and was immortalized by the late Hans Rosling in his *The Joy of Stats* television program on the BBC in 2010:

You can see an animated version of the scatter plot that was used by Rosling on the BBC's YouTube channel:
`https://www.youtube.com/watch?v=jbkSRLYSojo.`

A **scatter plot** is sometimes called a bubble chart, but in Spotfire nomenclature, it's a scatter plot. A scatter plot is a really useful visualization that can represent multiple dimensions of data at once through its axes and by several other means.

In this section, we will build the scatter plot and then enhance it in various ways, showing some key data concepts and how to make use of them in Spotfire.

Building the scatter plot using population growth versus child mortality

Here's how to get started with building the scatter plot. If you are using the Analyst client, you can use Spotfire's AI-driven recommendations engine in order to get started (web client instructions will follow):

1. Open the data panel and select the column called **Annual Rate of Natural Population Increase (% increase per year)**.

2. The recommendations will pop out to the right. Scroll down until you find this one (showing the relationship between **Child mortality rate** and **region**):

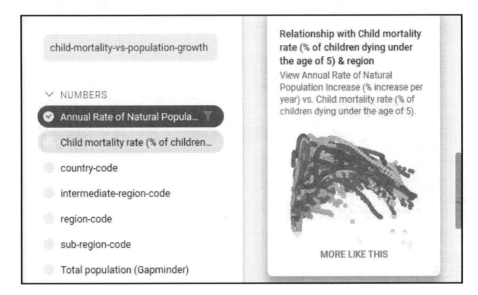

3. Add it to the analysis and click on the visualization you just added in order to hide the data panel.

Now for the web clients:

1. Open the data panel and select the following three columns:
    - **Annual Rate of Natural Population Increase (% increase per year)**
    - **Child mortality rate (% of children dying under the age of 5)**
    - **Region**

2. Locate the scatter plot recommendation and click **MORE LIKE THIS**:

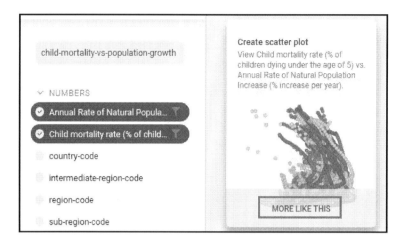

3. Once again, click **MORE LIKE THIS** on the scatter plot recommendation. In this case, we are telling Spotfire that we definitely want a scatter plot, but the various columns are not on the correct axes yet.

4. Add the bottom visualization to the analysis:

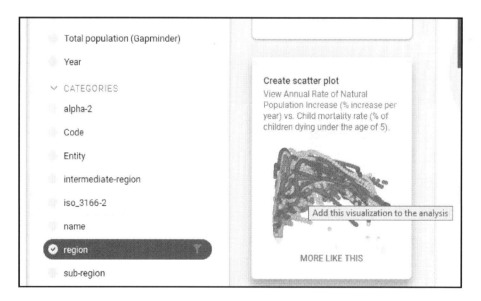

5. Hide the data panel by clicking on the visualization you just added to your analysis.

As we might expect, there's definitely a relationship between mortality rate, population increase, and region, but it all looks a bit confusing because data is shown for all years. There is a marker for every single data point. However, we can still see the progression of each of the countries' data through the years. We can make things a lot clearer by continuing to work with the analysis.

Region is useful to show as there's a really strong relationship between region and infant mortality and rate of population increase. However, the data becomes even more interesting if we switch to show each country as a marker on the scatter plot and add the dimension of population to the visualization. A scatter plot visualization is particularly appropriate for viewing lots of dimensions of data in one go! Let's complete the configuration of the scatter plot:

1. From the legend of the visualization, select **Entity** for **Marker by:**

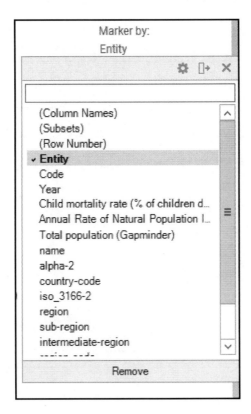

2. Take a look at the axis selectors—Spotfire has automatically applied an aggregation method to each of the axes—it needs to do this as it must group the data per entity (country). It's now showing multiple rows of data behind each marker on the scatter plot.

3. It's good practice to check and adjust the aggregation method that's being used—we can do this by pulling out the axis selector. Let's do that now and adjust both axes to show the **Avg (Average)** (if they are showing **Sum**):

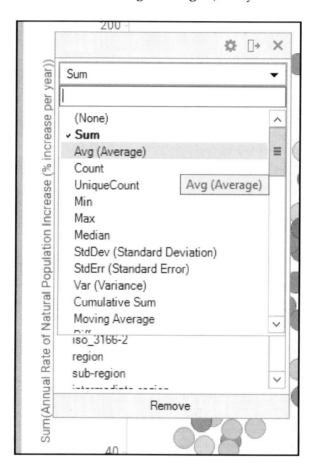

Aggregation methods: Spotfire's default aggregation method is **Sum**. My practical experience of real-world data suggests that **Avg (Average)** is more appropriate in most cases. Spotfire X added a user preference for this. I usually set mine to **Avg**. You can set this via **Tools | Options | Visualization (Analyst clients only),** or your server administrator can set it for all users in your organization.

Aggregation is the method by which Spotfire calculates measures over groups in the data. It groups data and applies the aggregation method to that group. There are lots of different aggregation methods—from **Sum** to **Average**, **Cumulative Sum**, and many more.

4. To show population as another dimension in the data, click the **Size by** legend item and choose **Total population (Gapminder)**. Adjust the aggregation method to Sum:

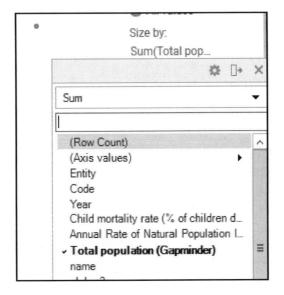

At this stage, we are using Avg for the aggregations on the x- and y-axes of the scatter plot and Sum for the size by. Since the x- and y-axes are showing percentage increases, it doesn't makes sense to sum these as we can never sum percentages! Additionally, each marker on the scatter plot contains the data for multiple years, so it doesn't make sense to sum the populations. However, as you are about to see, we are about to filter the data to an individual year, so summing the population data for each region will then be valid.

5. Open the filter panel (by clicking on the funnel icon in the toolbar) and find the **Year** column or open the filter from the data panel on the left (by clicking on the column name and then the funnel icon).

6. Right-click on the filter and change its type from a **Range Filter** to an **Item Filter**:

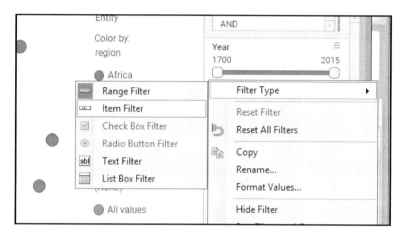

7. The data is most complete from the middle of the 20th century, so choose a year from that range, for example, **1974**:

8. Labelling marked data is also a nice thing to do—we can configure this by accessing the visualization properties and choosing to label by **Entity** (the web client is shown here):

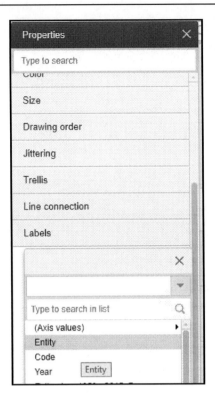

9. Here is the same dialog in an Analyst client:

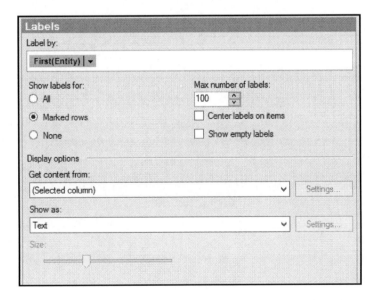

10. It's good practice to give visualizations a meaningful title, so double-click on the title bar and enter a new title—I suggest **Population Increase Rate vs Child Mortality Rate**.

11. You should end up with something that looks like this:

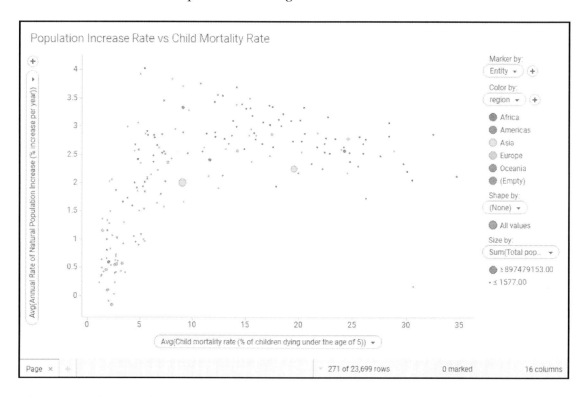

The chart is showing the relationships between child mortality, population growth, rate of population increase, and total population per country. The size of the markers indicates the total population and the color indicates the region. Combining the x- and y-axes along with marker size and color allows us to visualize four dimensions in the data simultaneously. It's also possible to add more dimensions to a scatter plot with shape, rotation, drawing order, and others, but we are not covering these in this chapter.

Try selecting **China** and **India** by marking them—hold down the *Ctrl* key as you click on them. They are the largest markers on the scatter plot:

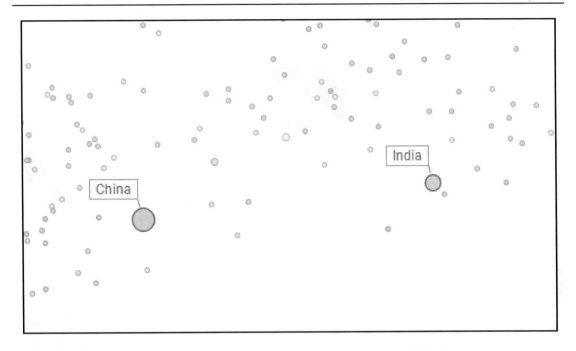

Note how much they stand out—not only because their markers are larger than other countries (as you would expect from their population sizes), but also because their child mortality is still comparatively high, as is their population growth. It's also interesting to inspect the countries at the bottom-left of the plot—they tend to be developed European countries. They have small populations, shrinking populations, and very low child mortality.

When following general good practice guidelines, it is a good idea to hide all visualization configurations that are not being used. To do this for the current example, right-click on the legend and uncheck the **Shape by** option.

Up until this stage, you have learned how to construct a scatter plot that shows multiple dimensions of data all at once. Along the way, you've learned some best practices around aggregation methods, visualization titling, and more.

Working with natural hierarchies in data

Data often contains natural hierarchies. One immediate example is date/time information. The highest (or least granular) level might be year. Then comes month, then day, hour, minute, and so on. There are also natural hierarchies in other types of data. In the example we are working with in this chapter, Region, Sub-Region, and Country form a natural hierarchy in the data. We can use this natural hierarchy to change the way we view the data, with Spotfire automatically being able to group or aggregate the data at any level within the hierarchy.

Hierarchies can be configured as columns in the data or by adding multiple columns to an axis selector. I'll show the former in the Analyst client and the latter in the web client. Add a hierarchy as a column (for Analyst clients only):

1. From the **Data** menu, choose **Add hierarchy...**.
2. From the **Available columns** selector, choose the following options (in the following order):
   - **region**
   - **sub-region**
   - **Entity**
3. Give the new hierarchy a name. I often choose something that really tells the user exactly what the hierarchy represents. In this case, I recommend **Region-Sub Region-Country**:

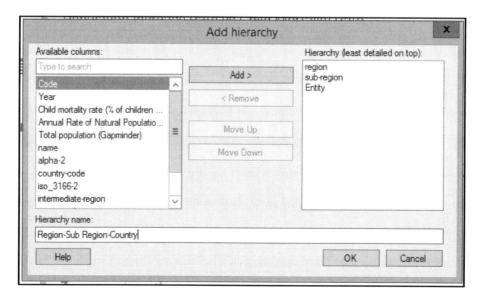

4. Click **OK**.

5. From the **Marker by** dropdown in the legend, choose the hierarchy you created in the last step:

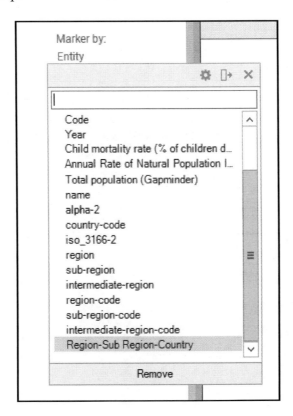

To create a hierarchy (all clients) using an axis selector, follow these steps:

1. Remove **Entity** from the **Marker by** selector (right-click and select **Remove all**).

2. Now, choose **region** for **Marker by**.

3. Then, add **sub-region** by clicking the + icon:

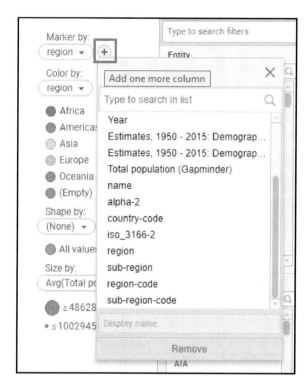

4. Choose **sub-region**.
5. Repeat this for **Entity**.
6. Finally, create a hierarchy by right-clicking on the axis selector and choosing **Create hierarchy**:

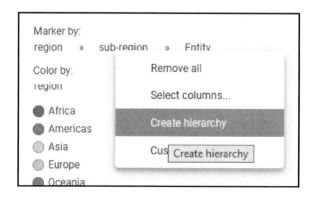

We'll be experimenting with navigating the hierarchy in the next section, *Gaining insight from the scatter plot*.

Before we finish with this section, there are a few recommended settings that I suggest we apply for best-practice purposes.

If you're using an Analyst client, you can set the minima and maxima for the axes showing gridlines and add a horizontal line at the origin of the y-axis), as follows:

1. Right-click on the visualization and select **Properties**.
2. Select the **X-axis** property page and set the following options:
    *   **Range Min**—0.00; **Max**—18.00
    *   **Show gridlines:**

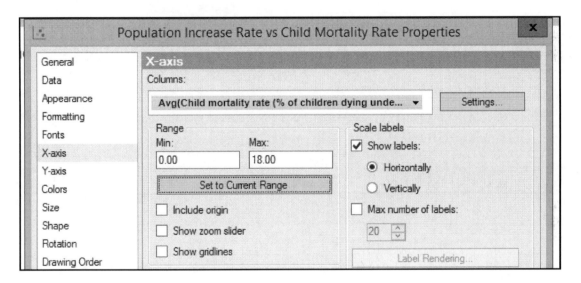

3. Select the **Y-axis** property page and set the following options:
   - **Range Min**—-2.00; **Max**—4.50
   - **Show gridlines**:

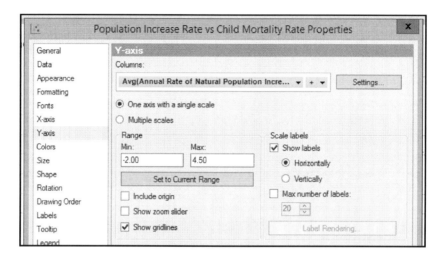

4. Select the **Lines & Curves** property page and set the following option:
   - **Horizontal line: 0.00**:

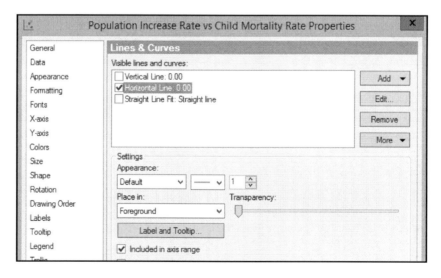

5. Close the **Properties** dialog.

Setting axis ranges is not always a good idea—in fact, I don't recommend it in most cases. However, in the next section, *Gaining insight from the scatter plot*, we'll be navigating through the years in the data to "animate" the scatter plot. Setting the axis ranges will be helpful as it will prevent Spotfire from auto-scaling them dependently on the ranges in the data. Of course, if you're using the web-based clients, you won't be able to set the axis ranges and will have to make do.

Finally, we should set the number formatting for the `Total population` column. This can be done in either the Analyst or web clients:

1. Expand the data panel and right-click on the column. If you're using an Analyst client, choose **Column properties**, then **Formatting**. If you are using a web client, choose **Formatting...**.

2. Then, set the formatting to the short number format and 1 decimal. Here is the dialog from a web client for illustration (Analyst clients have similar options):

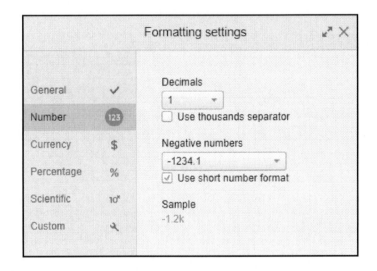

Notice that as you update the settings for a visualization, the changes happen immediately. The **Properties** dialog is not modal—this means that you can still interact with your Spotfire analysis as you adjust the properties.

The visualization should now look something like this (Analyst clients):

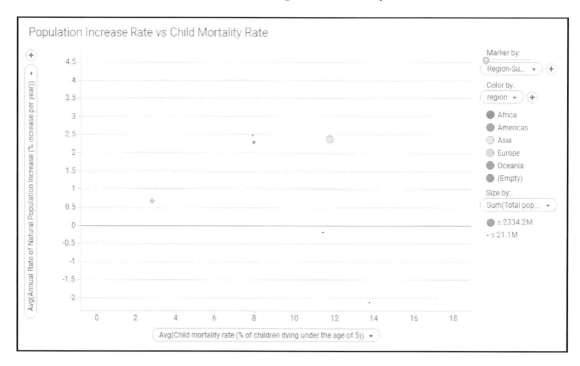

Gaining insight from the scatter plot

At this stage, in a few simple steps, we have configured a very useful visualization that matches the power of the visualizations shown by Hans Rosling. I'm now going to show you how to use its best advantages:

1. Experiment with adjusting the **Marker by** hierarchy slider. Notice how it changes the visualization. **Region-Sub-region** is shown here:

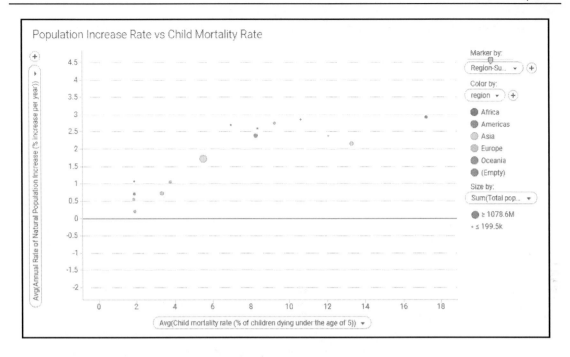

2. Change the hierarchy slider to **Region-Sub-region-Entity**:

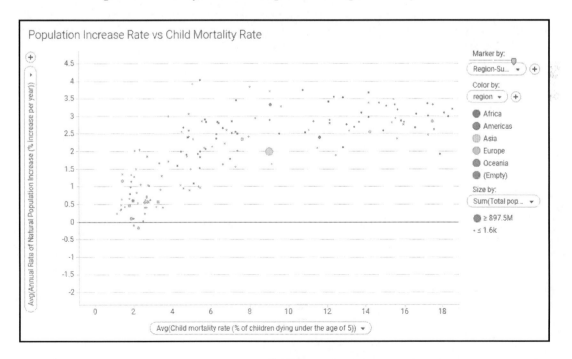

It's really interesting to see the clusters of points by continent. Experiment with the **Region-Sub-region-Country** hierarchy slider. Do you get a better view of how the regions compare in any particular view?

 More on aggregation: Notice that when you adjust the hierarchy slider, the number of points shown on the scatter plot changes. Spotfire is dynamically recalculating the aggregation of the values for the x-, y- and size-by axes (yes, size-by is considered to be an axis!) based on the grouping of the data. The x- and y-axes are using the Avg function to calculate the average; the size-by axis is using the Sum function. This makes sense in our case, as we always want to know the average rates of population growth and child mortality across a country, region, or continent, but we also always need to know the total population of that country, region, or continent.

Note that the developing world looks very different from the other parts of the world. Asia is also interesting to look at and the Americas give a very mixed picture.

Experiment with marking (selecting) various regions of the plot. Labels will be shown on the marked points because we set that option in the **Properties** dialog. It's not perfect, because the label is fixed to **Entity**, but it gives you a good idea. For an experiment, you could try using the UniqueConcatenate aggregation method for the label—that way, if you are showing a region or sub-region and you mark a point on the scatter plot, you will see a list of all the countries contained in the point. Right now, you just get the first one as that is the default aggregation method for categorical columns:

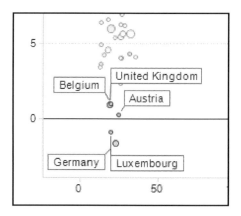

Recall that the scatter plot is showing four dimensions of data all at once: child mortality, population increase, population size, and country/region/continent. It's possible to visualize a fifth dimension (time) by moving through the `Year` filter. Open the `Year` filter from the data panel as before, and try clicking through the various years, one by one. You will see the scatter plot animate and show the time dimension.

You can play around here to reveal various depictions in the visualization:

- Click through the years in the filter and watch the various countries and regions move along the axes, jostle for position in the world order, and so on.
- Look out for major changes over short periods of time—keep an eye on countries such as China and India—they have had enormous population growth and massive reductions in infant mortality.
- Note the overall trend of the world. Better health care and education (we infer) over time has given rise to an overall positive trend in infant mortality and a reduction in natural population growth.

Recall that we set the limits of the x- and y-axes in the properties of the visualization so that we could use the filter to animate the visualization. If the axes had been left to auto-scale, they would have readjusted every time the filter was changed, which would not have shown a consistent picture of the data over each year.

This would be a good point to save the analysis file, if you haven't done so already.

Displaying information quickly in tabular form

The Spotfire **Table Plot** visualization is a simple way of visualizing tabular data. You can think of a table of data in the same way as a Microsoft Excel worksheet, but that's only the beginning. People will nearly always want to see the "underlying data," that is, the details behind any visualization you create. The table plot visualization meets this need.

It's very important not to confuse table in the general data sense with the Spotfire Table Plot visualization: the underlying data table remains immutable (unchanging), except in some special cases, and complete in the background; the table visualization is a highly manipulable view of the underlying data table and should be treated as a visualization, not a data table.

Let's create a table plot as a details visualization from the scatter plot we created earlier in this chapter:

1. Right-click on the scatter plot visualization, click **Create Details Visualization**, and then select **Table...**:

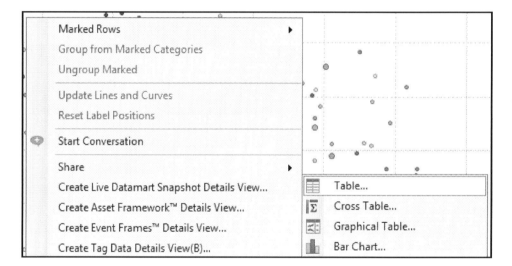

2. This will create a default table plot that displays details of the data that was selected in the main visualization.

3. Try clicking on or marking points (markers) in the main visualization and watch how the table plot changes. In this case, I have marked all countries in Oceania by clicking on **Oceania** in the legend:

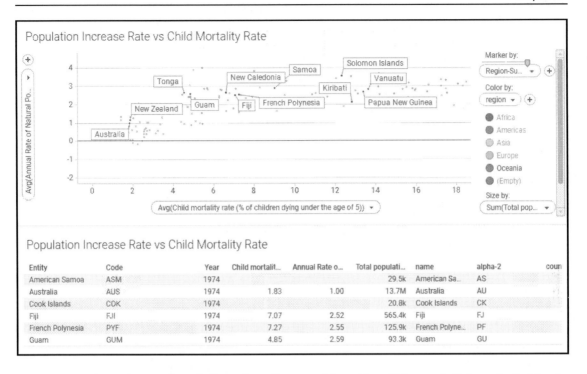

Population Increase Rate vs Child Mortality Rate

Entity	Code	Year	Child mortalit...	Annual Rate o...	Total populati...	name	alpha-2	coun
American Samoa	ASM	1974			29.5k	American Sa...	AS	
Australia	AUS	1974	1.83	1.00	13.7M	Australia	AU	
Cook Islands	COK	1974			20.8k	Cook Islands	CK	
Fiji	FJI	1974	7.07	2.52	565.4k	Fiji	FJ	
French Polynesia	PYF	1974	7.27	2.55	125.9k	French Polyne...	PF	
Guam	GUM	1974	4.85	2.59	93.3k	Guam	GU	

4. Adjust the **Region-Sub-region-Country** hierarchy slider and click on individual markers on the plot—notice how the table plot shows that a single (aggregated) marker in the scatter plot can contain multiple rows of data, or just one data row, depending on the level of aggregation being performed.

There is always more than one way to do the same thing in Spotfire, and this is particularly true for the manipulation of visualizations. Let's start with some very quick manipulations of the table plot:

- To move a column, left-click the column name, hold, drag, and drop.
- To make a column wider or narrower, hover the mouse over the right-hand edge of the column title until you see the cursor change to a two-way arrow, and then click and drag.

- To adjust the settings of an individual column, click on the column header. This causes a popup menu to appear:

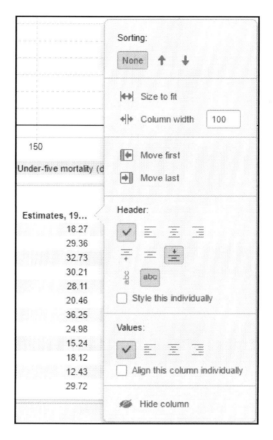

From this menu, you can do the following:

- Change the column sorting—**None**, ascending (from small to large values), and descending, respectively.
- Adjust column sizing (to fit the data or an explicit column width).
- Move the column to be the first or last shown.
- Adjust the header display. Two points of note: the tick mark means that the header should align the same as the underlying data (left for string data, right for numerical data, and so on); changing one of these settings will affect all columns. If you want to change the setting of a single column, make sure that you check **Style this individually** before adjusting the setting.

- Adjust the value alignment—as for the header display.
- Hide the column.
- Set the row height (only in Analyst clients) by right-clicking the column header and choosing **Row Height**:

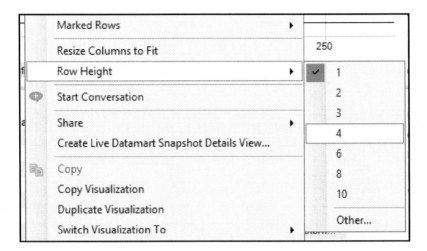

These and other properties of the table visualization are also accessed via **Visualization Properties.** As you work through the various Spotfire visualizations, you'll notice that some types have more options than others, but there are commonalities and an overall consistency in convention.

Visualization properties can be opened in a number of ways:

- By right-clicking on the visualization, which is a table in this case, and selecting **Properties**
- By going to the **Edit** menu and selecting **Visualization Properties**
- By clicking on the cog icon in the top right-hand corner of a visualization
- By clicking the **Visualization Properties** icon in the icon tray below the main menu bar

It's beyond the scope of this book to explore every property and option. The context-sensitive help provided by Spotfire is excellent and explains all the options in detail.

Enriching visualizations with color categorization

Color is a strong feature in Spotfire and an important visualization tool, which is often overlooked by report creators. It can be seen as merely a nice-to-have customization. However, color can be the difference between creating a stimulating and intuitive data visualization and an uninspiring and even confusing corporate report. Take some pride and care in the visual aesthetics of your analytics creations!

Let's take a look at the color properties of the table visualization. These are only available in the Analyst clients (however, you can still choose a pre-configured color scheme, or choose colors from the legend of a visualization if you're working in web-based clients):

1. Open the table visualization properties and select **Colors**, and then **Add** the **Total population (Gapminder)** column:

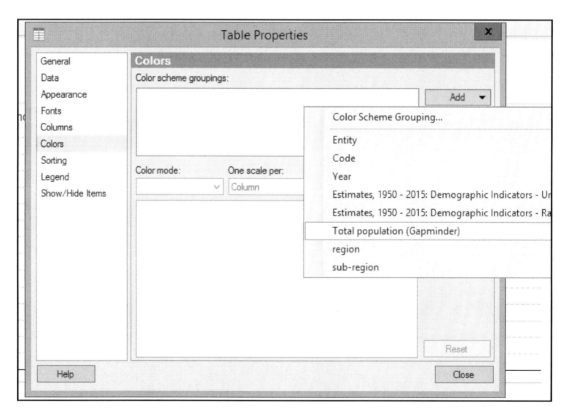

2. Now, you can add points and color rules, or adjust the color gradient. To adjust the existing color gradient, just click on the box next to the **Max** point and pick a new color, and do the same with the **Min** point:

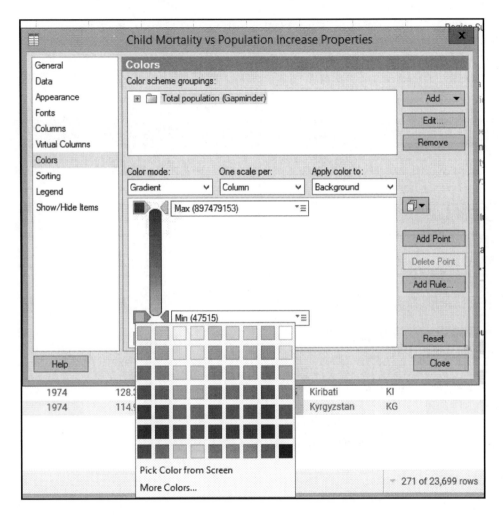

3. To add a point with a color indicating the average, click **Add Point**. Spotfire will add a point with a specific value, so we need to change it to show the average. Click the drop-down to the right of the point and choose **Average**, then select a color that you'd like use to indicate the average within the gradient. This book is in grayscale, so it's difficult to represent the colors accurately, but I recommend starting off at a deep color for higher values, leading to a lighter shade of the same color for the average. Then, choose a totally different color for the minimum value, but one that does not clash with the gradient from high to average values:

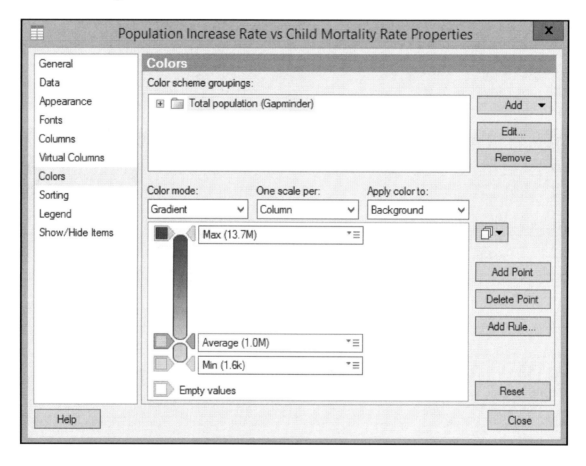

You can also use some built-in color schemes in Spotfire—just click the icon that looks like several sheets of paper to expand the menu:

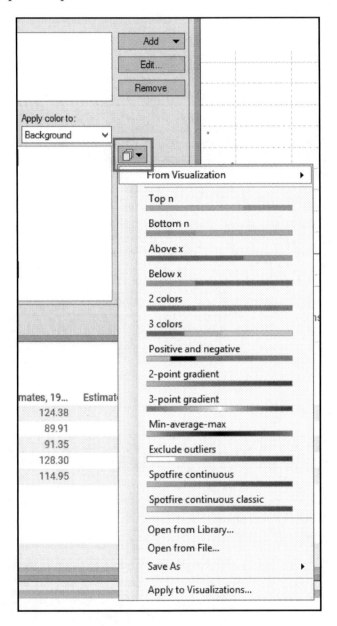

Out of interest, just look at the difference between the spread of the average and the max and the min and the average. I suspect that China and India really skew the population figures. In fact, we can check this out:

1. Close the dialog and return to the main visualization.
2. Select all the data in the scatter plot.
3. Sort the `Total population` column by descending. Now, look at the data:

Population Increase Rate vs Child Mortality Rate

Entity	Year	Child mortalit...	Annual Rate o...	Total population (... ▼	name	sub-region	region
China	1974	8.99	2.00	897.5M	China	Eastern Asia	Asia
India	1974	19.52	2.24	607.6M	India	Southern Asia	Asia
United States	1974	1.96	0.60	217.1M	United States ...	Northern Ame...	Americas
Russia	1974	3.25	0.57	133.4M	Russian Feder...	Eastern Europe	Europe
Indonesia	1974	14.20	2.56	130.9M	Indonesia	South-eastern ...	Asia
Japan	1974	1.40	1.16	109.5M	Japan	Eastern Asia	Asia

You can see from the values that China and India are indeed responsible for skewing the data—their populations significantly outnumber those of the next two countries—USA and Russia. Note that I was still looking at data for 1974 at this point. Your results will be different if you are looking at a different year.

Now would be a good time to save your analysis file.

Visualizing hierarchical data using treemaps

Most data has natural hierarchies within it. So far, we've discussed `Region`, `Sub Region`, and `Country`. We used them on the scatter plot to allow the consumer of the visualization to navigate the different levels of the hierarchy, and group (or aggregate) the data at each level.

It's also possible to visualize the hierarchy directly using a treemap. A **treemap** is a hierarchical visualization and allows easy navigation up and down through the different levels and is the only Spotfire visualization, at the time of writing, that supports clicking up and down through the hierarchy on the visualization itself.

Let's create a treemap showing the relative infant mortality between the different `Regions`, `Sub Regions,` and `Countries`:

1. Add a new page by clicking on the + sign at the bottom of the Spotfire window:

 It's good practice to give your pages a meaningful title, since Spotfire just names the pages `Page, Page (2)`, and so on. You can rename a page by double-clicking its title.

2. Choose a treemap from the visualizations pullout:

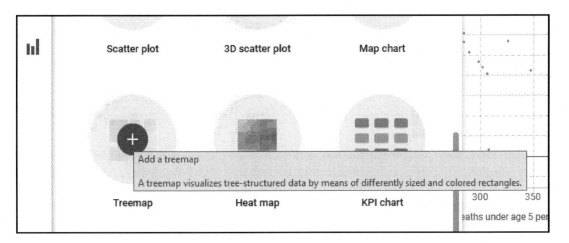

Helpfully, Spotfire chooses the `Region, Sub Region, Country` hierarchy for the treemap. The defaults that are chosen for the other axes are a reasonable starting point too, but let's explore them in detail. Here's what you should see in Spotfire at this point:

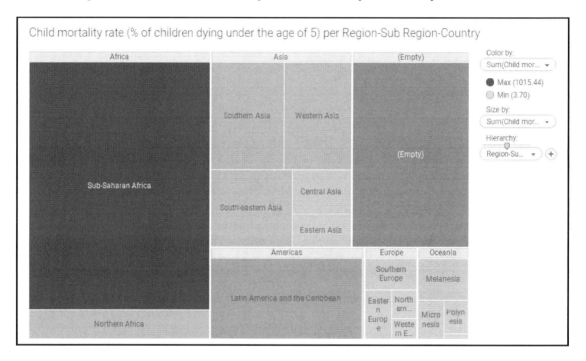

The preceding screenshot shows the following elements:

- **Hierarchy** axis: This axis determines how to split up the data into the various blocks that you can see in the visualization. You can change how the blocks are shown by using the hierarchy slider, as per the scatter plot you created earlier on in this chapter. Experiment with the slider and see how it changes the display of the hierarchy and the detail it goes into.
- **Size by** axis: This axis determines the size of the blocks in the visualization. Spotfire has automatically chosen the column that estimates child mortality. However, the `Sum` aggregation is not correct:
  - We need to change it to `Avg`. Please do this now, for both the **Color by** and **Size by** axes.

Of course, if you've already set Spotfire's option to use Avg as the default aggregation (as I recommended), then you won't need to complete this step!

- Let's choose some more appropriate colors for the **Color by** axis, too. You may think that a gradient from red to green is a good idea, but I tend to find that red to green color schemes don't look very nice as the two colors clash badly. I usually prefer a darker shade of a color to represent something that is "bad" and a lighter shade of the same color to represent something that is "good":

    1. Click on the **Max** color icon on the legend and choose a color:

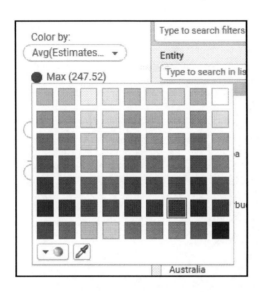

    2. Click on the **Min** color icon and choose another color. Spotfire will automatically apply a gradient to the colors.

- Although you won't be able to tell in the printed book (it's a grayscale book), I have chosen a dark brown to represent the **Max** and a light orange to represent the **Min**. You could, of course, get more creative with the colors by adding rules or points to the gradient—for example, to differentiate between above and below average regions, as per the earlier example in this chapter. If you want to do this, please right-click on the axis selector for the color axis (in the legend) and click **Properties**.

If you can't see the colors here, you can download the graphics bundle containing the color images. Please visit the *Preface* for more details. If you're reading this book on a color e-reader, you'll see the images in color on there.

Now, let's explore the data a bit more by using the navigational aspects of the treemap:

1. Each of the headings of the groups in the treemap are clickable. Try clicking on a header, for example, for **Asia**. The treemap will update, as follows:

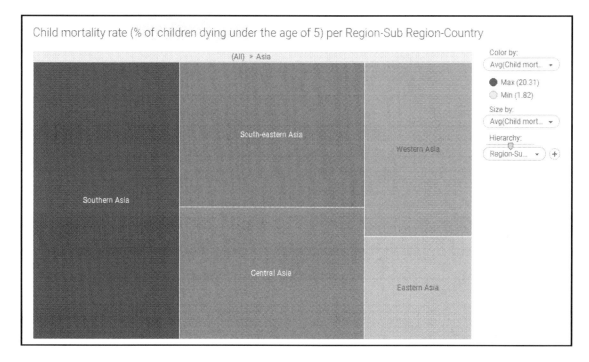

2. Note the treemap navigator at the top of the visualization. It is like a breadcrumb trail and will always show you where you are within the hierarchy. If you click **All**, you will be taken back to the highest level within the hierarchy.

3. Of course, it's possible to change the level of detail shown on the hierarchy by changing the slider on the hierarchy axis, too. In this case, I have slid it all the way to the right in order to show sub-regions and countries:

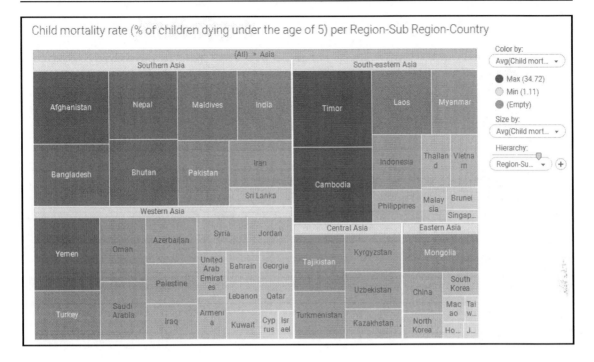

There are a few things you need to know about treemaps:

- A treemap can be used as a source for a details visualization, so you can drill into the details of any of the sections of the treemap in your data if you have a large amount of structured, hierarchical data.
- A treemap is very useful for an at-a-glance view of the relative importance or weight of many categories of data. However, don't forget to provide another means of comparing the categories if you need to compare absolute values.
- A commonly asked question is—"Can I change the text in the boxes to show something other than the name of the category within the hierarchy?". The answer is "No"—I'm letting you know at this stage to save you time searching various online forums, and so on! However, I do know that TIBCO listens to customer requests, so later, if you feel this would be a useful addition to the Spotfire product, please submit an idea to the TIBCO ideas portal (or vote up an existing one). You can find the TIBCO ideas portal at `https://ideas.tibco.com`.

Remember! The human brain is not very good at comparing areas visually. Take care when using a treemap not to rely on the sizes of the boxes in the map to represent absolute values. Just like pie charts, do not rely on the sizes to indicate true relative values. Use a bar chart or similar instead!

Summary

In this chapter, you've learned about the basic structure of data in Spotfire and how it's strongly typed. You've also learned how to combine two datasets to enrich your data with additional columns. Continuing with the theme of data, you learned about hierarchical data in Spotfire and how to work with it.

The scatter plot was shown throughout this chapter—you saw how we used it to reconstruct a famous bubble chart showing population growth and how we built it up, step by step, into a fully featured, interactive visualization. You've also learned some hints and tips for producing best-practice visualizations in Spotfire and some more about how to gain insight from those visualizations.

The next chapter covers dashboarding and how to answer the "What?" and "Why?" questions of analytics. It also covers another real-world example of how to use Spotfire to get a deep understanding of what's going on in your data!

Impactful Dashboards! 3

The first two chapters showed you how to work with data and create visualizations. This chapter is all about building impactful dashboards and analytic applications. An analytic application brings analytics to the masses: providing users with an application that they can use to get work done, which is driven by analytics and has analytics at its core.

It's all very well to produce a set of impactful or cool visualizations that shows you a picture of the data. However, it's really worth spending some extra time considering how the analysis is presented and how easy it is for you and others to change options and parameters in order to guide other users through the analysis.

Even the most static dashboard-style report will usually benefit from the inclusion of some form of user-definable parameters, and a visually appealing and well-annotated analysis will draw people in and encourage engagement. Visualization titles, information and instructions, and good overall layout and organization are essential design principles.

In this chapter, we will cover the following topics:

- KPI charts - the basis of any analytics dashboard
- Framing your analysis using text areas
- Custom expressions
- Document properties
- Property controls
- Marking
- Enabling end users to configure a KPI chart interactively
- Drilling into the KPI chart
- A deep dive into the insights you can find in a dashboard
- Publishing a dashboard to Spotfire Web, with a brief introduction to the Spotfire library

At the end of this chapter, you will be ready to share your work with others by publishing it to Spotfire's Web clients!

 Note: From now on, I won't be explaining how to perform each and every step if I have covered the topic in previous chapters, but if you need reminding how to import files into Spotfire, please refer to `Chapter 1`, *Welcome to Spotfire*.

KPI charts

KPI charts provide an at-a-glance view of key performance indicators (KPIs). They also work really well on mobile devices and are an ideal way of presenting information to users at all levels. CEOs and top-flight executives love them!

I like to divide analytics into the "What?" and the "Why?", First of all, what's going on? What's happening? What's your data telling you? Then, there's the "Why?"—why is something happening?

An example might be as follows:

* What? Sales are down this month compared to last month.
* Why? There was a dip in sales in one particular region.

KPI charts display the "What?" and allow drill-in to other visualizations to reveal the "Why?".

The KPI chart divides data up into individual KPIs that show a measure (value in data) divided and aggregated over a category. KPI charts are pretty special in Spotfire as they behave differently (in some ways) to most other charts—for good reason. Follow along with the example in the following section and all will become clear!

Constructing a KPI chart

This example will show how to construct a simple KPI chart showing stock prices of the Standard and Poor's 500 list. For more information on the S&P 500, please review this Wikipedia page:

`https://en.wikipedia.org/wiki/S%26P_500_Index`

Alternatively, use this shortened link:

`http://bit.ly/2ODeEvV`

For the example, we will be downloading an example dataset from Kaggle and joining it to another dataset that's been downloaded from GitHub that will allow us to categorize the companies in the S&P 500 into their industry sectors.

Please download the S&P 500 data from this link (you will need to log in to Kaggle):

`https://www.kaggle.com/camnugent/sandp500`

Extract the downloaded `.zip` file, and then download the list of S&P companies and their categories from GitHub:

`https://github.com/datasets/s-and-p-500-companies/blob/master/data/`
`constituents.csv`

Alternatively, use this shortened link:

`http://bit.ly/2U6akeG`

(Credit to Rufus Pollock and the Open Knowledge Foundation).

Reminder—to download the file from GitHub, you will need to follow these steps:

1. Navigate to one of the URLs that was provided previously.
2. Right-click on the **Raw** button and click **Save link as...** and save the file somewhere on your computer where you can import it into Spotfire.

Now, let's load the data into Spotfire. The process of loading the data is exactly the same, whether you are using the web or Analyst clients:

1. Import the `all_stocks_5yr.csv` file into Spotfire, accepting the default column types.

2. Add the `constituents.csv` file as columns to the `all_stocks_5yr` data table. First of all, drop in the options by clicking the import bar—you can see where I clicked:

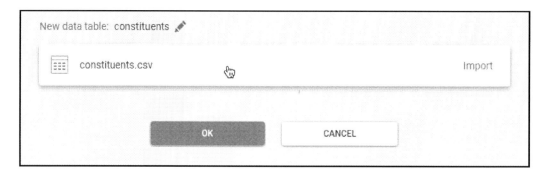

Choose **Add as columns to:**

3. Click the cog wheel to open the **Match columns** dialog:

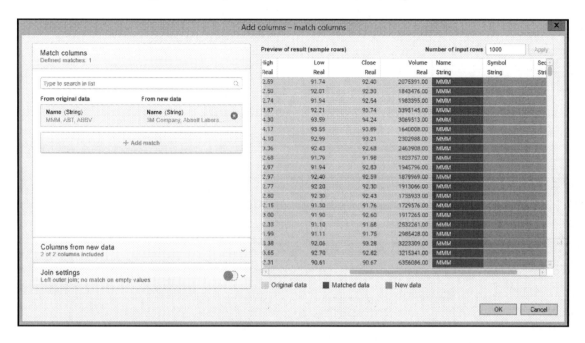

4. By default, Spotfire matches on column name and type, but the recommended match isn't what's needed in this case, so the preview doesn't show any matches in the data. Remove the suggested match and add a new match between **Name (String)** and **Symbol (String)**:

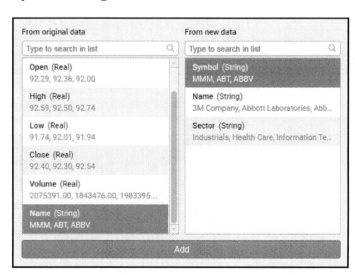

5. Use the default settings—2 of 2 columns, left outer join. Notice how the preview shows that the match is now working correctly:

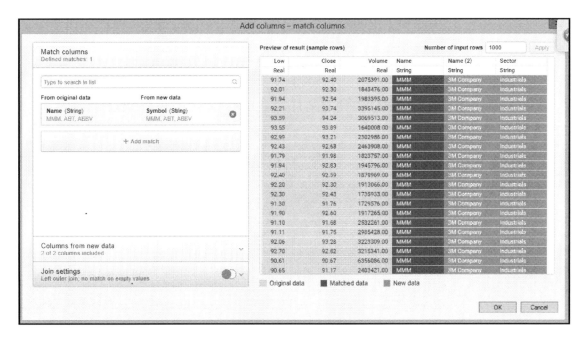

6. Click **OK** to close the dialog and **OK** again to add the data to the analysis.

7. If you're interested, take a look at the data canvas by clicking on the button on the bottom-left of the Spotfire window (highlighted). You should see something like this:

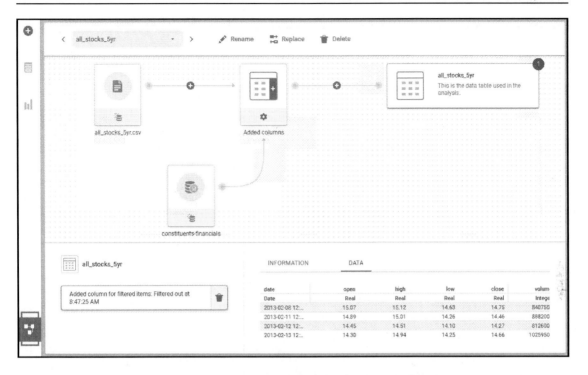

8. If you did open the data canvas, you'll need to close it again by clicking on the data canvas button once more. Now, add a KPI chart from the visualizations flyout:

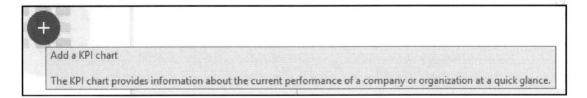

A default KPI chart will be added to your Spotfire analysis. Now, we can begin by configuring the KPI chart using the following steps:

1. Right-click on the box that's showing figures and a sparkline (mini-line graph) and click **KPI Settings:**

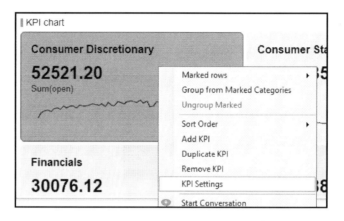

2. Let's start by configuring the values of the KPI chart—the properties dialog will open to the correct place for us to do this. Set the following properties:
   1. **Value (y-axis): Avg(close)**
   2. **Time (x-axis): Date(Year >> Month >> Day of Month):**

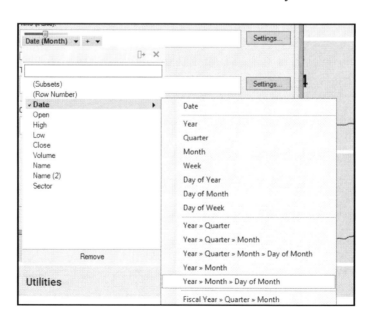

3. **Show time in tile**: (checked).
4. **Tile by**: **Sector**.
5. **Comparative value**: **Avg(volume)**. Here's the completed configuration for the **Values** part of the KPI chart:

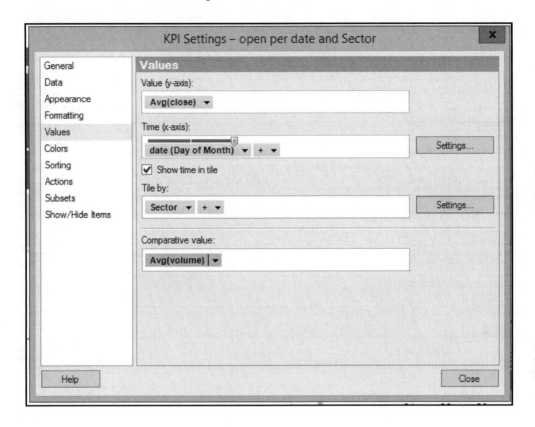

3. Select the **Formatting** property page and set the format for the value axis to show **Currency**. Check the checkbox to use the short number format and choose **USD**:

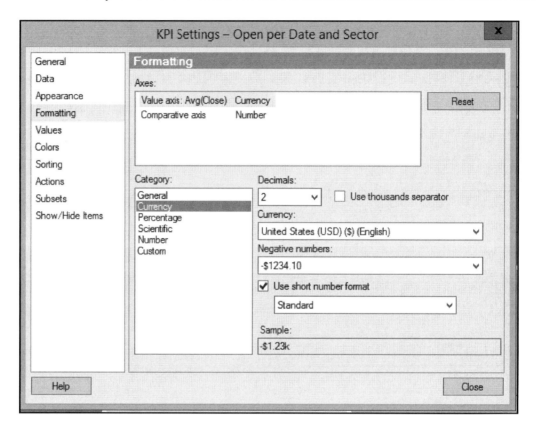

4. Set the formatting for the comparative axis in the same way, but this time, choose number formatting.
5. Click close on the properties dialog. You should see something like this:

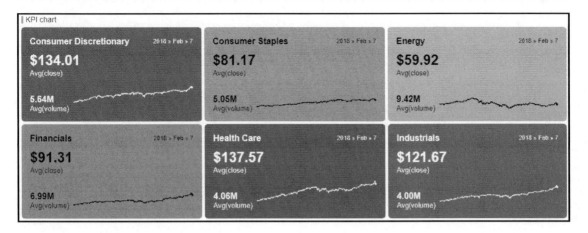

The KPI chart is looking good so far, so let's pause to discuss some important aspects of the chart before configuring it further:

- The KPI chart is divided into "tiles". Each tile represents a category in the data. In our case, we joined the constituent data so that the industry sectors could be represented in an easy-to-view format. Showing all the individual symbols in a single KPI chart is too much information to digest at a glance.

- KPI charts show a trend over time with the sparkline. A **sparkline** is a small line chart with the purpose of showing a general trend, without the full details. A sparkline is very efficient in the amount of screen space it uses. In this case, we have chosen to keep the y-axis of the sparklines the same for all categories—this allows for a direct comparison between the categories, but we could choose to show individual scales, which would give a greater indication of trend in each category, but not allow direct comparison between the categories.

- There are two values shown in each tile the KPI chart:
  - **Value**: This is the "large" value shown on the top-left of each tile
  - **Comparative value**: This is the smaller value shown at the bottom-left of each tile

- The value (top-left) is always based on the data at the latest time point. In my case, the value shows the average closing price on February 7, 2018—the date is displayed in the top-right of each tile. The KPI chart needs special care if the data isn't complete and the latest dates are different across the categories, but we will discuss this later on in this chapter.

- The comparative value is designed to show any other value—in our case, we have selected **Avg(volume)**. It's important to note that this is the average volume (per day, as that is how the data is stratified) for all stocks in each sector since "the beginning of time."
- The **(Empty)** tile is just present because some of the stock symbols are not listed in the constituent data, so they have not been allocated an industry sector. This is not a problem for our example, but you may wish to fix issues like this in the real world.

 It's especially important to remember the difference in how the values are calculated, so I'll say it again! Most Spotfire visualizations aggregate data over time, but the (main) KPI chart value is calculated on the latest data point.

Coloring, sorting, and other customization of the KPI chart

The KPI chart looks pretty good right now, but there are other settings and customizations we can apply to see if they would be useful.

To color the KPI chart by value, perform the following steps:

1. Right-click on the KPI chart and select **KPI Settings**.
2. Select the **Colors** property page.
3. Make sure **(Value axis values)** is shown for the **Columns** for coloring.

4. You can choose a Spotfire default coloring scheme by clicking the pull-out that looks like multiple sheets of paper:

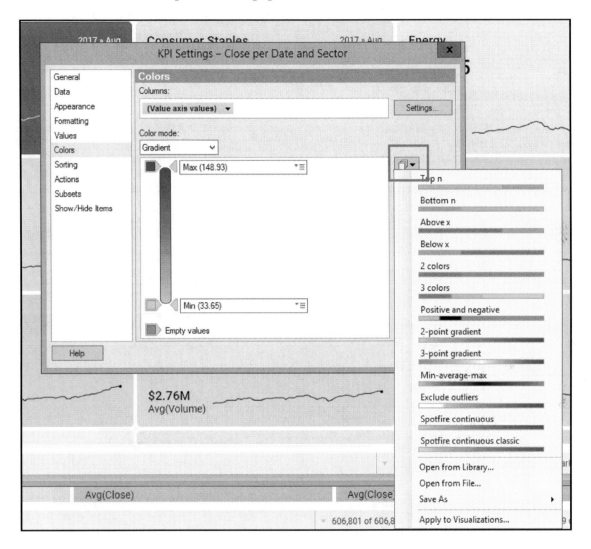

5. We can refine the color scheme by choosing some suitable colors. I chose green for the **Max** value to indicate that a high closing price is good; red for **Min**, indicating that a low closing price is not so good; and yellow was chosen for **Average**.

6. We can also choose a default color scheme in Spotfire web clients:

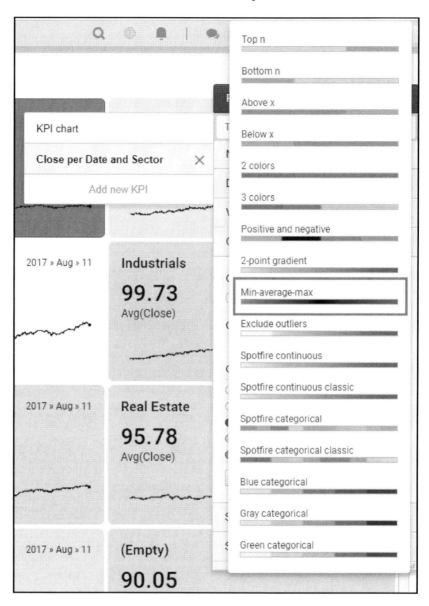

We should sort the KPI chart by value to show the highest closing stock first. There are a couple of steps that need to be followed. In the Analyst client, do the following:

1. Reopen the **KPI Settings**, if they're not already open.
2. Select the **Sorting** property page.
3. Click the **Sort tiles by** dropdown and choose **(Axis values)** | **(Value axis values)**:

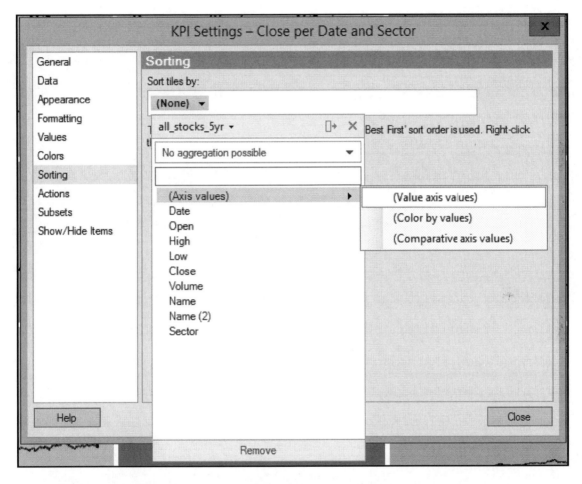

Note that this doesn't immediately apply the sort order to the KPI chart since there is no sort order defined. We need to define whether the sort is ascending or descending from the KPI chart itself. In our case, I think it makes sense to show the best industry sector first.

4. Close the **KPI Settings** dialog and right-click on the KPI chart.

5. Click **Sort Order**, then choose **Best First**:

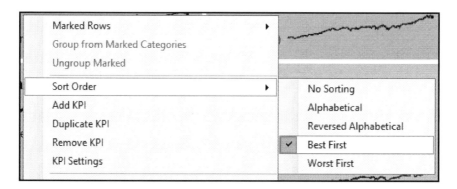

This will sort the KPI chart by the sort order that was defined in the KPI settings (descending in value).

In the web clients, the steps are broadly similar. Now that we have configured the KPI chart, wouldn't it be nice to allow end users to configure the chart interactively—even Spotfire Consumer users? Remember—Spotfire Consumer users do not have the ability to configure charts—everything is read-only. The next section will show you how to allows all users to choose which measure the KPI chart displays.

Enabling end users to configure the KPI chart interactively

Imagine the following scenario: you've just configured a KPI chart showing **Avg(close)**—well, that's exactly what you've done right now, so it shouldn't be too hard to tax your imagination! Then, you want to publish the KPI chart to others in your organization. The trouble is, it may not meet the needs of others.

What if they are interested in the average opening price of the stock instead of the closing price? What if they want the sum rather than the average? All these options would show different pictures of the data, and we can't expect every user of a Spotfire chart to go digging into its settings in order to change what's shown on an axis.

Fortunately, Spotfire has an easy way of adding controls and customization to visualizations. Discussing these will introduce a number of important Spotfire concepts, so I'll discuss them briefly first to give you some background and then pull them together in an example.

Framing your analysis using text areas

Spotfire's **text area**, though not strictly a visualization, is as important as any of the visualizations on your analysis page. In terms of insertion on the page and maneuvering within the layout, the text area behaves exactly the same way as a visualization, so treat it as one.

In its simplest form, the text area can be used simply to add some text to support your analysis: a title and brief description or some usage instructions. You can enter text plainly or take advantage of the text area's underlying HTML base for more sophisticated presentations. If you don't know much about HTML, the W3Schools website (http://www.w3schools.com/html/) is an excellent starting point. It's not that difficult to pick up some basic techniques.

The text area is much more than just a text area. In a text area, you can embed property controls such as input fields or drop-down menu controls. You can also embed calculated values, images, URLs to external content, action buttons, filters, and some simple visualization elements.

We will create a text area in the next example and use it to configure the KPI chart. Before we get to that, however, we need to introduce the concepts of **Custom Expressions**, **Document Properties**, and **Property Controls**.

 Important note: Text areas can only be added and configured using Spotfire's Analyst clients. Once configured, they can be used to drive analyses for web client (Consumer) users.

Spotfire custom expressions

So far, we have selected columns and aggregation functions on visualization axes. These are selected by the (now familiar) axis selector dropdowns. Behind the scenes, Spotfire is translating the selections made by you into an "expression." This expression determines how Spotfire aggregates or displays the data on a visualization.

It's possible to see the expressions behind the visualizations by right-clicking on an axis selector on a visualization or a visualization property page. For example, if we revisit the KPI chart we just created, we can see the expressions that drive the data that is shown. It's then also possible to customize any of the expressions therein.

A simple example of an expression is as follows:

```
Avg([Close])
```

What does this represent in Spotfire? Simply put, Spotfire will calculate the average of the **Close** column and display it. You can access the expressions wherever you see an axis selector. For the preceding KPI chart, try right-clicking on the **Value (y-axis)** selector and clicking **Custom Expression...**:

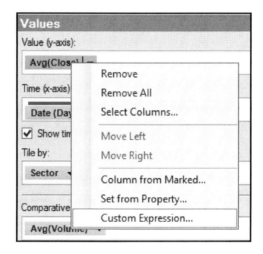

In Analyst clients, you'll see the full expression editor pop up:

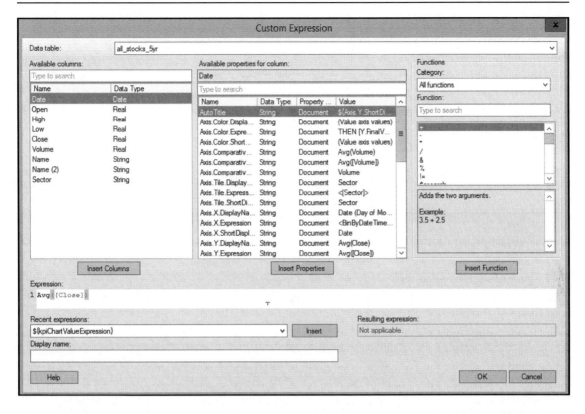

Study the dialog briefly—the individual parts of it will be discussed in more detail later on. We will be using a custom expression in the next example.

In the web client, the expression editor is simpler—it doesn't have so many options or hints to help you, but it's only designed to enable editing of simple custom expressions:

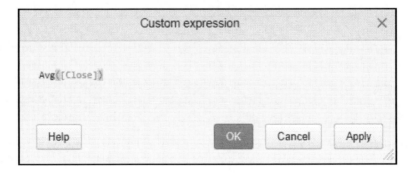

Spotfire document properties

Document properties are key to the use of user inputs and other controls. As we'll see shortly, you can create new document properties in the course of creating controls, but you can also access all document properties directly, creating new ones and editing existing ones through the main document properties dialog.

A document property is "global" to the Spotfire document. In Spotfire nomenclature, the document is the currently open analysis file. A document property can be thought of as a value that is stored in the document. It can be used to control or configure various aspects of the analysis.

 Important note: Document properties can only be configured using Analyst clients.

You'll find document properties under the **File** menu options. Select **Document Properties** and then the **Properties** tab:

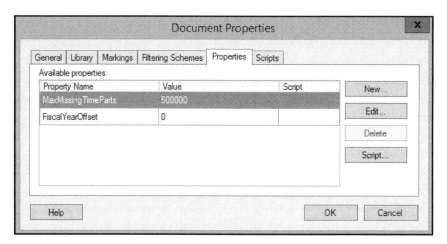

Don't worry about the **Script...** button for now. Scripting is covered in `Chapter 11`, *Scripting, Advanced Analytics, and Extensions*. Stick to the **New...** and **Edit...** buttons for now. When creating a new property, you need to enter the following details:

- **Property name**: You must give the property a unique name with no spaces. You cannot change this once the property has been created, but you can delete the property and start again.

- **Data type**: You must choose a data type from the drop-down list. You cannot change this once the property has been created.
- **Description**: This is optional and only required for information purposes. You can change it later.
- **Value**: This is optional for strings, but you'll need to enter some initial value for numbers, dates/times and Booleans. The value of a document property can be changed as often as you like after it has been created.

Once a document property exists, you can use it as the basis for a property control or reference it directly in a custom expression. A dollar sign and braces are used when referencing a document property, for example, `${ExampleDocumentProperty}`. This is very useful functionality, as we are about to see.

 Document properties cannot have spaces or special characters such as underscores in their names. When naming properties, it's good practice to use what's known as `UpperCamelCase`, concatenating the words you want to use and starting each with a capital letter. Try to cultivate a logical and consistent approach to naming properties such that the name is self-explanatory.

There are also a couple of predefined document properties. They are called `MaxMissingTimeParts` and `FiscalYearOffset`.

`MaxMissingTimeParts` allows you to specify the maximum number of missing time parts that should be allowed to be replaced using the **Compensate for missing values** setting, which is available on the **Appearance property** page of some visualizations.

`FiscalYearOffset` specifies the number of months from the start of the calendar year to the start of the fiscal year. For instance, a value of -1 specifies that the fiscal year starts in December of the previous calendar year, whereas a value of 2 specifies that it starts in March of the current calendar year.

Spotfire property controls

Property controls are input controls that can be used to set the values of document properties. There are various types of input control—dropdowns, multiselect boxes, text input boxes, action buttons, and so on. The palette of controls that's available in Spotfire may seem limited on the surface, but the controls are configured in ways that are extremely powerful and allow for the creation of sophisticated analytics applications. Property controls are contained in text areas.

Bringing it all together – interactively configuring the KPI chart

So, how do we bring together the concepts of text areas, document properties, property controls, and custom expressions?

Easy! We are going to use them to provide a configurable KPI chart that allows us to change what is shown on it.

 This example is only possible to follow within Spotfire Analyst clients.

Follow along with this example, as we add a text area, a property control, and wire everything up together:

1. Add a text area to the current page by selecting it from the new visualization pullout:

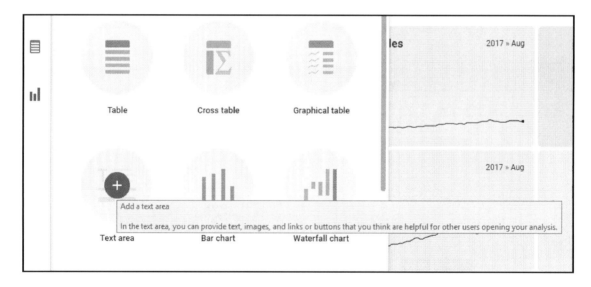

2. Move the text area above the KPI chart and resize it to a reasonable size by clicking and dragging the divider between it and the KPI chart.

3. Click the pen icon on the top right-hand corner of the text area to edit it. Note that the icons are not visible until you hover over the top right corner of the text area:

4. A new dialog will pop up. Add a drop-down list control to the text area by clicking the **Insert Property Control** button and choosing **Drop-down list**:

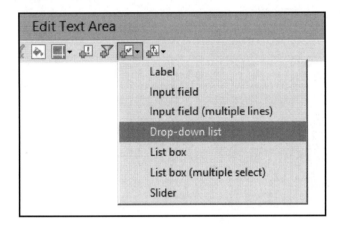

5. A further dialog will pop up that will allow us to configure the property control. First of all, we need a new Document Property that can be configured by the property control. This Document Property will then control the KPI chart. Click the **New...** button.

6. A dialog will open. The Document Property must be named. As we already stated, it's important to give meaningful names to **Document Properties**, so call it `KPIChartValueAxis`. All the other settings can be left as per the default:

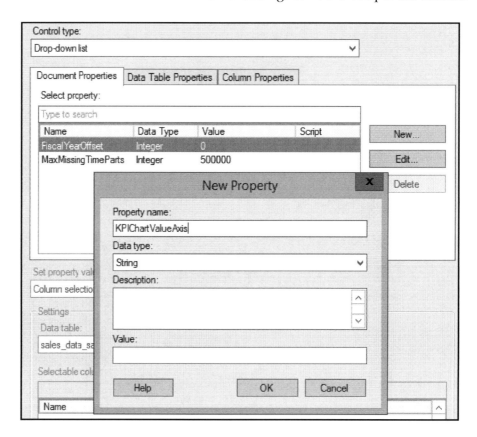

7. Click **OK** to close the dialog box for the new Document Property.
8. Choose to set the property values by **Expressions**:

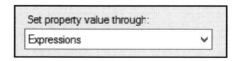

9. Click on the first **Display Name** field in the table and enter `Avg Open`. Then, use the carriage return/*Enter* key on the keyboard to move to/add the next row. Fill in all the values as per the following screenshot:

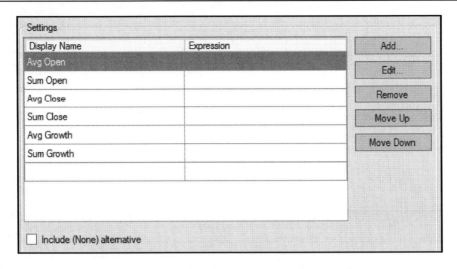

10. If you click the **Add...** button instead of using the carriage return key on the keyboard, Spotfire's expression editor will be shown. You can enter the **Display name** in the box at the bottom of the editor. I haven't asked you to fill in any expressions just yet as it's general good practice to enter the display names ahead of the expressions because it gets you thinking about what you want to show without worrying about how to show it:

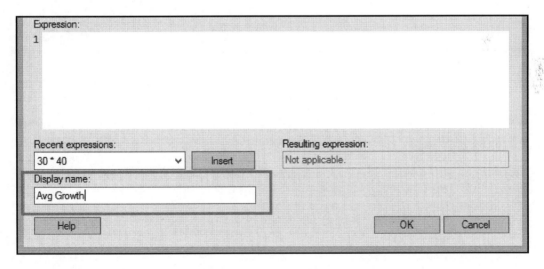

11. Now, select the first row in the table and click the **Edit...** button:

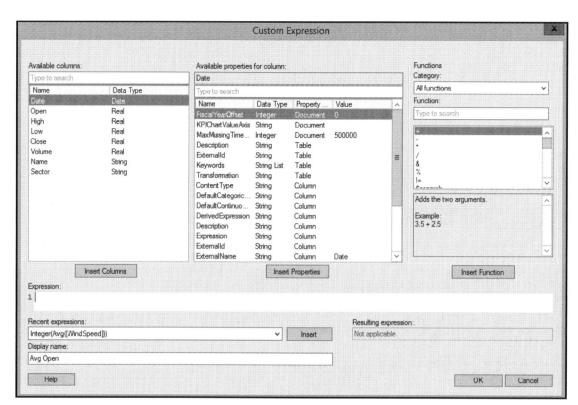

12. You'll notice that available columns, properties, functions, and so on are all shown in the dialog. For now, we will be using the columns and functions part of the expression editor.
The expression we want to end up with is as follows:
Avg([Open])

13. On the **Functions Category** dropdown, choose **Statistical functions**:

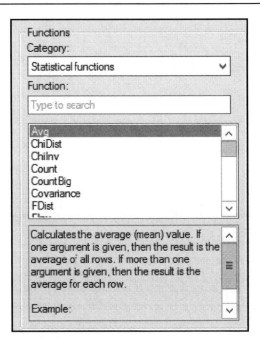

14. Select the **Avg** function and click **Insert Function** (or double-click on the **Avg** function).

15. Now, move to the **Available Columns** part of the dialog, click the open column, and click **Insert Columns**.

16. You should now find that the **Expression** reads as follows:

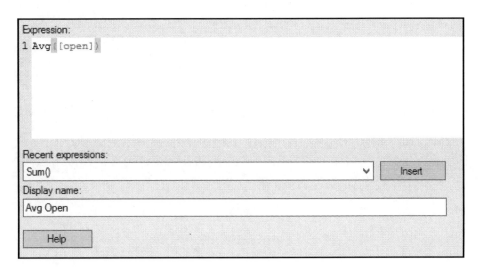

17. Click **OK** on the dialog to close it.

18. Now, follow the same steps for each of the other expressions in the drop-down control. They should be as follows (**Display Name : Expression**):

  - Avg Open: Avg([open])
  - Sum Open: Sum([open])
  - Avg Close: Avg([close])
  - Sum Close: Sum([close])
  - Avg Growth: Avg([close] - [pen])
  - Sum Growth: Sum([close] - [open])

19. Note that in order to enter the minus symbol, you will have to edit the expression directly inline. Spotfire has auto-complete with column names and functions, and so on.

20. You should end up with a list of expressions that looks like this:

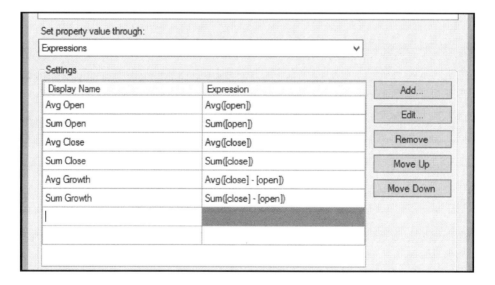

21. Click **OK** on the dialog.

22. Finally, we should add a hint to the user. Place the cursor in front of the drop-down control and enter KPI Chart Value:

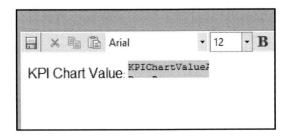

Feel free to adjust the text size, font, color, and so on.

23. Close the Text Area editor. Click **Yes** on the dialog that asks if you want to save changes.

Now that the property control has been configured, it's necessary to set up the KPI chart so that it uses the expressions from the control. We can do that by following these steps:

1. Right-click the KPI and choose **KPI Settings...**.
2. Right-click the **Value (y-axis)** selector and choose **Custom Expression...**:

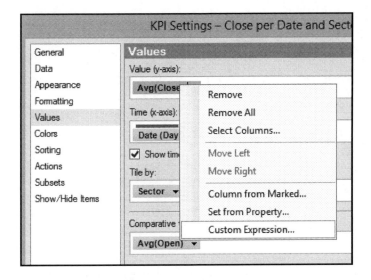

You might think that **Set from Property...** might be a good option to choose here. This works in some cases, but it won't work here—it works if the property is just a reference to a column or similar, but we are doing more than that—we are specifying an aggregation function and a column. Spotfire doesn't know that, so it will generate an invalid expression if we choose **Set from Property...**.

3. Highlight and delete the current expression.

4. Now, we get to use the **Available properties for column part** of the custom expression editor dialog. Scroll through the list of properties and select **KPIChartValueAxis**, and then click **Insert Properties**:

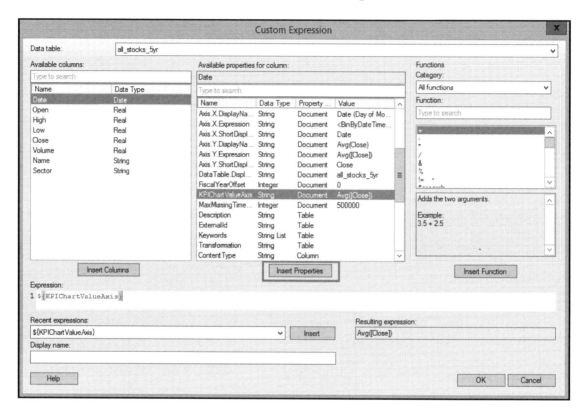

Recall that KPIChartValueAxis is the name of the document property that was created at the time the drop-down property control was created and designed.

5. Take a look at the **Resulting expression** part of the dialog. This shows the **decoded** value of the current value of the expression. The expression that's now used for the value axis of the KPI chart is ${KPIChartValueAxis}.

The syntax for document properties in custom expressions is a $ sign with curly brackets that encloses the document property name. In some cases, you'll need to **escape** document property values, for example, if the document property contains a string that represents the name of a column and you need Spotfire to translate the string into a valid column name. Escaping document properties is done like this: `$esc(${PropertyName})`.

6. Click **OK** on the **Custom Expression** editor dialog.

7. Now, try choosing different values on the drop-down control. You should see the KPI chart updates to show whatever is chosen. In the background, Spotfire is substituting the custom expressions that we have designed in the control into the KPI chart value axis.

8. Finally, it's good practice to hide the title bars of text areas (and other visualizations) if they serve no purpose. Hiding the title bars makes the dashboard or analysis much cleaner. To hide a title bar, open the **Text Area Properties** and uncheck **Show title bar**:

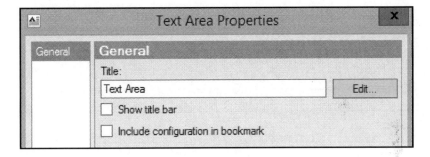

To recap—this example has shown how to provide the ability to change the configuration of a Spotfire visualization on the fly. This enables a nontechnical user or consumer of a Spotfire analysis to customize how they view the analysis without needing a Spotfire Analyst client. In addition, by providing property-control-based configuration of an analysis, you are guiding the end user of the analysis to get the best value out of it.

Now would be a good time to save your dashboard!

Drilling in to the KPI chart

Remember the introduction to the section on KPI charts? I stated that KPI charts give you the answer to the "What?" question. Now, let's look at the "Why?" of analytics.

Answering the "Why?" question can be a lot more challenging than answering the "What?". Sometimes, significant creativity is required, but here's a checklist of things you might wish to consider:

- What types of visualizations will best show a detailed view of the data?
- How can I slice and dice the details visualizations to show a complete picture?
- Can additional value be gained by showing multiple, related datasets side by side?

We will build a line chart details visualization that shows historical data over time. By way of an example, I will walk you through the thought processes that go into making the line chart more and more insightful and useful. Before I do that, it's time to cover another key Spotfire concept in detail—that of marking.

Marking in Spotfire

In Chapters 1, *Welcome to Spotfire*, and Chapter 2, *It's All About the Data*, we covered the basics of marking but it now warrants a more in-depth explanation since it's such a key concept in Spotfire.

We created details visualizations by right-clicking on a main visualization and selecting **Create Details Visualization**. This is the standard method of enabling drill-in from one visualization into another. However, behind the scenes, the drill-in capability is implemented via a concept known as **marking**. In other analytics tools, this is often called brushing and linking. Similar terminology may also be used. The example that follows will show you how to configure a details visualization manually by explicitly specifying the marking scheme to use.

The concept of marking is that data is **marked** or **highlighted** temporarily on one visualization (by using the mouse or touch). The same data, related data, or linked data is then shown elsewhere within the analysis. Spotfire will either simply highlight marked data on multiple visualizations, or it will restrict data on some visualizations based on data selected in another. The concept of a details visualization is the latter concept. Data that is marked on one (main) visualization is used temporarily to limit the data shown on other visualizations to the subset of data marked in the main visualization.

There are a few key rules to be aware of with marking:

- Spotfire analyses can have multiple marking schemes
- Marking can be used to set up a parent-child relationship between visualizations
- Multiple visualizations can share the same marking schemes
- Multiple marking schemes can be used to restrict data on visualizations (it's even possible to use Boolean logic—data must be in all markings or just one or the other)
- Marking data does not affect the underlying data in any way
- Marking of data can work between multiple, related data tables (note that we have not discussed data table relations yet—this topic is covered in Chapter 8, *The World is Your Visualization*)

 You can edit markings stored in a Spotfire analysis file by using the **File | Document Properties** dialog, then navigating to **Markings** in Analyst clients or from the **Edit** menu in web clients.

Building a details visualization using marking

The steps for building a details visualization using marking are slightly different for the Spotfire Analyst and web clients, so I'll point out how they differ along the way.

Reopen the KPI chart example file if you closed it earlier and follow these steps:

1. Add a new line chart visualization:

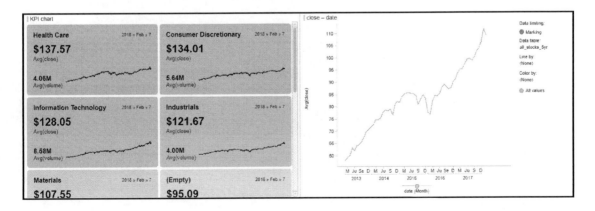

Great—now, notice that it shows all the data for all the KPIs together—it's the summary of the entire dataset. That may not be what we want right now, but this is what we are about to configure!

2. Using the **Color by** selector for the line chart (the selector is in the legend), choose **Sector** from the dropdown:

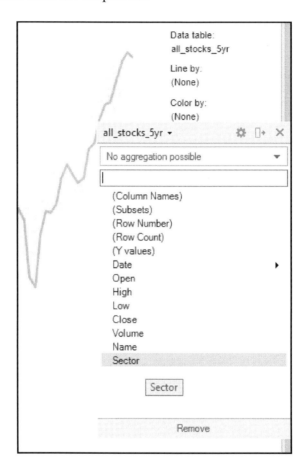

3. Choose **Avg(close])** for the *y*-axis for the line chart.
    Wow—that looks different! Notice that choosing a column to color by has split the data into multiple lines. One for each sector:

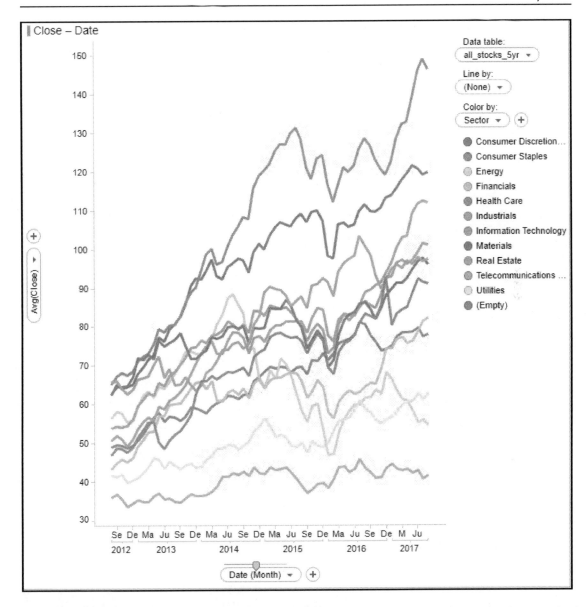

If we had changed the **Line by** setting of the visualization, it would have also been divided into one line per sector, but the colors would not have been set - all the lines would have been gray. In effect, color has been used to segment (or slice/dice) the data into its separate categories. These categories now match what is shown in the KPI chart. We will see, a little later, how we can use line by and color by together to get an even deeper understanding of the data.

So far, the line chart shows all data. Let's update it to show just the data that corresponds to marked tiles in the KPI chart by configuring marking:

1. The KPI chart is going to be the master visualization and the line chart for the details visualization. So, right-click on a KPI tile and choose **KPI Settings** (Analyst) or **Properties** (web).

2. Navigate to the **Data properties** and check the **Marking** scheme that's being used. It should be the default and is just called **Marking**:

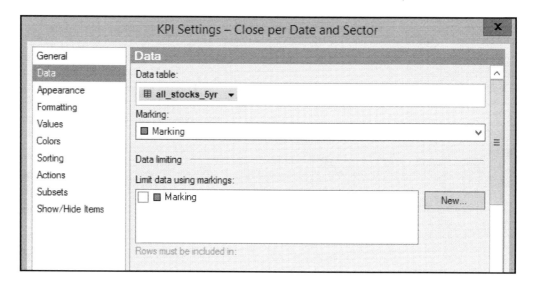

 Checking the marking scheme that's used in the master visualization is always a good step—it's just good practice to check what's going on before proceeding to the next step.

3. Close the KPI chart properties, then right-click on the line chart and choose **Properties**, or click on the cog wheel in the top right-hand corner of the visualization.

4. Navigate to **Data properties** and find **Marking**.

5. In the **Data limiting** part of the dialog, select the checkbox to limit the data by **Marking**:

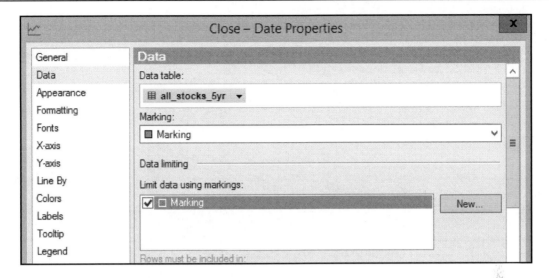

6. In Analyst clients, I recommend that you also choose to show all data if no items are marked in the master visualization:

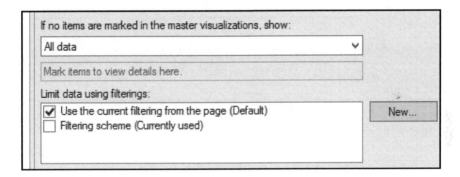

As we previously stated, this option is not available in the web client.

 Notice that the line chart also uses the same marking scheme as the KPI chart, so everything you mark in the KPI chart will also be marked in the line chart. This is very confusing for anyone using the analysis, and it doesn't look great. We will fix this issue in the following set of steps.

In the meantime, close the visualization properties and return to your dashboard. Try clicking on KPI tiles. Notice how the line chart updates to show the details of the data that belong to each tile that you mark.

Now, let's add another marking scheme (Analyst clients):

1. Right-click on the line chart and choose **Properties**. Navigate to the **Data** page and locate **Limit data using markings**.
2. Click the **New...** button.
3. Choose a suitable color and name for the marking scheme and click **OK**:

4. Now, choose the new marking scheme for the line chart:

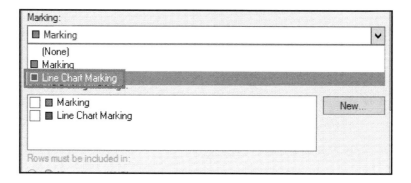

We can add a new marking and configure the line chart to use it in web clients by following these steps:

1. Choose **Edit markings...** from the **Edit** menu.
2. Click the **+** icon to add a new marking scheme. You can rename it by clicking the pencil icon once it's been created (if you feel so inclined!):

3. Return to the line chart properties and choose **Marking (2)** as the marking scheme for that visualization.

Finally, I suggest that you experiment a bit with marking some KPI tiles and observing what happens to the line chart. It should behave just like any other details visualization.

Deep dive – what insights can the dashboard reveal?

I expect that some stocks may be more volatile than others and some may grow better than others. Please note that, as I am writing this, I do not know what insights I am going to uncover ahead of time—you are following me live as I use the power of Spotfire to find fresh insights in the data:

1. Try clicking on some individual KPI tiles—notice that the line chart will update to show details for the data that corresponds to the KPI that has been clicked. The line chart shows the detailed trend of the KPI over time.

2. What if you want to view multiple KPI tiles at the same time? Most Spotfire visualizations support click-and-drag marking, where you mark an area on the chart to show the details underneath the area that's been marked. The KPI chart works slightly differently.

Hold the *Shift* key on your keyboard to select multiple KPI tiles at once. Hold the *Ctrl* key to select and deselect KPI tiles individually.

Selecting multiple KPI tiles will allow you to compare them together. Here, I have selected **Consumer Discretionary** and **Consumer Staples**:

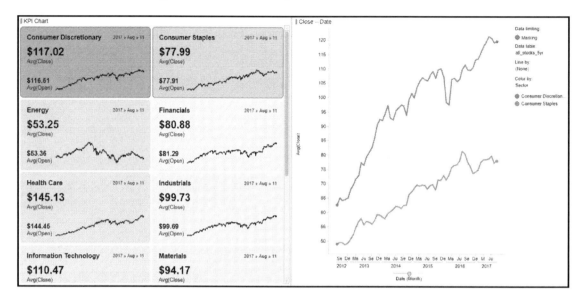

Notice that the two trends are shown side by side in different colors on the line chart. From the line chart, the following insights are clear:

- The value of **Consumer Discretionary** is always higher than **Consumer Staples**
- The trend of **Consumer Discretionary** is less stable than **Consumer Staples**—there's a big dip around January-March 2016

These insights might lead to a direct action from this chart alone! For example:

- An investor that wishes to make short-term, larger gains may choose to invest in unit stocks in **Consumer Discretionary**
- A more cautious investor, for example, one heading toward retirement, may choose to invest in stocks in **Consumer Staples**

We can take this analysis even further by drilling in to the makeup of the individual industry sectors. Right now, the line chart shows the difference between various KPI tiles, but does not yet provide any insight into *why* one industry sector might be trending differently from another.

Let's enable the splitting of the data by stock as well as sector by creating another line chart and splitting it by stock name. We can duplicate the line chart so that we can create another from scratch:

1. Right-click on the line chart and choose **Duplicate Visualization**.
2. Now, split the right-hand chart by name as well as sector—choose **Name** from the **Line by** selector:

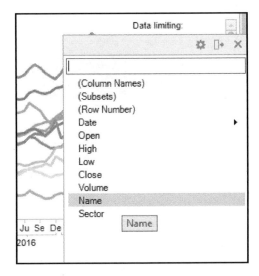

Interesting! Look at the screenshot of the second line chart now:

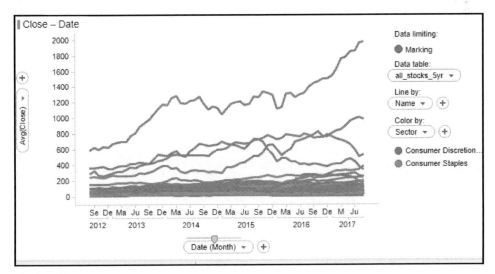

It's pretty clear that some **Discretionary** stocks are indeed generally higher than the **Staples** stocks—look at how the **Staples** stocks are all bunched at the bottom of the visualization. Notice also that there is one stock that is head and shoulders above the rest—both in terms of its overall value and in the magnitude of its growth. Right now, we don't know which stock that is, but it can be found easily enough.

Simply hover the mouse over the line chart and particularly, the line at the top:

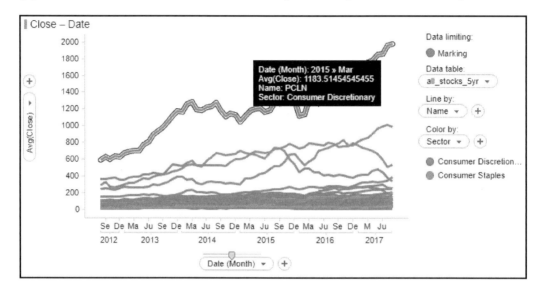

So, the top performing stock is **PCLN**—this is the **Priceline Group** (from 2012 to 2017 it has trebled in price). It should be far from me to give financial advice in a Spotfire book, but... you can draw your own conclusions!

I'd really like to remind you of one other nice feature. In `Chapter 2`, *It's All About the Data*, the concept of natural hierarchies in data was introduced. Time/date data is one of the most interesting and useful natural hierarchies there is, and here we have used it for the first time. Think about it—time and date information is split up into this kind of hierarchy:

- **Year**
- **Month**
- **Day**
- **Hour**
- **Minute**
- **Second**
- **Millisecond**

However, it could also be split up as follows:

- **Year**
- **Quarter**
- **Month**
- **Day**

In addition, there are concepts of fiscal years, quarters, months, and so on.

Spotfire has a native understanding of such date/time hierarchies, and we can use that to our advantage by following these steps:

1. Drop-down the *x*-axis selector on the second line chart and choose:
   Date, then **Year >> Quarter >> Month >> Day of Month**:

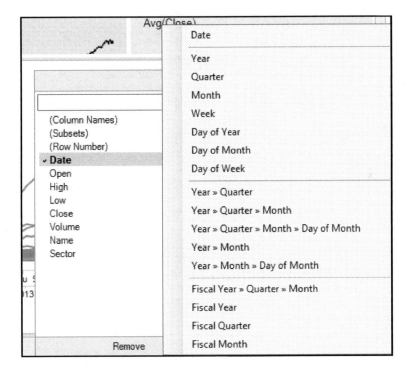

2. Now, adjust the hierarchy slider on the axis. Try all the different levels of the hierarchy in turn and watch what happens to the line chart. Spotfire will automatically aggregate the line chart at each level. Here is the highest level (**Year**):

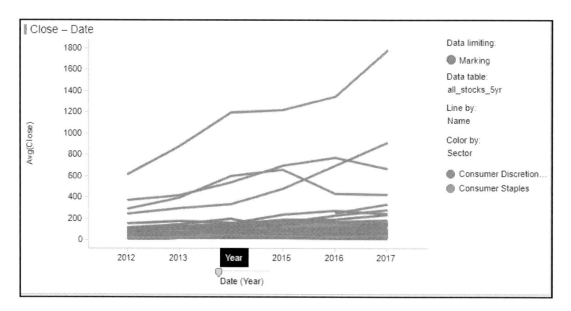

The next level is **Quarter**:

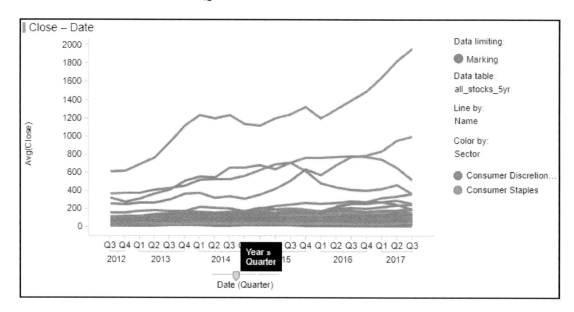

Now **Month**:

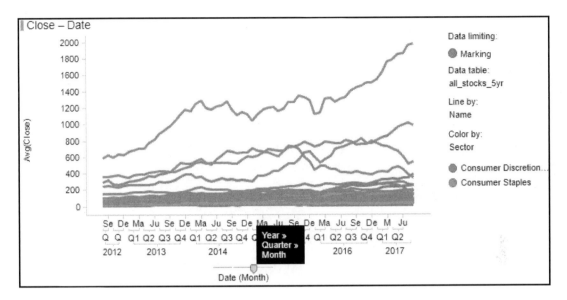

And finally, **Day of Month**:

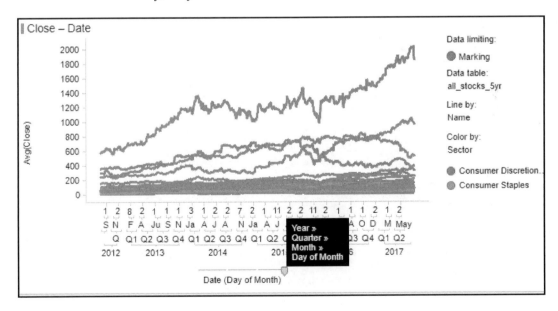

Notice how each line is aggregated at the level currently selected in the hierarchy—the line is smoother at the less detailed levels and more jagged at the more detailed. Higher levels of the hierarchy are useful for looking at overall trends and minimizing local effects (rapid changes that don't affect the overall statistical significance of the trend too much). Lower levels are useful for examining the detail and looking at variations—peaks and troughs over time.

Finally, let's hone in on some detail and try to understand more about why there is a dip and a rebound in the value of **Consumer Discretionary** stocks at around January 2016. Was it caused by PCLN on its own or was there a sector-wide issue leading to a crash and a rebound?

How can we look at this area of the visualization in more detail? Spotfire's zoom sliders will allow us to do this really easily.

If you are using a Spotfire Analyst client, perform these steps:

1. Right-click on the visualization and choose **Visualization Features | X Zoom Slider**:

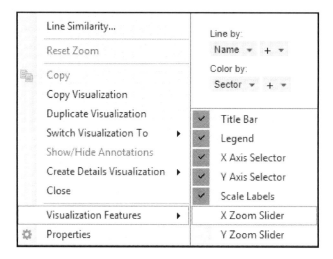

2. Do the same again for the **Y Zoom Slider**.

In web clients, perform the following steps:

1. Right-click on the *x*-axis of the line chart and choose **Properties**.
2. Check the **Show zoom slider** checkbox:

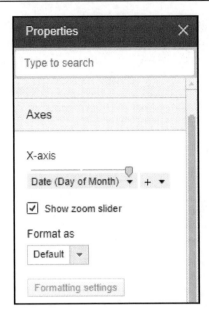

3. Close the **Properties** dialog.
4. Do the same with the *y*-axis and enable its zoom slider.

Now, you can experiment with the zoom sliders to explore various features of the data in detail. It really does look like PCLN's dip and rebound is confined to January to March 2016. I wonder what happened during that time:

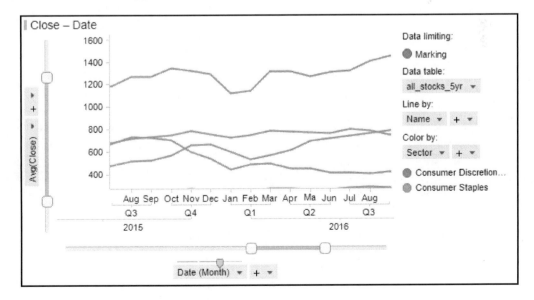

In fact, I think the dip and rebound isn't big enough to affect the overall average that much—remember that the same trend was found overall for this industry sector. We can easily test this hypothesis by removing the effects of PCLN from the analysis:

1. Click on the line representing PCLN. This will mark it.

2. Right-click on the visualization and choose **Marked Rows** | **Filter out**:

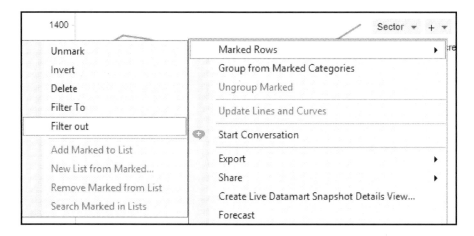

3. Now, look at the line chart on the left. The dip and rebound is still there! So it can't be due to PCLN alone:

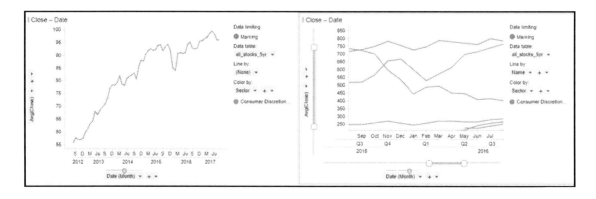

That makes me think. Could it be that, in fact, **Consumer Staples** is the industry sector that bucks the trend? It might be... let's just check:

1. Go back to the KPI chart and select some more industry sectors—I have chosen the following:
   - **Consumer Discretionary**
   - **Consumer Staples**
   - **Energy**
   - **Financials**
2. Look at the line chart trends now:

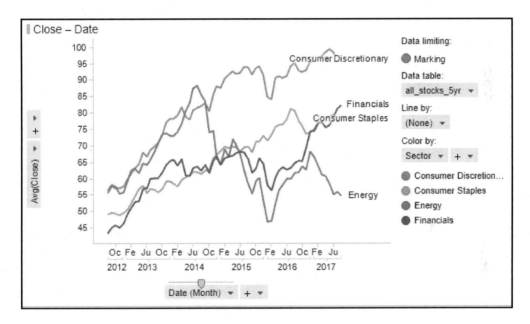

It would seem that the only sector unaffected at that time (in this subgroup anyway) is **Consumer Staples**. However, notice that it has a dip and rebound a little bit later than the other industry sectors.

I have also added labels to each line—the setting for this is available in the visualization properties—go and take a look and try turning them on for yourself.

The updated line chart suggests to me that there must have been a problem with the stock market as a whole in January-March 2016. In fact—googling "stock market crash January 2016" does point to a bit of a crash and rebound in the first quarter of 2016—see how our analysis enabled us to identify this and explore the details of it?

If I were doing this analysis again and knowing what I know now, I may well have just produced a single line chart with the average of all stocks over time—I leave it as an exercise for you to do if you so wish!

In summary, I know that it may seem that focusing on PCLN may have been a "red herring"—that is, of no real value, and that my initial assumptions about the markets (that in some way, **Consumer Discretionary** was different from the other sectors, and that PCLN was leading to this difference) were wrong.

However, doing this kind of exploratory analysis is a very useful technique when working with analytics. I have also enjoyed showing you how to drill in to details and configure Spotfire visualizations "live" without being worried about designing them ahead of time. How can you know how to design something if you have no idea what you need to design ahead of time?

Having a hunch and following it, only to be proved wrong, is just as valuable as having a correct assumption in the first place. Go with your instincts. Investigate the data. See what it reveals!

 Now would be a good time to save your analysis file.

Publishing the dashboard to Spotfire Web

One of the key aspects of Spotfire is that it is very straightforward to publish an analysis to the web so that it can be consumed by many more users than just you or your immediate team members.

Note that if you are using a Spotfire Web client to author your analysis, saving the file online saves it directly to the Spotfire library, so you have already published it (if permissions are set correctly)!

However, if you are using a Spotfire Analyst client, it's a really simple matter to publish it for use by Spotfire Consumer users. This makes it available to a wider audience—potentially hundreds or thousands of users. Many Spotfire users even expose their analyses to the internet!

The following example of publishing an analysis applies to Spotfire Analyst and requires that you have a Spotfire web deployment up and running. This could be a Spotfire Cloud instance or an on-premises installation of Spotfire. If you do not have anywhere available where you can publish the analysis, please do still read through the example, as it may provide you with food for thought if you should want to scale up the use of Spotfire in your organization in the future.

Let's deploy the analysis now:

1. If you are not online to a Spotfire server, please close Spotfire and reopen it, logging in to a server that you have access to. You can tell if you are online by checking the globe icon in the toolbar:

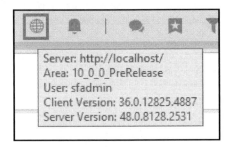

2. From the File menu, choose **Save As | Library item...**:

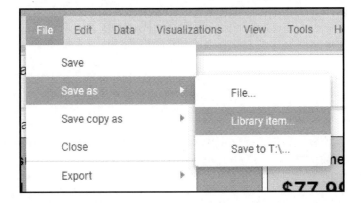

3. Spotfire's library browser will open by way of a **File, Save As** dialog:

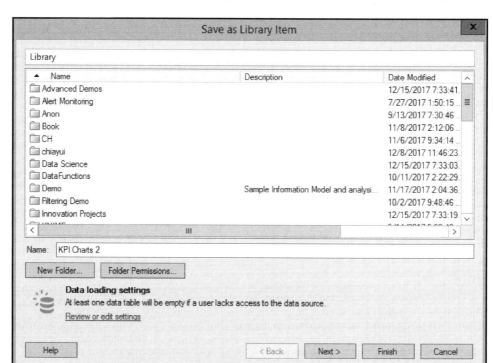

 Spotfire's library is its in-built file store. It has already been mentioned in the earlier chapters of this book. The library is stored on the Spotfire server and is shared by all users that use the particular server. The folders have a sophisticated permissions model and can store Spotfire analysis files, data files, database connections, information links (for Spotfire's database abstraction model), and more.

Notice that the library browser has opened at the root (highest level) of the library in my case. It's a good idea to have a well-thought-out folder structure within the library, so let's create a new folder for our dashboard.

 Do you have the right permissions to save in the library? If your server is managed centrally, you may already be provided with a folder in which you can save your analysis. If you don't have a suitable folder, or the permissions to save to the library, then please contact the administrator of the server asking for the requisite permissions!

4. Click the **New Folder...** button (note that you may need to move to a lower level folder within the library for which you have write permissions). We will cover what happens if you try to save to a folder in which you do not have permissions.

5. Enter the **Name** of the folder. In my case, I have chosen to name it `Sample Dashboards`:

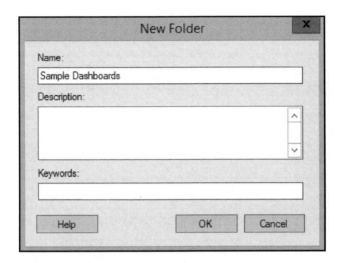

6. Click **OK** on the dialog.

7. The Spotfire library browser will open the new folder you have created. Before we go any further—did you notice the **Data loading settings** warning at the bottom of the **Save as | Library item...** dialog?

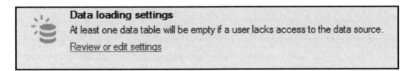

It's important to heed the warning! In `Chapter 1`, *Welcome to Spotfire*, it was discussed that if you do not embed the data in your Spotfire analysis file, any user that doesn't have access to the original source data will not be able to open it. In this case, we have loaded data from CSV files, so it's unlikely that your intended users will have access to the CSV files that were used to create the dashboard. Let's fix that now!

8. Click **Review or edit settings**.

9. In the dialog that pops up, update the data table settings to match the settings I have used here:

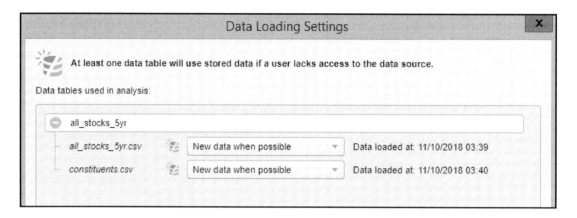

I have chosen **New data when possible**. This means that if the file exists, it will be reloaded/updated when you load the file. Otherwise, Spotfire will use the stored (embedded) data in the analysis.

Remember that we loaded a single data table by joining multiple files. If the files were loaded as separate data tables and joined them afterwards, this option will always re-execute the join when the dashboard is opened. Of course, this has a performance penalty and is something to consider when handling large data volumes, but it could be useful in order to keep various parts of the data up to date—you could have a static data table joined to another table that changes frequently, for example.

It's important to notice that any updated data files will not be reloaded automatically **UNLESS** they are in exactly the same folder that you originally loaded them from. This means that another user would have to specify the data file locations if they wished to update the dashboard with new data.

Now that the warning has been dealt with, let's go ahead and save the file!

10. Choose a filename and click **Next >** on the dialog.

11. The dialog will now enable you to enter a description and some keywords. These are optional, but I have filled in some examples:

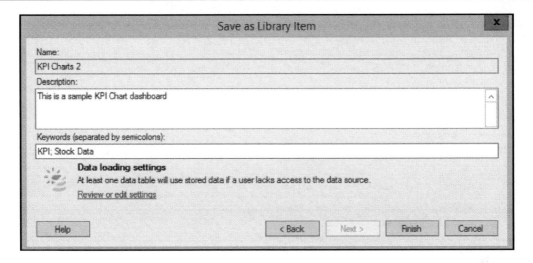

12. Click **Finish**.

Spotfire will save the file to the library. That's all it takes to publish an analysis to the Spotfire web client so that it can be opened by a Spotfire consumer.

Let's take a quick look at this dialog—there are some useful functions herein:

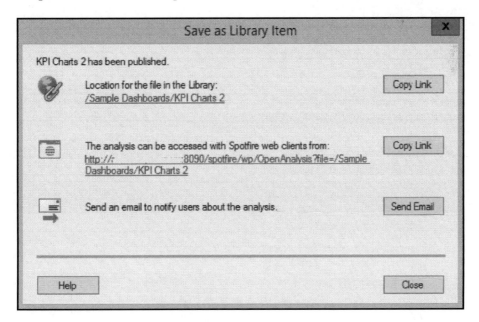

You can see the location of the file in the library—the first link that's shown is just the path of the file. You can use this to open the file using Spotfire Analyst.

The second link is the link to the analysis within the Spotfire web interface.

The third option is to send an email to notify other users about the analysis.

Try clicking the second link—a web browser should open up that shows the dashboard:

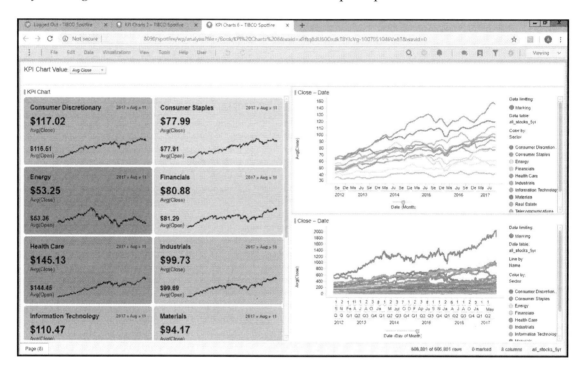

Now, check the property control that was created in the previous example—does the KPI chart update to show whatever is selected? If so, congratulations! You have successfully created and deployed your first Spotfire dashboard, and it is available for other users to consume (if the permissions have been set correctly).

Summary

This chapter has provided an introduction to producing impactful dashboards in Spotfire. Dashboards show answers to "What?" questions of analytics. Drill-in visualizations from dashboards show answers to "Why?" questions. The KPI chart was covered in detail with a real-world example.

You have learned how to use the versatile text area to embed descriptive information and user inputs. You have also learned how to get details of marked items.

Together, we explored some more ways of using details visualizations and the features of Spotfire to gain insight from visualizations. My original assumption of the data was invalid, but I showed that and then guided you through how I worked out what was really going on.

You are well on your way to creating guided analyses and dashboards. Indeed, I hope that the first three chapters have given you a solid understanding of how to get some relevant data into Spotfire, build some visualizations of that data, and enable end users to interact with and customize the analysis. Spotfire is fundamentally an exploration tool, and it's important that you keep exploring and expanding the concepts you are learning. Be curious!

Chapter 4, *Sharing Insights and Collaborating with Others*, builds on the work we've covered in the first three chapters. It gives examples of how to collaborate with your team members using Spotfire, and much more. I hope you find it useful!

4
Sharing Insights and Collaborating with Others

Collaboration is all-important these days. Working in a vacuum on any project is seldom productive. In the modern world, we all share updates via social media and the like and feed off each other for ideas, insights, and project updates and management.

In addition, we sometimes find we are drowning in too much data. **Spotfire** helps you get to the details that matter in your data. Then, when you've found them, you can share the details with your colleagues using the various built-in functions designed to assist with this. It allows sharing of context and data together.

This chapter will describe these collaborative functions and demonstrate how to use them. The topics covered are the following:

- Bookmarks
- Annotations
- Conversations

Bookmarks

Bookmarks are traditionally used in paper books to identify where you've got to. The same goes for bookmarks in Spotfire. They capture the current state of the analysis that you are working with and allow you to recall various parts of the state.

Bookmarks work fairly similarly in Spotfire's web and analyst clients—the differences will be pointed out in the example that follows:

1. Load one of the analysis files you created in a previous chapter. For the purpose of this example, I will use the KPI chart example created in `Chapter 3`, *Impactful Dashboards!*.

2. If you recall, toward the end of the example, I marked **Consumer Discretionary**, **Consumer Staples**, and **Energy**, and **Financials** on the KPI chart, by holding down *Ctrl* and clicking the tiles. Do the same again:

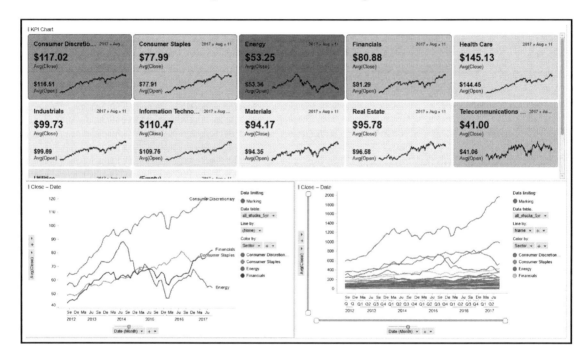

3. Now change the hierarchy slider on the x-axis of the right-hand graph to `Date(Quarter)` and zoom in on the right-hand side so that you can see the data for **2016** and **2017** only.

4. Filter out the line for PCLN (hover over the lines and find it—it's the top one—mark it, right-click, and select **Marked Rows-Filter Out**) and adjust the x-axis zoom slider. PCLN is the outlier in the data as it's so much higher than the other lines:

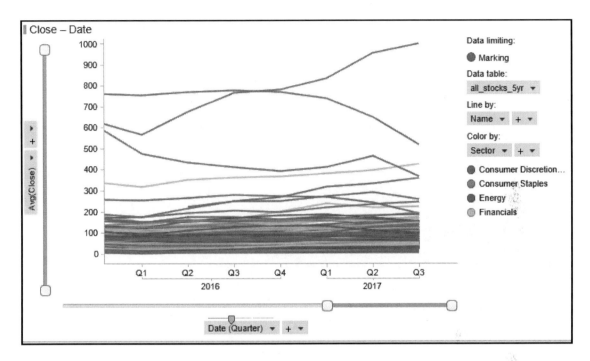

5. Now, let's capture that as a bookmark. For analyst clients, click the bookmark icon on the toolbar, then enter a name for the bookmark and click the + button:

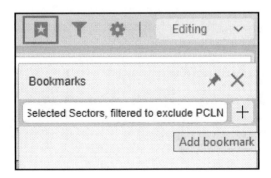

6. For web clients, the process is similar, except the bookmark icon looks different. Note that you won't be able to filter out PCLN by filtering out marked rows unless you switch to **Editing** mode (top-right of the screen). You can, however, filter it out by using the requisite filter in the filter panel:

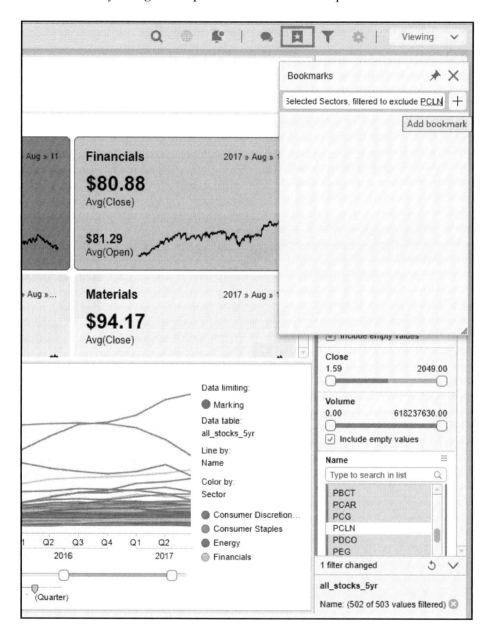

7. The bookmark captures the current state of the analysis and can be recalled at any time. It's like a snapshot in time. Now try changing some other settings. It's up to you exactly what you do, but you might try resetting the filters or marking some different tiles in the KPI chart. Also, try changing the left-hand line chart to show `Avg(Volume)` rather than `Avg(Close)`. Here is what my analysis looks like after I have changed some settings:

8. Capture a second bookmark—in my case, I am calling it `Other Sectors, showing volume`:

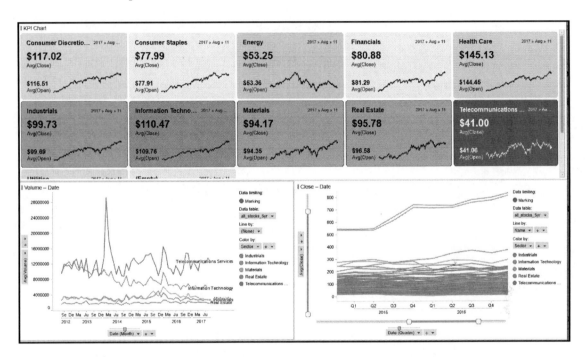

9. Finally, if you are using an Analyst client, you can create a special type of bookmark that captures only certain settings. In my case, I want the visualization configuration, and layout to be captured, but nothing relating to the data itself. This time, right-click on the + button and choose **Add Bookmark Special....**

10. I have deselected everything to do with data:

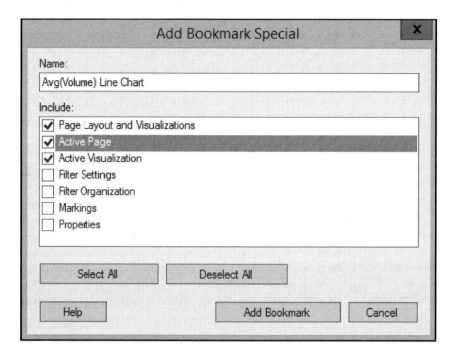

11. Click on the **Add Bookmark** button.

So, now that we have created some bookmarks, what can we do with them? We can apply them as is or select only certain settings to apply, or we can use them to perform actions when a user clicks a button. We can also make bookmarks public, so others can make use of them:

1. Click the first bookmark created from the bookmarks menu—notice that the page updates to show the settings you first created. Note how the analysis returns to the very first state when you did all the marking and filtering, zoom slider adjustment, and so on.

2. Next, let's apply just parts of the second bookmark—click on the drop-down arrow on the bookmark and choose **Apply Special**.

The following shows a screenshot from the Analyst client:

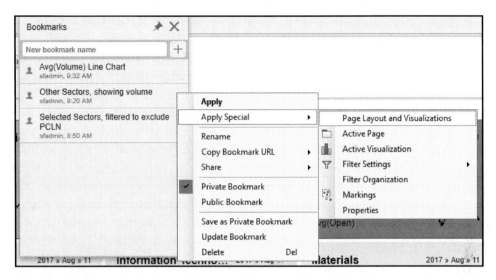

This screenshot shows the web client:

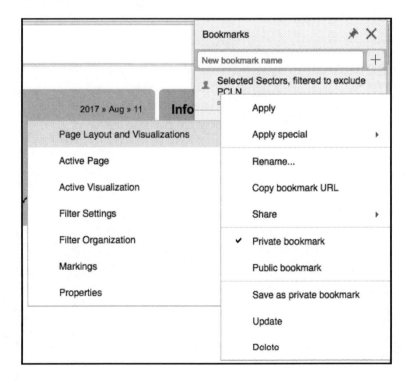

3. Choose **Page Layout and Visualizations**. Notice how the filtering and marked data does not change. I'll discuss in a moment why bookmarks are so useful, but finally, let's try assigning a bookmark to a button. Note, this is only possible in Analyst clients.

4. Right-click on the text area at the top of the page and choose **Edit Text Area**.

5. The text area editor will open. Now click the **Insert Action Control** button:

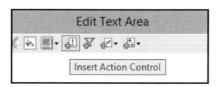

6. Enter a **Display text**, then expand the **Bookmarks** section of the **Available actions** box and choose the **Avg(Volume) Line Chart** bookmark and add it to the **Selected actions** box:

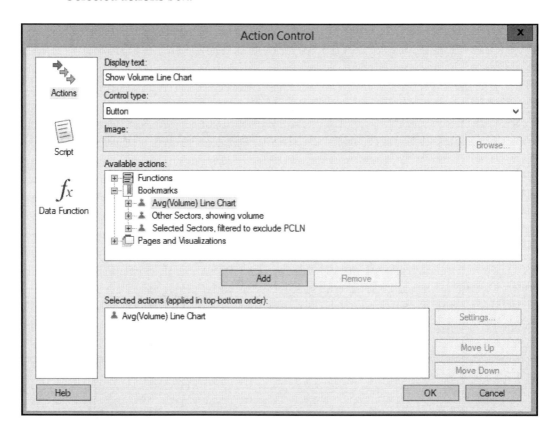

7. Click on the **OK** button, save the text area, and return to your analysis.

8. Now try applying one of the other (not the **Avg(Volume) Line Chart**) bookmarks in the list manually, then click the button you just created.

See what happened? Now you have created a button that sets a new visualization configuration that shows something different from the default. Of course, in the real world, you might create several bookmarks, each capturing a separate set of settings for the visualizations on screen.

By default, bookmarks are created as **Private Bookmark**. This means that only you can view and apply them. However, if you right-click on the bookmark (Analyst) or expand the menu (web), then you can make the bookmark public so that others can view and apply them:

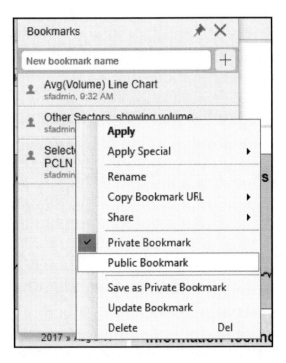

 Should you make bookmarks used for buttons public or private? Good question... My recommendation is to make them private. That way they don't get in the way of other users' bookmarks. Note that even if you make them public, they cannot be updated by other users.

So... now that you understand how to work with bookmarks, what purpose can they serve and why did I suggest that you create three different ones?

- Bookmarks are an excellent way of saving the state of an analysis and returning to it at a later stage—for example, if you are in the middle of experimenting with finding some insights in the data; or, if you have found something interesting and don't want to lose that thought!
- Bookmarks are a great way of sharing configurations, data, and insights with other users. However, other features of Spotfire can be even more useful than bookmarks! They are covered later in this chapter.
- Bookmarks are great for capturing the setup of an analysis, so that you can guide a non-expert user through an analysis that you created, step by step, or highlighting useful ways of looking at the data. They also help with analytic application development.
- Why the third bookmark, with special settings? This was designed to show the use of bookmarks for guided analysis. Did you notice that when you created the action button, you couldn't choose which parts of the bookmark to apply? The **Settings...** button is grayed out, so if you only want certain settings of the bookmark to be applied, then you need to make sure you set only those settings when you create the bookmark.

Advanced topic – key columns

There's one important caveat with bookmarks. If you want bookmarks to capture markings between data updates, then you must allocate key columns to the underlying data table. Otherwise, Spotfire won't be able to determine which rows of data to mark as it won't have any reference to know which rows to mark when the data is updated.

Setting key columns is only available in Analyst clients. Let's set them now:

1. Click **Edit** | **Data Table Properties.**
2. Make sure the default data table is selected.
3. Locate the **Key columns for linked data:** box and click the **Edit...** button:

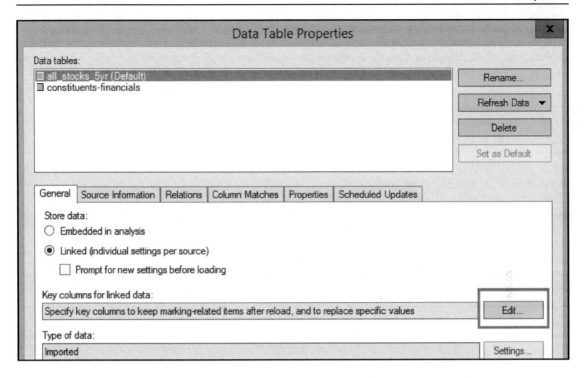

4. We need to find columns that uniquely identify the rows in the data. Unfortunately, Spotfire thinks that **Name** and **Sector** might be suitable, but neither of these, nor their combination, uniquely identifies every row (there are rows for every date for each **Name**). To fix this, choose **All columns** from the **Limit available columns to:** dropdown.

5. Add the **Name** and **Date** columns to the **Selected columns:** box in the dialog:

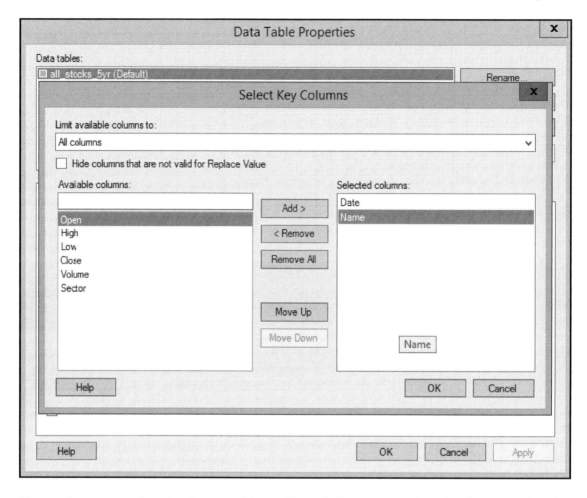

Now, when you update the data, marking will mark these rows when the data is updated and you apply the bookmark. If you didn't do this, Spotfire would not be able to identify the rows and so wouldn't apply any marking at all. Remember that marking using bookmarks in Spotfire is chiefly for the purpose of capturing the exact current state of the marking.

Imagine you marked all rows for PCLN, saved a bookmark, and then next time the data was updated, you wanted Spotfire to mark all rows for PCLN including any newly available data. This wouldn't be possible, since Spofire does not support "symbolic" marking currently. This use case is far better achieved by using filtering rather than marking.

Annotations

Annotations are a useful function that you can use to explain aspects of a Spotfire analysis. They can be placed anywhere on a page and can be styled too. Annotations are also useful for producing infographics in Spotfire, as we will see later on.

You can continue with the same analysis as before. It doesn't really matter what we do with annotations, so I just want to introduce you to the concept. Let's get started:

1. If you are using the Analyst client, click the **Visualizations** menu and select **New annotation...**:

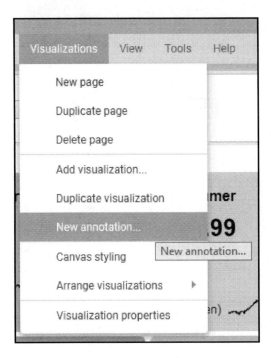

2. If you are using the web clients, you will first need to switch to the **Editing** mode by clicking the dropdown in the top-right corner of the Spotfire application. Then the steps are the same as the ones following.

3. Spotfire will place the annotation on the page. You can drag it wherever you want and start editing. Here, you can see I've started typing a description of the KPI charts:

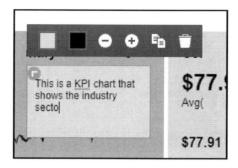

4. I'm not going to talk you through all the steps to configure an annotation, but I will mention them in brief. From left to right, the controls are as follows:
   - Background color—a standard color chooser (including eye-dropper—Analyst clients only)
   - Foreground color—as for background color
   - Decrease font size
   - Increase font size
   - Duplicate the annotation
   - Remove the annotation

Annotations can be resized horizontally—they will resize vertically automatically. The angle bracket in the top-left corner of the annotation will hide the annotation—it can be shown again by clicking on its icon left in place on the page.

Another potential use for annotations is to produce infographics. You can match the colors in the annotations to the colors you use in visualizations and produce some pretty nicely styled visualizations with real impact!

Conversations

In Spotfire, **conversations** are bookmarks on steroids! With conversations, you can have contextually aware discussions with colleagues looking at the same analysis. You can comment on the visualizations and record any marking or filtering or other configuration to explain the context of the conversation or any kind of insight or finding in the data.

Let's look at the KPI example again. Conversations work exactly the same whether you are using the Analyst or web clients. The example I am showing here requires **Editing** mode in order to prepare the visualizations. I'm editing the visualizations to make them more useful:

1. Change the bottom right-hand visualization to show color by **Name**:

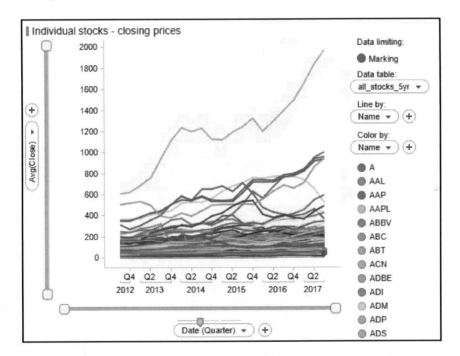

2. Right-click on the line graph and select **Create details visualization**. Choose a **Bar chart**. I recommend you add labels to the bar chart by right-clicking to go to the visualization properties. I also recommend setting the bar chart to show side-by-side bars

3. Change the **Filter type** for the **Date** column to a **Range Filter**:

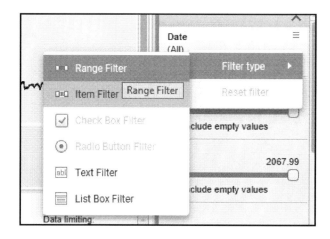

4. Here's what I have:

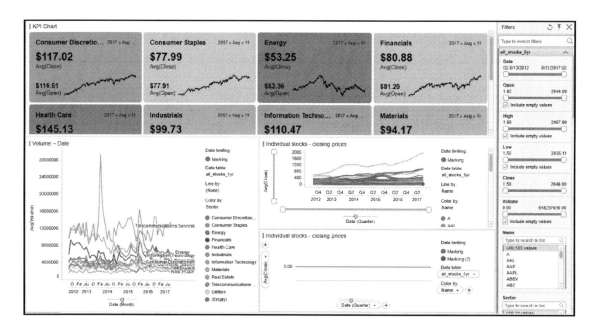

5. Save the analysis. Now let's apply some filtering and marking and capture that as part of a conversation!

6. Mark the **Consumer Discretionary** KPI tile to select that industry sector:

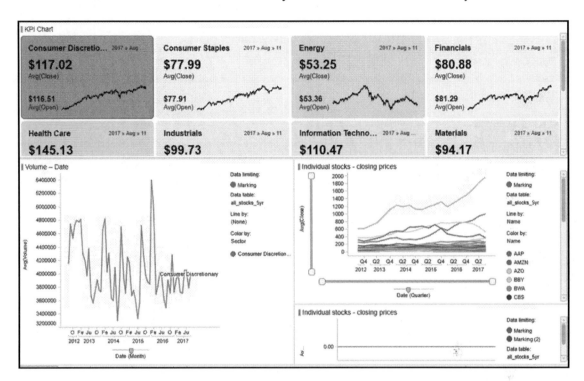

7. Let's focus on AMZN—one of the fastest-growing stocks. Mark it by clicking on **AMZN** on the legend on the right-hand side line chart.

8. Filter to the last couple of years of data only. My data only covers 2012-2017.

9. Here is what I have ended up with:

10. Save the analysis file so it takes the changes you have made.

11. Now, let's start a conversation! Click the Collaboration icon on the toolbar. It will open a small window that can be used to start a conversation:

12. Click the bar chart in order to make it **active**. Then click the **+** sign to start a conversation. Enter some text:

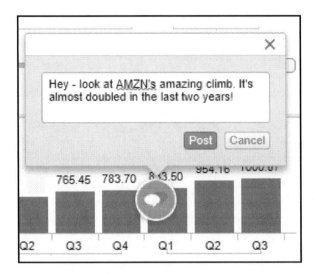

13. Click the **Post** button. You can move the green conversation icon wherever you want on the page, but I recommend you place it near or on the visualization you want to highlight.
14. You don't have to do this, but in order to illustrate the point, I'm now going to log in as another user and open the same analysis (on the web) and see what happens.
15. I have logged in as a different user—one called `sales1`. Initially, there is no sign that there is a conversation associated with the analysis, but if I click the Collaboration icon, a green speech bubble appears against the bar chart:

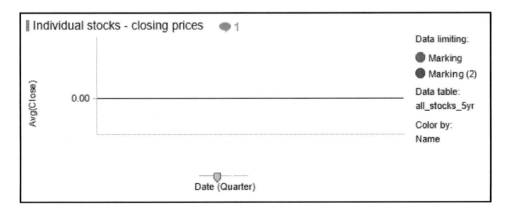

16. If I click the bubble, the **Conversations** panel opens. I can then click on a conversation to open it:

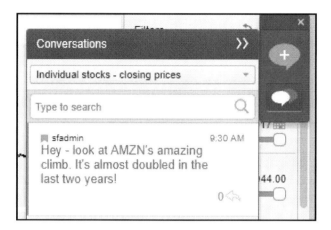

17. Clicking the conversation text applies the filtering and marking settings and opens the conversation attached to the visualization:

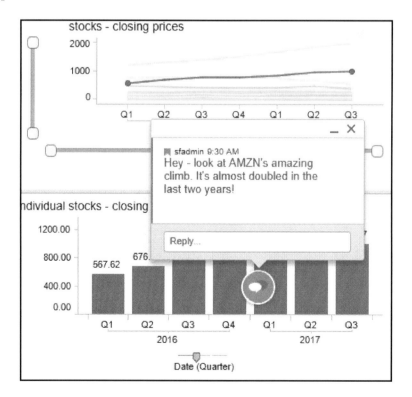

18. Recall that I am now logged in as the `sales1` user. I can now do some more analysis and reply to the conversation. I have chosen to mark **FOX** in the line chart in order to compare it with **AMZN**:

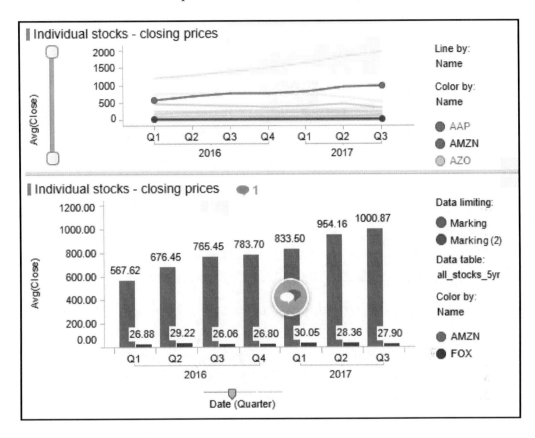

19. Now I can reopen the conversation by clicking on the grey bubble and entering my reply. Notice the checkbox that enables me to choose whether I should save the analysis state in the reply. I'm going to leave it checked:

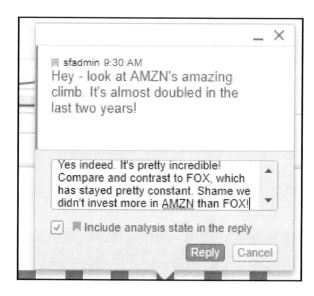

20. Now let's return to the original user (`sfadmin`). If I open the conversations panel, I can see that there's a new reply:

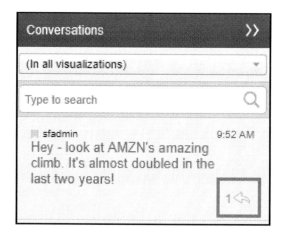

21. If I then click on the arrow, I can expand the conversation and apply the analysis state that the `sales1` user was working with:

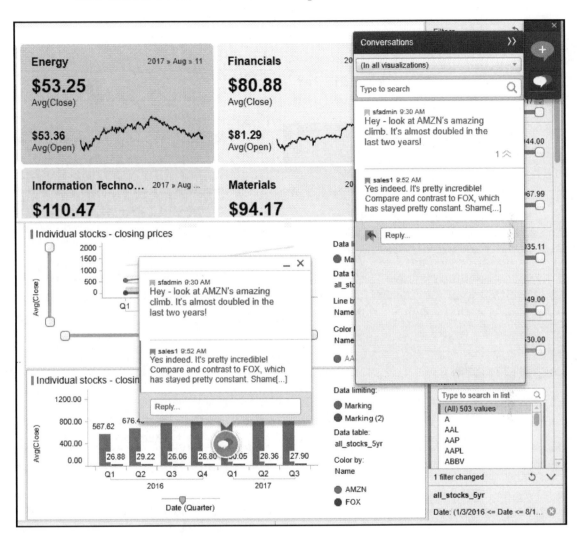

22. One final point—if `sfadmin` were now to reply to `sales1`, the **Conversations** panel would update to show a refresh icon. Clicking this will bring in the latest replies to the conversation:

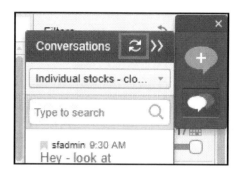

Note that you don't need to save the analysis in order to use conversations. The **Conversations** panel will always update without needing to load or save.

The **Conversations** feature is a really nice way to discuss specific insights and findings within your Spotfire analyses. The conversations are context-aware so you can see what others see. Marking and filtering are captured, much like bookmarks. It's really useful for collaborating with colleagues to analyze data and take action from it.

Summary

This chapter has provided an introduction to the collaboration features in Spotfire—bookmarks, annotations, and conversations.

Bookmarks are great for storing and retrieving the state of an analysis—they are very flexible in that they can store all sorts of things about it. You can also choose only to store or retrieve certain settings, such as the visualization configurations, for example.

Annotations allow you to describe parts of an analysis file and provide hints to other users. As mentioned, you can also use them to create infographics in Spotfire.

Conversations allow context-aware discussions around the data in an analysis. The conversations store the current analysis state and can be retrieved at any time!

The next chapter is a reference for all the visualizations available in Spotfire. I've explained some of the amazing things you can do with Spotfire, so now it's time to expand your knowledge and inspire you to do some more creative work with visualizations!

Section 2: Spotfire In Depth

This section will go over important Spotfire topics in more depth—it covers some real-world instances of working with visualizations and goes into depth about how to configure them to deliver the best value. It also gives an introduction to the Spotfire architecture and how it all fits together.

This section will also cover how to work with data in detail, and it will cover some visualization types that haven't been worked with elsewhere in this book.

In this section, the following chapters will be covered:

- Chapter 5, *Practical Applications of Spotfire Visualizations*
- Chapter 6, *The Big Wide World of Spotfire*
- Chapter 7, *Source Data is Never Enough*
- Chapter 8, *The World is Your Visualization*
- Chapter 9, *What's Your Location?*

5
Practical Applications of Spotfire Visualizations

Spotfire is universally adaptable. There's usually a way to display any kind of data in a meaningful visualization in Spotfire. However, how do you know which type of visualization to use? How can you configure a visualization to best represent the data that you're working with? How can you get the fastest results and insights from the data? What should you **not** do with each visualization type?

In this chapter, we will cover the following topics:

- Some real-world examples of some common Spotfire visualization types
- What to use each visualization for
- The pros and cons of the visualization types
- Some configuration hints and tips
- Common pitfalls and things to avoid

Bar charts

Bar charts are one of the most useful and versatile visualization types in Spotfire. Let's go over them here:

- **Good for visualizing**: Any type of data that is split into categories. Examples of categories include the following:
    - Product category
    - Sales region
    - Car make and model
- **Don't use for**: Generally, visualizing continuous data on the x-axis is not recommended (as you will see in the following example), unless you are interested in the general shape or trend of the data.
- **Pros:** Really easy to construct, configure, and interpret.
- **Cons:** If you have lots and lots of categories, there simply isn't enough space on the categorical axis to show all the labels, so you will need to use techniques such as zoom sliders and hierarchical axis selectors. See Chapter 8, *The World is Your Visualization*, for more information on constructing hierarchies from axis selectors.
- **Summary**: Bar charts are the go-to visualizations in Spotfire. Think bar chart first!

We typically use bar charts to represent numerical data that's split into categories. Bar charts are very useful for showing numerical values in an easy-to-consume way.

Bar charts can also show several dimensions of data at the same time. You can choose to **Color by** values and trellis by columns, in order to produce an at-a-glance view of data that is both accurate and straightforward to interpret.

There are some things to watch out for, though!

Things to watch out for with bar charts

First, we must be careful with summing averages.

This is always something to be aware of. If you are using `Avg` as an aggregation function, then it probably doesn't make sense to use a stacked bar chart. Consider the following example:

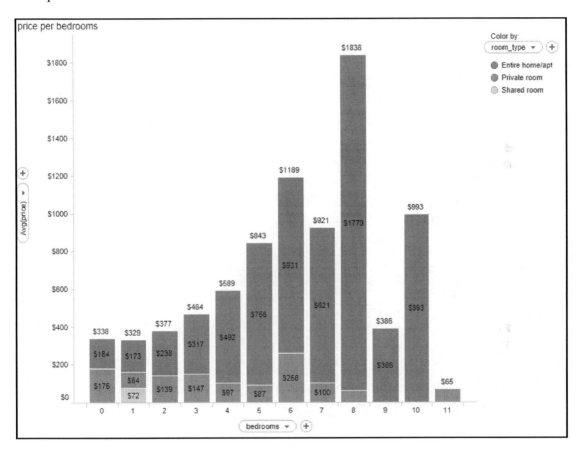

I've labeled the bars to explain why this visualization may be confusing. The preceding visualization shows the pricing of Airbnb data in a stacked bar chart. It is colored by **Room Type**. Notice how the bar segments show the `Avg` (price). That's what we want! However, if you look at the total bar height and the value axis (y-axis), you'll see that the average of the segments in each bar is summed to the total bar height. This doesn't make much sense. Summing the averages is invalid mathematically and misleading at best. It's far better to use a side-by-side, or 100%, bar chart:

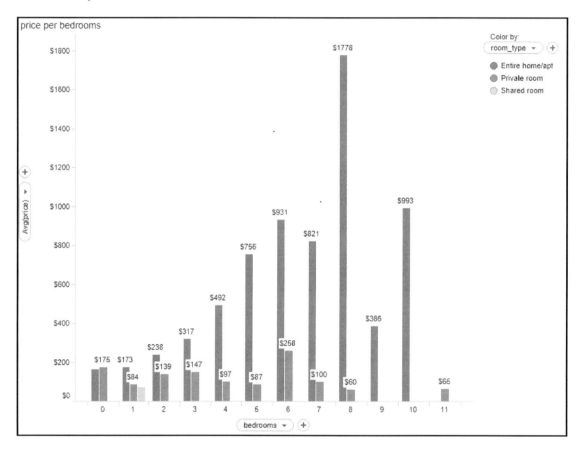

That's better! The chart is no longer misleading. I have left the labels on the bars, but it would probably be better to remove them for clarity.

While we're on the subject, watch out when using 100% stacked bars; if you use this mode, you can only ever compare the bottom split of the categories directly, as they have a common baseline.

Before we leave this example, notice how the bars are nice and wide. This is because I have set the x-axis to be categorical. By default, Spotfire sees the number of bedrooms as a continuous variable, since it's an integer. However, if the x-axis is continuous, the bar chart is rendered like this:

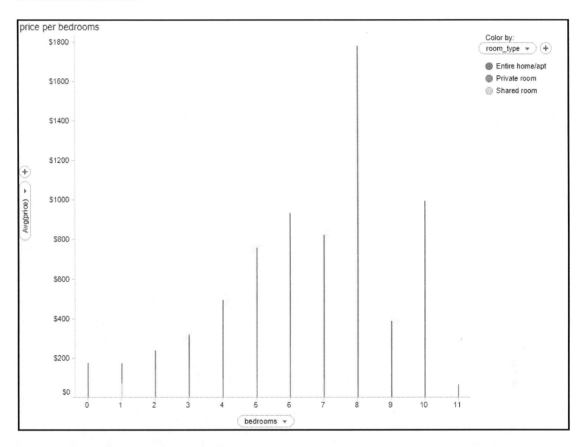

Oh dear. This visualization doesn't work very well. Even though I have specified side-by-side bars, all the bars are superimposed, so it's not possible to (easily) see the different values for the different room types. They are superimposed because each bar must be placed exactly on the point of the x-axis where that integer value is represented, and therefore, coloring by room type creates separate bars, all overlapping each other. Using a categorical axis is much better. As you can see, we have separate categories—0 to 11!

One more thing to be aware of: when using numerical values as categories, there is a risk of missing values on the axis. For example, if the data doesn't contain any values for four bedrooms, the value of four will be entirely missing on the categorical axis, as shown in the following graph (I deleted all the rows with four bedrooms):

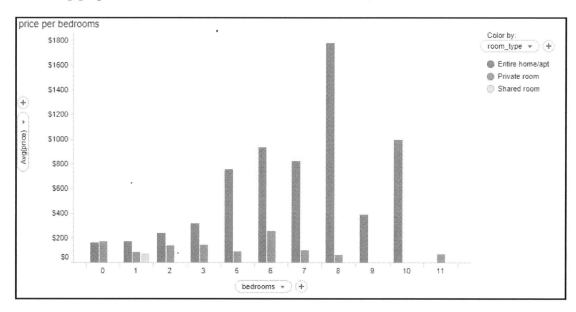

This is not a fault with Spotfire—just because you and I read the numbers sequentially, does not mean that Spotfire can understand that they are sequential. Spotfire just displays the distinct categories. However, if this is a problem, a potential fix could be to insert some empty data. In this case, we could add a row to the data with four bedrooms, but with all other values empty. This could be done by using the Add Rows operation in Spotfire to add the empty row from another data source, for example, an Excel or CSV file.

Finally, if the values were filtered out (not deleted), there is an option you can choose by right-clicking on the axis to show all values—not just filtered values:

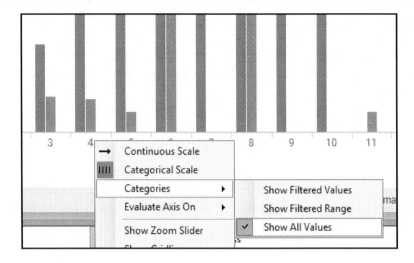

This will lead to a gap in the x-axis, like this:

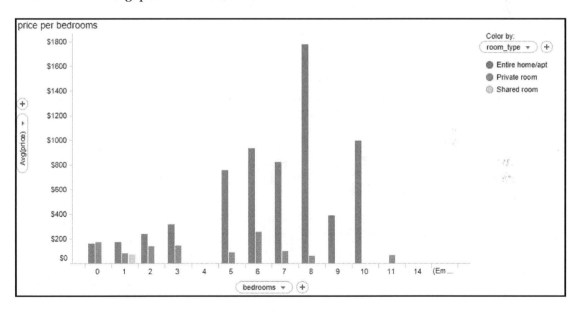

Just be aware of these issues and take care not to produce misleading visualizations!

Bar chart summary

The bar chart is definitely one of the most useful visualizations in Spotfire. Use bar charts to visualize continuous data by category; group the data; or visualize multiple dimensions in the data all at once. Bar charts are usually preferable to pie charts. Just watch out for the following:

- Don't accidentally sum averages using a stacked bar chart (this is true everywhere in Spotfire, and for analytics in general).
- Don't use too many categories.
- Make sure that using 100% stacked bars makes sense; don't use them for comparing multiple categories. You can only ever directly compare the bottom category.

Combination charts

Combination charts are extremely useful for visualizing multiple series of categorical and trend information together. They are covered in more detail in `Chapter 8`, *The World is Your Visualization*. One thing to be aware of is a current limitation in Spotfire, whereby it's not possible to choose which series share which y-axis scales. At the time of writing this book, this is a feature under consideration in Spotfire. Currently, you can either split out all scales so that each series has its own scale, or you can share a single scale between all series:

- **Good for visualizing**: Multiple series of data simultaneously. You can visualize bars and lines together on one chart.
- **Don't use for**: Data that has multiple scales that do not sit well together.
- **Pros**: Gives you the ability to view multiple series together.
- **Cons**: As we mentioned previously, you cannot choose how to split or share scales between series.
- **Summary**: Combination charts are great for visualizing simple (and compatible) series of data together.

Cross tables

Cross tables are a bit like pivot tables. You can configure them on the fly, just like any other Spotfire visualization. Cross tables are great for displaying aggregated information at a glance, in tabular form.

Hierarchy sliders are also useful for producing cross tables that can be configured on the fly, even in the Spotfire Consumer client:

- **Good for visualizing**: Any data that you want to aggregate and show in a tabular format. Cross tables are also great for showing multiple aggregations in the same table. You can, for example, show percentages, totals, and absolute metrics, all together.
- **Don't use for**: Randomly distributed data with lots and lots of categories and empty values. A mostly empty cross table plot is annoying to work with!
- **Pros**: Great for showing the values of aggregated data.
- **Cons**: As I will explain shortly, there are some important things to note about how cross tables work, particularly when it comes to grand totals.
- **Summary**: Great for showing aggregated data in a nicely tabulated format, but good design is important; for example, for the choice of columns to show on each of the axes, any coloring used, and the use of grand totals.

Cross table grand totals

Cross table grand totals are extremely useful. They are also important to understand. You **must** use them properly. When they are used unwisely, they can be confusing. When they're used incorrectly, they can be downright wrong!

Here is a cross table showing some Airbnb data:

Note that I have not colored the cells. I would recommend that you do; color helps differentiate the values in the cross table. Perhaps the most effective way to do this is to only color the cells that are significant—maybe the top or bottom *n*, or outliers, and so on. A lot of color confuses, but color, when used effectively, is extremely useful!

Also, notice how I have built hierarchies on the vertical and horizontal axes. The hierarchy sliders allow a consumer of the data to change the levels of the hierarchy, in order to summarize the data at the different levels in the hierarchy.

The cell values are representing the average price of the Airbnb rentals. Now, look at the grand totals. The grand totals are correct; they show the average value of all the values shown in the columns of the cross table.

Grand totals – underlying values versus sum of cell values

There are two settings for calculating the grand totals of the cross table: underlying values or the sum of cell values. Here is the configuration for the cross table:

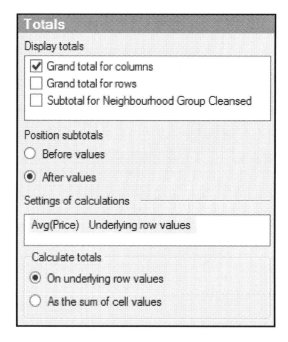

It's very important to understand the distinction between the different methods of calculating the totals. If I change the setting to **As the sum of cell values**, the cross table will now look like this:

Price per Neighbourhood Group Cleansed » Neighbourhood Cleansed and Property Type » Room Type

Property Type » Room Type (Room Type) ▾ ⊕

Neighbourhood Group Cleansed	Bed and breakfast		Boat	Cabin	House		
	Entire home/...	Private room	Entire home/...	Entire home/...	Entire home/...	Private room	Shared room
Bronx	-	-	-	-	$120.70	$50.87	$29.00
Brooklyn	$175.00	$125.50	-	-	$201.80	$71.17	$34.07
Manhattan	$300.00	$119.13	$399.00	-	$300.70	$82.48	-
Queens	-	$330.14	$156.67	$110.00	$174.91	$62.83	$35.31
Staten Island	$180.00	-	-	-	$166.11	$46.89	$34.00
Grand total	$655.00	$574.77	$555.67	$110.00	$964.21	$314.24	$132.37

Avg(Price) ▾ ⊕

Oh dear... as I also showed with the bar chart example in this chapter, Spotfire is now summing the averages. The summing of averages is almost never a good idea! Now that I have chosen this setting, Spotfire will sum whatever is shown in the cross table. This is fine if the aggregation that's being used for the cell values can be summed, but is not good otherwise.

So, why the different settings?

Underlying values

In this mode, Spotfire will use the values in the underlying data table to generate the grand total. It will apply the same expression to the grand totals as it does to the cell values. So, in my example, each cell value will be the average of the `Price` column for each of the categories represented by that cell. The grand total will be the average of the `Price` column for all the data in the table.

In most cases, you should use this mode. However, there are some cases where it doesn't work and will lead to incorrect results, so you need to be aware of this.

Sum of cell values

If you choose this setting, Spotfire will sum the values shown in the cross table. No matter what aggregation you use for the cell values, Spotfire will always sum the values for the grand total. This is so important that I have said it twice!

You should use the sum of cell values setting when the calculation of the column values aggregation depends on the grouping of the data shown in each cell, and you could get different results depending on the underlying values.

Imagine the following scenario: I am an import/export company, and I just need to know the absolute value (the magnitude) of the volume of imports, minus exports for each year. Then, I want to know the grand total. It's a very contrived example, but bear with me.

The expression for the values axis is as follows:

$$Abs(Sum([Imports]) - Sum([Exports]))$$

Let's think about the math for a bit. You can see that the value of this expression will depend on the subset of the data that is used within it. *Abs* is the key here (absolute value—the result is always positive). Each category will be based on a subset of the data; the sums are calculated for each category, and then *Abs* is applied over the top.

If we then sum the values over the whole table, the results are likely to be different. This is due to the *Abs* part of the expression. Its results will depend on the grouping of the data that it is operating on.

Here are two cross tables that illustrate this point:

Underlying Row Values

	(None)
Year	Abs(Sum([Imports]) - Sum([Exports]))
2004	436
2005	425
2006	381
2007	298
Grand total	1542

Abs(Sum([Imports]) - Sum([Exports]))

Sum of Cell values

	(None)
Year	Abs(Sum([Imports]) - Sum([Exports]))
2004	436
2005	425
2006	381
2007	298
Grand total	1540

Abs(Sum([Imports]) - Sum([Exports]))

The top cross table uses the underlying row values for the grand totals. The bottom table uses the sum of the cell values. You can do the math if you like! I'll give you a clue: the bottom one is correct. The top one is incorrect, because the expression is aggregated at different levels in the hierarchy of the data for the cell values and for the grand total.

Cross table summary

Cross tables are great for showing the absolute values of aggregated data. They are very flexible and powerful. However, you need to be careful when using grand totals.

Use the underlying row values if the cell values expression can be applied to the grand total and it doesn't matter what level the data is grouped at.

You can (and should) use the sum of cell values if you only want to sum what you see in the cross table itself.

I am not suggesting that one method is better than the other; I merely want to show you some things you need to be aware of when using grand totals. If you are unsure, I recommend that you construct a simple cross table with a small number of values shown. Test each setting and check the math. That's what I did in order to construct the preceding example.

Scatter plots

The scatter plot is the next most useful chart type in Spotfire. Other visualization tools may call them bubble charts or differentiate between scatter plots and bubble charts in some way. Well, in Spotfire, they are all called scatter plots!

A scatter plot is primarily used for visualizing multiple continuous variables together. In fact, you can visualize at least four dimensions of data with ease. However, there's still a responsibility on the author or designer of the plot to make good choices as to which dimensions to show. Let's explore the scatter plot further:

- **Good for visualizing**: Multiple dimensions of continuous and categorical data. Excellent for showing relationships and patterns in data.
- **Don't use for**: Very large amounts of randomly distributed data; you'll just get a mess.
- **Pros**: Ability to visualize several dimensions in the data, all on a single chart.
- **Cons**: Randomly distributed data can be difficult to interpret. Lots and lots of markers on a scatter plot can be difficult to understand, especially if they overlap.
- **Summary**: Scatter plots are great for visualizing lots of dimensions simultaneously.

Let's take a look at a scatter plot that's showing four dimensions:

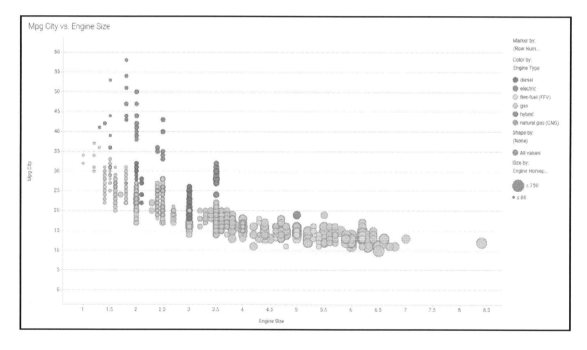

This scatter plot is visualizing vehicle fuel economy. It's currently showing four dimensions:

- `Mpg City` is shown on the y-axis; this is the target column that I want to understand
- `Engine Size` is shown on the x-axis
- `Engine Horsepower` is the size-axis, that is, each point is sized relative to the minimum and maximum value in the column
- `Engine Type` is the color-axis, that is, each engine type is given a color, in order to represent the different categorical values in the column

This chart is pretty nice and clear. There are some clear insights into the data, such as the following:

- City fuel economy is related to engine size, engine horsepower, and engine type.
- Electric cars aren't shown (unfortunately). Since their engine size is empty, they cannot be shown on a continuous axis. We can fix this later.
- Notice that there is also a relationship between the engine size and the horsepower—the points on the scatter plot get larger in correspondence to the increase engine size. This is to be expected, as in general, larger displacement engines produce more power.
- The relationship between the engine size and `Mpg City` is not linear. Notice the wide spread of the smaller engines; see how the hybrid cars have much better fuel economy for the same engine size. Note how (at the lower end of engine size) there are only a few distinct values of the engine size, but larger engines tend to be a wide mix of sizes.
- Look at the outlier on the far right of the visualization. Which car could have an 8.5 liter engine? (It's actually a Dodge Viper). Interestingly, its fuel economy is not much worse than most of the other large engine cars.

I am fascinated by cars; in fact, they've been a long-term hobby of mine, so I could mine this data for much longer!

Now, let's look at some of the potential issues with this visualization, and how we might address them:

- Look at the midsection of the scatter plot. It looks like a lot of the markers are obscured. It seems to be the flex-fuel markers that are most affected. It may be that we are most interested in flex-fuel cars, so they are of greater importance than the other fuel types. There are a couple of ways this can be addressed:
  - The markers can be brought to the fore by clicking on **flex-fuel** in the legend. This has the effect of marking the flex-fuel markers and fading the others to the background:

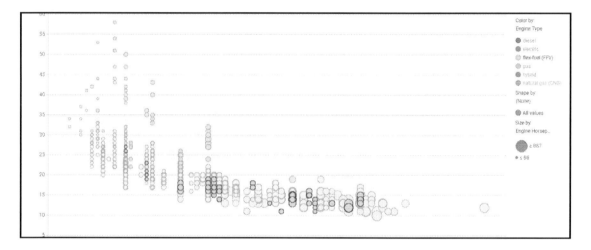

- The drawing order can be adjusted; this is done by visiting the property pages of the scatter plot and choosing a column for determining the drawing order, and then setting a custom sort order for the column (in **Data** | **Column Properties**). Here are the results of doing this (and unmarking the marked data):

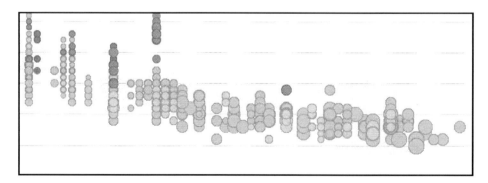

I found that I had to put flex fuel at the bottom of the values in the custom sort order dialog, so that it showed up in front of the other markers.

- Finally, we can try to apply jittering to the scatter plot. I don't really recommend it, as it can confuse the picture. Using it means you can't read the values accurately across the axes where you are using jittering. Jittering works by randomly displacing the markers in a horizontal (and/or vertical) direction. Jittering is available on the **Appearance** property page of the scatter plot visualization. Here is the result of some jittering:

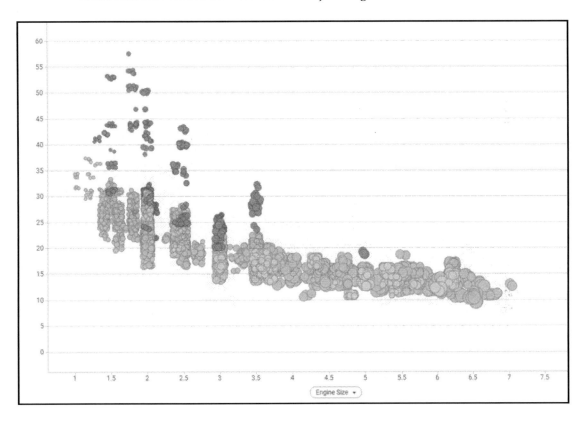

See what I mean? You can still see the clusters of data around the smaller engine sizes, but the larger engine sizes are all merged together, so it works less well there.

- The electric cars aren't shown on the scatter plot. This is because the engine size of electric cars is empty. It's not even zero. This can be artificially fixed by visiting the **Data Panel** and setting a value to replace the empty values. Note that I have selected the column and clicked on the cog-wheel to get to the column settings:

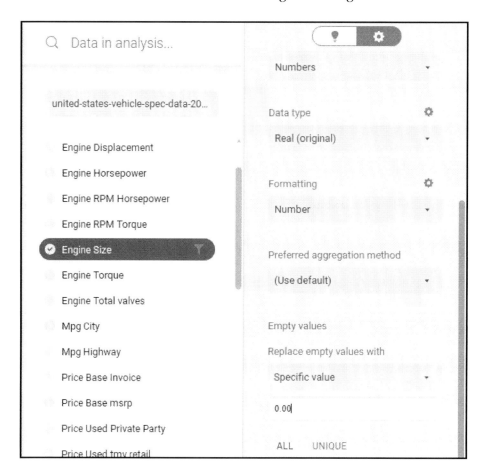

Now (some of) the electric cars are shown:

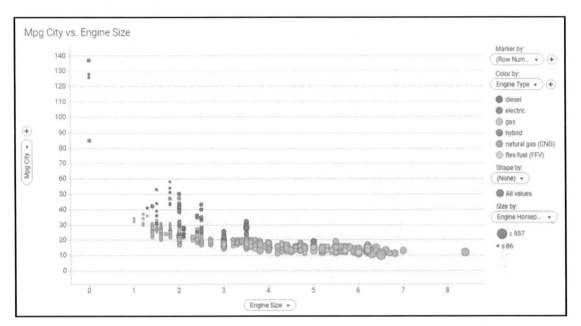

By looking at the rest of the data, I can tell that there is also missing information for Mpg City for some electric vehicles so they still don't show on the scatter plot. Since electric vehicles don't use liquid fuel, this might make sense, or I could choose to fix the issue by choosing an arbitrary value (say zero, or even a value that's significantly larger than the maximum) for the column, or by some other means, but this would be a data management issue in the real world.

It's also possible to represent more dimensions in a scatter plot. In addition to the methods we have explored thus far, the following methods can be explored:

- **Shape**: The shape of the markers can represent another dimension
- **Marker rotation**: This can be used to indicate the directionality of a dimension
- **Line ordering**: You can connect markers with the same values and order the line according to a column value
- **Trellis**: This splits up the visualization according to other columns; in fact, you can use up to three columns

The drawing order could represent another dimension in the data. However, this can be difficult to interpret.

Here is an example of using trellising and size by in order to show the vehicle size category, automatic transmission type, valve gear configuration, and engine configuration. I filtered out the empty values and focused on some key data in order to make the visualization a bit simpler to interpret, but it does show the principles at hand. Also, note that I have kept all the y-axes of the trellis panels at the same scale throughout, so that it's possible to directly compare each of the categories of vehicle and vehicle configuration. I've pushed the complexity of this example as high as it should normally go. There's a lot of information being shown:

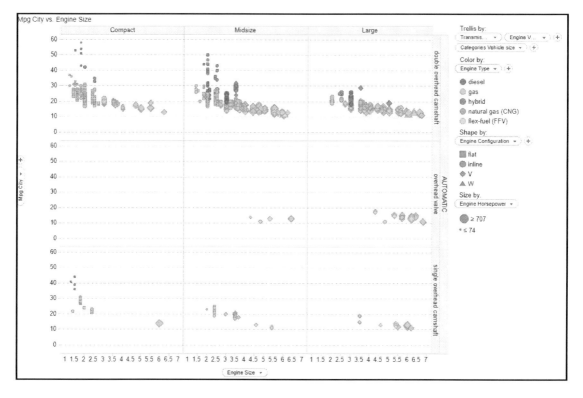

Finally, also note that I adjusted the sort order of the vehicle size category; as the standard, alphabetical sort order would have them in the order of Compact, Large, and Midsize. This is probably not what would be required. I am illustrating this so that you can think about it when you're designing your own visualizations.

You can set the column sort order by accessing the properties of a column. Right-click on the column in the **Data Panel** to do this.

Line ordering

Line ordering works best with time-based data. I've opened up the data we first looked at in `Chapter 2`, *It's All About the Data*: the gapminder data on the rate of population increase versus under-five mortality. I've filtered to Cambodia, as it appeared to be one of the more interesting tracks through time:

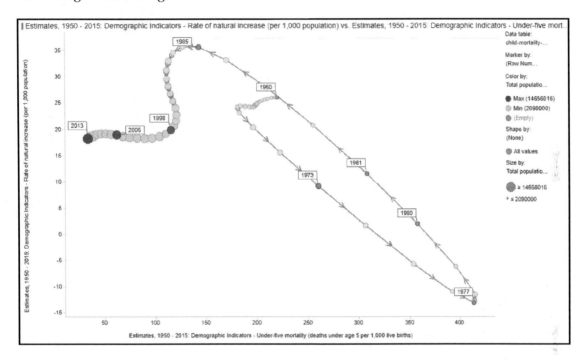

Notice Cambodia's journey through time, and see how the scatter plot represents it in a way that's really clear! Do you see where Cambodia started in 1950 and progressed to really high mortality and slow population increase through 1977, followed by a rapid escalation in population increase and an associated decrease in infant mortality? Population growth peaked in 1985/6. Both measures finally settled down by about 1988.

I wonder what happened to Cambodia in 1977 to reverse the trend?

Looking at Wikipedia, it seems that the Communist Party, Khmer Rouge, had something to do with it. The party was in power from 1975 to 1979. A large number of deaths were reported during that time. Take a look at the following quote from Wikipedia:

> *"The Khmer Rouge regime was highly autocratic, xenophobic, paranoid, and repressive. The genocide was in part the result of the regime's social engineering policies. Its attempts at agricultural reform through collectivization led to widespread famine while its insistence on absolute self-sufficiency, even in the supply of medicine, led to the death of many thousands from treatable diseases such as malaria. The Khmer Rouge's racist emphasis on national purity included several genocides of Cambodian minorities. Arbitrary executions and torture were carried out by its cadres against perceived subversive elements, or during genocidal purges of its own ranks between 1975 and 1978."* (https://en.wikipedia.org/wiki/Khmer_Rouge)

It appears that there was a post-Khmer Rouge baby boom, as well! I do find it fascinating when I spot something in the data using Spotfire and can then follow up my findings with hard evidence.

How did I configure the line connections? Simple: there's a visualization **Property** page just for line connections. Here are the settings I used:

Density plots

The AI-driven recommender in Spotfire will often suggest density plots, typically under **MORE LIKE THIS**:

I'm looking at some Airbnb data here. I've selected the price as the target column and clicked through to **MORE LIKE THIS** for `Price` versus `Bedrooms`. Notice how the recommender has produced the density plot second to the scatter plot. If I add the density plot to the analysis, I get the following:

The recommender heuristics have also trellised the density plot by `Room Type`. Let's see what's going on here:

- The density plot is being represented by a scatter plot with special configuration.
- The markers are tiled (to see how this is configured, see the **Markers** property page of the scatter plot).
- The markers are colored by row count.

Creating a density plot in this way demonstrates the versatility of the scatter plot. Configuring it in a certain way has enabled an entirely new type of visualization to be represented in Spotfire. Even more, Spotfire's recommender has applied all the settings for that configuration automatically!

This visualization shows that there are definitely clusters of Airbnb with small numbers of rooms and low price. The gamut of price ranges is much more varied for the entire home/apt category of property than any other. There are not many shared rooms!

A density plot is similar in some ways to Spotfire's heatmap visualization. Heatmaps are discussed in Chapter 8, *The World is Your Visualization*). The main advantage of the density plot over a heatmap is that it's perhaps easier to interpret than a heatmap. The scatter plot visualization is also more flexible in its configuration than a heatmap, so you have more options for extending the density plot plot.

Other types of visualization with scatter plots

It's possible to construct all sorts of other visualization types using scatter plots. You can even think of the scatter plot as an x-y grid. If you would like to visualize points on an x-y grid, you can load the data and place the columns on the x and y axes. Here is such an example: each row of data has x and y coordinates corresponding to a map location. As a result, plotting them gives a pretty good approximation of the shape of the US! It's worth mentioning that map charts should generally be used for geographical analysis. This will be covered in Chapter 9, *What's Your Location?*:

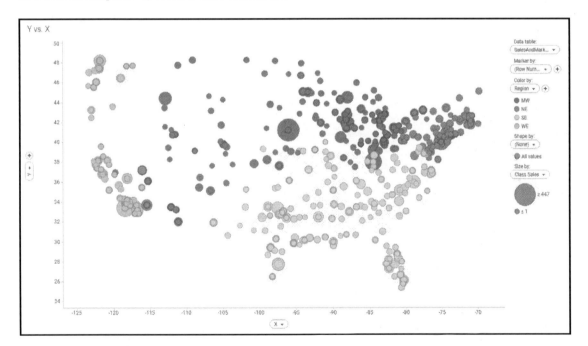

You can use scatter plots to represent geological structures, symbolic mapping, Gantt type charts, and much more. Please visit the TIBCO community for further resources at `https:/ /community.tibco.com`.

I haven't mentioned three-dimensional scatter plots yet. These are great for visualizing structures in three-dimensional, but I don't recommend them for static visualization. You really need to be able to animate or rotate the scatter plot in order to understand them properly.

Three-dimensional visualizations can be misleading, due to the effects of perspective on objects that are some distance away from the viewpoint. Perspective (out of necessity) makes the objects smaller. Are they really smaller, or are they smaller just because of perspective? Also, selecting markers on a three-dimensional visualization is challenging on a two-dimensional visualization canvas. How should marking behave? How do you translate the two-dimensional representation of a marking rectangle to a three-dimensional space?

One more important point about three-dimensional scatter plots: they don't work in the Spotfire web client. It would be frustrating to spend a lot of time developing a three-dimensional scatter plot using Spotfire Analyst, and then attempt to deploy it to the web, only to find it doesn't work! Would this be frustrating? Yes, it definitely would. Trust me—I am speaking from experience.

Scatter plot summary

Scatter plots are so versatile! They are great for viewing multiple dimensions of data in one visualization. It's possible to visualize all the dimensions at once and to present a lot of information in one place. It's also possible to get carried away and produce a scatter plot that's too complicated! I think my final example of using vehicle data (the one that shows trellising) was borderline too complicated.

Scatter plots are also immensely adaptable to all sorts of data and visualizations. I haven't produced a full reference of all the different types of data and visualizations you can represent with a scatter plot; that topic alone would probably fill the rest of this book!

Line charts

Line charts are commonly used for visualizing time-series data, that is, data that changes over time. Their main purpose is to identify a trend in continuous data. Some examples could be to visualize the following:

- Population trends over time
- Sensor readings from manufacturing equipment
- Sales/production data over time

In fact, line charts are also one of the most commonly used visualizations for streaming (live) data. Streaming data was introduced in Spotfire X, and will be covered further in Chapter 12, *Scaling the Infrastructure; Keeping Data up to Date*:

- **Good for visualizing**: Time-series data, or data where one variable changes in response to another.
- **Don't use for**: Visualizing lots and lots of time series simultaneously—you'll get a very confused picture of the data! Please don't use line charts with a categorical x-axis (unless that category is time, of course)! It just doesn't make sense for one category to feed to another, unless (of course) there is a natural progression between stages. Using a categorical x-axis where there is no natural progression implies a nonexistent relationship and order.
- **Pros**: Simple to understand; de facto visualization for time-based data.
- **Cons**: If not designed carefully or showing too many lines at once, line charts get messy.
- **Summary**: Use line charts when you are looking at some kind of trend.

Let's look at some example line charts. Again, continuing with the gapminder data, we can visualize the infant mortality and natural rate of population increase by putting both measures on the y-axis of a line chart and trellising it. I am also using the same treemap to subset the data; remember, too much data on a line chart is horrible. I'll show you that in a minute. For now, here is a line chart that works:

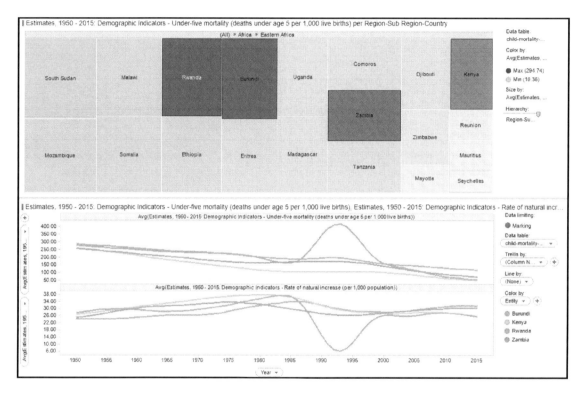

Once again, we can see that Rwanda had a problem in the early 1990s. It's clear to see, but there's nothing in the visualization that identifies the problem as a statistical outlier, like the box plot did!

The other countries all follow a similar pattern to each other. Now, let's go and get this really wrong, in order to show you what **not** to do!

I've now deselected everything and set the hierarchy in the treemap to the most detailed level:

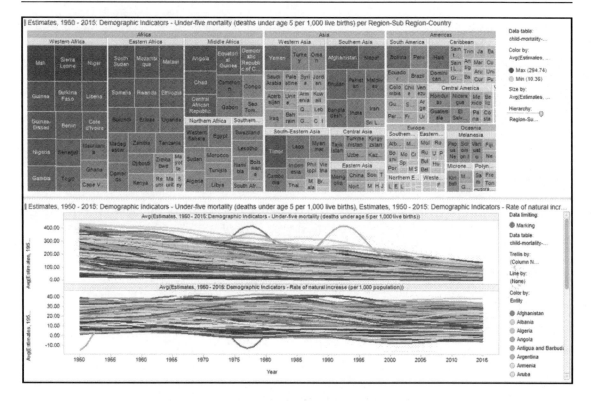

Hmm... what a mess! I did say it would get messy. It's almost impossible to discern anything from the line charts. Also, note that the treemap is pretty difficult to understand. The treemap is easy to fix by adjusting the hierarchy slider.

Fixing the line chart is a bit harder. I think that the best way to do this is to change the **Color by** option to the same hierarchy that's used for the treemap. If I do this and set it to the highest level (by continent), then I get something that looks like this:

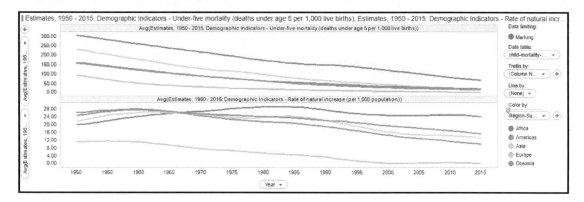

I'm much happier with that! We can now follow the trend at whatever level we have set for the hierarchy. The only challenge is that there are now two hierarchy sliders: one for the treemap and one for the line chart. We can't synchronize them without getting clever with a property control and a document property. There isn't space in this chapter to detail how to do that, but for reference, here is the custom expression I used for the hierarchy expression on the treemap and for the color by expression for the line chart:

```
<PruneHierarchy([Hierarchy.Region-Sub Region-Country],${hierarchyLevel})>
```

`hierarchyLevel` is the name of the document property I created. I attached a property control to that document property.

In summary, use line charts wherever you need to visualize a trend, look at data over time, or look at the relationship between two continuous variables. Avoid using categorical variables for the x-axis unless there is a very clear progression between stages (for example, in a process).

Pie charts

A pie chart displays categorical data as segments of a pie. It's a very common type of visualization, and it is often used in infographics in the media. However, I am not a huge fan of pie charts. They are poor for visualizing large numbers of categories, as the eye cannot differentiate between the different sizes of the segments:

- **Good for visualizing**: Not much, really! Pie charts are best restricted to dashboards, where you need a proportional view at a glance. However, if you **must** use a pie chart, make sure it is only for small numbers of categories.
- **Don't use for**: Visualizing more than, let's say, four categories, or for representing proportions accurately.
- **Pros**: Reasonably good at representing proportional data for a small number of categories. Bar charts generally do a better, more accurate job of this.
- **Cons**: Really bad for representing large numbers of categories. They don't give any idea of the size of a population or the size of the data being visualized.
- **Summary**: Pie charts are best avoided. Use them for dashboarding scenarios, to represent three or four categories (maximum).

Here is an example of a (reasonably) good pie chart:

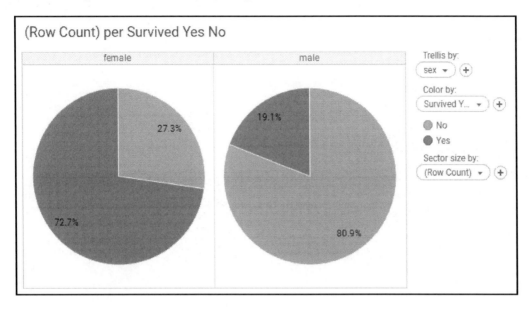

This pie chart is fine; it's clear, and it shows the relative proportions of the survival rate of passengers on the Titanic. Also, there is a huge difference between the sector sizes. Even so, without the labels, we still wouldn't be able to accurately determine the relative areas of the pies. More often than not, most people usually just read the labels on a pie chart, rather than look at the proportional areas that are represented.

If you refer back to Chapter 1, *Welcome to Spotfire*, you'll recall that the survived column contained 1 or 0. In order to display a more meaningful pie chart, I have created a calculated column to replace these values with Yes or No respectively. The expression for the calculated column is If([survived] = 1,"Yes","No").

Here is an example of a very bad pie chart:

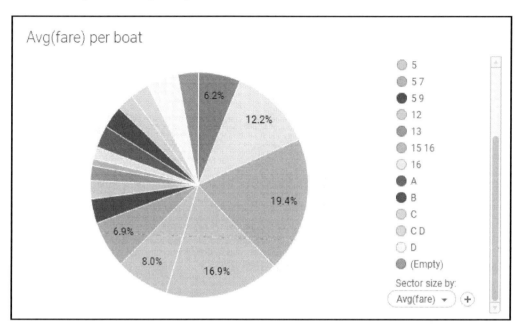

This pie chart is pretty hard to understand! It shows the average fare paid for passengers in each of the lifeboats on the Titanic. Note that I filtered some of the data, in order to produce a more interesting chart.

Let's go over what's wrong with the pie chart:

- There are too many categories. The smaller categories are too small for their labels.
- Anyone interpreting this chart needs to cross-reference the colors to the legend to find out which lifeboat corresponds to which sector.
- There are several sectors that are of a similar size, but the eye cannot differentiate properly between their respective areas and understand the proportions correctly. Look at the 16.9%, 19.4%, and 12.2% sectors. It's impossible to compare them in any meaningful way.
- It's a crazy way to look at the average fare paid by passengers on the boats! It's difficult to understand what this visualization is even trying to represent. It doesn't even give a good idea of the spread of the average fare paid per passenger.
- It's far better to produce this visualization using a bar chart, or even a cross table sorted by fare.

Before we leave the topic of pie charts, I'd just like to mention donut charts. A donut chart can be thought of as a pie chart with a hole. Often, the donut chart has some figure or metric in the middle. Being able to represent an overall metric does give an idea of the size of the data or population being represented. However, when interpreting a donut chart, you still have to calculate the absolute values in your head when given the overall population size and the proportions together.

Having said all that, however, donut charts are a reasonable way of representing information in a dashboard, where you need information at a glance. However, they still suffer the same issue as pie charts, in that it can be difficult to differentiate between the different proportions. Here is an example of a donut chart that was created in Spotfire, using the JavaScript visualization extension:

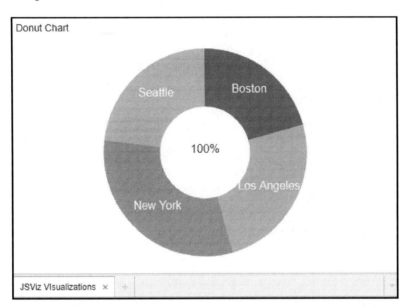

Even though this donut chart isn't a terrible example, it's rather difficult to see the difference in sector size between Seattle, Boston, and Los Angeles. Just be careful, and think really hard about whether a pie or donut chart is indeed the best way to represent your data!

The JavaScript visualization extension is further discussed in `Chapter 12, Scaling the Infrastructure; Keeping Data up to Date`. You can also go and read up about it at `https://community.tibco.com/wiki/javascript-visualization-framework-jsviz-and-tibco-spotfire` and (shortened) at `http://bit.ly/2XTtnXY`.

Box plots

Box plots are one of the least-often used visualizations in Spotfire, in my experience. This is a shame, as they are incredibly powerful! Box plots allow you to see the shape of the data at a glance. Chapter 8, *The World is Your Visualization*, also covers box plots in more detail, but I want to introduce them here first and discuss where and why you might use them:

- **Good for visualizing**: Distributions of data, particularly for visualizing differences in the distributions among different populations or cohorts of data. They are particularly useful for visualizing patient healthcare information; for example, charting blood pressure or QTc interval (indicating interruption of the heart's rhythm) during the course of a clinical trial.
- **Don't use for**: Randomly distributed data; you'll just get a mess, just like the scatter plot.
- **Pros**: The ability to visualize several distributions, all on a single chart.
- **Cons**: Box plots have less fine-grained control over the formatting and layout of the visualization than other Spotfire visualizations. However, there are some options that are extremely useful, which I will detail in this section.
- **Summary:** Box plots are great for visualizing lots of distributions simultaneously.

Whenever you are measuring a population or taking readings of a naturally occurring phenomenon, it is likely to have some kind of distribution. The most common distribution is the normal distribution, and you will see it in such measures as the blood pressure of a patient population.

You can think of a box plot as the distribution being turned on its side. The actual detail of the distribution is hidden in the boxes, as the boxes represent specific statistical segments of the data. Therefore, the box plot reduces the amount of screen real estate that is required to view the distributions, and it allows for an easy comparison between different categories. Let's return to the gapminder data on infant mortality and population growth.

The following box plot shows infant mortality for the entire world, for each of the years from 1950 to 2015:

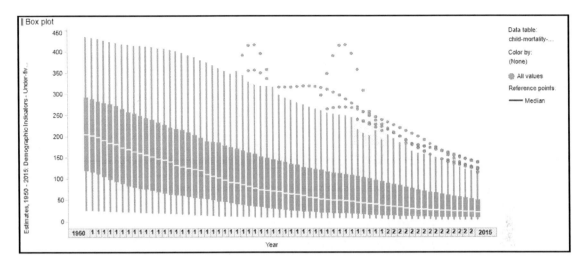

Look at that! There are several insights to be gained from this visualization. Here are a few that I can think of:

- It's clear that infant mortality is decreasing globally over time. This is shown by the overall downward trend of the heights displayed for each year.
- It's also clear that the gap between the countries of the world is closing. Healthcare is improving, so infant mortality is decreasing globally. There are probably other reasons for this, too, such as poverty decreasing, better water supplies, and so on.
- There are definitely some countries that are outliers (the dots above the bulk of the visualization); they appear to have unusually high infant mortality rates for a few years.

Let's explore the outliers a bit more. Unfortunately, it's not possible to label them on the box plot visualization, but I have created a details visualization and marked the first set of outliers:

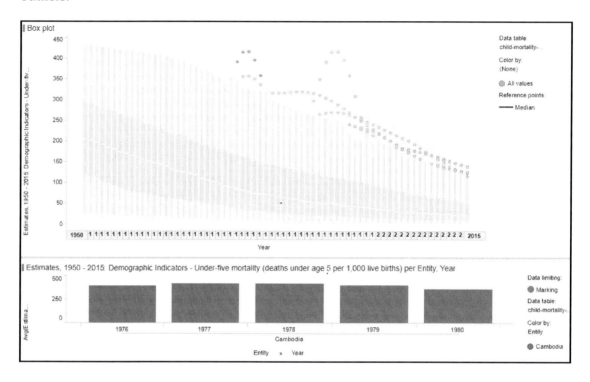

Interesting! It's Cambodia again. Note that in the previous example, where I highlighted Cambodia, I just eyeballed the data in the scatter plot. Here, I have used statistical methods to identify and call out unusual data.

Furthermore, I am able to mark all the outliers and produce a year-on-year view of all the countries that fall significantly outside the rest of the world:

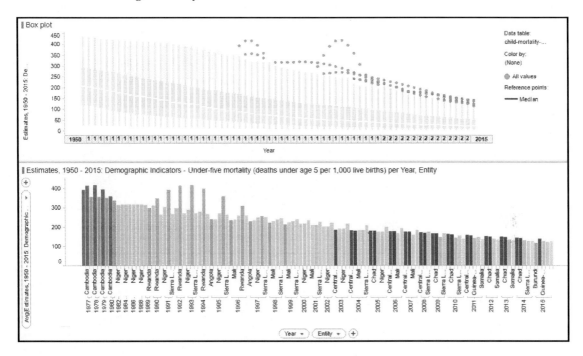

Again, notice the overall downward trend; there is still an improvement in the worst-performing countries.

How to further interpret a box plot

You may be wondering what the sections of the box plot mean. Here's a clipping from Spotfire help that explains them:

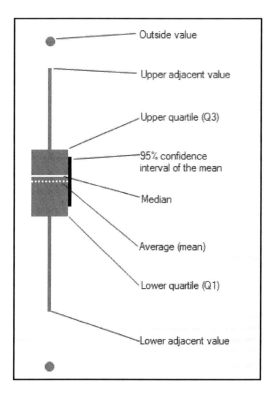

Not all the statistics are shown by default; you can enable or disable them and customize the coloring and line styles through the **Reference points property** page for the box plot.

It's beyond the scope of this book to describe what all these statistics mean and how they are defined. Suffice it to say, the box plot allows you to evaluate the distribution of your data, understand where the data is centered, and understand where the bulk of it lies. How do the outliers vary? How much of the data is statistically significantly lower or higher than the lower and higher quartiles, and so on? Even without a statistical understanding, the box plot is really easy to interpret!

More box plot options

There are some more options for box plots that I'd like to explore:

- **Show distribution**: This is available in the **Appearance Property** page. You can turn it on in order to help explain the boxes on the box plot, but I don't recommend its usage in the real world. My own opinion is that it is confusing, because it doesn't correspond with the histogram drawn alongside the box plot:

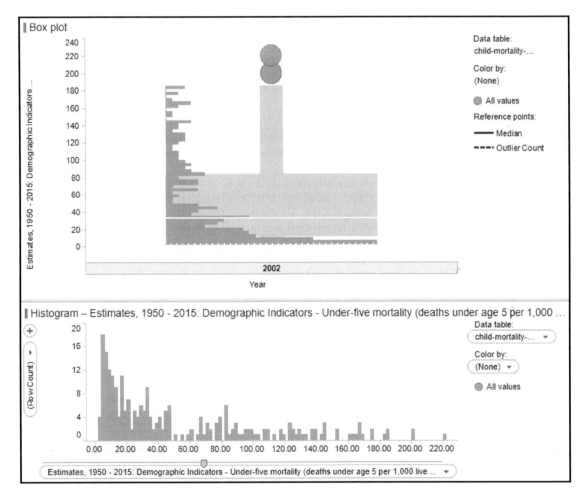

The histogram and the distribution that's been superimposed onto the box plot show the same data, but that fact is not immediately apparent.

- **Color by**: The box plot works differently than other visualizations in Spotfire. You cannot highlight single values in a box plot by color; all you can do is apply different colors to the box plots, as split by the columns on the x or trellis axes. This can be used effectively to color certain categories differently from each other, or to produce a visual effect. The color will be applied to the whole category and cannot be used to highlight or split individual values in the box plot.

- The list of reference points in the box plot properties is extensive! It's beyond the scope of this book to go into each one in detail, so please study the Spotfire help for more information. It's possible to get really creative with how the points are represented: by lines or by markers, and by setting colors for each reference point. You can create some nice effects and really highlight the reference points and draw the human eye to the most important ones.

The statistics table underneath the box plot gives summary statistics of interest. Here is an example box plot that shows the statistics table with various measures enabled:

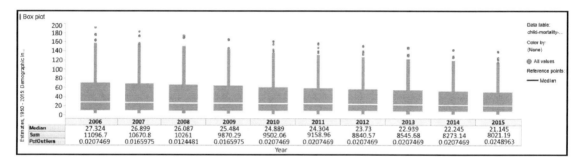

You can switch the individual statistics on and off via the **Statistics Table** page of the box plot configuration.

Box plot summary

Box plots are really powerful! Use the power of the built-in statistics to show the shape of your data. Rapidly identify outliers; compare distributions over time or other categories.

Treemaps

Treemaps are also under-utilized, in my opinion! They are extremely useful visualizations for navigating hierarchical data. This was already described in Chapter 2, *It's All About the Data*, but I'd like to expand on what was said there:

- **Good for visualizing**: Hierarchical data. You can size each box in the treemap by a value in your data and navigate up and down the levels of the hierarchy interactively. They are great for collapsing large amounts of data into a single view. They are also great for setting up navigable hierarchies, so that users can sub-select parts of the data really easily.
- **Don't use for**: Hierarchies with lots and lots of levels; you'll get confused. Hierarchies where the amount of data in some categories is really small compared to the others (you'll end up with lots of tiny boxes that you can't interpret).
- **Pros**: The ability to view hierarchical data at a glance!
- **Cons**: Treemaps can only show the name of the category in the box. It isn't possible to label the boxes by any other value. You can size/color the boxes however you want, but you cannot choose how to label the boxes.
- **Summary**: Treemaps are great for visualizing or navigating hierarchical data.

Treemaps are also the only visualization in Spotfire that supports in-place drilldown and drill-up. Most other visualizations work on the principle that you set up a master-detail relationship between the visualizations. With a treemap, you can drill down into the hierarchy and then drill back up to the higher levels, all with the click of a mouse. You can, of course, still set up a master-detail relationship between a treemap and other visualizations.

I have used treemap visualizations to provide users with the ability to select categories of data. The size and color are almost unimportant in this case, as they don't provide the user with analytic value—they are just a visual clue as to which categories are the most important.

Let's return once again to the gapminder data. I have a hierarchy representing the region, sub-region, and entity (country). This hierarchy is shown in the treemap, and I have chosen to size by infant mortality. It's therefore possible to select different regions in the treemap and view box plots for each of the regions I have selected. I have also trellised the box plot visualization by the hierarchy:

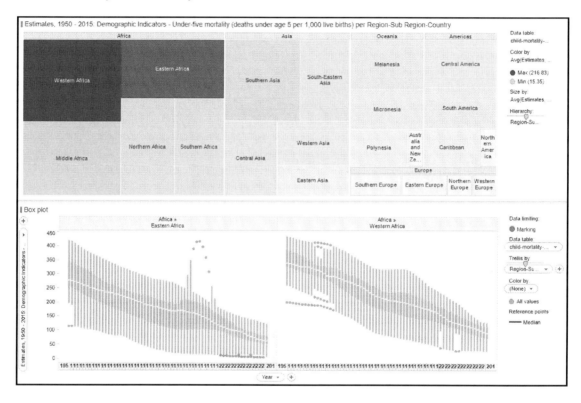

Now, it's really straightforward to compare any two regions, just by selecting them on the treemap! Here, you can see that I am comparing Western Africa and Eastern Africa. There's definitely a higher disparity with Western Africa. It's also interesting to note that some low outliers are starting to appear in later years. You can also see the rise and fall of one outlier in Eastern Africa. That outlier is `Rwanda`. Unfortunately, it also corresponds with rather disturbing events—a civil war and a genocide.

To summarize, treemaps are very useful for navigating hierarchical data. They are the only Spotfire visualization that supports in-place navigation through hierarchies.

Waterfall charts

Waterfall charts are not referenced anywhere else in this book, so I will cover them now. Waterfall charts exist primarily for a single use case: to show profit and loss across various categories or over a time period. The idea behind a waterfall chart is that it shows the individual contribution of each category (or time period) to the overall total, while showing the overall total at the end.

That being said, profit and loss calculations and visualizations are extremely useful to almost any business. So, don't ignore the waterfall chart! You should also consider a waterfall chart whenever you have a measure that is changing and you need to know how much it changed by overall, how much each event changed, or the event that contributed the most to that overall change. Let's go over them now:

- **Good for visualizing**: **Profit and loss** (**P&L**) data—any process changing over time or being affected by different categories of events.
- **Don't use for**: Data that's been split into many categories—the picture gets confusing and hard to follow.
- **Pros**: Simple to interpret—de facto visualization for P&L data.
- **Cons**: Waterfall plots work in a slightly different way from other Spotfire visualizations. The overall picture you get is dependent on the ordering of the categories (this is true of any visualization, but could cause unintended consequences with a waterfall plot).
- **Summary**: Use waterfall charts for displaying P&L data (mostly).

Here is an example of a waterfall chart in Spotfire:

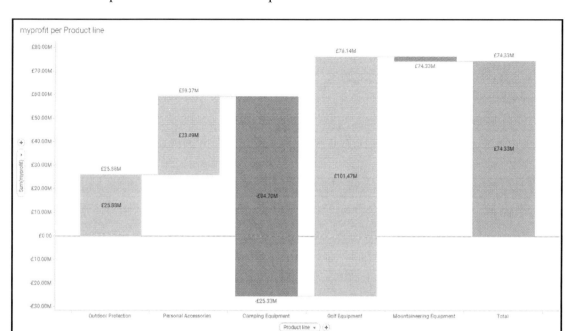

How did I configure this? The y-axis is a continuous variable. The bar height is the sum of `myprofit`. If `myprofit` is positive, the bar will go up. If it is negative, it will go down. Each bar starts where the previous one ends. The total profit is the bar on the far right. I would interpret this chart as follows:

- All product lines returned a profit, except for `Camping Equipment` and `Mountaineering Equipment`
- `Golf Equipment` returned the largest profit overall, making up for the losses incurred by `Camping Equipment` and `Mountaineering Equipment`
- `Outdoor Protection` and `Personal Accessories` were reasonably profitable
- The overall profit was £74.33 M

How was the coloring of the waterfall plot done? Easy! Spotfire comes with a default coloring scheme for waterfall plots. You don't have to change it unless you don't like it. It defaults to green for positive, red for negative, and blue for the overall total. In fact, Spotfire does a pretty good job of configuring a waterfall chart with zero, or next to zero, configuration.

Now, let's go over some warnings about using the waterfall chart:

- Notice that I have enabled labels for the blocks (bars) and the totals. The block (bar) for `Mountaineering Equipment` is too small to fit the block label. There's no current solution to this. Just be aware that this may make it hard to determine the absolute value of each of the bars if they are too small.
- The sort order of the column that's used on the x-axis can significantly affect the apparent findings. Let's adjust the order slightly:

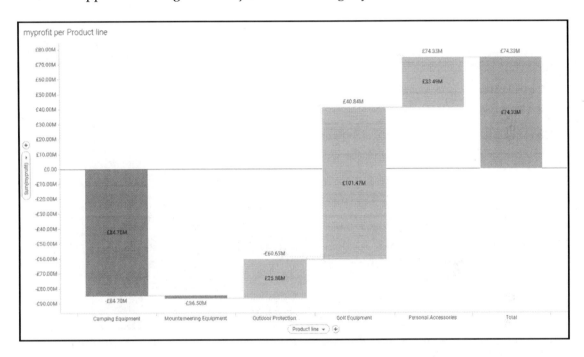

Now, the picture looks totally different! The data is just the same, though. I would say that it's much harder to see that the profit from the `Golf Equipment` made up for the loss from `Camping/Mountaineering`. All I did was change the sort order of the product line column!

Let's look at one more example:

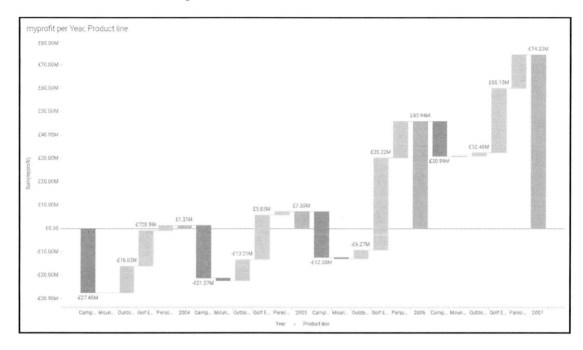

I have added `Year` on the x-axis. To me, this produces a more compelling visualization. There's a time-based element to it, so I now know that the visualization is showing P&L over time, but is also split by category. Therefore, I get the best of both worlds.

Waterfall plots are great for displaying P&L data, or some other process that's changing due to certain events or categories. I would caution against using waterfall plots with purely categorical information on the x-axis. It's far better to have a time component!

Graphical tables

The graphical table visualization is a bit like a cross table, in that it shows aggregated data, but it can show it in a graphical form. Alongside regular table columns, you can add sparklines, calculated values, conditional icons, and bullet graphs.

Graphical tables are unusual in the Spotfire world; KPI charts and graphical tables are the only visualizations that support direct actions when you click on them. You can set up actions that are triggered when a user clicks on an element in a graphical table. Those actions could be to apply a bookmark, navigate to a page, execute a data function to perform some statistical analysis, or automate Spotfire with IronPython.

That being said, I don't really recommend the use of graphical tables unless you have a specific need for automating actions from a visualization, producing bullet graphs or icons, or want to show several different representations of the data in each row. I prefer using KPI charts over graphical tables. Don't forget that you can show sparklines, values, and much more with KPI charts:

- **Good for visualizing**: Data at a glance. Sparklines show trends over time; bullet graphs show values against targets; icons can highlight particular rows in the graphical table or show an overall trend using up/down arrows.
- **Don't use for**: Lots and lots of categories! A graphical table that doesn't fit nicely on a page in Spotfire is not a good graphical table. The end users of Spotfire dashboards won't want to scroll beyond a page or so of a table.
- **Pros**: Great for showing lots of things about your data at a glance.
- **Cons**: Not so good for showing lots of categories. Sparklines and bullet charts do not have scales, so they are only suitable for showing the overall shape of the data or relative values; bullet charts can be difficult to interpret without a scale or key (legend). Spotfire does not show a legend for the bullet chart, so you would need to produce one manually and put it in a text area.
- **Summary**: Look at KPI charts first. I would recommend only using graphical tables if you really need bullet charts.

Graphical table visualization types

Sparklines are miniature line charts. You could, for example, create a graphical table of countries with a sparkline showing the interest rate in each country over time:

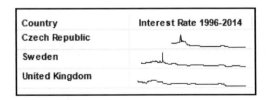

Calculated values are simply calculations, usually involving aggregation of the data. For example, we could list baseball teams and provide a column for the total runs scored.

Conditional icons, such as upward and downward arrows, can be associated with a rule, such as above or below average, or if a trend is upward or downward:

Team	Stolen Bases	Above/Below Average
LA Angels	146	⬆
LA Dodgers	42	⬇
Milwaukee	45	⬇
Minnesota	85	⬆

Bullet graphs are a miniature representation of how one variable compares to another. The vertical bar represents variable 1 (a target, perhaps), the horizontal line represents variable 2, and the color shading can be configured to represent points of interest, such as percentages:

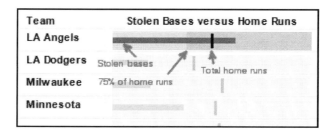

By now, you should be pretty familiar with how to configure Spotfire visualizations, so I'm not going to walk you through setting these visualizations up from scratch. Please visit the Spotfire online help if you need further information or guidance.

Graphical table summary

In short, use a KPI chart instead of a graphical table. Only use a graphical table if you need a bullet chart and there's nothing else that will do!

Taking action from KPI charts or graphical tables

There are all sorts of other actions you can take from the user clicking on an item in a KPI chart or graphical table.

Note: you can only configure actions if you're using a Spotfire Analyst client. Actions cannot be set up using a web-based client.

Here are some example actions:

- Perform various Spotfire actions—reset filters, filter to marked rows, navigate to a page, apply bookmarks, and so on
- Execute IronPython scripts
- Execute a statistical data function

You can build up a series of multiple actions, in order to achieve the task you want. Here is an example:

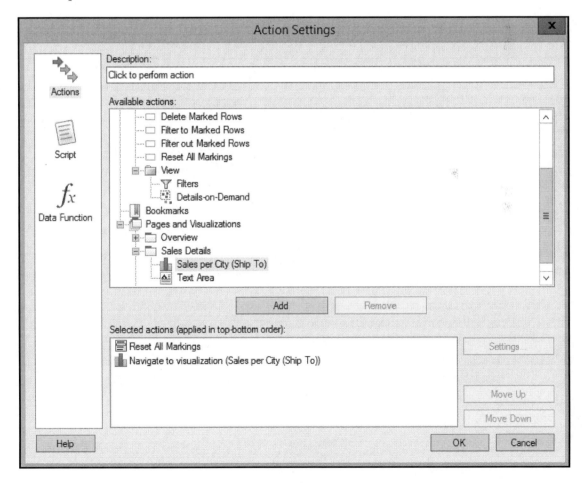

The important thing to remember (and it doesn't appear to be documented anywhere) is that clicking on the visual element in the KPI chart or graphical table marks the data first, then executes the actions. This is important because it allows the action to act upon the data that has been marked. For example, a data function (see Chapter 9, *What's Your Location?*) would be able to know which row(s) of data the user was interacting with, or an IronPython script could determine which rows of data are marked, and then do something with that data.

Other visualization types

KPI charts are covered in Chapter 3, *Impactful Dashboards!*.

Heatmaps and parallel coordinate plots are covered in Chapter 8, *The World is Your Visualization*.

Map charts have a chapter to themselves, so I won't cover them here. Please read Chapter 9, *What's Your Location?*, for more details.

Summary

This chapter has given you some practical suggestions about when you should use the different types of visualizations provided in Spotfire. It is based on my experience of working with various customers and use cases, in different industries. You are free to take your own route, and I'm sure you'll end up with your own favorite visualizations!

I have also provided some hints and tips for configuring the visualizations, some common pitfalls and mistakes to avoid, and some thoughts about good design.

Some important takeaways from this chapter are as follows:

- Bar charts, cross tables, and scatter plots are probably the most versatile visualizations. You can do so much with them!
- Avoid pie charts (most of the time).
- Think carefully about which visualization type you should use in a given circumstance.
- Don't sum averages.

- Be careful with cross table grand totals—watch out for aggregations at different levels not giving results that add up properly.
- It is possible to incorrectly configure visualizations, to give either misleading results or results that are just wrong!
- Test the results from your visualizations.

In the next chapter, we will take a break from data and analysis and look at the Spotfire platform as a whole. We'll be looking at some administration topics, and also at tools such as automation services.

6
The Big Wide World of Spotfire

It's time to take a break from the world of analysis and visualization and learn something about the Spotfire environment. So far, the focus has been on the detailed work of the analyst or report author, but Spotfire is much more than an analysis tool for individuals; it is an enterprise application with multiple components. This chapter is primarily targeted toward the Spotfire administrator. However, Spotfire Automation Services is covered in detail, so skip to that bit if you need to run an automated job in Spotfire to load some data, export a PDF, or send an email.

If you are not an administrator, I recommend that you skim read this chapter so that you have an understanding of the general concepts and can come back to it for future reference—or take the book to a meeting with your IT organization so that you can understand what's going on!

I also recommend that you read the part of this chapter on scalability—one day, you may wish to deploy your analysis to hundreds or thousands of users, so an understanding of how Spotfire scales will be very useful. Please refer to `Chapter 12`, *Scaling the Infrastructure; Keeping Data up to Date*, for a full reference on how to define the rules for how Spotfire intelligently scales for web analysis.

 Note: if you are not a Spotfire administrator, you won't be able to follow along with the examples showing the administration tools (either in Spotfire Analyst or via the web-based administration console). However, you may well have access to be able to build Automation Services jobs.

You will find comprehensive architecture and administration documents online (`https://docs.tibco.com/`), but this chapter will introduce the main components of the Spotfire analytics framework. You will learn about the main Spotfire administration tasks, how to distribute dashboards and analytic toolkits to a wider audience, how to monitor the use and performance of the system, and how to automate repetitive tasks, such as refreshing data and sending PDF reports.

In this chapter, we will cover the following topics:

- An overview of Spotfire components and architecture
- Scalability of Spotfire's Web Player
- A quick guide to administration manager
- Using the library administration interface
- Automating tasks using Automation Services
- A detailed overview of the Spotfire administration console—including a real-world example of how to troubleshoot the loading of a scheduled analysis

An overview of the Spotfire platform

The Spotfire platform uses a client/server architecture in which users analyze their data using the various Spotfire clients (desktop, web, and mobile):

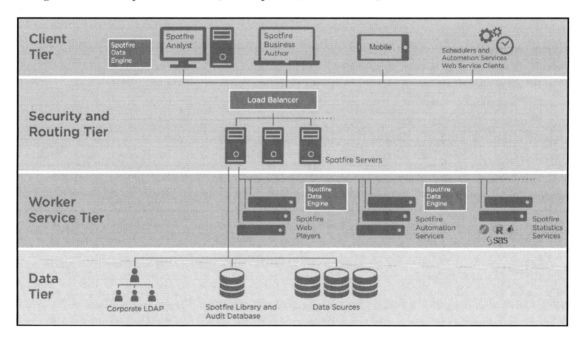

The main components are discussed as follows.

Spotfire server

This is the central part of the Spotfire architecture. It is a Java Tomcat web application that runs on Windows or Linux. It is the administrative center of any Spotfire environment. It provides the tools for configuring and administering the Spotfire environment and, through the various Spotfire clients, enables users to access their data, create visualizations, and share them with coworkers or with the world. The Spotfire server enables the following activities:

- Authenticates and authorizes Spotfire users
- Provides access to analyses and data stored in the Spotfire library
- Provides access to external data sources, including Oracle and SQL Server databases, or most **Java Database Connectivity (JDBC)** sources, through information links
- Makes sure that analyses are loaded with updated data according to schedules that are defined by the administrator
- Provides storage (in the Spotfire database) for configurations, preferences, analyses, and so on
- Manages the traffic through the Spotfire environment to optimize performance, and in accordance with rules that are defined by the administrator
- Distributes software updates
- Monitors the health and activities of the Spotfire environment and provides diagnostic information both in the server interface and through downloadable logs

Spotfire database

The **Spotfire database** stores all the account administration and configuration information needed to make Spotfire work. The Spotfire server requires a database in order to work. It also stores the Spotfire library, which looks to the user like a hierarchical filesystem to organize and store analysis files. The Spotfire database can be built in Oracle or Microsoft SQL Server.

Nodes and services

Nodes and services are crucial for enabling the Spotfire web clients and Automation Services (discussed in subsequent sections). The node manager architecture hosts service instances of Spotfire Web Player and Automation Services. The architecture provides industry-leading scalability and reliability, with intelligent routing of users based on a simple and powerful set of rules that can be configured. Nodes and services must be installed on Windows servers.

Spotfire Web Player(s) and Business Author

Instances of Spotfire Web Player are installed within Spotfire nodes. Spotfire Web Player is the zero installation (for the end user) consumer interface to Spotfire. It also supports Spotfire Business Author, with web-based authoring of Spotfire analyses. All users of the web clients log in directly to the Spotfire server. From there, the server delegates the work of providing the analyses to an appropriate Web Player server.

Spotfire Automation Services

Spotfire Automation Services is a tool for automating certain Spotfire tasks into jobs that can be run on demand or to a schedule. Service instances of Automation Services are also hosted within Spotfire nodes. It's perhaps easiest to think of Automation Services as headless, Spotfire clients that don't display a user interface. There are some standard tasks that can be performed to refresh data, export data, images, or PDFs, notify users by email, and so on.

Spotfire Analyst clients and mobile clients

The Spotfire Analyst and mobile clients are discussed in detail in `Chapter 1`, *Welcome to Spotfire*.

Spotfire Statistics Services

Statistics Services is a lightweight, flexible server that provides a communication layer, a service layer, and a **TIBCO® Enterprise Runtime for R (TERR)**, S-PLUS, or open source R engine pool, among other features. Spotfire statistics Services does not include user interface features. You can also use external engines, such as SAS and MATLAB, if you have access to the corresponding software. Statistics Services can be deployed as a standalone server against which you can run analyses in one of its engines, or it can be deployed as part of a Spotfire stack. Statistics Services is also covered in Chapter 13, *Beyond the Horizon*.

Geeky information—**Spotfire's data engine**: At heart, I'm a true computer geek! I love to know what's happening under the hood and how anything and everything works. So, here's some information that appeals to my inner geek: Spotfire has a really unusual feature—a highly optimized in-memory data engine. It's actually a database that is specifically built for the extremely fast slicing and dicing of data. It supports the calculation of aggregated visualizations on large volumes of data in seconds. It has all sorts of caching algorithms and optimizations particularly suited to working with Spotfire. The installed clients and web clients all use the data engine.

Spotfire Web Player scalability

Spotfire's web architecture scales amazingly well. The Web Player shares parts of the analysis files and data between multiple users in order to make the most efficient use of the hardware resources available.

Furthermore, the node manager and service instance architecture has many benefits over traditional load balancing. The chief advantage is that it is context-aware. Traditional load balancers have variations on round-robin or least utilized sharing algorithms (and more besides, but we will focus on the simple ones for the purposes of this example). In the case of these traditional load balancers, they will assign users to individual servers in turn (round- robin) or allocate a new user to the least used server in the cluster.

The disadvantage of the traditional load-balancing scheme is that, eventually, all the servers will most likely become overloaded. Here's an example (with two nodes, A and B, in a cluster/resource pool):

- User Asad wants to load the `Sales Analysis` file—the load balancer notices that server A is not utilized, so will assign Asad to server A.
- User Mary also wants to load the `Sales Analysis` file. In this case, the load balancer notices that server B is less utilized than server A (since Asad is already using it) and so will assign Mary to server B.

This has the result that the `Sales Analysis` file is loaded on server A and server B. Both servers consume the same amount of memory, and there is no opportunity for Spotfire to share memory and data between Asad and Mary.

Imagine that this scenario continues, with new users requesting more analysis files. Very soon, all analysis files will be loaded on both servers and they will suddenly be out of resources.

A far more efficient routing scheme is described as follows (and this is what Spotfire does):

- User Asad wants to load the `Sales Analysis` file. The Spotfire server will know that both servers A and B are not utilized, so Asad will be directed to server A. The analysis will then be loaded on that server.
- As before, Mary also wants to load the same analysis file. The Spotfire server knows that the analysis is already loaded on server A, so it will direct Mary to server A.

In this case, Asad and Mary share the same server and the same data. They consume fewer resources overall than if they were spread between both servers.

Spotfire also supports routing based on a specific analysis file, user group, geographic location, and so on. The rules are applied in priority order, similar to mail-sorting rules. Rules can be disabled or mapped to a different resource pool. Finally, the rules can be scheduled—effectively turning a routing rule into a scheduled update. By this mechanism, analysis files can be preloaded on selected instances in a resource pool. They will then open instantly and can have data refreshed at specified intervals (or the refresh could be triggered by an external system via a web service call to the Spotfire server).

The rules for routing and scheduling are covered in more detail in `Chapter 12`, *Scaling the Infrastructure; Keeping Data up to Date.*

A quick guide to administration manager

The **administration manager** (Spotfire Analyst clients only) is a tool that's available only to Spotfire administrators, to control how each Spotfire user uses the system and its components. It is accessed through the **Tools** menu. The number of Spotfire administrators in an organization is normally very small. This section is included to give you some sense of how Spotfire is administered at an enterprise level.

 Basic user administration is also available via Spotfire's web-based administration console. The steps and principles shown here are broadly similar, regardless of whether you are using the administration console or the tools in Spotfire Analyst.

Spotfire, like many other computer systems, allows you to organize users into groups and those groups into hierarchies of groups. Groups are used to organize users into categories of a common purpose, which could be to do with functionality or with access to particular data.

Spotfire uses the concept of a license to define functional granularity within a system. The term can be confusing. It is related at a high level to the product licenses that are purchased for a given Spotfire implementation, such as Spotfire consumer and Spotfire Analyst licenses. However, it also refers to elements of functionality that fall under those product licenses. For example, a Spotfire administrator can restrict the visualization types that are available to a group of users who otherwise have full Spotfire Analyst licenses.

Using the **Users** tab of administration manager, an administrator can do the following:

- View the group membership and licenses of an individual user
- Change the group membership of an individual user

 The management of user accounts and passwords and the authentication of login events can be enabled in a variety of ways in Spotfire. Account management can be handled solely within Spotfire or delegated to another authority such as Microsoft Active Directory, which is used to manage and authenticate users in an enterprise Windows environment. It's beyond the scope of this book to explore this aspect of user administration.

Using the **Groups and Licenses** tab, an administrator can do the following:

- Create groups
- Assign users to groups
- Assign licenses to groups

Using the **Preferences** tab, an administrator can do the following:

- Assign configuration preferences to groups

Users

To look up the current assignment of groups and licenses of an individual user, you need to do the following (assuming you are logged in as an administrator):

1. Open the **Users** tab in **Administration Manager**, enter a search string for the user of interest using the asterisk symbol as a wildcard, and click on **Search**. All users matching the search string will appear in the left-hand window; select the one of interest:

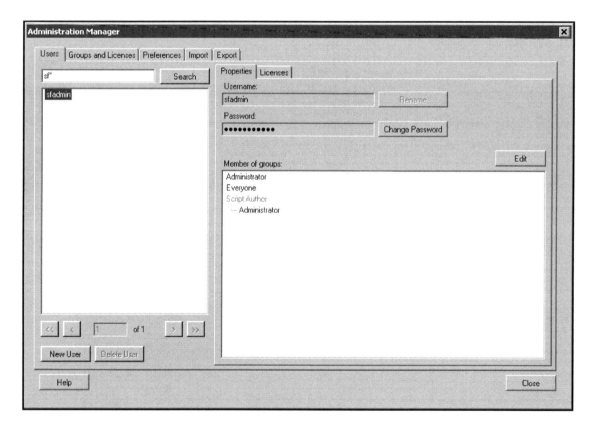

2. The **Properties** tab shows the user's group membership. To make a change, click on the **Edit** button. You will be presented with a simple dialog that allows you to add available groups to or remove groups from the user's profile.

3. The **New User** and **Delete User** options may not be available, depending on how user authentication has been set up in your system.

4. The **Licenses** tab shows the user's licenses, which cannot be changed from this dialog; you need to move to the **Groups and Licenses** tab to do that.

Groups and licenses

As an exercise in creating new groups, assigning users to groups, and assigning licenses to groups, let's work through the following scenario:

1. Open the **Groups and Licenses** tab in **Administration Manager**, and click on the **New Group** button. Create the groups Marketing Department and Finance Department. You want to create these groups as top-level groups, not as part of a hierarchy:

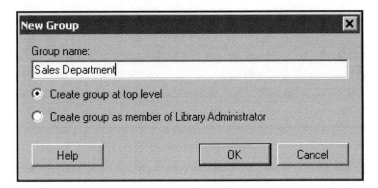

2. Now, select the group **Marketing Department** group, and create a new group as a member of this group. Name it `Marketing Librarians`. Create a second group called `Marketing Spotfire Consumers`. Do the same for the **Finance Department** group. The following screenshot shows what you should have when you are finished:

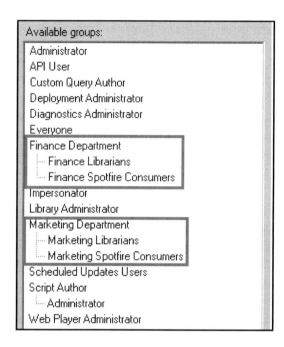

3. Select the group **Finance Department**, switch to the **Licenses** tab, and click on the **Edit** button:

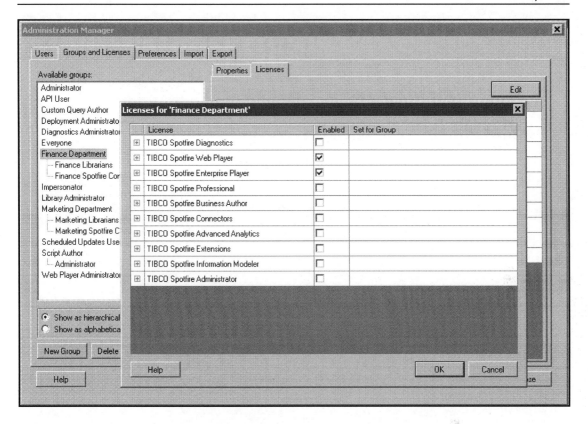

4. Check the **TIBCO Spotfire Web Player** and **TIBCO Spotfire Enterprise Player** checkboxes under the **Enabled** column. Click on **OK** to save the changes. Repeat for the **Marketing Department** group.

 All groups within **Finance Department** and **Marketing Department** will inherit the licenses you granted.

5. Now, select the **Finance Librarians** group, click on the **Licenses** tab's **Edit** button, expand the **TIBCO Spotfire Administrator** license by clicking on the plus symbol next to it, and check the **Library Administration** option, but not the **Administration** option. Click on **OK** to save the changes, and repeat for **Marketing Librarians**.

6. Select the subgroups you created and, in turn, select the **Properties** tab and click on **Edit Members** to add users to each group.

We created containers for two different departments, each with a report consumer group and a more privileged library administration group.

Special user groups

Some special groups exist for administration purposes. They allow users or other groups to be assigned certain permissions. They define standard roles for administering and using Spotfire. Each special group enables a set of licenses that correspond to an administrative or user role. To give a user the ability to administer certain aspects of the Spotfire platform, the user must be a member of that group, either by direct inclusion or by being a member of a user group that is also a member of the special group.

Note that some roles require not only membership in the special group, but also that a specific license be enabled for the group.

The following are the predefined groups:

- **Administrator**: All users who need administrator privileges on Spotfire server, including the ability to manage users and groups, must belong to this group. Membership of this group grants all the permissions described in this section, in addition to the administration of preferences, licenses, and the user directory. This group must also have the Spotfire administrator license enabled to fully administer the Spotfire system (to access the administration manager tool in Spotfire Analyst, as well as all areas of Spotfire server).
- **Library administrator**: Membership of this group grants full permission for the library. It overrides all folder permissions set in the library, granting full control over content. It also includes the permission to import and export library content. All users and groups that need administrative privileges in the library must belong to this group or the administrator group. This group must also have the Spotfire library administrator license enabled to be able to administer the library (to get access to the library administration tool in Spotfire Analyst).
- **Deployment administrator**: Membership of this group grants permission to deploy packages to the server. Note that these users can deploy to any area on the server, as well as delete any existing deployment. Members of this group can access the deployments and packages area of Spotfire server.

- **Diagnostics administrator**: This group grants permission to view server logs and diagnostics, as well as to set logging configurations. Members of this group can access the monitoring and diagnostics area of the server.
- **Scheduling and routing administrator**: Membership of this group grants permission to create scheduled updates and routing rules. Members of this group can access the scheduling and routing area of the server. Users of an account that execute scheduled updates must be members of this group. By default, the scheduledupdates@SPOTFIRESYSTEM account is a member of this group.
- **Automation Services users**: This group grants permission to schedule Automation Services jobs on the Spotfire server and to execute Automation Services jobs on the server manually, using the Automation Services job builder or the client job sender.
- **Custom query author**: This group is granted permission to save scripts written in custom query languages (used with database connectors-see Chapter 10, *Information Links and Data Connectors*), as trusted to the library. An authorized custom query author **must also** have the custom query in connections license enabled to get access to the required user interface.
- **Script author**: Members of this group have permission to save scripts as trusted to the library. An authorized script author **must also** have the Author Scripts license enabled. Scripts that are executed by Spotfire server can essentially do anything that deployed packages can do. Therefore, this permission should only be granted to trusted users.
- **API user**: All users who require access to the deprecated Spotfire server public web service API must be members of the API user group.
- **Everyone**: This group always contains all users in the Spotfire implementation. No users can be removed from this group, but you can set licenses for the group if you want to.
- **System account**: This group cannot be edited. It contains the system accounts that are used internally in the Spotfire environment.

Preferences

The **Preferences** tab allows a Spotfire administrator to assign default settings and preferences for visualizations to any or all user groups. Examples would be the default font for labels and the marker shape for scatter plots. Users can, however, override these preferences.

Using the library administration interface

The **library administration** interface is a tool that's available only to full administrators or users who have been granted the **TIBCO Spotfire library administration** license. It is accessed through the **Tools** menu.

The Spotfire library is a repository of analysis files arranged in a folder-like hierarchy for distribution to the enterprise. It can be accessed from both Spotfire desktop clients and the Spotfire Web Player. Although all the items in the library are actually stored in the Spotfire database, the library works very much like a Windows filesystem.

The library administration interface allows a library administrator to create folders and hierarchies of folders, to move and copy analysis files between folders, and, most importantly, control who has access to each folder.

There is a special, built-in group called **library administrator**, and members of this group have full control of the entire library. If you want to delegate control just to parts of the library, along departmental lines, for example, you must create a separate group and grant it a TIBCO Spotfire library administration license. This is what we did while exploring the administration manager tool. You can then restrict the access of this group to certain folders in the library, effectively making those users departmental-level library administrators.

Folder permissions

Let's continue with our finance and marketing departments scenario. We'll be setting library folder permissions for different user groups:

1. Open **Library Administration** from the **Tools** menu (assuming you are logged in as a member of either the administrator or library administrator groups).
2. Click on **New Folder** to create a new folder and call it Finance; do the same for Marketing. You can give the folders descriptions if you wish, but it's not essential.
3. Select the newly created Finance folder and click on the **Edit...** link next to **Permissions for Selected Folder**. The dialog that opens allows you to decide which users or user groups can access the contents of the folder to various degrees of privilege:

The built-in administrator and library administrator groups implicitly
have full control over all `Library` folders, irrespective of any permissions
that are set explicitly.

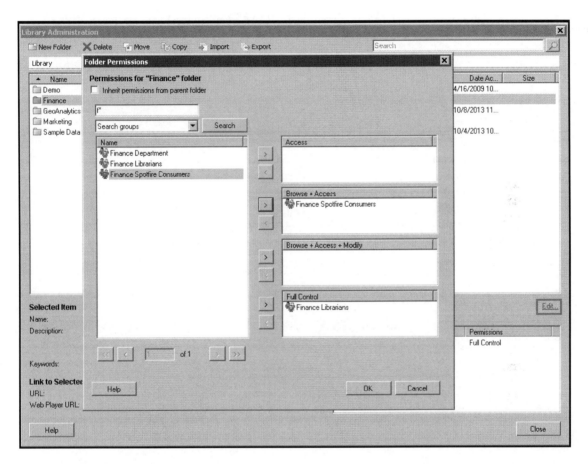

Uncheck **Inherit permissions from parent folder** if you want to start a
new inheritance hierarchy. Otherwise, you will not be able to remove, for
example, the Everyone group, which is applied to the root of the library
by default.

4. Search for the **Finance Department** groups. Select **Finance Spotfire Consumers** and add it to the **Browse + Access** panel. Select **Finance Librarians** and add it to the **Full Control** panel. Remove all other groups from the **Permissions** windows.

5. Do the same for the **Marketing Department** folders, and then remove the Everyone group from all other root folders.

 For security reasons, I would recommend removing the Everyone group from all root folder permissions and only adding the group back on a case-by-case basis, if ever.

With this setup, when Finance Department users log in, they will only see their departmental folder and any subfolders to which they have been granted permission. Although finance librarians have the elevated privilege of library administration, they too will only see the departmental folder. The difference is that they will be able to create new folders under that folder and control which groups and users have access and at which level. The control of user accounts and group membership remains with the Administrator group.

Import and export

As a library administrator, you can also import and export individual files or entire folders with all their subfolders.

To export, select the folder or file of interest and click on the **Export** button. The selection will be exported as a ZIP file to a file directory location that is predetermined by a configuration setting on the Spotfire server. The default location is the installation directory of the Spotfire server, but it is possible to set up a network share and use that as a more communal area.

 All items in the library have an underlying unique identifier called a **Globally Unique Identifier (GUID)**, which is retained when exported.

To import, click on the **Import** button and browse to the exported package, which must be in the configured import/export directory. When importing a package back into the library, it's possible that either the name or the GUID of an object in the import package is identical to an existing item at the target location. You must choose one of the three following rules to resolve any conflicts:

- **Automatically assign a new name or GUID to an imported item**: A (2) is appended to the name of the imported item, and it is given a new GUID
- **Replace existing item**: The imported item assumes the name and/or GUID of the target item
- **Keep existing item**: The item is not imported

The same rules are used when simply copying or moving items around the library, except there is no potential GUID conflict in such cases, just a potential name conflict. When importing and exporting between multiple server environments, it's good practice to use **Replace existing item** because it ensures that any Spotfire analysis files that use the items imported to the library will continue to work without modification.

Automating tasks using Automation Services

Automation Services is a very useful tool to automate certain Spotfire tasks. You can think of Automation Services as a special **headless** Spotfire client that runs on a server. Spotfire has a scheduler built in to the administration console as of Version 10.

Some great things you can do with Automation Services include the following:

- Load the latest data from an information link or file in the library—in this way, the Spotfire file becomes a **cache** for data and can store the data without having to query the external data source every time it is opened. This can also be achieved (in a different way) by using scheduling and routing.
- Export images or PDF files.
- Send emails to users containing visualizations, a copy of the analysis, link to the file on the web, PDF files, and so on.
- And much more...

The **Automation Services Job Builder** is found under the **Tools** menu. You use this job builder to create an Automation Services job. Custom tasks can be created using the **software developer kit (SDK)**, but this is an advanced topic for Spotfire developers with programming skills:

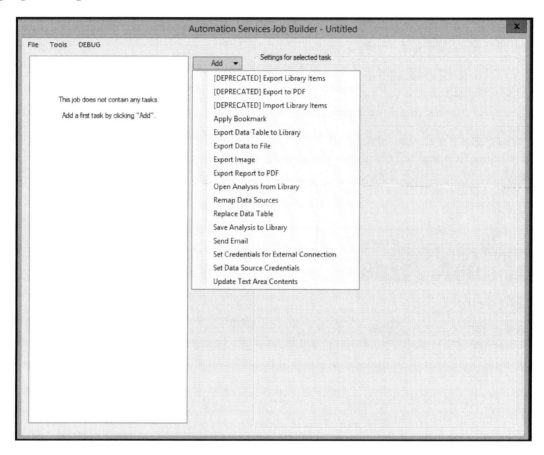

You can see from the list that the job builder offers a diverse range of tasks. Some are backend administration tasks, such as setting data source credentials or remapping data sources; others help to provide updates to people, such as emailing them with a message and including images from an analysis file, a Web Player link to the file, or even an embedded analysis file.

When you select a task to add, a dialog window for that task opens to allow you to enter the relevant details. As you add tasks, they build up as a list in the job builder's window. You can remove individual tasks at any time, and you can move them up and down the order.

When your job is complete, you can use the job builder's **File** menu to save the job as an XML file or to the Spotfire library. If you want to use Spotfire's built-in scheduler, you must save the job file to the library.

An XML file can be edited directly, but it can also be opened in the job builder for editing. That's an easier and safer way to make changes to a job. It's possible to get really clever with job builder XML files and use an external tool to generate them (for example, to parameterize Automation Services jobs), but the mechanism to do that is outside the scope of this book.

Running Automation Services jobs

There are several different ways to run Automation Services jobs:

- By selecting **Execute Locally** or **Execute on Server** from the job builder's **Tools** menu—these methods are normally used for testing only.
- By setting up a schedule on the Spotfire server (a detailed tutorial follows in the *Spotfire administration console* section).
- By calling the Automation Services REST API (new in Spotfire 7.13): `https://docs.tibco.com/pub/spotfire_server/7.14.0/doc/api/TIB_sfire_server_REST_API_Reference/`.
- By running the `Spotfire.Dxp.Automation.ClientJobSender.exe` command-line tool. This tool is available by downloading the Automation Services product from `https://edelivery.tibco.com`. The syntax to run a job is as follows:

```
"Spotfire.Dxp.Automation.ClientJobSender.exe" <Spotfire Server>
<Path to job XML file>
```

Here is an example:

```
Spotfire.Dxp.Automation.ClientJobSender.exe
http://spotfireserver C:\myJobs\job.xml
```

The Spotfire administration console

It is beyond the scope of this book to provide a full reference guide to the Spotfire administration console, but it will be covered briefly here.

> More details (particularly on scheduling and routing) can also be found in `Chapter 12`, *Scaling the Infrastructure; Keeping Data up to Date.*

The administration console is the default view that a Spotfire administrator receives when they log in to the Spotfire server using a web browser:

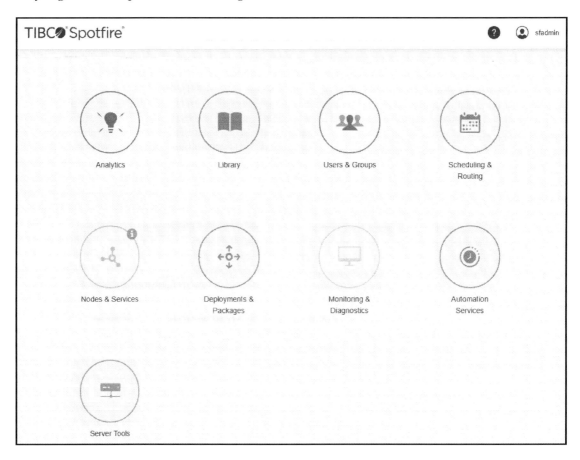

Most users will not see this initial screen—they will be shown the **Analytics** view by default, since they are not administrators. Notice that there is currently a notification on my system attached to **Nodes & Services**.

Let's explore each of the options in turn.

Analytics

As stated, this is the default view that non-administrator users will be presented with. It is usually configured to start with a blank analysis file into which data can be loaded (as of Spotfire 10). This requires that the user has the Business Author license. To view the Spotfire library from this view, you can either add a new file from the library or select **View library** from the **File** menu.

Library

From the **Library** browser, users can find a preexisting analysis file or data file, data connection, and so on, and open it.

Users and groups

A simple interface for managing users and groups, its functionality is a subset of the functionality that's available via the **Tools | Administration Manager** in the Spotfire Analyst client. I suspect that in the fullness of time, the tool built into the Analyst client will be entirely superseded by the web-based administration tool, but that is not currently the case. I won't cover the functionality that's available here as it would be covering the same ground that has preceded this. However, I would recommend using the web-based **Users & Groups** interface for adding new users or moving users between groups, or when a Spotfire administrator needs to check group members without needing to start the Analyst client.

Scheduling and routing

This is where the rules for smart routing are configured and where scheduled loading of Spotfire analyses is configured. This section of the administration console warrants a full explanation, so it will be covered in detail in `Chapter 12`, *Scaling the Infrastructure; Keeping Data up to Date*. However, I would like to explore a real-world example. The scenario is that I have some large files that take a long time to load. I also want the data to be kept up-to-date regularly. So, I have added some rules and schedules to load two files:

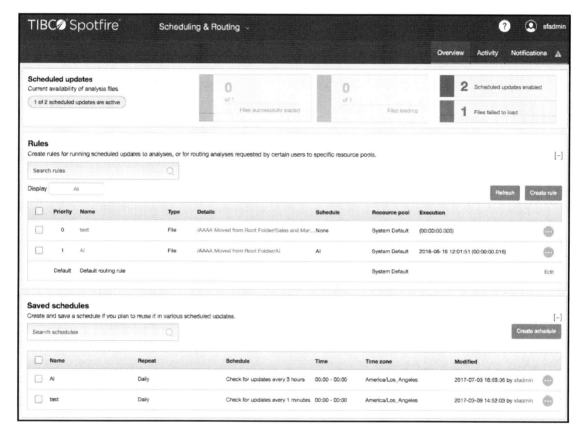

In this case, notice that one file failed to load; the other is inactive. The failure to load needs further investigation.

In fact, let me do it now and write it up as I follow through the troubleshooting—sometimes, I feel that working through a live example of a problem is so much more helpful than when everything goes smoothly:

1. Click on the name of the **test** rule:

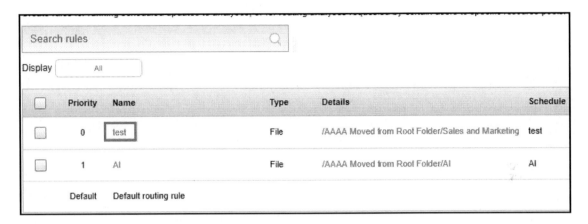

2. This takes me to the page where I can see the details of the file load/refresh activity. Here is the entry in question:

3. The server cannot load the analysis! I wonder why not?
4. Click on the **Overview** tab at the top of the page to go back to the overview of **Scheduling & Routing**:

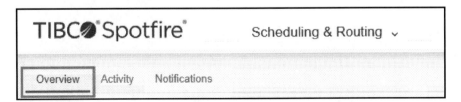

5. Let's try loading the file manually. Click the link to the file under **Details**:

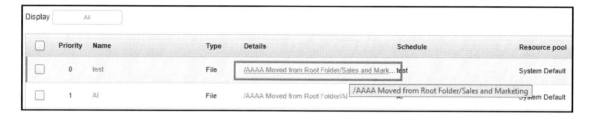

6. Interesting—it loads perfectly!

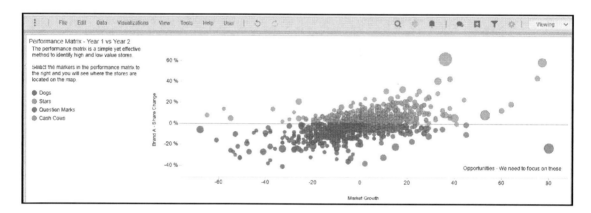

7. Close the analysis (by selecting **Close** from the **File** menu and then closing the resultant page) and return to the **Scheduling & Routing** page. Click **test** to go back to the details of the file load/refresh activity and find the entry that failed.

8. Click **View diagnostics & logs**:

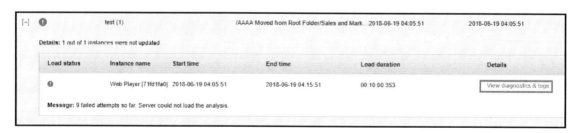

9. This takes me to **Monitoring & Diagnostics**, which will be covered in more detail shortly. Browse to the Web Player instance and click **View logs**:

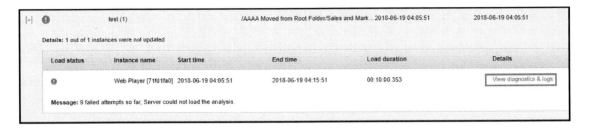

10. Now for the scary bit! A log file... If I browse through the log file, I can find an entry that reads like the following screenshot:

```
ERROR;2018-06-19T08:08:11,440-07:00;2018-06-19 15:08:11,440;ee0e02f3-c274-47ba-88be-d1bf629bf662;1908048316ROOk;WorkThread 36;scheduledupdates@SPOTFIRESYSTEM;Spotfire.Dxp.Web.
Spotfire.Dxp.Framework.Library.LibraryException: The file '067d2bb7-f347-4a34-84c6-f11ff5b6c5f5' could not be found or accessed.
   at Spotfire.Dxp.Web.LibraryAnalysisFileProvider.GetFileInfo(Guid id)
   at Spotfire.Dxp.Web.Library.ScheduledUpdates.Item.InternalPerformUpdate(UserSession userSession, UpdateFileInfoCache cacheUpdater, DateTime startTime)
   at Spotfire.Dxp.Web.Library.ScheduledUpdates.Item.PerformUpdate(UserSession userSession, UpdateFileInfoCache cacheUpdater)
```

11. It seems that the file could not be found or accessed. Now, I know that the file exists as I clicked on it and loaded it. So, for some reason, it must not be accessible. Aha! I know that I am logged in as the admin user while in the Administartion Console, but scheduled updates use a different user. Let's go to the library administration tool in Spotfire Analyst, logging in as an administrator (**Tools | Library Administration**):

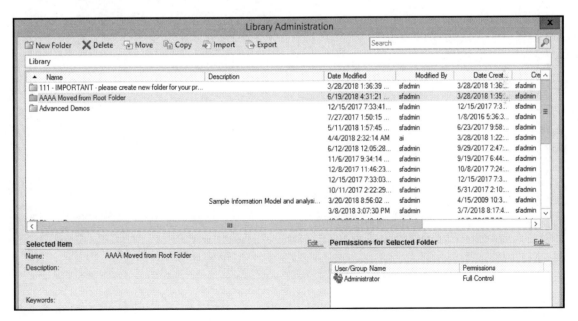

12. Indeed—that would appear to be the problem. The folder in question is only accessible to users in the Administrator group. So, let's fix this by editing the permissions.

13. Click **Edit...**.

14. Search for `sched*` to find the **Scheduled Updates Users** group and give the group **Browse + Access + Modify** permissions to the folder:

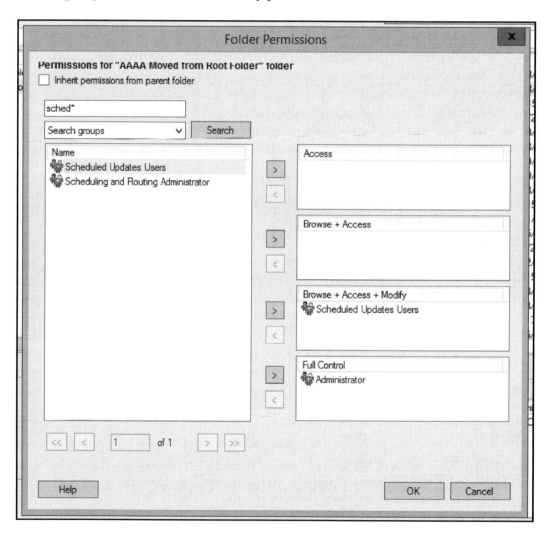

15. To confirm that this has fixed it, we can go back to the administration console and confirm that the file has been loaded properly.

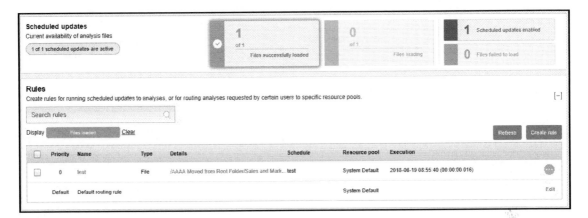

We can do this by clicking on the green box showing how many files have been loaded successfully.

Nodes and services

The **Nodes & Services** section of the administration console allows Spotfire administrators to see the entire infrastructure of nodes and services that are running on the Spotfire platform.

Once the node managers have been installed on all nodes, there is no need to visit every node server in turn to configure them or to set up new services:

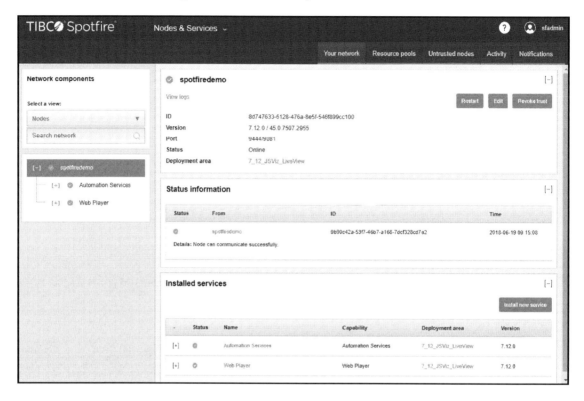

Here is a screenshot of a simple configuration—on the left are the details of the nodes that are installed and their running services. From here, you can install new services on nodes and see which deployment area is being used currently (more information on deployment areas follow). Clicking on the running instance of **Web Player** leads to the following view:

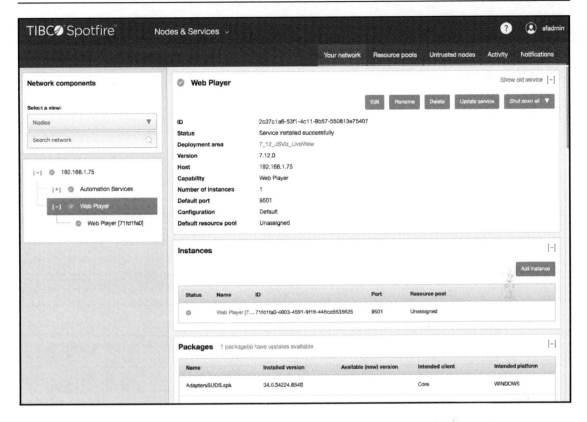

Of interest in this case is that there is a package that has an update available. The administrator should update the service in order to install the update. It is also possible to edit, rename, delete, or shut down the service instance.

The view for Automation Services instances is similar to that of the Web Player instances, so it is not shown here.

Deployments and packages

The feature of deployments and packages makes maintaining a large Spotfire infrastructure so much simpler than many other enterprise-class applications. The Spotfire server manages the deployments and packages centrally. Any updates to any of the Spotfire clients are pushed to the clients, without the need for a reinstall on an end user's PC, or for visiting the Web Player servers.

Here is a screenshot of the **Deployments & Packages** on a server I use for my own purposes. Note that I have a lot of deployment areas! I use this server heavily and depend on it for testing and developing Spotfire extensions. I often have to connect to the server with different versions of Spotfire:

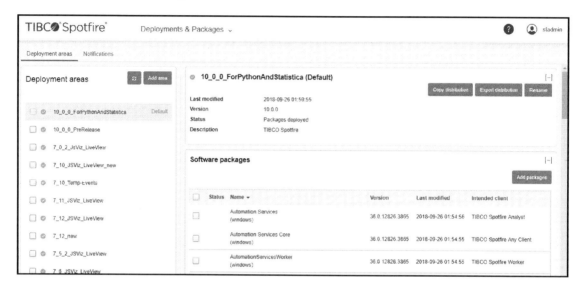

 Deployments: A deployment area is defined as a container for a number of Spotfire packages.
Packages: A package is defined as a package of components that make up a part of Spotfire's functionality. Packages are part of the standard Spotfire distribution, but can also be built as extensions for Spotfire.

It's pretty easy to work with deployment areas, so I'll just cover the main tasks in turn so that you can grasp what they are for and what they do:

- Add a deployment area—useful if you are performing an upgrade to Spotfire in your organization. This will create a blank deployment area. You could also use it to create a specialized deployment area that has a set of extensions that you only want to deploy to a selected group of users. It is possible to restrict a user group to a particular deployment (via users and groups in the administration console—though not from the administration manager in the analyst client).
- Delete a deployment area.
- Rename a deployment area.

- Make a deployment area the default—anyone that logs in to the server for the first time will be presented with this deployment area as their default.
- Export distribution—this is useful for copying deployments between servers. The distribution will be exported as a `.sdn` file and can be used with the **Add packages** functionality in a new deployment area.
- Copy distribution—I find this really useful—I often deploy extension packages to a particular distribution and then want to use the packages in a later version of Spotfire. I can simply copy the distribution (with all the extension packages) to a new deployment area and then add the new Spotfire deployment over the copy, so that the new deployment area contains the core Spotfire deployment and the extension packages. This avoids having to deploy the extension packages individually.
- Clear area—clears the packages in a deployment area.
- Add packages—this functionality is used to add a new Spotfire deployment (the standard Spotfire packages are provided in a `.sdn` package, supplied with the Spotfire server installation). Simply add the `.sdn` file to the deployment, validate, and save the deployment area. The same applies with extension packages. These are normally provided as `.spk` files and are added to the deployment.

> A note about adding packages and distributions to a deployment: once packages and/or distributions are added to a deployment, the deployment area must be **Saved**. No changes will be made until the save operation is complete. Spotfire also offers the option to validate the deployment area. This checks that all prerequisites and dependencies are satisfied. Saving the deployment area also validates before saving. When saving the deployment area, you will be asked to update its description.
> It's extremely important to name deployment areas sensibly. The deployment area is the first thing that users are required to choose when they log in to Spotfire, so the name should be something simple and easy to understand.

Monitoring and diagnostics

We have already seen how **Monitoring & Diagnostics** can be used to troubleshoot an issue with an aspect of the Spotfire infrastructure. A few more key areas will be highlighted here:

Download global Spotfire troubleshooting bundle—this is very helpful to TIBCO support—if you are having an issue with your server infrastructure, TIBCO support will often request a global troubleshooting bundle. Just click the link at the top of the page—Spotfire will attempt to collect all the information it can and bundle it into a single file that can be provided to TIBCO support.

The status of Web Player instances can be seen at the bottom of the page. Currently, the instance on this server is **AVAILABLE**. If resources are a problem, this will change to **STRAINED** and finally **EXHAUSTED** if the Web Player can no longer accept connections. At this point, it would be prudent to investigate which analyses or users are consuming all the resources or to consider adding new nodes and services to your Spotfire infrastructure.

The **Instances** view gives really detailed information on what has been loaded:

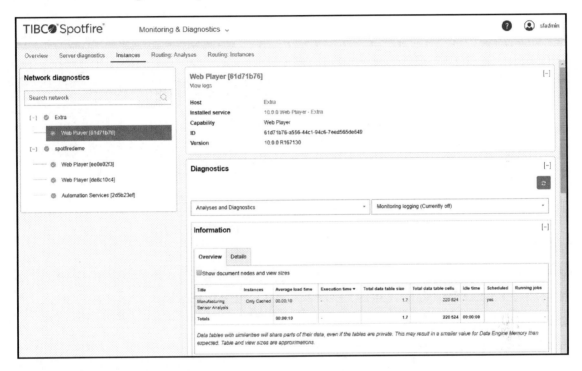

I have clicked on a **Web Player** instance. I can see things like the load time, execution time, data table size, and so on. Total document node count is interesting as it gives an idea of the complexity of the analysis. The **Details** tab gives information about which user is using which analysis and some further details that also indicate how much is being shared between users.

Automation Services

As we mentioned previously, it is now possible to schedule Spotfire Automation Services jobs from within the administration console:

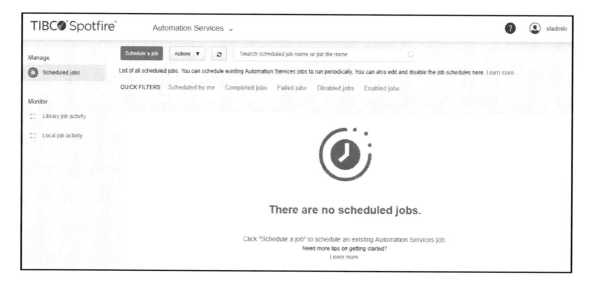

Right now, there are no scheduled jobs, so let's go ahead and create one:

1. Load Spotfire Analyst and create a new job by using the **Automation Services Job Builder**. A full tutorial for this is not provided, but here's a screenshot of a simple job that I have created. Its purpose is to load a file and send a sample email:

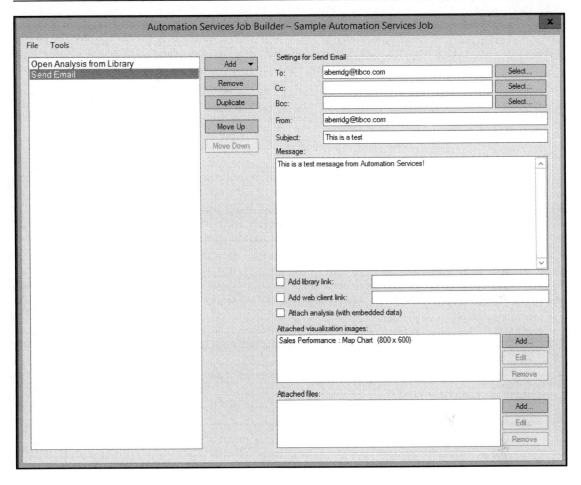

2. Test the job by running it on the server by clicking **Tools | Execute on Server**.

3. Now, save the job into the Spotfire library.

4. To schedule the job, click **Tools | Manage Job Schedule**.

5. This will open the Spotfire administration console in your web browser. The following view is presented:

6. Now, it is necessary to add a schedule. Click the **Add schedule** button and fill in the details:

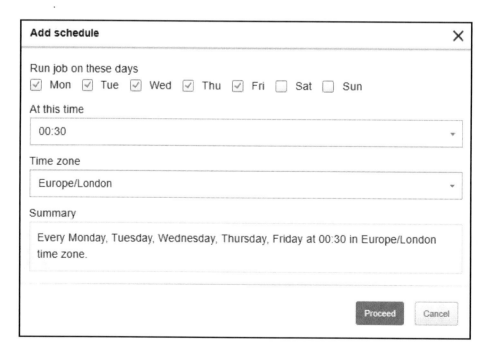

7. Click **Proceed** to save the schedule.

8. You can add further schedules as you wish. Save the job. You should then see something that looks a bit like this:

9. You can run the job right now by clicking its checkbox and choosing **Run** from the **Actions** menu.

10. Once the job has completed successfully, you should see the **Last status** column update showing **COMPLETED**.

11. You can monitor the job history by clicking **Library job activity** and then selecting the job in the list. Here is the history of the sample job:

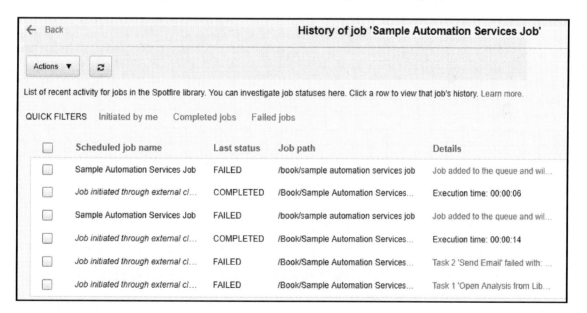

You'll notice that it failed when run through the scheduler. I'm not going to go through all the troubleshooting steps in detail, so I will cover them briefly here. As in the previous example in this chapter, I think it's sometimes useful to cover some real-world troubleshooting steps when things don't work out properly!

12. I clicked the link in the **Details** column for a failed job. This showed the properties of the job:

13. I was then able to click on the link for the **Job ID**. This took me to the log files for the Automation Services instance.

14. By scrolling through the log, I was able to locate the error. This error was that the job file didn't seem to exist.

15. By reading through the log file some more, I noticed that the task was running as a special user: `automationservices@SPOTFIRESYSTEM`. Ah! I should have realized... Never mind—there is an easy fix.

16. Visit the Spotfire library administration dialog in Spotfire Analyst and allow the **Automation Services Users** group account to **Browse + Access** the folder that contains the job file:

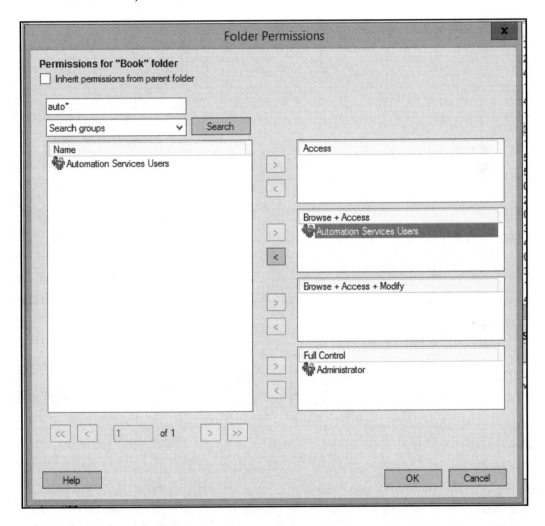

17. It was also necessary to apply the same permissions to the folder that contains the analysis file itself.

18. Did I get the email? Yes! Here it is:

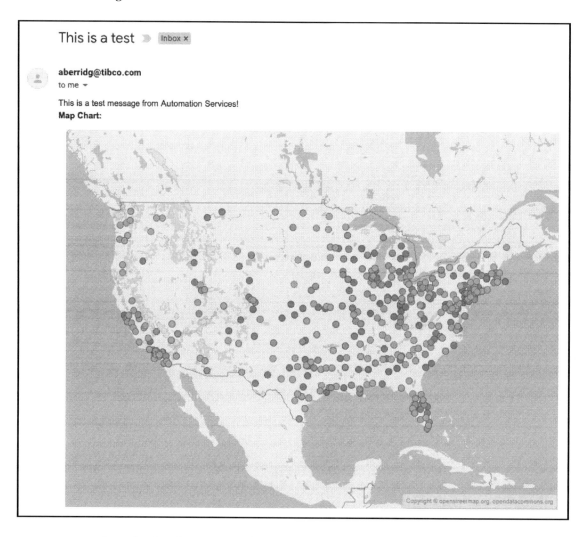

In order for Automation Services to be able to send an email successfully, the Automation Services instance must be set up correctly by an administrator. Instructions on how to do this are available via the online documentation. I was able to find the instructions by searching for `Spotfire Automation Services SMTP`. There are also some useful instructions at this URL:

`https://support.tibco.com/s/article/Automation-Services-How-to-s et-SMTP-and-Send-Email-details.`

Summary

This chapter has covered the overall Spotfire architecture and infrastructure. Although primarily targeted to Spotfire administrators, many interesting and useful topics were covered that benefit Spotfire end users too.

We looked at the main Spotfire components and how these work in harmony to provide unparalleled scalability and availability; we also covered some simple administration topics and concepts. In addition, a real-world example of troubleshooting an issue with **Scheduling & Routing** was shown.

Automation Services were covered in some detail, along with a practical example of scheduling a job on the server. Again, a real-world example of troubleshooting an issue was covered.

The online documentation is always a good reference resource, so I recommend that you visit `https://docs.tibco.com/` if you want to know more about anything that was covered in this chapter.

In the next few chapters, we are going to return to the world of data analysis and visualization!

Source Data is Never Enough 7

Any analysis, no matter how clever or imaginative, is only as good as the underlying data. The previous chapters have touched on the underlying data for visualization. This chapter will discuss different methods for preparing data for visualization. We will demonstrate how to use Spotfire's data-wrangling and calculation capabilities as one method.

There are many different tools and methods available for preparing and storing data for visualization. Spotfire has built-in data wrangling—this is a good choice for ad hoc data analysis, but when should you use it over any other method?

When creating production-or enterprise-grade analyses in Spotfire, it's usually good practice to do as much heavy lifting as possible in the source systems by using data virtualization or putting the data into some kind of warehouse (in this, I include big data systems and the like).

However, as a creative Analyst and data explorer, you will often have a need to modify and transform data after it arrives in Spotfire, and Spotfire is a great tool for doing so. Additionally, you may not have IT resources available in your organization, so you may be entirely reliant on Spotfire for data transformation. That's fine, because Spotfire is excellent at manipulating data and, as such, gives you lots of flexibility to reach the analytic insights you seek. Note that any involved transformations such as unpivot or pivot can only be performed using Spotfire's Analyst client, so don't get frustrated if you can't complete the examples in this chapter if you are using Spotfire's web clients!

In this chapter, we will cover the following topics:

- Creating metrics using calculated columns
- The Spotfire data canvas
- Key data concept-dimensional hierarchies
- Categorizing continuous numerical data using binning functions
- Slicing and dicing data using hierarchy nodes
- Key data concept-tall tables versus wide tables
- Transforming data through pivots and unpivots

Technical requirements

In order to follow along with the examples in this chapter, please download the airline delay data from here:

```
https://www.transtats.bts.gov/Tables.asp?DB_ID=120DB_Name=Airline%20On-
Time%20Performance%20Data.
```

Alternatively, use the following shortened link:

```
http://bit.ly/2uuWh3l.
```

This chapter uses the Reporting Carrier On-Time Performance data (1987-present) for January 2018.

Creating metrics using calculated columns

Probably the most fundamental and useful data manipulation tool provided by Spotfire is the ability to create calculated columns in data tables. A calculated column is created by writing an expression that references other columns in the table, document property values, and values that you supply, or **hard code**. The expression can be a simple piece of arithmetic, such as dividing one column by another to get a proportion, or a more complex piece of conditional logic. Once created, a calculated column can be used exactly like any other column.

Important note: You can use expressions for calculations in calculated columns, or you can use them within visualizations (for example, for axis expressions). Calculated column expressions **DO NOT recalculate** based on filtering. However, expressions that are used in a visualization **DO recalculate** based on filtering. So, if you need calculations to reflect the state of filtered data, make sure that you use them directly in visualizations, not as calculated columns in the data table.

Basic metric

In this example, we will create a very simple metric to show the amount of time that's made up in the air. I fly a lot with my job, so it's interesting to see how much time is made up in the air. If a flight leaves late, does it still arrive on time, or even early? Or does it lose time in the air and arrive even later? Let's see:

1. First of all, import the data into Spotfire. It's a CSV file, with straightforward data types, so accept the default import settings.
2. Click **Data** | **Add calculated column...**:

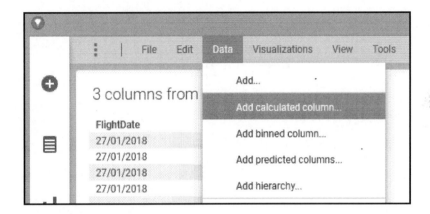

3. The **Add calculated column** window will be shown. This window is the expression editor—it's used for calculated column expressions and also for expressions in visualizations.

   If you are using a Spotfire Analyst client, the expression editor is more fully featured than the one available in the web clients. In the Analyst client, you can add columns to the expression editor by double-clicking their names or just by typing. Spotfire will auto-complete column names, functions, and properties. You can only type or paste if you are using the web clients. This example shows the Analyst client editor.

4. Use the following expression:
   ```
   Integer([DepDelay] - [ArrDelay])
   ```

5. Name the column `TimeMadeUp`:

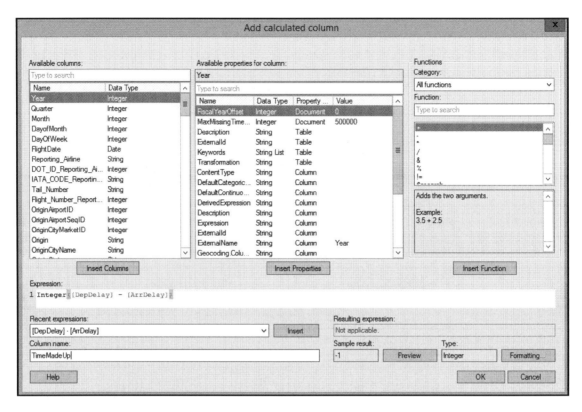

6. Click **OK** on the dialog.
7. Create a table plot by choosing it from the visualization pullout from the left-hand side of the Spotfire window. Select the following few columns (from the visualization properties) in order to check that the results are as expected:

5 columns from On_Time_Reporting_Carrier_On_time_Performance

Reporting_Airline	FlightDate	DepDelay	ArrDelay	TimeMadeUp
UA	27-01-2018	-13.00	-12.00	-1
UA	27-01-2018	-4.00	-18.00	14
UA	27-01-2018	-2.00	1.00	-3
UA	27-01-2018	-9.00	-8.00	-1
UA	27-01-2018	-14.00	-24.00	10
UA	27-01-2018	-7.00	-19.00	12
UA	27-01-2018	27.00	19.00	8
UA	27-01-2018	8.00	-23.00	31
UA	27-01-2018	-5.00	-22.00	17
UA	27-01-2018	-7.00	-18.00	11
UA	27-01-2018	-6.00	-14.00	8
UA	27-01-2018	-9.00	-13.00	4
UA	27-01-2018	-8.00	-15.00	7
UA	27-01-2018	1.00	-2.00	3
UA	27-01-2018	-1.00	-25.00	24
UA	27-01-2018	-3.00	-28.00	25
UA	27-01-2018	-7.00	-19.00	12
UA	27-01-2018	-14.00	-21.00	7
UA	27-01-2018	-7.00	-11.00	4
UA	27-01-2018	-4.00	-28.00	24
UA	27-01-2018	-3.00	-18.00	15
UA	27-01-2018	-10.00	-43.00	33
UA	27-01-2018	-18.00	-23.00	5
UA	27-01-2018	-1.00	-14.00	13
UA	27-01-2018	-5.00	-29.00	24
UA	27-01-2018	-12.00	-10.00	-2
UA	27-01-2018	-9.00	-34.00	25

That looks good! You can see that `TimeMadeUp` is positive if the arrival delay was less than the departure delay. Negative values for `DepDelay/ArrDelay` indicate that the flight left early. Right now, I'm not concerned whether the flight was delayed or not— only if any time was made up while the plane was in the air.

8. To access the column expression, I'd like to remind you of the data canvas. The data canvas is accessible at any time. Click on the data canvas icon—it's the bottom button on the left-hand panel of the Spotfire client. Here is how your data canvas should look:

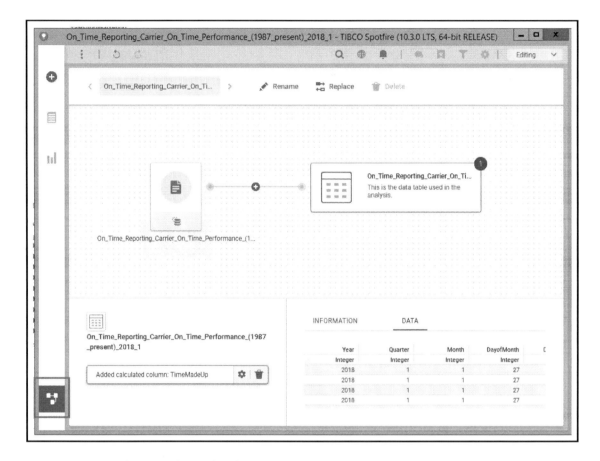

 TIP

When you have the data canvas open, you can't immediately create new visualizations or view the data panel. You'll need to dismiss the data panel by clicking the button again. The data canvas is available in the web clients and Analyst clients.

9. To access the column expression, make sure that the main data table is selected by clicking on it, and then click the cog icon:

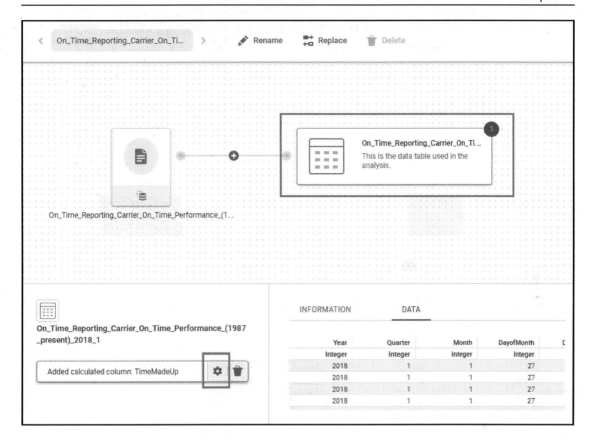

Note that you can't edit the calculated column in Spotfire's web clients. If you need to change the calculated column, you'll need to delete it via the data panel.

Now that we have created the calculated column, let's dissect the expression. Let's look at the expression again:

```
Integer([DepDelay] - [ArrDelay])
```

Let's try to understand this expression:

- Spotfire calculated column expressions work across the whole data table; thus, Spotfire will apply the expression to every row of the table.
- Spotfire expressions are not like Excel formulas! You do not reference individual cells in the data table—in fact, you can't. There are some things you can do to calculate various values that are grouped by category and the like, which will be covered later in this chapter.

- The calculation for the number of minutes made up during the flight is as simple as the arrival delay, subtracted from the departure delay.
- I surrounded the calculation with the `Integer()` function as most math functions (if not all) in Spotfire return real values (with decimal places), rather than integer values. This avoids having to adjust the formatting for the column.

Now that we have created a simple calculated column, let's move on to creating a dynamic metric in the next section.

Dynamic metric

It's also possible to create dynamic metrics in Spotfire—that is, calculated columns that use document properties as part of their expression. By employing such a method, you can give end users the ability to change a calculated column by interacting with property controls in a text area. This, of course, also applies to expressions that are used in visualizations.

Continuing with the airline delay example, I will now show you how to create a dynamic column that determines which columns are used to sum up the different types of delay in order to view the total delay time to the airline:

 You will only be able to do this in a Spotfire Analyst client, since you cannot create or edit text areas in the web clients.

1. Recall that in `Chapter 3`, *Impactful Dashboards!*, we created a text area with a drop-down property control in order to dynamically configure a visualization. Refer to that chapter if you can't remember how to create a text area.
2. This time, we are going to create a **List box (multiple select)** control, so choose that option from the action control dropdown:

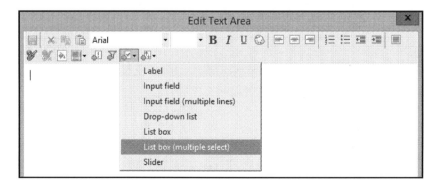

Important: In this example, we are creating a multiple select list box control. This is the only way to create a document property that can contain multiple values. You cannot create a multi-value document property from the **Document Properties** dialog in Spotfire.

3. Create a new document property of type string and call it delayMetrics.

4. Now, set up the columns to be used for the property control. You can choose the individual columns or use an expression to select them. When you've finished, the dialog should look something like this:

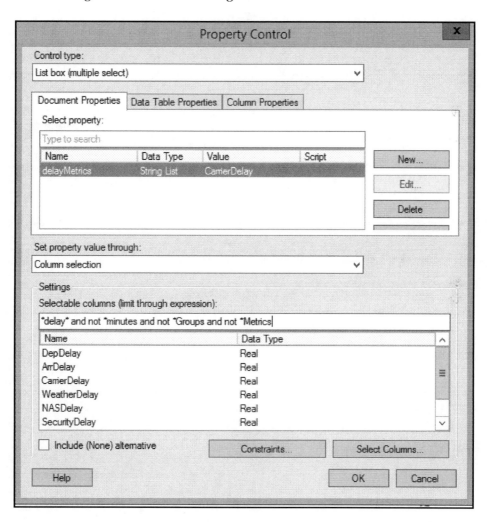

5. Now, let's create a calculated column that uses this expression. Once the property control has been added, select a few of the values in it. You'll see why I asked you to do this shortly.

6. Add a calculated column and use this expression:

> **$map("[${delayMetrics}]", "+")**

7. Now, look at the resulting expression part of the dialog. It should give you an output similar to the following:

> `[CarrierDelay]+[DepDelay]+[ArrDelay]`

What's happening is that Spotfire is expanding the expression in the editor into the final expression that will be used in the calculated column. By selecting multiple values in the control, you can check that the final expression is correct and is what you expect.

In this case, we are just adding up the values for the selected delay columns. The expression uses the $map function—this maps a list-valued property to a single string. In our case, it concatenates the individual values of the property into a string, with the values separated by the + operator.

> You can use the expression editor to create a $map expression automatically just by clicking on the property in the list of properties in the dialog. However, that wouldn't have worked in our case as it would have created an expression like this: $map("sum([${delayMetrics}])", ",").
> Unfortunately, the expression then maps to this: sum([CarrierDelay]),sum([DepDelay]),sum([ArrDelay]).
> This is not valid as a calculated column expression. It would be valid as a visualization axis expression and would have created three different axes, and not summed all the values like we wanted in the example.

8. Name the calculated column DelayMetrics and click **OK** on the dialog.

9. Now, create a visualization that shows the results of the calculated column. We will create a cross table:

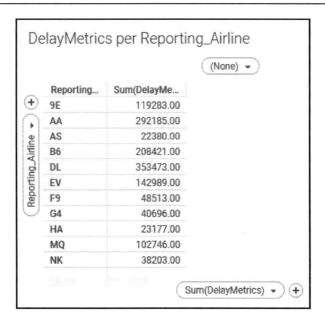

10. Experiment by selecting some different values in the property control and see how the values of the displayed metric change.

We have built a calculated column that is recalculated based on a user's selection. You can use all sorts of clever tricks with this mechanism to provide dynamically calculated columns. I would tend to steer you toward using this sort of technique in visualization expressions rather than calculated columns where you can.

 Calculated columns do not respond to filtering changes. Visualization expressions do, however. Be careful!

Categorizing continuous numerical data using binning functions

You can also create custom columns in Spotfire through binning. Chapter 1, *Welcome to Spotfire*, introduced the concept of binning numerical values. You can do the same for calculated columns. Create binned columns from the **Data** menu—just choose **Add binned column**. A binned column is just a way to turn a continuous set of values—usually numeric, but not always—into a set of discrete (categorical) values or bins.

Recall that the age column from the Titanic data was binned in `Chapter 1`, *Welcome to Spotfire*. Adding a binned column gives you access to a much richer way of binning a column rather than right-clicking on an axis selector and choosing **Auto-bin Column**. However, please remember that the calculated column will not respond to filtering (this is so important that I feel the need to repeat it lots!).

The **Add binned column** dialog will create a new calculated column. You could create such a column by using the dialog and then copying the expression to a visualization. Here is an example of the dialog:

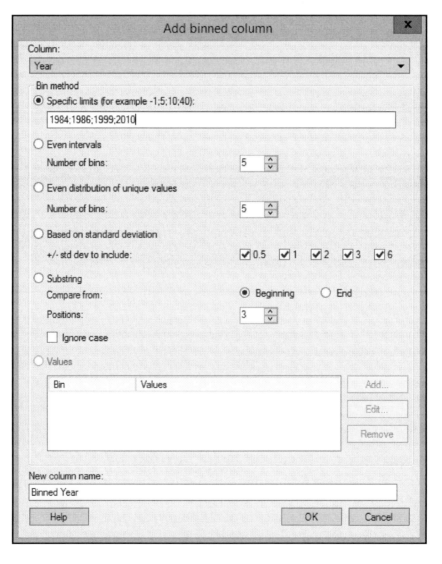

The dialog has the following methods for creating a binned column:

- **Specific limits**: It creates an expression like this:

```
BinBySpecificLimits([column name], value 1, value 2, ..., value
n)
```

This method allows you to define each bin boundary explicitly; any values below or above your minimum and maximum values are placed into bins automatically as well.

- **Even intervals**: This creates a number of bins with even intervals with this kind of expression:

```
BinByEvenIntervals([column name], number of bins)
```

This method allows you to focus on the number of bins and not worry about the distribution of values.

- **Even distribution of unique values**:

```
BinByEvenDistribution([column name], number of bins)
```

This method allows you to focus on the distribution of values, still dividing the values into bins, but telling Spotfire to create the bin boundaries to equalize the distribution.

- **Based on standard deviation**:

```
BinByStdDev([column name], scaling factor 1   SD, scaling
factor 2   SD, ..., scaling factor n   SD)
```

This method is similar to a specific limits method, except you refer to a scaled list of standard deviation values.

- **Substring**:

```
BinBySubstring([column name], number of characters from
beginning or end of string)
```

This method allows you to categorize string values into bins based on a defined number of characters from the beginning (positive number) or end (negative number) of a string.

- **Values**:

```
case  when [column name] in ("value1", "value2") then "Bin1"
else [column name] end
```

This method uses a case statement to bundle multiple individual (categorical only) values into single values. Note how the expression isn't actually a binning operation! Also, notice how the expression does a straight copy of any values not explicitly coded in the case statement.

 Binning can affect the shape of the data that is displayed. It can have a significant statistical effect on what you see. It's important to be aware of this and to use a binning strategy that makes sense. I don't recommend any binning strategy over another—you just have to be careful about which you choose and how many bins you choose. Use binning to display overall trends and patterns in the data, but do not use it if you need to show absolute values or spot outliers easily.

Slicing and dicing data using hierarchy nodes

As we mentioned previously, Spotfire expressions do not work in the same way as Excel formulas. Expressions must work over the whole of the data that's currently in scope (be it the whole data table or a grouping within a visualization).

Spotfire provides a set of OVER functions to allow you to aggregate data over the **nodes** of a hierarchy in a data table. At its simplest level, the OVER function is a means to define at what granularity you wish to aggregate values.

The nodes of a hierarchy are the unique values in each level of the hierarchy. Perhaps the easiest type of hierarchy to think of is a date. The levels of the date hierarchy could be year/month/day. The nodes at each of the levels are the unique values at each level in that hierarchy. So, given a date column, you could imagine the nodes as the individual boxes that are shown in this cross table (DayOfMonth has been filtered to the first few days of the month in order to illustrate this point more clearly):

Year	Month	DayOfMonth
2007	Jan	1
		2
		3
		4
		5
		6
	Feb	1
		2
		3
		4
		5
		6
	Mar	1
		2
		3
		4
		5
		6
	Apr	1
		2
		3
		4
		5
		6

Date (Day of Month)

Now, let's move back to the airline delay example. To illustrate the simplest type of OVER expression, you could calculate the average delay in minutes for every airline as a calculated column using the following expression:

```
Avg([ArrDelayMinutes]) OVER [Reporting_Airline]
```

As each airline has more than one row in the data, you would end up with the following result:

2 columns from On_Time	
Reporting_Air	**AvgDelay by Airline**
9E	16.45
9E	16.45
9E	16.45
B6	23.75
B6	23.75
B6	23.75
B6	23.75
B6	23.75

See how Spotfire has grouped the data per airline?

I wouldn't really recommend doing this kind of aggregation within the data table. It would be far better to use it within a visualization expression on an axis.

There are many other OVER methods for use in custom (visualization) expressions and calculated columns. The in-line help in the Spotfire client provides details and examples for each. The **Functions** panel in the custom expression dialog also provides basic descriptions and syntax. However, I sometimes find the help confusing, so I will debunk some of the language that's used in the help and provide practical examples as to how to use some of the more common OVER methods.

LastPeriods

LastPeriods applies an aggregation over the last values of the hierarchy. It is commonly used to calculate moving averages:

```
Agg(column) OVER LastPeriods(n, hierarchy)
```

The Spotfire help describes the `LastPeriods` method as applying an aggregation over the current node and `n-1` previous nodes in the hierarchy. To explain this in simple language, it calculates the aggregation over the previous values in the hierarchy for the column (or axis) specified. It can be used, for example, to calculate a 7-day moving average as a visualization axis custom expression:

```
Avg([ArrDelayMinutes]) OVER (LastPeriods(7,[Axis.X]))
```

As with any such expression, I recommend testing it, so this example will show how to do this.

Here's how I showed the expression on the y-axis of a bar chart and then used another bar chart to verify that the expression is correct. First of all, here is the complete bar chart, limited to a single airline:

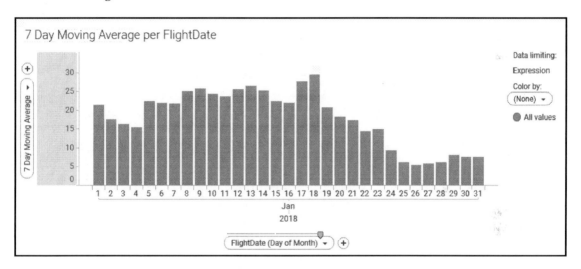

Now, I have selected the first seven bars and created a details visualization showing the average arrival delay in minutes, turning on labels so that we can see what's going on!

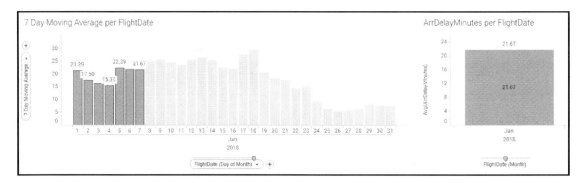

That looks good! Notice how the last bar has the same value as the average of all the bars. That's what we should expect from a moving average. A moving average smooths out the influence of single values on a particular day—for example, you may be interested in looking at the average trend over time. If I add the average arrival delay per day, the visualization looks like this:

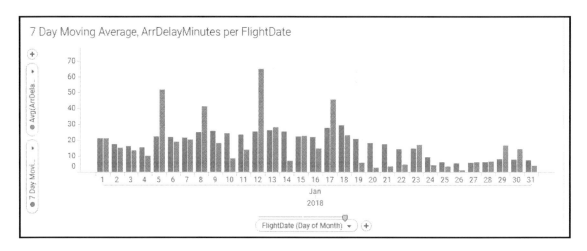

Notice how the average per day is much more "peaky" than the moving average. It makes it much harder to spot the overall trend over the month.

We could argue that calculating the moving average over the first few days is incorrect and that the value should only be shown if 7 days' worth of values have been accumulated. This can be achieved if you replace the expression with the following:

```
Avg([ArrDelayMinutes]) THEN If(Count() OVER
(LastPeriods(7,[Axis.X]))=7,[Value],null)
```

Everything after the THEN clause is a **post-aggregation expression**. A post-aggregation expression uses the value returned by the previous expression. See where [Value] is specified? That's where the value returned by the first expression is used in the post-aggregation expression.

Finally, Spotfire has built-in advanced aggregations on the visualization axis selectors. I could have chosen a moving average for the ArrDelayMinutes column on the y-axis of the bar chart, like this:

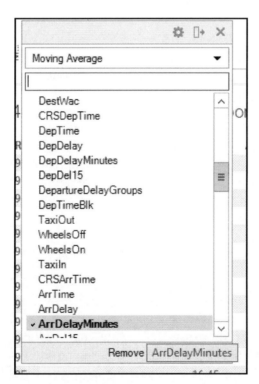

The resulting expression that was auto-generated by Spotfire was as follows:

```
Sum([ArrDelayMinutes])
THEN Avg([Value]) OVER (LastPeriods(10,[Axis.X]))
THEN If(Count() OVER (LastPeriods(10,[Axis.X]))=10,[Value],null)
```

However, this did not produce the results I was expecting. We need to replace the Sum with an Avg.

The advantage of using the advanced aggregation option is that it does all the hard work of constructing the full expression by using OVER and THEN for us. Using the advanced aggregations and then inspecting the generated expressions is also a good way to learn how the aggregations work.

PreviousPeriod

PreviousPeriod calculates the value of an aggregation over the previous period in a hierarchy. It is commonly used to calculate the change from one period to another:

```
Agg(column) OVER PreviousPeriod(hierarchy)
```

The PreviousPeriod method allows you to populate the rows for one node/period of the hierarchy with an aggregation on the previous node/period. In itself, this displacement is not particularly interesting, but if we use it in a calculation, we can determine changes in value from one period to another. For example, say we'd like to see the difference between the average arrival delay for one week and the average arrival delay for the previous week. We would use the following expression:

```
Avg([ArrDelayMinutes])
THEN [Value] – First([Value]) OVER (PreviousPeriod([Axis.X]))
```

The first part of the expression calculates the average delay in minutes. The second part subtracts the value of the previous period from the current value. The First function just picks the first value that's returned by the Avg function. All OVER functions must operate on an aggregation. The result of this expression is shown in the following graph. Note that, like I did previously, I have created a simple "test" visualization in order to verify that the calculation by the OVER expression is correct:

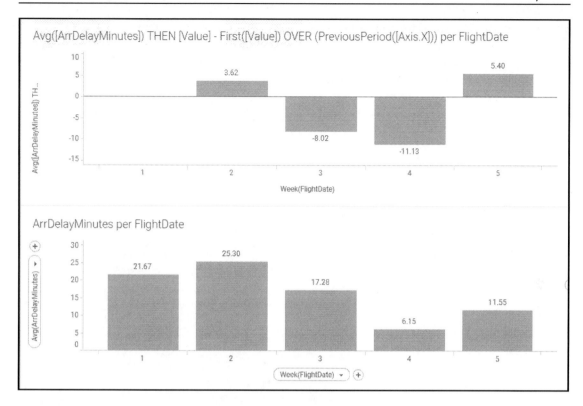

If you subtract the previous value from the current value in the bottom bar chart, you'll see that the corresponding bar in the top bar chart is correct.

Notice how I am frequently using Spotfire to check its own results. I recommend that you do this too—it can save a lot of heartache later on!

ParallelPeriod

ParallelPeriod compares values across parallel periods in a hierarchy:

```
Agg(column) OVER ParallelPeriod(hierarchy)
```

What if we want to calculate a month-on-month analysis for this year's figures against last year's? For example, how does June this year compare with June last year? That's where the `ParallelPeriod` method comes in. It allows us to get a value in a previous period at the same level of the hierarchy. Note that the `ParallelPeriod` method only goes up one level in the hierarchy. If you want to navigate more than one level, you can use the `NavigatePeriod` method that's shown in the next section.

For this example, I have taken some more airline delay data covering 3 years and applied the following expression to the y-axis:

```
Avg([ArrDelay]) THEN [Value] - First([Value]) OVER
(ParallelPeriod([Axis.X]))
```

Here is the resultant visualization:

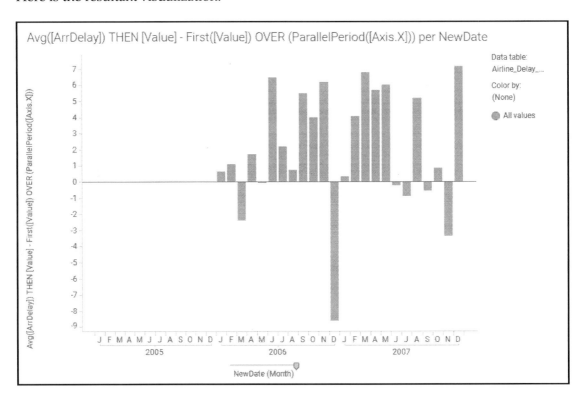

The visualization shows each month compared with the same month in the previous year.

You're probably wondering what exactly the difference is between `PreviousPeriod` and `ParallelPeriod`. `PreviousPeriod` is simply the previous period in the same node, whereas `ParallelPeriod` traverses the hierarchy to a parallel node. This is best explained the following diagram:

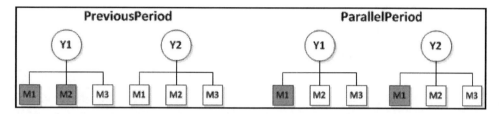

Of course, the `ParallelPeriod` doesn't just need to apply to dates. You can use it to navigate other types of hierarchies, too. For example, you could apply it to product categories and subcategories or to sales regions and countries.

NavigatePeriod

`NavigatePeriod` is a more advanced specialization of navigating hierarchies—you can specify the period, how far in the hierarchy you want to navigate, and the period level for the aggregation:

```
Agg(column) OVER NavigatePeriod(hierarchy, node/period name, period
displacement, period level for aggregation)
```

The `NavigatePeriod` method is a fully flexible hierarchy navigation method. It allows you to specify the period level or node you want to use; how much, if any, you want to move forward or backward; and the level at which you want to aggregate, zero being the top level, incrementing by one for each level into the hierarchy. In fact, the `ParallelPeriod` example that we used previously can be replicated with `NavigatePeriod` like this:

```
Avg([ArrDelay]) THEN [Value] - First([Value]) OVER
(NavigatePeriod([Axis.X],"Year",-1, 1))
```

`Year` specifies the period, -1 calls for a displacement by one period back, and 1 specifies the month as the aggregation period since Month is the first level in the hierarchy.

You could also replace the `PreviousPeriod` example with `NavigatePeriod` like this:

```
Avg([ArrDelayMinutes]) THEN [Value] - First([Value]) OVER
(NavigatePeriod([Axis.X],"Week",-1))
```

AllPrevious and AllNext

These methods apply the aggregation over all the previous or next values in the column or hierarchy:

```
Agg(column) OVER AllPrevious(hierarchy)
```

`AllPrevious` is commonly used to calculate a cumulative sum. Previous means "sorted by the defined sort order of the column/hierarchy." `AllNext` is the inverse of this—that is, sorted in the reverse order.

The `AllPrevious` method is typically used to calculate a cumulative sum. In fact, you can choose a cumulative sum as an aggregation on a visualization axis. Spotfire will set the expression to one that uses `AllPrevious`.

Previous and next

These methods apply the aggregation over the previous or next values in the column or hierarchy. They are commonly used for determining the differences between the current value and a previous or next value:

```
Agg(column) OVER Previous(hierarchy)
```

For example, this expression calculates the difference between the current value and the previous value on a bar chart:

```
Avg([ArrDelayMinutes]) THEN [Value] – Avg([Value]) OVER
(Previous([Axis.X]))
```

Thus, here is the bar chart that shows the day per day difference for the average arrival delay in minutes for a single airline over the course of a month:

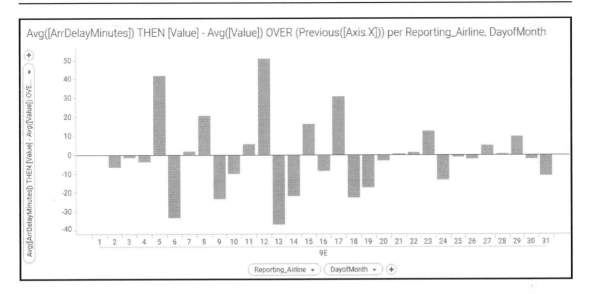

With these methods, you can optionally specify how many values you would like to navigate backwards or forwards:

```
Avg([ArrDelayMinutes]) THEN [Value] - Avg([Value]) OVER
(Previous([Axis.X],2))
```

In this case, the expression will use the value of 2 days ago to calculate the difference. Now, this could get confusing to an end user of your analysis, so make sure that you make it clear what's going on! I would recommend using a meaningful visualization title or description, or some text in a text area.

Intersect

This method finds the intersection of two or more columns or hierarchies:

```
Agg(column) OVER Intersect(hierarchy)
```

Consider a scenario where we need to calculate the worst delay for each airline on each day (given 1 month's worth of data). You might think that multiple OVER functions would work—something like the following:

```
Max([ArrDelayMinutes]) OVER [Reporting_Airline] OVER [DayofMonth]
```

However, this is wrong! Spotfire cannot combine OVER functions like this—even a nested aggregation wouldn't be correct either, as we can't do a THEN following an OVER expression.

What we need to do is find the intersection between the values of the columns or hierarchies. This has the effect of grouping the data based on two of the columns. If you are familiar with SQL syntax, you can think of the `Intersect` method as being roughly equivalent to the `GROUP BY` clause in `SQL` when grouping by multiple columns.

The `Intersect` method on its own is probably most useful when used in a calculated column. In fact, Spotfire is using the `Intersect` method internally, for example, when it draws a bar chart with a **Color by** axis. It needs to group the aggregation shown on the y-axis by two categories—the x-axis and the **Color by** axis.

So, the calculated column expression to calculate the worst delay for each airline on each day is as follows:

```
Max([ArrDelayMinutes]) OVER (Intersect([Reporting_Airline],[DayofMonth]))
AS [Worst delay for each day]
```

Note the `AS` clause. This just names the column.

I have tested this by showing bar charts of `Min([Worst delay for each day])` and `Max([ArrDelayMinutes])` for one airline:

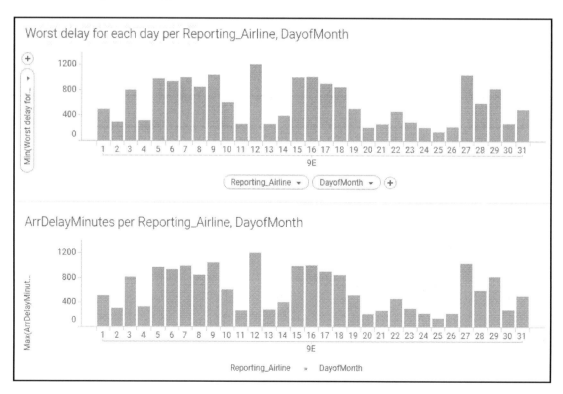

The bar charts are functionally equivalent—remember what I said about Spotfire using the `Intersect` method internally? In the bottom bar chart, it is performing the intersection between `Reporting_Airline` and `DayOfMonth` and then applying the `Max` aggregation over the intersection for the y-axis values.

The top bar chart needs an aggregation method in order to show a single value for each grouping of values in the data table. I have chosen `Min`, but `Max`, `First`, `Last`, or `Avg` would have all yielded the same result.

If you're still not sure what's going on here, study this cross table:

ArrDelayMinutes per Reporting_Airline and DayofMonth

Reporting...	1	2	3	4	5	6	7	8
9E	496.00	300.00	803.00	318.00	969.00	934.00	993.00	841.00
AA	1159.00	1778.00	1648.00	383.00	927.00	971.00	861.00	974.00
AS	178.00	397.00	452.00	234.00	170.00	210.00	150.00	118.00
B6	292.00	482.00	379.00	322.00	603.00	1473.00	887.00	383.00
DL	281.00	923.00	911.00	820.00	1179.00	796.00	482.00	701.00
EV	780.00	710.00	270.00	805.00	1142.00	560.00	888.00	1454.00
F9	465.00	872.00	431.00	205.00	327.00	230.00	1253.00	556.00
G4	616.00	408.00	360.00	243.00	489.00	278.00	661.00	380.00
HA	136.00	154.00	1717.00	462.00	1316.00	107.00	97.00	78.00
MQ	565.00	684.00	524.00	356.00	460.00	543.00	611.00	669.00

Max(ArrDelayMinutes)

Again, Spotfire is using the `Intersect` method internally. Each intersection is represented by a cell in the cross table. An intersection is a single, combined grouping for the columns shown on the vertical and horizontal axes. Spotfire will apply the `Max` aggregation to all the values of `ArrDelayMinutes` within that grouping.

If you add the `Parent` method to the intersection, Spotfire will use the next level up in the hierarchy to perform the intersection.

Finally, the combination of `Intersect` and the other methods can be extremely powerful.

Over methods in calculated columns versus axis expressions

The syntax for the `OVER` methods is different depending on whether you are working with calculated columns or axis expressions. In axis expressions, you can refer to axes like `[Axis.Color]` or `[Axis.X]`, for example.

In calculated columns, there is some special syntax for referring to hierarchies. If I have a hierarchy called [Region.Country], it would be referred to as [Hierarchy.Region.Country] in a calculated column expression. You can, of course, just refer to a column.

Be careful when using OVER aggregations in calculated columns—you will most likely get duplicated values as results (which you will need to aggregate with Min, Max, First, and so on) when displaying them. However, they are extremely useful when building up complex calculation strategies.

The aggregations in calculated columns will also NOT respond to filtering. Again, I make no apologies for repeating this fact. It's just so important!

If you're struggling with constructing a calculated column that uses OVER expressions, it can be helpful to build the expression (or parts of it) as a custom expression on a visualization axis and then translate it into a calculated column expression. For example, you'd replace [Axis.X] with the name of the column that contains the hierarchy you are working with.

Over method summary

The OVER methods are extremely powerful—just think of them as methods to reference the various parts of the data that aren't already grouped as elements of a visualization (for example, bars, markers, and so on), or to calculate values between these elements. You can also use them to calculate values between rows of a data table by using them in calculated columns.

I have merely scratched the surface here. It's beyond the scope of this book to cover every possible permutation or combination of OVER methods. If you have a specific query for using an OVER method, I suggest that you post a question on the TIBCO Community.

Don't forget that Spotfire contains some sample OVER expressions as advanced aggregation functions for visualization axes. Feel free to experiment with these—you can always use one of the built-in expressions and then modify it to suit your needs.

Other calculations in Spotfire

The expression language in Spotfire is extremely powerful, but again, it's beyond the scope of this book to document each and every one of the functions and how to use them. However, I'd like to add a few hints and tips here:

- The rich expression editor in Spotfire is great for building custom expressions. It performs auto-complete and inline syntax editing, for example. It also contains context-sensitive help on each of the functions.
- In addition to the built-in functions, you can extend the palette of calculations by using **TIBCO Enterprise Runtime for R (TERR)** aggregations, TERR expressions, and TERR custom calculation methods.
- Be careful when creating expressions with document properties (and other types of properties). If you choose a property from the list of document properties, Spotfire will insert a default syntax into the expression. This won't work in some cases as Spotfire doesn't know the context of your expression. You may have to surround an expression with quotes, escape it ($esc), or perform some other adjustments to it before it works as intended.
- Use the **resulting expression** box in the editor to "unpack" any expression that uses a document property (or any other kind of property) within it.

There really is so much you can do with calculations in Spotfire. Have fun exploring!

Data manipulation – where, why, and how?

As mentioned in the introduction to this chapter, it is generally considered good practice to transform your data, including merging from multiple sources, before it arrives in your analysis tool. However, you might not have this facility or access to good data integration tools, or perhaps you just want to explore something quickly to follow an analytical hunch. Spotfire provides some easy-to-use and powerful data transformation tools.

In brief, here is an overview of some different data transformation methods and a short explanation of when you would use each of them:

- **Data wrangling in Spotfire**: This is great for ad hoc data analysis–load data into Spotfire, transform it, filter it, add calculations, and so on. You can also use data wrangling to design a data workflow for implementation in another tool later on.

- **Data virtualization:** TIBCO produces a tool called **TIBCO Data Virtualization (TDV)**. TDV creates virtual databases that can be queried by Spotfire and other tools. It doesn't create copies of the underlying databases—it creates virtual layers that just appear to an application as databases. It supports intelligent caching and query optimization. It can also query and join all sorts of data sources—from files to big data and everything in-between.

- **Data pipelining or data science tools:** Some data pipelining and data science tools can write native **Spotfire data files (SBDF)** to the Spotfire library or write the files to the filesystem. Some examples are TIBCO Statistica, TIBCO Data Science Team Studio, and KNIME. These tools can be used to load data, transform it, run statistical modeling over the data, and write it somewhere it can be easily kept up to date and accessed by Spotfire analyses.

- **Extract, Transform, and Load (ETL) tools:** There are lots of ETL tools in the marketplace. These extract data from source systems, transform the data, and then load it into a warehouse, a big data database, or an other similar system.

Let's look into how you can merge data from multiple sources.

Merging (joining) data from multiple sources

When merging data into an existing data table, the first thing you have to decide is whether you are adding new columns or new rows. Then, you must define how the datasets are related. If you are adding new columns of data, you must define the key columns in each table that link the two datasets uniquely for the columns you add. If you are adding new rows of data, you must match or map the column names. When defining key columns and mapping columns, the names that are used in the two tables can be different as long as you know that their values and data types are equivalent.

Adding columns to existing data tables was covered in Chapter 2, *It's All About the Data*.

Adding rows to an existing data table is straightforward if the column names match. If they don't, you'll need to map them. An example usage of adding rows could be combining multiple Excel worksheets or workbooks into a single data table for analysis.

Here is an example of an add rows operation. This example simulates an add rows operation by loading the Titanic data, then adding the same data again as new rows:

1. Load the Titanic data in the same way as described in Chapter 1, *Welcome to Spotfire*.

2. Add new data and choose the same dataset. Spotfire will present an information bubble and description:

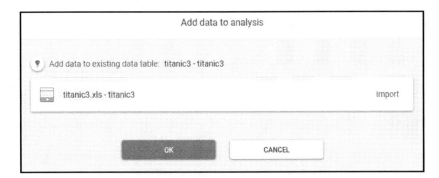

3. At this point, you don't need to do anything, as all the columns match up since it's the same data! But let's explore the settings.
4. Click **Import**. This expands the settings for the import operation.
5. Click on the **Add rows to** dropdown. This reveals the following options:

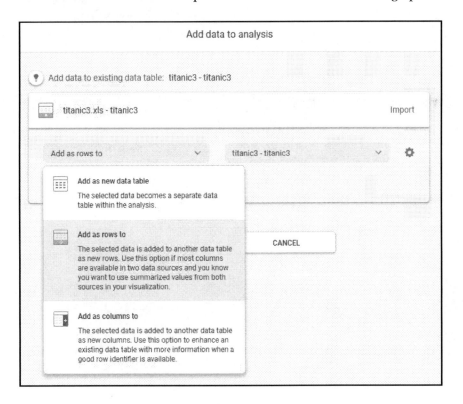

6. Since we are adding rows, accept that option and click the cog wheel icon. The settings for the add rows operation will be displayed:

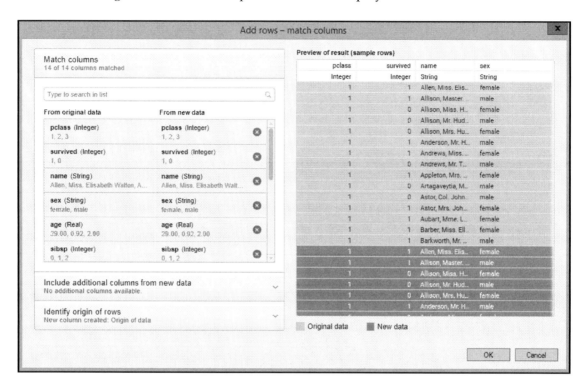

7. Perhaps the most interesting part of this dialog is being able to identify the origin of the rows. Using this option, as illustrated in the following screenshot, will add a column to the data table, which will contain `Original data` for the rows from the original import of the data, and `New data` for rows from the data that was added subsequently:

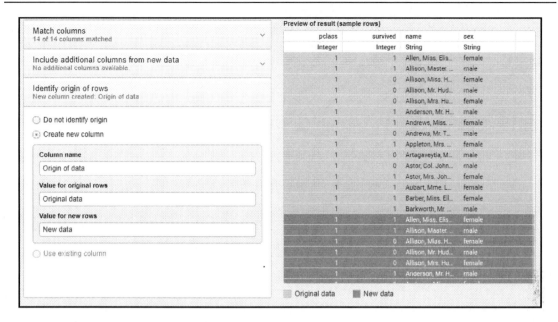

8. Once the new rows have been added, the data canvas shows the operation, like this:

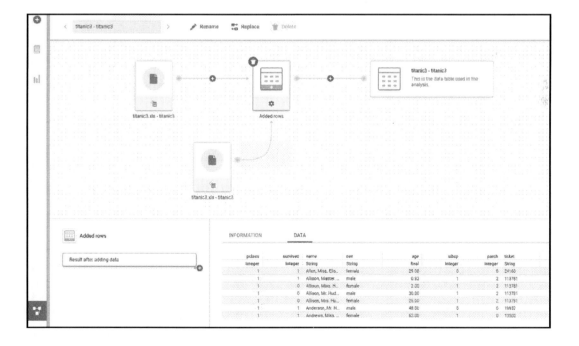

Using the data canvas, you can see each of the operations being performed on a data table at a glance. You can also edit the operations by clicking on the cog wheels after selecting the part of the workflow you'd like to work with.

Tall tables versus wide tables

Data tables are row-by-column matrices, and obviously they can range in size from one row by one column to many rows by many columns. You might have come across the colloquial expressions **tall table** and **wide table**, or even **tall, narrow table** and **short, wide table**, or some variation thereof.

These expressions are a handy way of describing the fundamental way in which the data is structured or categorized in a table. In a tall table, a list of categories is contained under a single column and a second column lists values associated with each of those categories. In a wide table, each category gets its own column and the associated values appear under it.

Consider the airline delay data we used previously in this chapter. As it stands, the data is wide. There is a column for every type of delay, for example:

8 columns from On_Time_Reporting_Carrier_On_Time_Performance_(1987_present)_2018_1							
FlightDate	Reportin...	Flight_Number...	CarrierDelay	WeatherDelay ▾	NASDelay	SecurityDelay	LateAircraftD...
03/01/2018	HA	50	35.00	1682.00	0.00	0.00	0.00
07/01/2018	OO	4656	0.00	1347.00	0.00	0.00	0.00
22/01/2018	OO	4289	0.00	1186.00	24.00	0.00	0.00
12/01/2018	OO	4623	0.00	1148.00	28.00	0.00	0.00
12/01/2018	9E	3510	0.00	1132.00	71.00	0.00	0.00
22/01/2018	OO	4446	0.00	1084.00	4.00	0.00	5.00
22/01/2018	AA	2532	0.00	1042.00	48.00	0.00	108.00
22/01/2018	DL	2037	0.00	1032.00	0.00	0.00	0.00
17/01/2018	OO	4765	0.00	1031.00	0.00	0.00	0.00
22/01/2018	DL	694	0.00	1016.00	77.00	0.00	0.00

As a tall table, it looks very different:

On_Time_Reporting_Carrier_On_Time_Performance_(1987_pre				
FlightDate	Reporting_Air...	Flight_Numbe...	Delay Category	Delay Value
01/01/2018	G4	1704	CarrierDelay	7.00
01/01/2018	G4	1704	WeatherDelay	0.00
01/01/2018	G4	1704	NASDelay	8.00
01/01/2018	G4	1704	SecurityDelay	0.00
01/01/2018	G4	1704	LateAircraftDe...	0.00
01/01/2018	G4	1712	CarrierDelay	12.00
01/01/2018	G4	1712	WeatherDelay	0.00
01/01/2018	G4	1712	NASDelay	13.00
01/01/2018	G4	1712	SecurityDelay	0.00
01/01/2018	G4	1712	LateAircraftDe...	5.00
01/01/2018	G4	1713	CarrierDelay	0.00
01/01/2018	G4	1713	WeatherDelay	0.00

Each type of structure has its advantages. You will find a true mix of tall and wide tables out in the real world, and you'll need to know when to use one over the other in your analytics.

Tall tables

Tall tables contain lists of categories and corresponding values. Tall tables tend to be narrow—they have lots of rows but few columns. They have the following benefits and drawbacks:

- Useful if you want to compare multiple series of data. For example, you can use the category column to separate the data.
- Useful if you need a flexible structure, whereby visualizations can just accept whatever categories you feed into it and you don't want to reconfigure your visualizations every time a new category is added. You can just add a category as a new set of rows.
- (Potentially) easier to calculate values across rows and categories.
- Not so good if there's a lot of data repetition throughout the table—it's probably better to have a wide table.

Wide tables

Wide tables contain lots of columns—one per category. They are generally more common than tall tables (in my experience) and have the following benefits and drawbacks:

- Easier to use than tall tables for charting the progression of data through a category
- Can sometimes be more efficient for storage than tall tables
- Not as flexible as tall tables—adding a category to the data involves creating a new column

Regardless, your real-world analytics experience will help you decide which format to use for the various tasks you would like to complete. I usually find that if I can't make sense of the data or I find it hard to make a decent visualization using it, it's probably in the wrong format and I need to transform it from a tall table into a wide one or vice versa! We'll cover how to do this in the next section.

Transforming data structure through pivots and unpivots

You can use **pivot** to transform tall tables into wide tables and **unpivot** to transform wide tables into tall ones. Spotfire has in-built transformation methods that we will cover in this section. You can also use a pivot to reduce the granularity of a data table permanently by summing up to a higher level.

With Spotfire, you can run the transformation on an existing table, or create a new table as a copy of the original.

To transform data in place (on top of the original data table), use the **Transform data...** option from the **Data** menu. To create a transformed copy of the data table, go through the **Add data** process and choose **Other**. From there, you can choose an existing table as a data source for a transformation.

If you're working with a blank analysis and you know you need to transform the data ahead of visualizing it (and you are sure you don't need the original format data), apply the transformation to the data table. If you feel that you are likely to need the original data and the transformed data, create a linked copy of the data table.

If you have existing visualizations built on the original data, then you'll need to create a linked copy. If you don't, all the existing visualizations will cease to work, since the structure of the data changes as a result of the transformation.

It's useful to know that Spotfire will rerun any transformations on data tables when the original source data is reloaded or updated so long as the data remains "linked." If you embed the data, then the data becomes static in the analysis file and will not be recalculated.

Unpivot

Let's see what happens when we unpivot the airline delay data table. In this case, we will add a new table as a linked copy of the original so as not to break the existing visualizations:

1. Click the **+** sign on the left of the Spotfire window.
2. Choose **Other** for the data source.
3. Click the existing data table to create a linked copy:

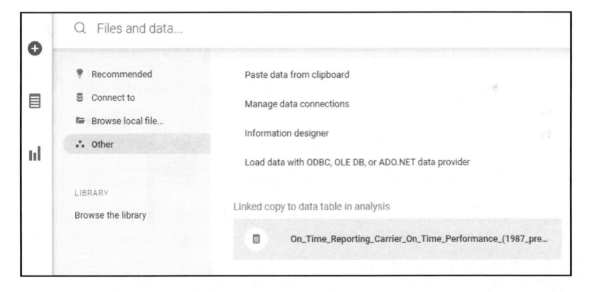

4. Pull down the settings for the new data table by clicking on its name (or the **Import** word):

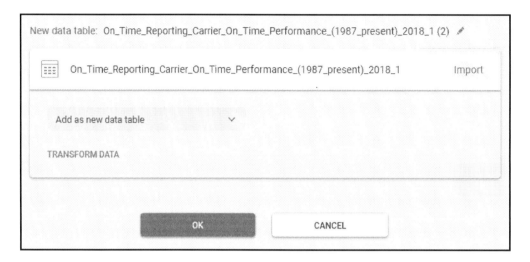

5. Click **TRANSFORM DATA**.
6. Choose **Unpivot** and click **Insert**.
7. You'll be presented with the **Unpivot Data** dialog. Don't be worried if it looks daunting! Let's plough on and then you should see how it all works.
8. Choose **FlightDate, Reporting_Airline**, and **Flight_Number_Reporting_Airline** as columns to pass through—this will copy the columns directly into the destination data table.
9. Choose **CarrierDelay, WeatherDelay, NASDelay, SecuirtyDelay**, and **LateAircraftDelay** as the columns to transform. You can search for these columns by entering `Delay` in the **Available Columns** search box.
10. Use `Delay Category` for the **Category column name**.
11. Use `Delay Value` for the **Value column name**.
12. You can choose to exclude empty rows. When you've finished working with the settings of the unpivot operation, you should end up with a dialog that looks like this:

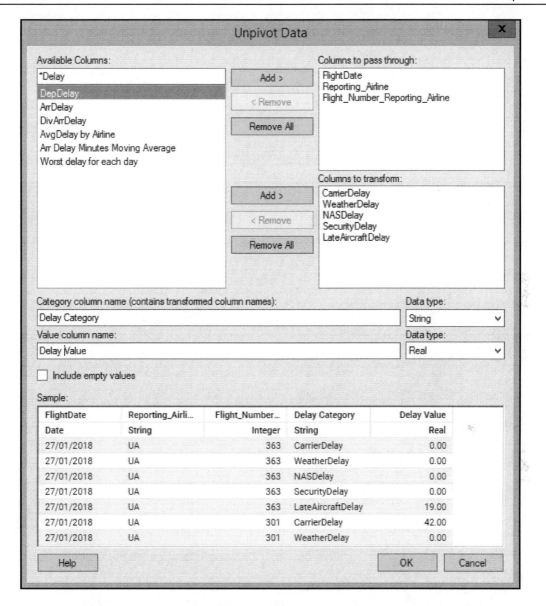

13. Click **OK**, then **Close**, then **OK**. Notice that, in the final step, Spotfire shows that the unpivot transformation has been added.

14. Now, look at the dashboard I created with the transformed data:

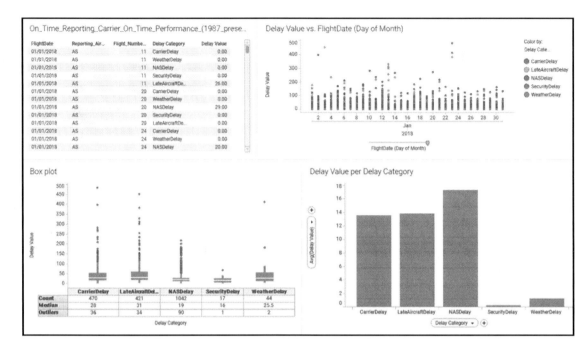

15. I've done a few things to tweak the display—for example, I limited the data in the box plot to `[Delay Value] > 0` and filtered to one of the more interesting airlines.

Study the resultant dashboard—notice that each of the delay columns is now represented as a row in the data table. Also, notice that I was able to place the delay category directly as an axis. As an exercise, why don't you try and construct the same visualizations on the wide data? I found it possible, but it took a lot of extra work!

Pivot

The pivot transformation produces a wide table from a tall table. In order to do this, Spotfire must be informed about how you would like to aggregate the data. The pivot transformation is a little more difficult to understand and configure than the unpivot. We can pivot the unpivoted table back into something that resembles the original table (or at least as far as is possible with the columns that were copied over):

1. Add a linked copy of the second (unpivoted) data table.
2. This time, choose the Pivot transformation.
3. Configure the dialog like so:

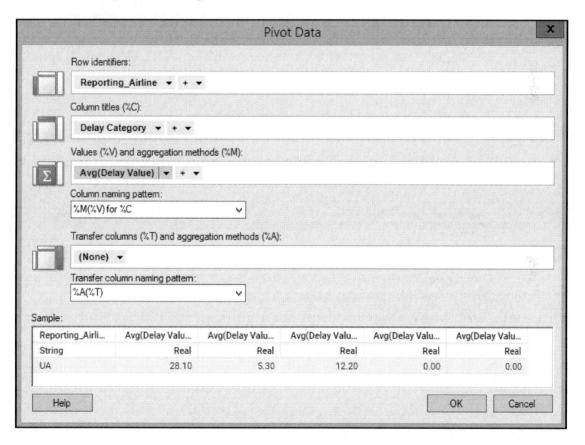

4. Looking at the preview, do you see what's going on here?

- The row identifiers are used to group the data. I have chosen just to use `Reporting_Airline` to identify the rows. This means that any aggregation of the data will occur at that level.
- `Delay Category` is chosen for the column titles. This is what will transform the row-based data into columnar data and the row values back into column values.
- The value and aggregation method I have chosen is `Avg(Delay Value)`—as described, this aggregation will be performed over the reporting airline.
- Look at the **Column naming pattern**—this describes how Spotfire will name the new columns.

To familiarize yourself with the column-naming setting, play around with the patterns and watch how the preview changes. Also, consult the Spotfire help if you want to find out more.

Other transformations

Spotfire has a whole host of transformations that you can apply to your data tables. I'm not going to document them all here—please refer to the Spotfire help if you need more information. Some of the operations you can perform are as follows:

- Calculate and replace column (use this if you want a calculated column but don't want to show the original source column)
- Calculate new column (adds a new calculated column)
- Change column names (provides an easy way to rename columns)
- Change data types
- Data function (runs a statistical function on the data)
- Exclude columns
- Filter rows
- Normalization (normalizes data so it falls between)
- Pivot
- Unpivot

- Group categorical data together with different values into a single value
- Replace a specific value (replaces a value in a data table—note that this option requires that a **primary key** or **composite primary key** is defined on the table)
- Replace value (replaces all occurrences of a value in a column with another)

You can replace specific values by double-clicking on a table plot cell. You can also group categorical values by marking them, right-clicking on them, and choosing **Group from Marked Categories**. Replacing values is available in Spotfire Analyst and web-based clients. Grouping data is only available in Spotfire Analyst.

Finally, before we leave the topic of transformations, you can always go and check the data canvas in order to view or edit any transformations you have performed on the data.

Summary

This chapter covered the topic of calculations and the transformation of data. We focused on some advanced calculations using some of Spotfire's OVER methods and gave examples of adding rows to existing tables and pivoting and unpivoting data tables.

We covered the differences between calculated columns and custom expressions in visualizations—remember that calculated columns do not recalculate based on filtering!

Moving beyond basic visualization building, we explored Spotfire's built-in data-wrangling functions to create and manipulate tall and wide tables through pivot and unpivot operations.

Spotfire's versatile and comprehensive suite of data-modeling tools offers excellent flexibility. It can be used to support the data discovery needs of an individual Analyst; it can also support an enterprise business intelligence deployment on top of a data warehouse; and it can help an experienced Analyst create a sophisticated guided analysis of large data collections for small and enterprise-wide audiences alike.

In the next chapter, you will learn about some important topics when working with data in Spotfire—it discusses data relationships, annotating visualizations with reference lines, and fitted curves. It also covers the final few visualization types that we haven't yet seen on our journey through the world of Spotfire!

The World is Your Visualization

8

This chapter ties up a few loose ends. It will introduce you to some key Spotfire concepts that we've not covered yet. My aim has been to take you on a journey through analytics and give you the benefit of my real-world experience with the tool. So, now it's time to pull things together a bit.

We'll be covering data relationships, where multiple data tables are related in Spotfire so that you can mark and filter between data tables. We'll also look at showing/hiding data and how to work subsets in order to find comparisons between different subsets of data.

We will visit the topic of annotating visualizations with lines, curves, and forecasts. Finally, we will be covering combination charts, heat maps, and their associated dendrograms, before finishing with parallel coordinate plots.

As we go through this chapter, I will begin to include some statistical concepts and topics. Spotfire makes it really easy to take advantage of these, even if you are not a statistician or a data scientist!

In this chapter, we will cover the following topics:

- Data relations and marking and filtering between multiple tables
- Column matching (for using multiple data tables in one visualization)
- Subsets
- Showing/hiding data in a visualization
- Annotating visualizations with reference lines, fitted curves, and error bars
- Visualizing categorical information and trends together in combination charts
- Visualizing complex multidimensional data using heat maps and dendrograms
- Profiling data using parallel coordinate plots

Data relations (between tables)

A great feature of Spotfire is that it allows freeform exploration between related datasets. You can mark data in one dataset and have other visualizations built on a different data table respond. You can also filter in one data table and the filtering will map to any dependent data tables.

Later on in this chapter, we will be producing a parallel coordinate plot that enables us to look at how various columns interact within European consumer price index data. To assist with navigating through the data, it's useful if lists of regions and zones are created and related back to the retail price index data.

 Two datasets are said to be related if they contain columns with the same values as each other. This is a key feature of relational databases and is known as a foreign-key relationship. Spotfire uses the concept of data table relations to represent foreign-key relationships.

Anyone can download consumer price index data (Harmonized Indices of Consumer Prices) from the European Commission's Eurostat website, at `https://ec.europa.eu/eurostat/web/hicp/data/database`.

Alternatively, use this shortened link:

`http://bit.ly/2Ucrh7u`.

In order to follow the example that we'll provide after downloading the data from scratch, you would have to perform some manipulations on the data, but I've done it for you for the mid-2014 data. I have also pivoted the data by geographical classification and Eurozone classification so that you don't have to! You can download the final datasets as `Eurozone HICP.zip` from here:

`https://community.tibco.com/wiki/tibco-spotfire-primer-sample-data`.

Alternatively, use this shortened link:

`http://bit.ly/2Vhfy3K`.

 Note that the file format for this data is `.sbdf`. SBDF is Spotfire's own file type—SBDF stands for Spotfire Binary Data Format. It's a highly optimized file format that is strongly typed, so there's no need for you to specify the column types when you load the data file.

Setting up relationships between data tables

Please download the data, unzip it, and follow along with these steps:

1. Load the three data files into Spotfire by browsing to them on your local file
   system. You can load them all in a single step by multi-selecting them from the
   File open dialog. Do make absolutely sure that you set each file to be a new data
   table, as shown here:

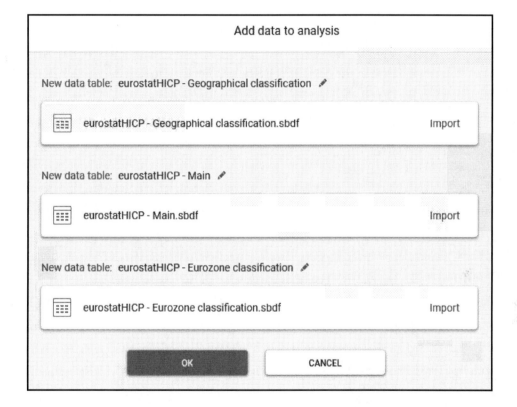

2. Once the data has been loaded, select **Data Table Properties** from the **Data** menu. This opens the **Data Table Properties** dialog:

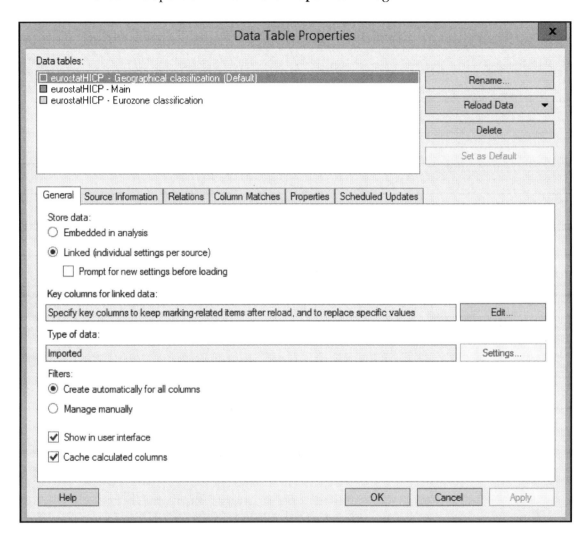

There are loads of useful things you can do with this dialog, but for this example, we are just going to focus on **Relations**.

3. Click the **Relations** tab to open it. By default, no relations have been defined, so we must go ahead and start to add some. Click the **Manage Relations** button. The following dialog will be displayed:

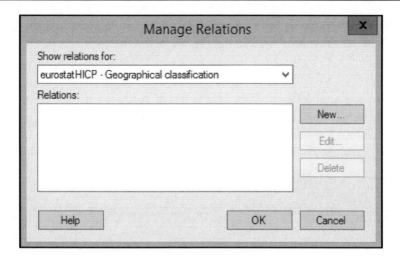

4. Select the Main table from the **Show relations for:** dropdown. This isn't strictly necessary, but it's helpful for later on.
5. Click the **New...** button.
6. Now, we can define the relations. It doesn't matter which way round the tables are, such as left to right, but let's be consistent and choose the Main data table as the left-hand table. So go ahead and set up the relation between the Main data table and the **Geographical Classification** table (I had to make sure that the Main table wasn't selected in the right-hand table dropdown first):

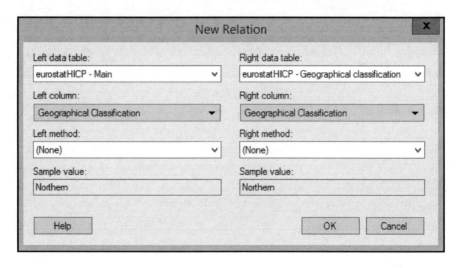

Make sure you choose the correct left and right columns—our example looks correct as you can see that the sample values match.

7. Now, do the same for the `Eurozone` table, matching the **Eurozone Classification** columns. The completed dialog should look like this:

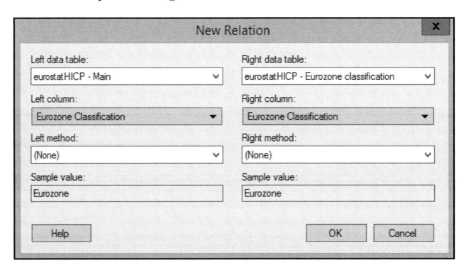

8. The **Manage Relations** dialog should now look like this:

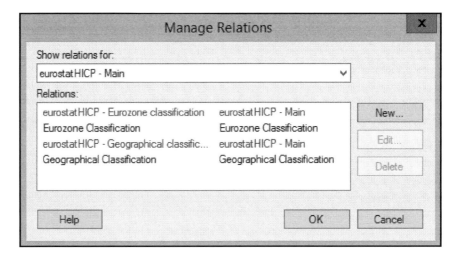

9. Click **OK** to close the dialog and then **OK** again on the **Data Table Properties** dialog.

The relationship between the data tables is established, so let's see how to configure marking and filtering between related data tables.

Configuring marking and filtering between related data tables

Now that we've set up the relations between the tables, we can use them in visualizations for marking and filtering, and explore how the relations improve our ability to work with the data by following these steps:

1. Add a table visualization and show the **Geographical Classification** table.
2. Right-click the visualization and choose **Create Details Visualization**. Choose a **Bar Chart**.
3. A new dialog will open that allows us to choose which related data table to use for the visualization. Select the **Main** data table:

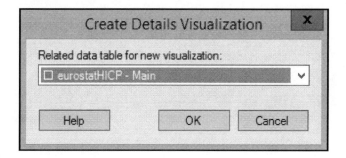

4. Click **OK**.
5. Now, explore what happens when you click on some rows in the geographical classification table—the details visualization updates based on the marked rows, just as if it was showing the same data table.

Let's move on to filtering:

1. Mark all the data in the **Geographical Classification** table so that you can observe what happens when you adjust the filters.
2. Show the filter panel (select **Filters** from the **View** menu).

3. Now, try adjusting a filter in the **Geographical Classification** table. In my case, I have deselected **Baltic** and **Eastern**:

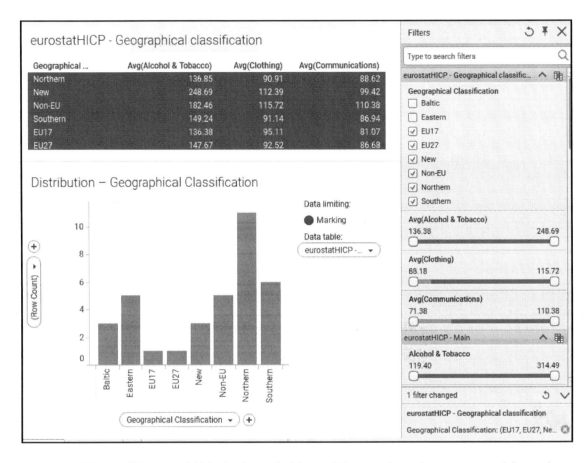

Oh—it didn't work! Notice how **Baltic** and **Eastern** have been removed from the table plot, but they are still present in the bar chart!

 The default setting for related tables is that the filtering in one data table does not affect related data tables. You may think this odd, considering that marking does affect related data tables by default, but there are some options for filtering that mean this makes sense.

Let's fix things so that filtering in one data table does affect another.

4. Locate the **Main** data table in the filter panel. In the top right-hand corner of the title bar for the table, you'll see an icon that shows two overlapping tables:

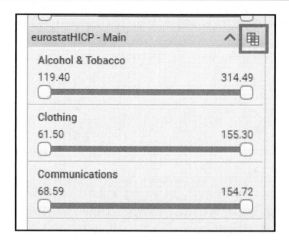

5. Click the icon. This will pop out a menu—locate the **Geographical Classification** table and expand it:

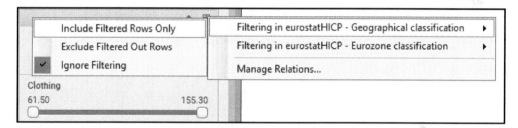

6. Now, click **Include Filtered Rows Only**.

7. Return to the analysis—notice that Baltic and Eastern are no longer shown in the details visualization.

The difference between the settings of **Include Filtered Rows Only** and **Exclude Filtered Out Rows** is rather subtle. The first option means that any rows that are in the child table (**Main**) but are not in the parent table (**Geographical Classification**) will not be shown in visualizations showing the child table. However, the second option means that any rows that are present in the child table but not in the parent will not be filtered out by any filtering performed in the parent. In other words, using **Include Filtered Rows Only** is a bit like an inner join, where rows will be shown only if the values of the columns match. **Exclude Filtered Rows** is equivalent to an outer join, where the filtering will never filter out rows that appear in one data table, but not the other.

Please reset any filters and save your analysis file—you'll need it later on in this chapter.

Mashing up data from different tables in a single visualization

Spotfire allows you to combine data from multiple tables in the same visualization and automatically matches any columns with the same name and data type. You can also manually match columns with different names or data types that you know to be equivalent.

If the columns that you want to use from the two data tables match, then the operation is very easy: you pick the columns you want from the table you want. Continuing with the HICP data we used in the previous example, let's explore this together:

1. In order to demonstrate this concept, let's create an issue with the data in the **Main** data table artificially. Open the data panel and delete the **Alcohol & Tobacco** column from the **Main** data table by right-clicking on it and choosing **Delete**:

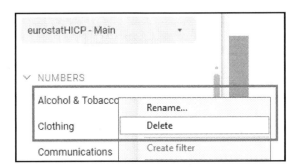

By deleting a column, we have made it no longer available in the table, so we cannot select it for the *y*-axis of a visualization.

2. Create a new bar chart using the **Main** data table—place **Geographical Classification** on the *x*-axis and leave (**Row Count**) on the *y*-axis.

3. Now, pull out the axis selector for the *y*-axis and look at the columns that are available. Notice that **Alcohol & Tobacco** is not available.

4. From the axis selector, click the **Main** data table—a dropdown will appear that allows you to select the **Geographical classification** table, where the **Average of Alcohol & Tobacco** is still available:

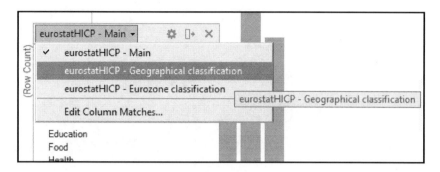

5. Choose the **Avg(Alcohol & Tobacco)** column.

6. Now, notice that the *y*-axis selector shows **Sum((Avg(Alcohol & Tobacco))**. If you've selected Avg as your default aggregation method, it will show **Avg((Avg(Alcohol & Tobacco))**.

In Chapter 5, *Practical Applications of Spotfire Visualizations*, we learned that summing averages is not really a good idea. In this case, it doesn't really matter because there is only one row of data for each geographical classification, so the aggregation method isn't important, but it's more correct if we choose Min instead, so please do that.

The Avg aggregation of the **Geographical classification** table was performed when I pivoted it originally.

To summarize this example: we have now brought in a column from another data table and shown it in the original visualization. We are neatly showing data from two data tables in a single visualization.

Please be very careful when you mash up data. It's possible to match on a column between data tables where the categorization of the data doesn't match, and this can lead to undesirable results, such as duplicate data.

Let's illustrate the problem with non-matching categorization by way of an example. In this case, I'm matching two tables with baseball players, where a player has played for two teams during his career. Matching is done on player name and the bar chart (horizontal) is showing the number of runs. Coloring is by team. The player Alex Gonzales appears to have scored two sets of 92 runs. This is obviously incorrect:

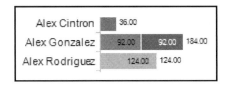

Finally, you can edit the column matches between tables—did you notice the **Edit column matches...** option? You can also edit column matches from the Data Property page within most visualization's property pages. I will also show how column matches are particularly useful—no, essential—when performing geocoding in map charts. This is covered in the next chapter, Chapter 9, *What's Your Location?*.

I would recommend closing the analysis and not saving changes (since we deleted one of the columns), that is, presuming you did what I suggested and saved it at the end of the previous example.

Comparing subsets of data

We saw in Chapter 1, *Welcome to Spotfire*, that trellising can be used to compare different subsets splitting the data by the values in various columns. Spotfire's Subsets feature allows for the comparison of subsets by filtering, marking, or a custom expression. Let's go through an example together. For the example, I have chosen the same US vehicles dataset that I first used in Chapter 5, *Practical Applications of Spotfire Visualizations*. You can follow along in your own dataset!

Here's how you can compare subsets of data in Spotfire:

1. Create a visualization. For this example, I have produced a visualization showing Mpg City per Transmission Type:

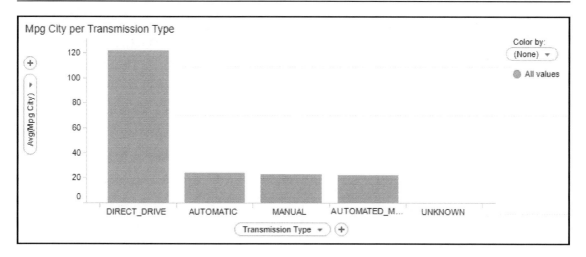

Recall that Mpg City is the measure of fuel economy when a car is being driven in city traffic. Higher Mpg is better.

2. Open the visualization properties and navigate to the **Subsets** page.
3. Select **Not in current filtering** and make sure that **Current filtering** is still selected. You should end up with a configuration that looks like this:

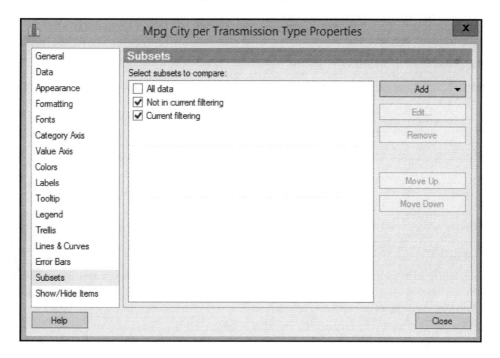

4. Close the dialog.

5. The first thing you should notice is that Spotfire has changed the color by axis of the visualization. It's now shown as **Color by: (Subsets)**:

Now, we can start to explore how to compare subsets by filtering. I'm interested in comparing the fuel economy of compact versus midsize/large cars.

6. Look at the following visualization. I have filtered out midsize and large cars and left compact cars in scope:

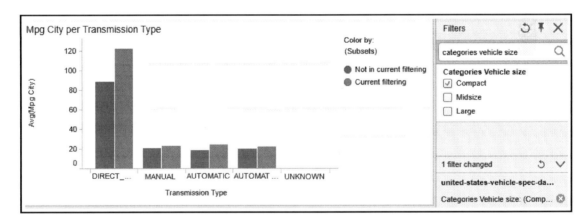

See how Spotfire shows the data for each of the subsets together? It's as we would expect—compact cars have better city fuel economy than midsize or large cars. The rows that are filtered out are shown in the `Not in current filtering` subset.

So, why have we used the subsets feature rather than any other method of comparing the different subsets of the data? We could have used color by or trellising, for example.

For me, one of the main reasons for using subsets with filtering is to provide maximum flexibility for an end user of your analysis. Think about it—if you give a user access to filters, the user can filter to any conceivable subsets within the data, without you having to design all the different possibilities for defining subsets into the visualization beforehand. This is a nice way of enabling free-form data exploration for all users—even web consumers!

You can also show subsets by marking, filtering scheme, or custom expression. I'm not going to document all these different options in this book—the Spotfire online help is very comprehensive on the topic of subsets.

Showing/hiding items of data

Suppose you are only interested in visualizing the most significant parts of your data in a visualization? For example, you might only want to see the top 5 or bottom 5 bars on a bar chart. Spotfire allows this and more with a flexible set of rules that can be used to show and hide the data in the visualization.

Let's work through another example. Again, I'm going to use the US vehicles dataset, but you can use anything you like! You can show/hide parts of your data by performing the following steps:

1. Let's begin with a visualization that's not too helpful as it stands, with all the data in it. I've created a bar chart that shows `Mpg City` for each model of car:

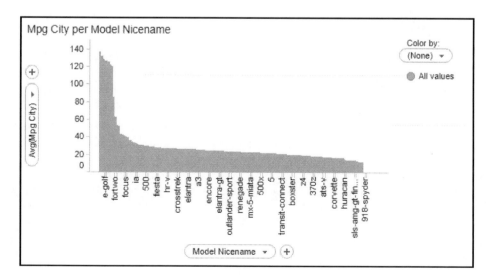

As it stands, the visualization isn't very helpful. It shows the shape of the data but nothing else. How can we isolate the cars that have the best city mpg?

2. Easy! Open the visualization properties and show the **Show/Hide items** page. There will be no rules defined, so click the **Add...** button to add a new rule.

3. Keep all the defaults except for the **Value**—I've entered 10:

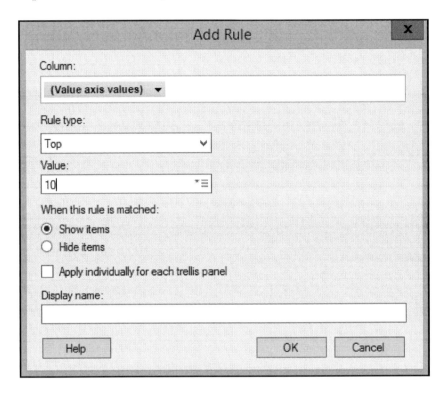

4. Click **OK** on the dialog and then close the visualization properties.

5. That's much better:

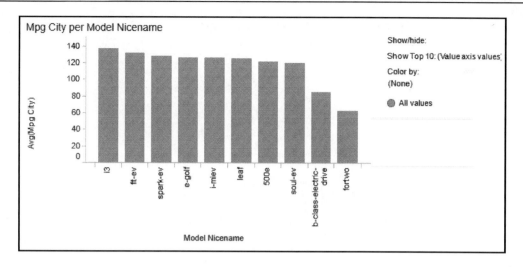

Notice how Spotfire displays the rules in the legend so that it's clear to anyone interacting with the visualization.

6. Now, revisit the **Show/Hide** property page and delete the rule for the top 10.

7. Add a new rule, but this time choose to show items where their value is greater than average:

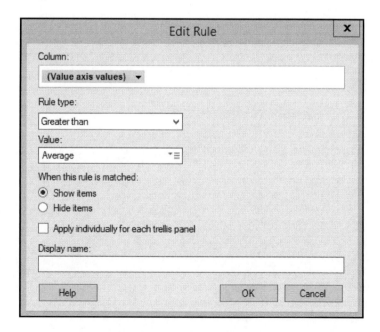

8. Setting the rule produces the following visualization:

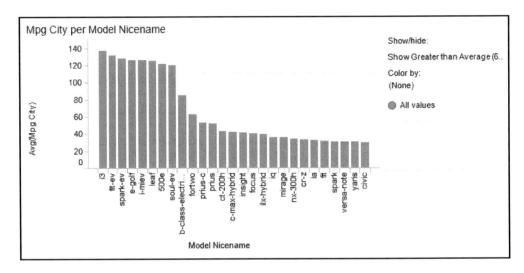

Using this rule has allowed us to isolate those cars with greater than average city fuel economy.

We can also apply statistical functions to the rule by specifying a custom expression for the rule.

9. Edit the rule again and click the dropdown for the **Value** box:

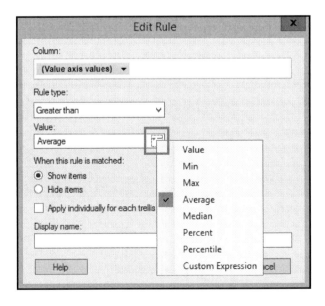

10. Choose **Custom Expression**.
11. This brings up the expression editor dialog. Enter the following expression:
    `P90([Axis.Value])`
12. Click **OK** on the dialog and close the visualization properties. The resulting visualization now looks like this:

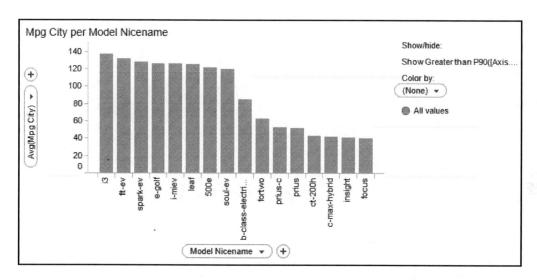

Why did I use the 90th percentile function? Just so that I could see the values that are greater than 90% of the rest of the values. So, in effect, the visualization shows the cars with city fuel economy in the top 10%.

Even though it's interesting enough to select the cars within the top 10% for fuel economy, it could be even more interesting to look at the absolute value of the 90th percentile as it would then give you a useful indication for the overall performance of the car industry (or however you wish to slice the data) for city fuel economy. This could be displayed as a calculated value in a text area or as a value in a KPI chart.

The examples here show how you can use the Show/Hide feature in Spotfire to show data in visualizations that meet certain criteria. The inverse is also true—you can hide data using the same process. I showed you how to create a simple top 10 rule, then a greater than average rule, and then a rule using a custom expression. The advantage of using a statistical function is that the amount of data shown on the chart varies according to the overall shape of the data being visualized, instead of being a fixed number.

Before we leave this topic altogether, note that using a custom expression also gives us the ability to use a document property to configure the rule—you could provide users of your analysis with a drop-down control that adjusts the rule in some way. For example, you could allow the user to choose between various statistical measures, or permit them to adjust the value of *n* for a top-*n* rule.

Annotating visualizations with reference lines, fitted curves, and error bars

Adding lines to a visualization can significantly enhance the information you wish to convey. You can add horizontal or vertical lines to indicate boundaries or various statistical measures. You can also add curve fits that "smooth" the data and show you the overall trend. Let's return to the stock market data that was first used in Chapter 3, *Impactful Dashboards!* For example, we may want to smooth out the fluctuations in the stock market and look at its overall performance over time. The example in this section will show you how to do that.

Fitted curves

Refer to Chapter 3, *Impactful Dashboards!*, if you've not already loaded the stock market data, or reopen the analysis file if you still have it! Follow these steps to add a curve to a visualization that shows the stock market performance over time:

1. Create a line chart visualization that shows **Avg(High)** over **Date**. It should look similar to this:

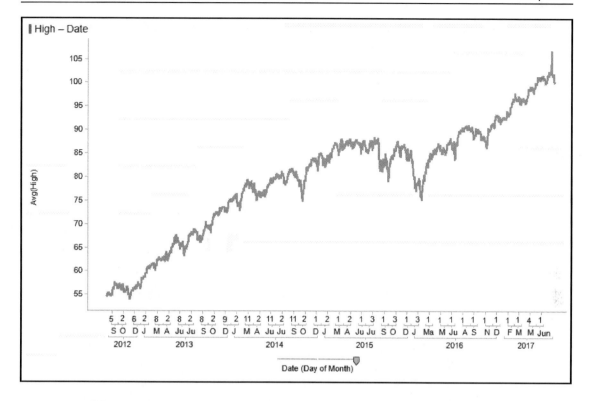

Notice all the peaks and troughs or "noise" in the data? We can add a fitted curve to the visualization to smooth it out.

2. Open the visualization properties and navigate to the **Lines & Curves** page.

3. Click the **Add** dropdown and choose **Polynomial Curve Fit...**:

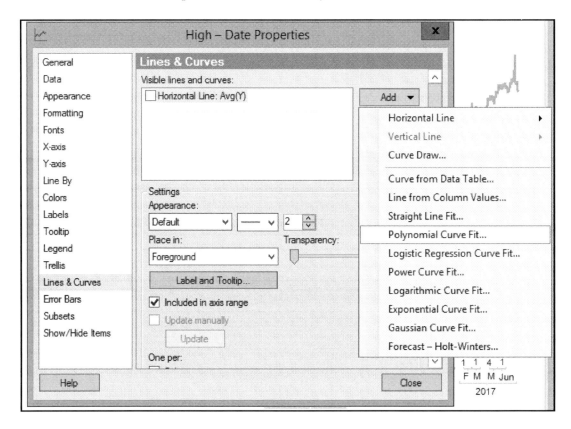

4. In the next dialog that's shown, Spotfire gives us the opportunity to specify the degree of the curve. You can think of this as how many twists and turns the curve makes over time, or how closely it follows the original data. I have chosen a degree of 3:

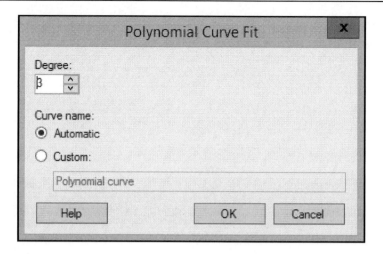

5. Click **OK**. Don't dismiss the visualization properties dialog just yet. I recommend labeling the curve. To do this, click the **Label and Tooltip...** button.

6. Select the checkbox to show the **Curve name**:

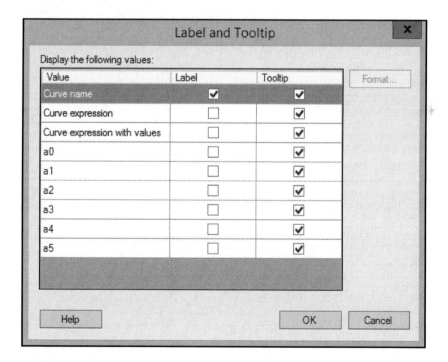

7. Click **OK**. Now, you can dismiss the visualization properties dialog. Your visualization should look something like this:

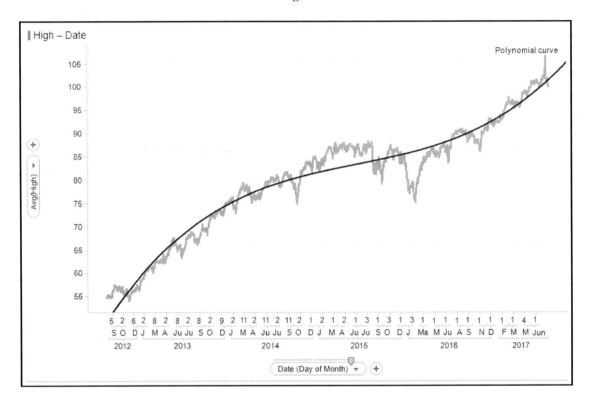

See how the curve follows the line of the original data but isn't affected by the individual ups and downs of the data?

You can also view the expression of the curve and export its data. To view the expression, hover over the curve—the default tooltip will show the expression and some other useful information that describes the curve.

8. To export the data from the curve, revisit the **Lines & Curves** property page for the visualization and click the **More** button:

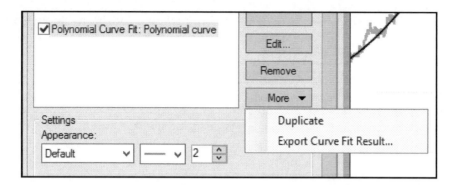

From there, you can export the curve fit result as a CSV file. Once you have exported the curve fit result, you can load it back into Spotfire and show it in another visualization.

 To be meaningful, a fitted curve should be supported by some underlying hypothesis or model. Do you expect a certain relationship between the two variables you are plotting? Always challenge such assumptions by exploring real-world relationships, as well as patterns in the data. Be particularly careful when using nonlinear fits: a high-order polynomial curve will closely fit the quirkiest data patterns, but the result may not really tell you anything meaningful about the real-world relationship between the variables concerned. For that, you need a more specific equation that actually models something that can be tested.

There are many other different types of lines and curves that can be used in Spotfire visualizations. I'll just briefly cover the main types I have used in various real-world applications of Spotfire:

- **Horizontal line**: A horizontal line can be used to represent a certain value in the data—it corresponds with a value on the y- (or value) axis of a visualization. It could, for example, represent the average, mean or median. It could also be used to segment a visualization into sectors.
- **Vertical line**: Be careful with vertical lines. They can only be used in visualizations with a continuous x-axis. However, in the right circumstances, they can be very useful. For example, a horizontal and a vertical line could be used to divide a scatter plot into quadrants.

- **Curve draw**: These can be used to draw a custom curve based on an expression that you enter. This type of curve is extremely flexible—you can use all the power of the Spotfire statistical functions, including using TIBCO Enterprise Runtime for R, to draw the curve. Any expression must map an x value to a corresponding y value.
- **Curve from data table**: This allows you to draw a curve from values in a data table. You could pre-calculate the values for the curve and use those values to draw the curve in the visualization.
- **Forecasting**: This is detailed in its own section, which we will go to now.

All the line and curve types are detailed in the Spotfire help—I recommend that you take a look if you want to know more about them—the preceding points is not a complete list!

Forecasting

I'd like to discuss **forecasting**—it's available as a curve type and applies to line charts or scatter plots with a continuous or date/time x-axis. Spotfire uses the **Holt-Winters forecast** for this.

 It's important to note that the data points must be spaced at equal distances, otherwise the forecast won't work. You can add forecasting via the **Lines & Curves** property page of a line chart, or you can simply right-click on the line chart and choose **Forecast**.

I've loaded a vehicle accident dataset covering 10 years' worth of data covering accidents in the UK from 2005 to 2015. It shows the number of accidents on the y-axis. The x-axis is set to show the month:

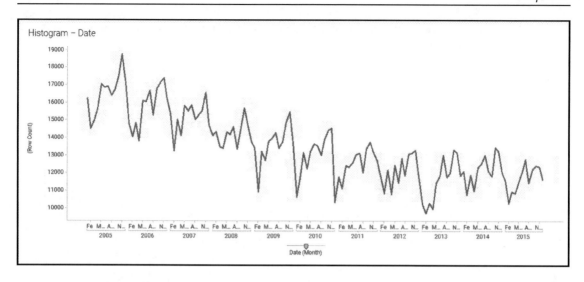

Notice how the data fluctuates seasonally over the course of each year, but the gradual overall trend is downwards. Forecasting can replicate this pattern in the data and forecast the accident rate over the next year, including forecasting the seasonal fluctuations and the overall downward trend. Here's how I have experimented with forecasting with this dataset. Feel free to follow along with your own, if you wish:

1. Right-click on the visualization and choose **Forecast**:

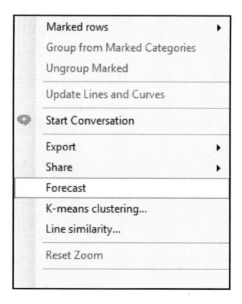

2. This applies what's known as a **Holt-Winters forecast** to the line chart:

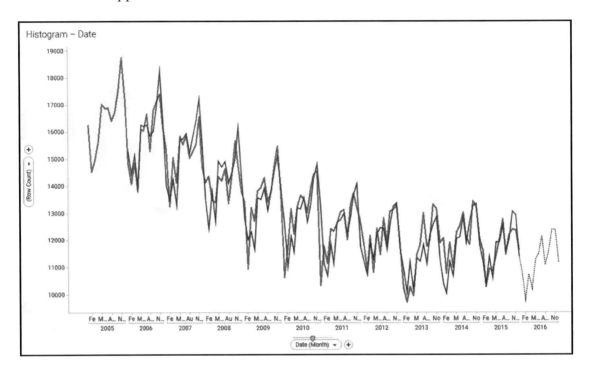

Notice that a fitted line has been applied to the existing data, after 1 year's worth. The dotted line at the right-hand side of the visualization indicates the forecast. The default settings have forecast the accident rate for the next 12 months.
Also observe how the forecasted line replicates the seasonal pattern in the actual data and how it continues the general trend downwards.
Now, let's customize the forecast a bit!

3. Visit the visualization properties and the **Lines & Curves** page. The defaults for the forecast show the fitted line and the forecasted line:

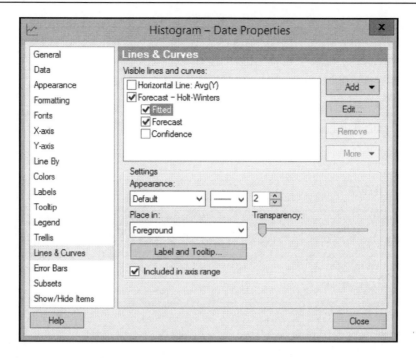

4. Adding the **Confidence** line can be useful—the default setting is the 95% confidence level. Here's how the confidence level is shown on the visualization:

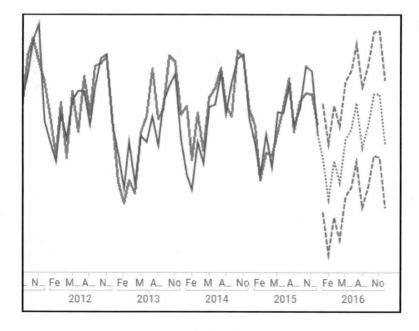

You can think of the confidence levels as measures of how much you can trust the forecast. In general, the further away it is in the future, the more uncertainty there is in the prediction. The confidence interval (difference between the upper and lower confidence curves) will depend on the length and variability pattern of the known portion of the time series, as well as on the parameters that are used for tuning the Holt-Winters forecast algorithm itself.

5. You can also experiment with the tuning parameters for the forecasting algorithm by editing the curve by selecting it in the **Lines & Curves** page and clicking **Edit...**:

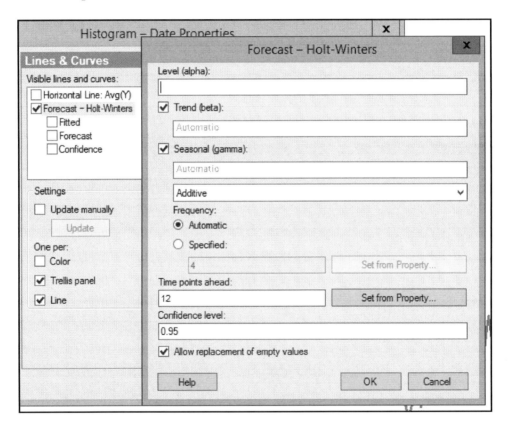

See how the defaults are set? Spotfire automatically chooses values for the tuning parameters so you don't need to. However, you can experiment with them, and once again, Spotfire's online help is great at explaining the **Level**, **Trend**, **Seasonal**, and **Frequency** parameters. However, it doesn't really explain the **Confidence level** so well, hence why I have explained it previously.

Before we leave the topic of forecasting, I'd like to add a few further points of interest. Spotfire uses its built-in statistical engine, TIBCO Enterprise Runtime for R, internally in order to run the forecasting algorithm. It's a pretty sophisticated algorithm, but it's not magic! The error in the forecasting is cumulative, so the confidence levels will get wider as the algorithm predicts further into the future. However, it's really easy to use and it requires no specialist knowledge to add the forecast to a visualization.

If, for any reason, the forecast cannot be calculated, Spotfire will let you know why by displaying a blue information icon in the top right-hand corner of the visualization:

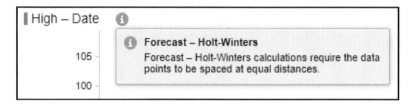

Finally, you can always customize the color and line type for the forecast, as with all other lines and curves.

Error bars

Error bars are used to illustrate the precision of a set of observations or measurements, and by precision, I mean the repeatability of a measurement. The tighter the precision, the more confidence you have that the average of your measurements is accurate to the true value.

For example, say you are a meteorological enthusiast who measures the temperature every hour, every day, and you want to plot the average daytime temperature over time. You could just plot the average or you could include error bars to indicate the range in your measurements.

Take, for example, hourly temperature data for a city over an entire year (one source of such data is the United States' National Climatic Data Center (http://www.ncdc.noaa.gov/cdo-web). You could make a straight plot of average monthly temperature against a month and also use a calculated column to define a nominal daytime dataset and plot those temperatures against months.

> You can use the DatePart function to define the daytime dataset. For example:
> ```
> If((DatePart("hour",[Date Time])>7) and
> (DatePart("hour",[Date Time])<18),[Date Time])
> ```

In each case, you could include error bars to represent the standard deviation in the data (all those hourly measurements). To configure the error bars, you need to do the following:

1. Open the visualization properties and select the **Error Bars** page.
2. Set the upper and lower errors by defining a suitable expression, such as StdDev([Temperature]) in each case.

It's pretty typical to use some statistical function of the relevant axis variable to define an error bar. You can also choose the color of the error bar or just keep the color the same as the marker:

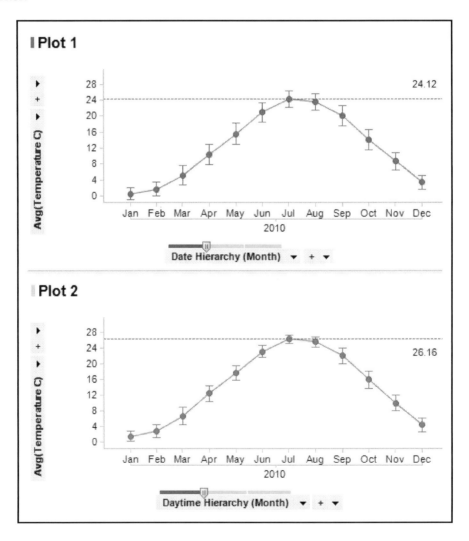

The second plot shows just the daytime temperatures and has much tighter error bars than the first. This shows that the line in the second plot is a more accurate representation of temperature at any point (that is the error is smaller).

Visualizing categorical information and trends together in combination charts

The **combination chart** visualization combines bar and line charts in one plot, allowing you to visualize categorical information and trends alongside one another. It might be viable to plot multiple lines or multiple bars, side by side, and that is indeed possible to do with a combination chart, but the contrast in visualization type can often provide a more striking comparison.

The **Pareto** chart, named after Vilfredo Pareto, and used extensively in Lean Six Sigma, is a classic example of a combination chart, where individual values are represented in descending order by bars, and the cumulative total is represented by a line. Let's construct a Pareto chart.

The data that's used here is `ParetoData.xlsx`, which you can download from `https://community.tibco.com/wiki/tibco-spotfire-primer-sample-data`.

Alternatively, use this shortened link: `http://bit.ly/2Vhfy3K`.

The Pareto data file contains some fictitious results for a survey asking why a website would drop down on search engine rankings. The results consist of nine ranked reasons and a corresponding citation count. After loading this data into Spotfire, we can create a Pareto chart in very little time by following these steps:

1. As a prerequisite, create a `Rank-Reason` hierarchy (with Rank as the highest level in the hierarchy and Reason as the next level) to put the reasons in order of importance. We'll use this hierarchy to create a cumulative sum using an OVER function.

2. Now, create a `Combination Chart` by clicking on the combination chart icon in the visualization flyout. Set the *x*-axis to the `Rank-Reason` hierarchy, and use the following custom expression for the *y*-axis (you can do this by right-clicking on the *y*-axis selector and choosing **Custom Expression...**):

```
Sum([Citations]) as [Citations], Sum([Citations]) OVER
AllPrevious([Axis.X]) as [Cumulative Sum]
```

Note that this custom expression creates two series as it's effectively two custom expressions, separated by a comma. Spotfire doesn't know how to separate these series on the combination chart yet, so you will get an error message to the effect that you need to use **(Column Names)** on the *x*-axis or to series or trellis by it. This is expected and will be fixed in the steps that follow.

3. From the legend, drop down the **Series by:** selector and choose **(Column Names)**. You'll notice that the two y-axis entries you have made are now represented as bar charts.

4. Click the bars icon for the **Cumulative Sum** in the legend and change the series to show line type. You can also change the colors that are assigned to each series (if you wish!):

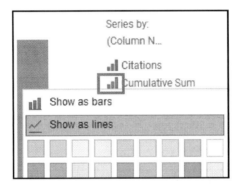

5. Open the visualization properties and, in the **Appearance** property page, select the option to show line markers. While you're there, I recommend that you increase the marker size and the line width a bit.

6. Now, insert a horizontal line equal to the 80% level of citations. Go to the **Lines & Curves** property page, check the **Horizontal Line** entry, and edit it to be a custom expression: `0.8*Max([Y])`. Give the line a custom name (80%) and make that label display on the chart by clicking the **Label and Tooltip...** button in the **Lines & Curves** property and checking **Label for Curve name**:

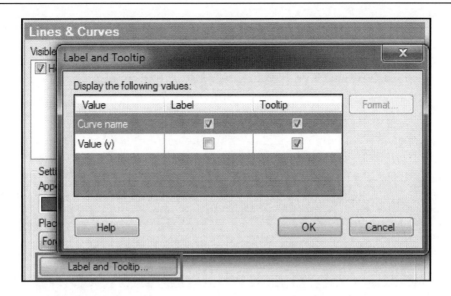

7. Finally, I recommend that you hide the *y*-axis scale labels—this can be done from the axis itself or from the *y*-axis property page.
   The chart visualizes the Pareto principle, or the 80/20 rule: ignore anything beyond the point at which the cumulative sum crosses the 80% line and focus on the things before that point. It's basically the law of diminishing returns. You should end up with something that looks like this:

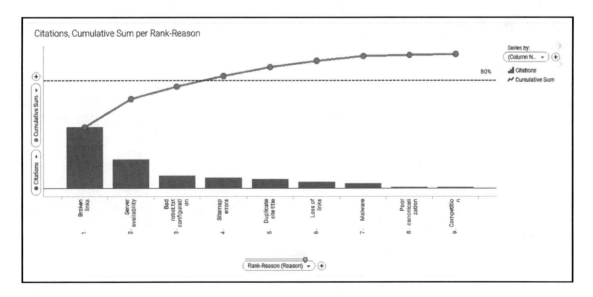

Do note, however, that the data in this example has been normalized so that both the reason and citations appear on the same scale and can share the same *y*-axis. Spotfire does have the ability to use an individual scale for each series, but it cannot mix and match individual series together on shared scales.

In the real world, it is likely that both series have different scales, so you may wish to normalize your data. Normalizing the data hides the absolute values but preserves the relationships in the data. This is why I have hidden the scale labels on the *y*-axis. I would recommend combining this visualization with another that shows the absolute values by way of a details visualization.

You can perform normalization using Spotfire's transformation methods.

Visualizing complex multidimensional data using heat maps

The **heat map** visualization is actually two visualizations in one. At a basic level, it is a simple heat map, which we will get to shortly; at a more advanced level, it is also a dendrogram, or tree-structured graph.

Heat maps

A heat map is very similar in concept to a cross table, or even just a spreadsheet, except instead of numbers, each cell is configured to display a color that reflects an underlying number. It provides a very intuitive representation of the relative values of complex multidimensional data. Compare the following visualizations (a cross table and a heat map) of monthly temperatures for a selection of American states. They are equivalent, except that one shows the actual temperatures in °C and the other shows a heat map to represent the temperatures:

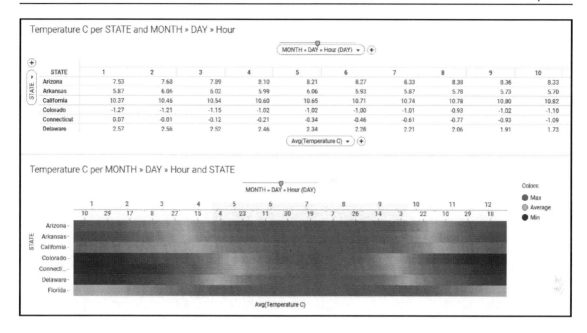

Temperature C per STATE and MONTH » DAY » Hour

MONTH » DAY » Hour (DAY)

STATE	1	2	3	4	5	6	7	8	9	10
Arizona	7.53	7.68	7.89	8.10	8.21	8.27	8.33	8.38	8.36	8.33
Arkansas	5.87	6.06	6.02	5.99	6.06	5.93	5.87	5.78	5.73	5.70
California	10.37	10.46	10.54	10.60	10.65	10.71	10.74	10.78	10.80	10.82
Colorado	-1.27	-1.21	-1.15	-1.02	-1.02	-1.00	-1.01	-0.93	-1.02	-1.10
Connecticut	0.07	-0.01	-0.12	-0.21	-0.34	-0.46	-0.61	-0.77	-0.93	-1.09
Delaware	2.57	2.56	2.52	2.46	2.34	2.28	2.21	2.06	1.91	1.73

Avg(Temperature C)

Temperature C per MONTH » DAY » Hour and STATE

I think you'll agree that the heat map shows the temperature data so much better!

Let's look at how to configure this heat map in Spotfire. For this exercise, we're going to use hourly normal temperature data downloaded from the United States' National Climatic Data Center (http://www.ncdc.noaa.gov/cdo-web). This data, which was collected across almost 10,000 stations from the period of 1981-2010, is not immediately usable. The temperatures (in Fahrenheit) have been entered as strings without decimal points and include flags. The station ID is given but not its location or name, and the data is in a wide format, with a column for each hour of the day, which makes it difficult to manipulate those temperature strings into numbers and convert to °C (which is how I like to look at temperature).

We need to download some additional information to cross-reference the station IDs to station names and states; we have to unpivot the data into a long, skinny form, with a single temperature column and multiple rows for the hours of the day; and finally, we have to manipulate the temperature strings to get them into numbers we can use. All this is mentioned in passing to illustrate the importance of data manipulation and transformation in the task of creating visualizations. Fortunately, you won't need to do any of this, and the final dataset (HourlyTemperatures.sbdf), which has more than 2 million rows, is available for download (as a .zip file) from the following link:

https://community.tibco.com/wiki/tibco-spotfire-primer-sample-data.

Alternatively, use this shortened link:
`http://bit.ly/2Vhfy3K`.

1. Load the temperature data into an analysis file.
2. Create a hierarchy for MONTH, DAY, and HOUR in that order.
3. Add a new heat map visualization.
4. Configure each of the axes of the visualization, as follows:
   - **X-axis**: The **MONTH >> DAY >> HOUR** hierarchy
   - **Y-axis**: **STATE**
   - **Value axis**: **Avg(Temperature C)**—of course, you may choose the Fahrenheit column if you like

   The *x*- and *y*-axes are the variables that will frame the heat map, with the *x*-axis representing the horizontal axis (the columns) and the *y*-axis the vertical axis (the rows). The cell values are the numbers that will determine the colors in the map.

5. Now, configure the colors via the legend or via the **Colors** property page if you wish. The default color scheme is a red-light blue-blue, where gray is the average, and red and blue are the maximum and minimum, respectively. The default color scheme actually works pretty well in this case anyway.

The result is the representation of a lot of data in a pretty coherent pattern of color. You can clearly see seasonal patterns and differences between states. For example, we can observe why Florida is called the "Sunshine State." See how it's hotter for longer in the year but doesn't get as cold as Georgia in the winter:

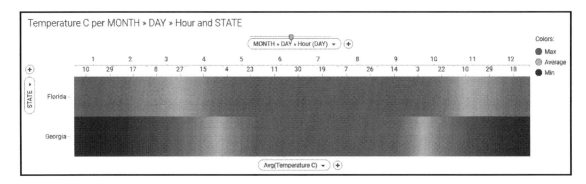

Now, look at the pattern for 9th January:

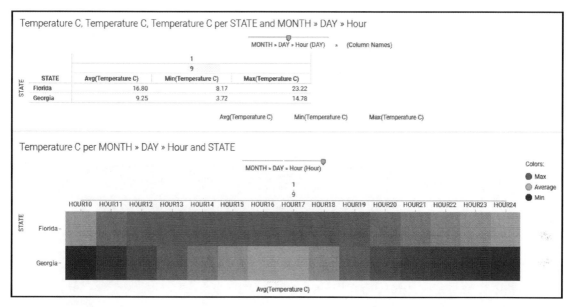

I prefer warmer weather, so I know where I'd rather be on that day! Also, notice that the heat map colors always reflect the current range of data in the visualization, so they are always relative to each other.

Finally, the fact that the heat map always shows relative values is important. In order that we can observe the absolute values, it can often be useful to represent the absolute values in another visualization alongside the heat map (or any other visualization that shows relative values only). For this purpose, I have added the **Min** and **Max** temperatures to the cross table and shown it in the previous example.

Dendrograms

A dendrogram is a tree-structured graph that can be added to a heat map to show hierarchical clustering. Spotfire offers a pretty advanced suite of clustering methods, distance measures, and other settings, including the option to import a dendrogram from a previous cluster calculation. It's beyond the scope of this book to explore these options, but the inline help in Spotfire is comprehensive.

We'll use the basic settings to illustrate the power and analytical beauty of a good dendrogram:

1. Open the visualization properties of the heat map you've already created, and select the **Dendrograms** page.
2. We're going to do a row-based clustering analysis on the states, so select **Row dendrogram** in the **Settings for:** dropdown and check the **Show row dendrogram** checkbox. If you want to verify or explore the settings for the **Calculated hierarchical clustering**, click on the **Settings...** button.
3. Select the option to update the dendrogram automatically:

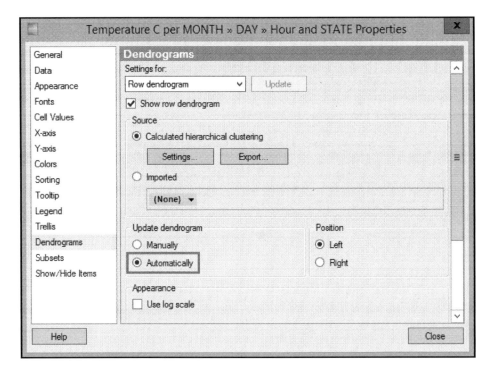

Due to the fact that some advanced calculations are being performed on the data, using automatic update may take a while with some datasets.

When you return to the heat map and reset any filters, you should see a very different picture, with the states organized into hierarchical clusters. You'll probably want a zoom slider to zoom in on areas of interest:

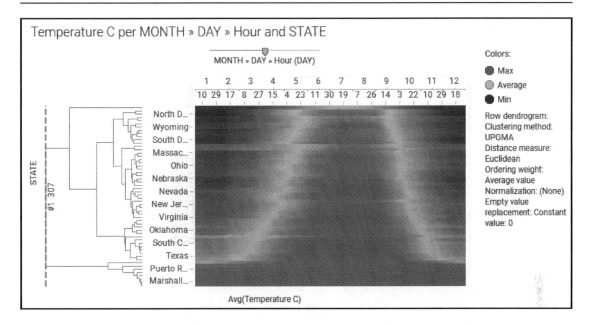

You can navigate this hierarchy by selecting individual nodes within it. There is a major early fork in the hierarchy, and if we take a close look at a *hot* fork, we can see how easy it is to navigate the dendrogram. We can select the part of the tree that contains the very hottest states within the US territories:

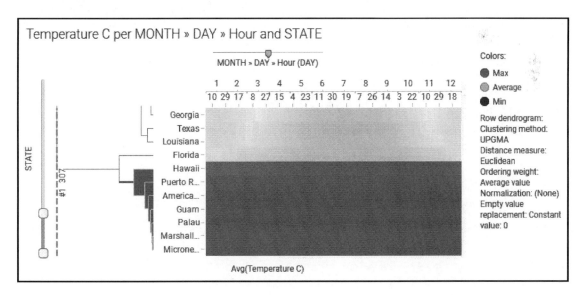

This shows that the hottest states all have very similar patterns of temperature.

 Selecting the dendrogram has the effect of marking the data that falls within the cluster that makes up that part of the tree.

The dendrogram is a useful tool for data mining and the discovery of patterns in large datasets, and Spotfire provides a rich suite of options for doing this type of analysis.

Profiling your data using parallel coordinate plots

The **parallel coordinate plot** visualization is used to compare a set of potentially diverse and unrelated properties that can nevertheless be attached to a themed series. A typical example would be comparing the specifications of a selection of desktop computers. The properties can be anything from keyboard color to processor speed, but they all apply to each PC in our selection.

The columns in a parallel coordinate plot are the properties we want to include, and their values, whether numbers or text, are normalized based on the value for numbers and an inferred value for strings based on natural string ordering. This normalization is the key to a parallel coordinate plot because it allows us to compare quantitative and qualitative information in the same plot. For example, if you include keyboard color and price in a comparison of 10 PCs, the color furthest down the sort order would be assigned the value of 100%, as would the highest price. The columns are plotted on the *x*-axis, and a line is created for each item in the series, showing how it compares with other items at each property point:

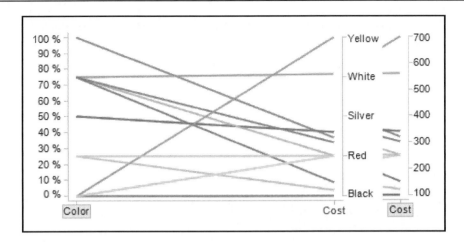

This type of plot is probably not appropriate for a high-level, executive presentation as it requires some explanation. It is fundamentally an interactive visualization for finding patterns in multivariate data, rather than a dashboarding or data analysis visualization.

It might look like a line chart, but there is no sequence or independent variable, that is, there is no timeline. In the very simple PC example, you could choose a color and then see the prices available or choose a price and see the colors available. The line running from color 0% (black) to cost 100% (700) is *not* a trend—it's just two unrelated comparison points.

Now, let's work through a more substantial example to demonstrate the configuration and use of a parallel coordinate plot.

In order to follow this example properly, please reopen the first example we worked on in the chapter, showing the Harmonized Indices of Consumer Prices. We will use it to create a parallel coordinates plot:

1. Add a parallel coordinate plot using the visualization pullout.
2. Make sure that the **Main data table** is selected.
3. Open the plot's visualization properties and go to the **Columns** page. From there, select the 12 price categories as columns, leaving behind **Country**, **Geographical Classification**, and **Eurozone Classification**.
4. Go to the **Colors** property and select **Country** as the column to color by. The **Line By** property should be left as **(Row Number)**.

5. Add three table visualizations alongside the main plot: one for the main
   `EurostatHICP` table but showing only the country, one for the `Geographical`
   table, and one for the `Eurozone` table. We will use these tables to interact with
   the parallel coordinate plot:

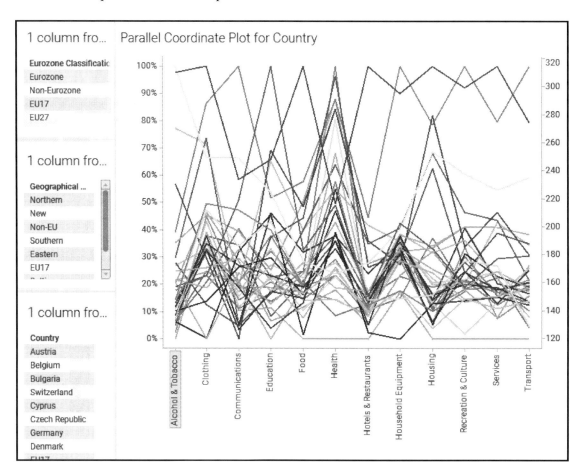

What does this visualization show? A lot of countries have experienced an increase in health prices, and we can perhaps discern a reasonably coherent bunch of countries toward the bottom of the plot, but that's about as much as you can glean through simple inspection.

However, we can interact with the plot using the left-hand tables to select items of interest, either individual countries or one of the classifications we've created. Select **Eurozone** in the **Eurozone** list. You can see that the **Eurozone** countries show a fairly consistent pattern except for Latvia and Estonia—identify them by hovering over the lines and using the tooltip:

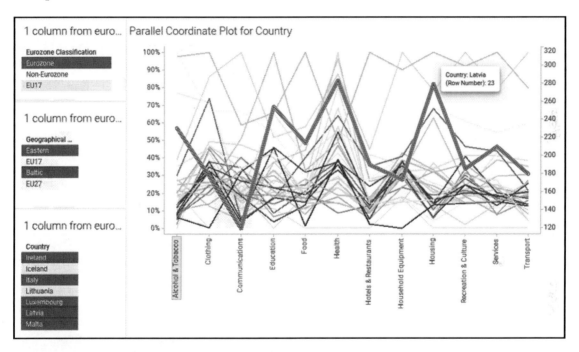

Latvia and **Estonia** have experienced relatively higher price increases in certain categories than the rest of the zone.

If you add in the other **Baltic** state, **Lithuania**, which is not in the **Eurozone**, you will see a common **Baltic** pattern:

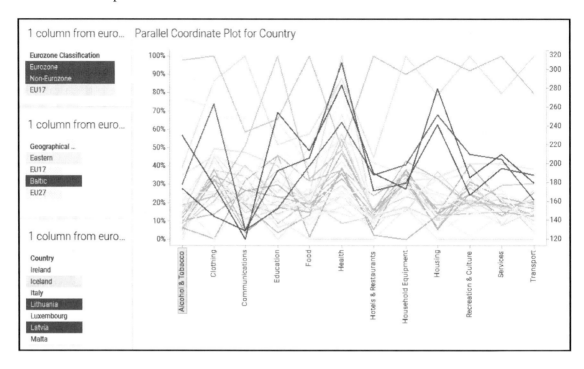

Interestingly, it's also evident that the Baltic countries have experienced the lowest inflation in communication costs in the entire dataset, which includes some non-EU countries and the United States.

We could go on for a while in this vein exploring patterns in the data. Once you have completed your exploration using a parallel coordinates plot, you would probably create a guided, interactive dashboard and some companion visualizations to present your conclusions, based on what you have found.

Summary

In this chapter, we have covered some more key concepts and a few visualization types that haven't been shown in other chapters. By now, you should have a good understanding of data relationships and also started to understand how to use some basic statistical capabilities within Spotfire.

Together, we have explored data table relations and column matches. We've also looked at some more key analytic capabilities within Spotfire-show/hide, subsets, reference lines, fitted curves, and forecasting. Remember that show/hide allows you to show or hide various parts of your data. Subsets allow you to compare different subsets as an alternative to trellising. Recall that subsets combined with filtering and marking are much more flexible than trellising. Fitted curves and forecasting are excellent tools for smoothing data and looking into the future, respectively.

Visualization-wise, we explored the combination chart and used it to superimpose categorical information and trends; we spent some time looking at the heat map and its companion, the dendrogram hierarchical clustering engine. The heat map and dendrogram are powerful tools for visualizing complex multidimensional data. Finally, we looked at the parallel coordinate plot as a good tool for exploring patterns in multidimensional data.

I'm really looking forward to the next chapter as it will be showing you how to use Spotfire's map chart visualization. It's one of the most powerful and flexible visualization types within Spotfire. The topic of map charts could fill an entire book on its own!

What's Your Location?

9

The first eight chapters of this book have shown you how powerful data visualization can be! We are all used to using **Geographic Information Systems (GIS)** such as Google Maps. It is much easier to give directions using an interactive map than using text instructions, and the language is universal. If you stretch your imagination just a little, you will also quickly realize that you don't have to confine your analysis to geographic locations. Any spatial context—a semiconductor wafer containing silicon chips, an MRI scan, an airport terminal—can all be mapped and combined with other data to perform spatial analytics.

In this chapter, will take a close look at the **map chart** visualization. You will learn how to use Spotfire's spatial analytics capabilities to overlay data on images and multi-layered maps, putting spatial and geographic contexts on your analyses. Along the way, you will learn about some important GIS concepts such as coordinate reference systems and geocoding.

The map chart is one of the most intuitive visualizations in Spotfire because it connects directly with our inherent spatial awareness. This is as close as it gets to representing data in a native human form.

In this chapter, we will cover the following topics:

- Map chart layers
- Getting started with map charts
- Coordinate reference systems
- Using geocoding to position data on a map
- Feature layers
- Using a data function to assist with geocoding
- Adding Web Map Service data to a map chart
- Creating custom maps using Tile Map Service layers
- Using the map chart for non-geographic spatial analysis
- TIBCO GeoAnalytics

Map chart layers

Spotfire's **map chart** visualization is a multi-layered visualization. Within a map chart, you can have multiple layers, all shown together. You can have more than one of each type of layer—the only limits are the memory and processing capability of your machine and the eventual complexity of the chart.

Map charts can have layers of the following types:

- **Map layer**: This is the default layer that' screated whenever you add a map chart visualization to your analysis.
- **TMS layer**: The **Tile Map Service** layer, for displaying map backgrounds as tiles—in fact, Spotfire uses TMS for its own default map layers. There are all sorts of things you can show with TMS layers, such as custom maps, satellite imagery, traffic information, and much more.
- **WMS layer**: The **Web Map Service** layer. A WMS can serve all sorts of features (such as bitmaps) or vector graphics such as points, lines, curves, and text. The output from a WMS can be displayed on a map chart. Examples might be geological information or weather information.
- **Marker layer**: Marker layers are a bit like scatter plot layers on a map chart, except the positioning of the markers is done by a coordinate reference system, not with x- and y-axes.
- **Feature layer**: Feature layers are defined by shapes and represent regions on a map chart.
- **Image layer**: Shows an image on the map chart—you can place markers on an image layer to represent all kinds of spatial analytics, such as traffic flow through an airport terminal, or chips on a semiconductor wafer.

It's extremely important to know that you can only interact with one layer at a time with a map chart; that is, you can only mark data in the interactive layer. You can set the interactive layer from the layers control in the map chart or from the map chart properties.

Getting started with map charts

When you create a map chart, a background map layer is created as a default base layer. The map chart will also be created with a marker layer that represents the current data you have loaded in your analysis. Spotfire will automatically choose which columns to visualize on the marker layer.

The map layer will be blank if you are not connected to the internet, as the tiles for the map layer are retrieved over the web.

Navigating the map chart is similar to any other online mapping tool, with zooming and panning via a tool pallet. You can also zoom in by double-clicking on the map chart or zoom in and out using the scroll-wheel on your mouse.

A map chart in Spotfire is an interactive visualization, just like all the others, so to support panning and zooming and marking data, it has **panning** and **marking** modes.

In panning mode, you can zoom in and out by using the mouse, drag the map to reposition it, and much more. In marking mode, clicking and dragging the mouse marks data just like any other Spotfire visualization. When covering marking in map visualizations, we will be looking at the various marking options—rectangular, circular, and lasso. All of these are useful in different circumstances.

Here is a sample map chart—I have loaded some Airbnb data for New York. Spotfire automatically places the markers on the map, as the data has latitude and longitude columns. Additionally, I have configured the map chart to show size and color by **Avg(price)** and set the drawing order to be by **Avg(price)** in order to show the most expensive properties on top:

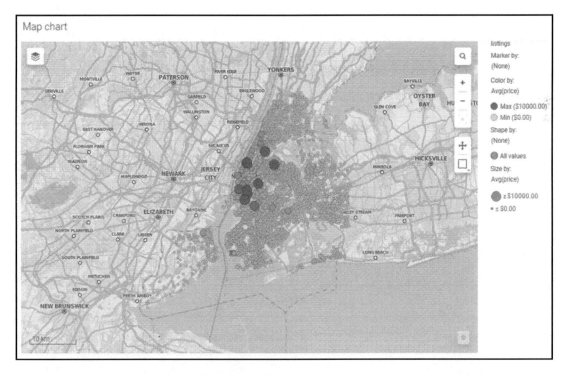

Look at the **Marker by** setting of the marker layer—it shows **(None)**. This means that no aggregation is being performed—one marker represents a single row in the data, that is, a single property. However, all the axes, other than those used for positioning markers, must use an aggregation method, even if no aggregation appears to be necessary (as in this case, since each marker represents a single row). I have chosen **Avg** because **Avg** will continue to work just fine if we do want to perform some kind of aggregation later on.

We will use the Airbnb data to experiment with the map chart, so go ahead and download a sample dataset—you can get the data from here:

```
http://insideAirbnb.com/get-the-data.html
```

Alternatively, you can get it from here:

```
http://bit.ly/2VlRRr5
```

The Airbnb data is pretty comprehensive—it is divided by major cities into manageable chunks. Please download a `listings.csv.gz` data file for a city of your choice. I recommend that you choose New York, as it's what I'll be using to demonstrate this example, but if you fancy a challenge, choose a different city! Let's get started:

1. Before we start building the map chart, let's look at how Spotfire has categorized the columns. Open the data panel.
2. First of all, look at the columns categorized by **CURRENCY**:

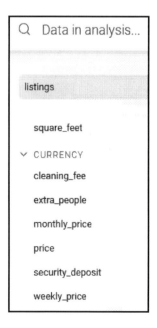

3. Spotfire has automatically categorized the currency columns—initially, I was skeptical about the `extra_people` column, but looking at the data, it does appear to contain currency information—it looks as if it is the fee for extra people to stay in the accommodation.

4. Now, look at the **TIME** columns:

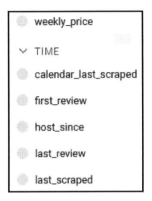

Yes—that looks about right!

5. Finally, let's look at the **LOCATION** columns. These are the most important when it comes to map charts (obviously):

Spotfire can use all of these columns to place markers on the map chart—we will look at the different ways of using the columns later on in this example—from absolute positioning to geocoding, along with fixing some real-world data issues along the way.

Of course, if Spotfire has miscategorized any columns, we can fix this at any point in time, as we covered in `Chapter 1`, *Welcome to Spotfire*.

There are two ways we could create the map chart—either we could add the map chart and then configure it manually, or we could use Spotfire's AI-driven recommender. The Airbnb data contains latitude and longitude for each of its listed rental properties. Using latitude and longitude will give accurate positioning on the map, and we will be using these to construct the first map.

You have to be using a fairly recent version of Spotfire X in order for it to show the relationship between latitude and longitude in the AI recommender, so you can either follow this example to see how this functionality works, or you can just create a map chart manually. Adding a new map chart manually will position the markers correctly, but I want to highlight the AI-driven recommender's capabilities in this area. We can follow these steps:

1. First of all, click the **price** column in the data panel.
2. If you are using an Analyst client, Spotfire will have already mined the data relationships for us—**bedrooms & cleaning_fee** are the strongest driver of price:

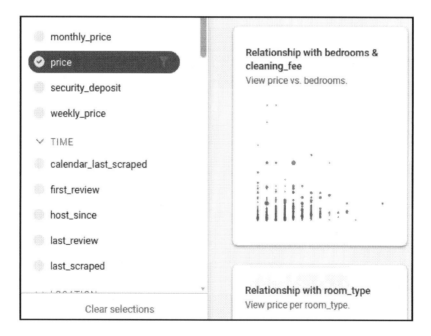

If you are using a web-based client, you won't get the AI-powered recommendations, so please follow this example in its entirety. You'll need to manually select associated columns rather than letting the **AI-Powered Recommendations** feature choose them for you.

3. We are interested in building a map chart, so scroll through the list of recommendations until you get to the first map chart. You should see something that looks like this:

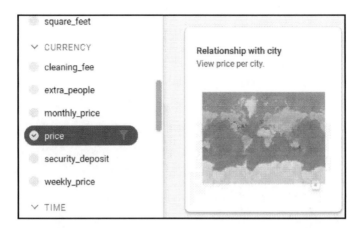

Oh dear! That doesn't look quite right, does it? I thought all the data was supposed to be in New York. This is an issue with geocoding (and with reality, actually, as city names are not unique across the globe). Spotfire doesn't know that the data should be restricted to New York City. Don't worry about what geocoding is at the moment—it will be covered later on in this chapter.

4. Continue to scroll down through the list of recommended visualizations until you get to the relationship with longitude and latitude (it's quite a long way down the list):

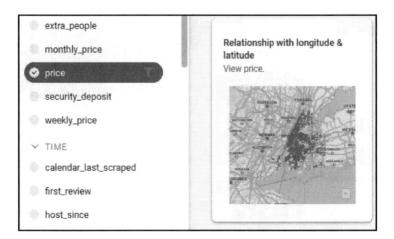

5. Add the map chart to your analysis. If you are using a web-based client, you can select price and latitude and longitude in the data panel—the same visualization recommendation will be shown.

6. Now that we have the map chart, we can start configuring it! Using the legend, adjust the size by and color by axes to show **Avg(price)**. Change the default colors too, if you like.

7. Setting the drawing order requires a little more work—we will need to edit the settings for the marker layer. To do this, click the layers icon in the map chart and right-click the **listings** layer to bring up the **Layer Settings** button:

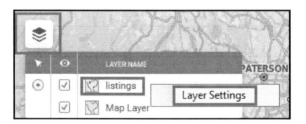

 The appearance of the layers button has changed in very recent versions of Spotfire—it will either look like this, or a gray box with the word **Layers** in it.

8. Click the button to open the settings for the marker layer.

9. Navigate to the **Drawing Order** property page and set the drawing order to be by **Avg(price)**:

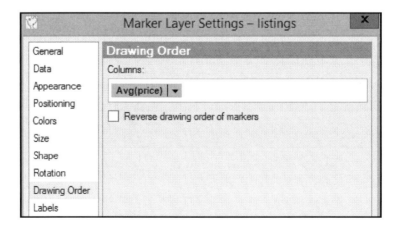

10. Close the dialog. Note that if you are using a web-based client, you can still set the drawing order by clicking the cog wheel in the top-right corner of the map chart and selecting the listings marker layer, or by right-clicking on the chart and choosing **Properties**.

11. You should end up with a map chart that looks pretty much like the example that was shown at the start of this section.

By following this example, we have seen how Spotfire shows map charts in the recommender and how it can identify relationships between a target column and location columns. Along the way, did you notice that the configuration for the marker layer looks very similar to the configuration for a scatter plot? That's because it is broadly similar—in fact, as we mentioned previously, the marker layer is analogous to a scatter plot, but the markers are positioned according to a coordinate reference system in the map chart.

Coordinate reference systems

Coordinate reference systems are used to project the three-dimensional Earth onto two-dimensional maps. There are many such models for expressing locations on Earth in a coordinate system. Spotfire supports more than you can ever hope to need, but the geocoding data tables provided by Spotfire are expressed in the coordinate reference system EPSG:4326 - WGS84, which we will use for all the geographic examples in this chapter. Don't worry about what this means for now; you can always go and look it up later.

Using geocoding to position data on a map

The Airbnb data contains location information in the form of latitude and longitude. This is very helpful for positioning the markers on the map. We can produce a marker for each property in exactly its location on the map. However, what if we wanted to aggregate the data by zip code or we didn't have a latitude and longitude in the data? That's where geocoding comes in. It's a way of translating a textual location into a latitude and longitude for positioning on a map.

We'll be using the zip code for geocoding in the first instance—it works reasonably well. Then, we'll start to experiment with the city. This is a lot more tricky, as the cities are not unique names globally and the cities have all been entered by hand. Ultimately, the positioning can only be as good as the underlying data allows.

A set of default geocoding hierarchies is provided with TIBCO Spotfire Server as a ZIP file. A library administrator can import this file into the library and make the geocoding files available to users (instructions can be found in TIBCO's server installation documentation). You can also load these geocoding files manually into an analysis file, or you can provide a third-party file. To do any geocoding, you must have a geocoding file from some source.

Geocoding using a zip code

Follow along with me as we explore creating a map chart that uses geocoding to position markers by zip code. If you're using a Spotfire web client, you'll be able to carry out similar steps and achieve the same end result, but I am going to focus on the Analyst client in this example:

1. Create a new page and add a map chart to the page. Spotfire applies default settings to the chart, including positioning the markers by latitude and longitude. We've already seen how that looks, so I haven't included a screenshot here.
2. Like before, set the **Color by**, **Size by**, and drawing order axes to **Avg(price)**. Alternatively, you could duplicate the original map chart we created earlier (right-click it) and drag it to the new page.
3. Open the settings for the marker layer and navigate to the **Positioning** page. Notice how Spotfire has automatically chosen longitude and latitude for the positioning:

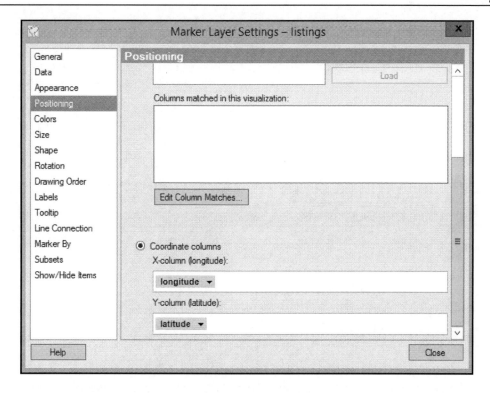

4. We are going to use a zip code for geocoding, so scroll back up to the top of the property page and choose **Geocoding** and select the `zipcode` column:

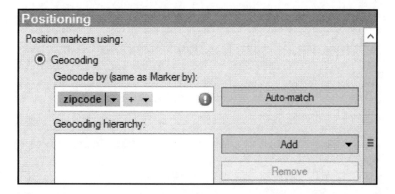

Notice the red warning symbol. If you hover over it, it will show that no geocoding tables have been specified. Let's fix that!

5. Click **Auto-match**.

6. Spotfire automatically recognizes that we have a zip-code column and so it will load the **USA Zip Codes** geocoding table. It will also automatically match the zip-code column in the data to the zip-code column in the geocoding table:

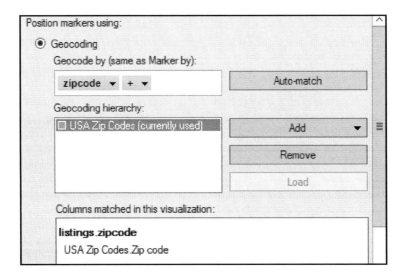

This is another example of column matching that was first introduced in Chapter 8, *The World is Your Visualization*. You can see that column matching is essential in this case and is a great application of using data from multiple data tables. Behind the scenes, Spotfire has loaded a built-in geocoding table and uses it to translate ther zip code into latitude and longitude to position the markers on the map.

Spotfire's geocoding tables are supplied with the Spotfire Server distribution on https://edelivery.tibco.com. If geocoding doesn't work at all for you, you'll need to contact your server administrator in order to get the geocoding tables loaded into your server's library.

7. Close the visualization properties dialog. You'll probably find that Spotfire will zoom out to show the whole of the US rather than focusing on New York:

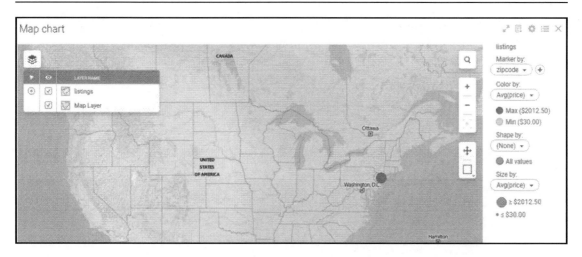

Why has Spotfire zoomed out to show the whole country? Because there are some issues in the data—it's a bit hard to spot, but there is one marker in southern California and there's another (potentially) rogue marker in the very eastern end of New York State. This suggests that there are some incorrect zip codes in the data. No matter—we can just exclude this data from our analysis by following these steps:

1. Using the panning and zooming capabilities in the map chart, zoom into New York City. If clicking and dragging the map doesn't pan it, you'll need to place the map in Panning mode by clicking the panning mode control:

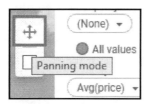

2. Now, mark all the data in the New York area. Before we can do this, we need to switch the map chart into marking mode by clicking the Marking mode control:

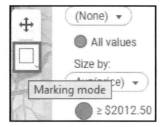

There are three different marking modes that you can use with a map chart—**rectangle** marking, **lasso** marking, and **radius** marking. Rectangle is the default and is the same as all other Spotfire visualizations. Lasso allows you to mark arbitrary areas on the map. Radius marking uses a circular shape for marking points on the map.

3. Right-click on the map chart and choose **Marked rows**, then **Filter to**:

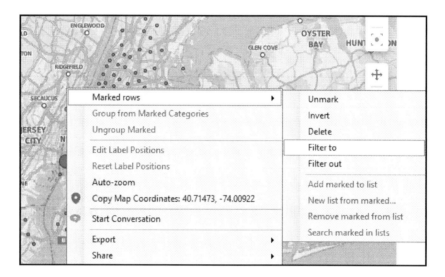

4. If you like, you can also click the Zoom to filtered items control to re-center the map:

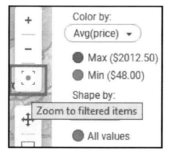

5. Great! Now, we have a map chart that shows just the markers that belong in the New York City area. They are grouped by zip code.

By grouping (and thus aggregating) by zip code, we have produced a marker for each individual zip code and so we are able to see where the higher-priced properties are located. There's a huge marker that's definitely the outlier—if you zoom in, you'll see that it's located right near the World Trade Center. This is unsurprising!

Case study – when geocoding doesn't work

Let's do some more work with geocoding. Remember when we got started that the recommended visualization for price versus city was not as expected? There were markers dotted all over the globe! We know this isn't right, but it's not Spotfire's fault. Its default geocoding that's been applied at a global level. As we mentioned previously, city names are not globally unique. The default Spotfire geocoding will prioritize cities based on their population or perform the best match it possibly can with the available data.

We can look into this and attempt some better geocoding using the `city` column. However, I need to disclose a spoiler at this stage: I wasn't successful! As it turns out, I discovered that the `city` column isn't properly coded—it's just manually entered information and contains lots of mistakes. Secondly, the geocoding tables don't match the data at the right level of city.

Even though I wasn't successful, I 'd like to take you through the process—it's a useful lesson and illustrates some more ways to use geocoding in Spotfire, and there are some great hints and tips for column-matching along the way:

1. Duplicate an existing map chart and move it to a new page.
2. Visit the **Positioning property** page for the marker layer.
3. Adjust the geocoding to geocode by city.
4. Click **Auto-match**.

5. Close the configuration dialog. You should end up with a map chart that looks like this. I have highlighted the warning triangle next to the chart title:

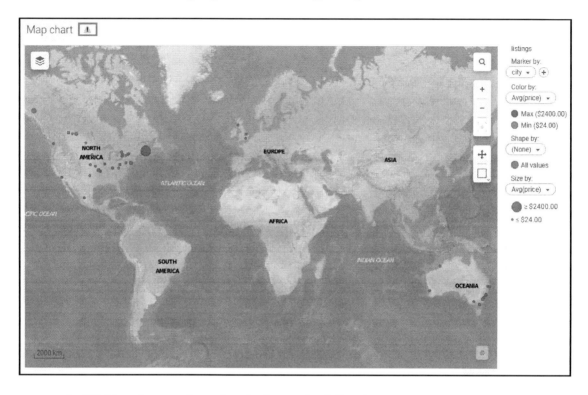

6. Clicking the warning triangle shows the following:

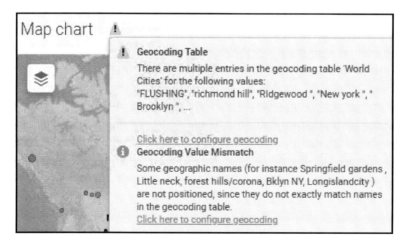

7. Spotfire knows there's a problem with the geocoding. Let's see how much of this we can fix! Click to configure the geocoding and let's continue where we left off...

8. First of all, remove the World Cities geocoding table. Remove any existing **Geocode by** settings.

9. Now, set geocoding to be by state, then city:

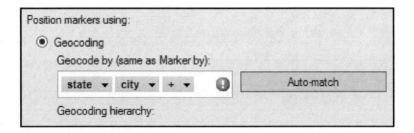

10. Next, manually add a new geocoding table by dropping down the **Add** button. Choose the **USA Cities** table:

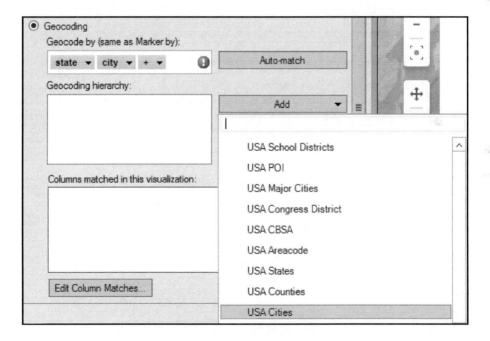

11. Happily, in my case, Spotfire automatically matched the columns that best match the columns in the Airbnb data. If you find that it hasn't, you'll need to edit the column matches and set them like this:

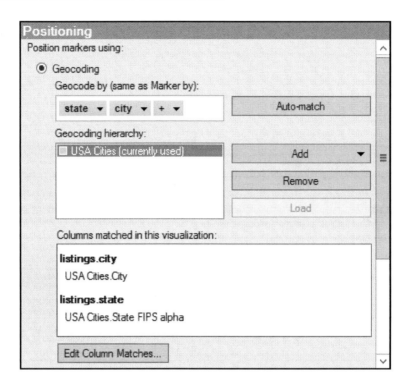

 In order to apply the `Upper(Trim([Value])` expression, you'll need to right-click the expression and choose **Custom expression....**

We also need to set the column match for state as follows:

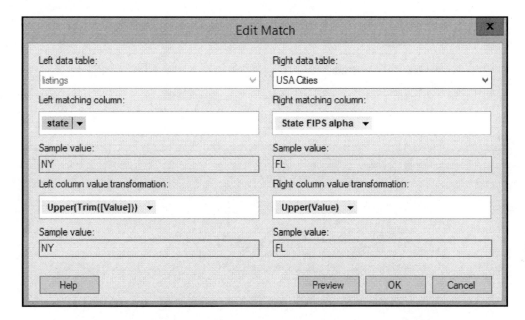

The column matches settings that are shown here are pretty interesting—consider what's going on for a moment: Spotfire's geocoding tables are "clean" in that each value is known to be correct. There are no leading or trailing spaces in the names of the cities or state codes, and they are all consistently and correctly spelled and capitalized. However, the Airbnb data is not so clean, so we need to apply the Upper and Trim functions to the city and state columns in order to give matching the best chance it can. Upper converts the textual data into upper case; Trim removes any leading or trailing spaces. We also apply the Upper function to the City and State columns in the geocoding table to make sure that the capitalization is consistent between the matches.

12. Let's return to the map chart. Yours should look similar to this:

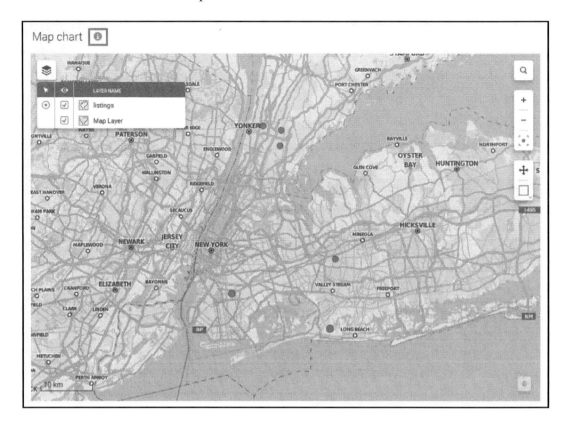

Note that I have highlighted the blue information icon next to the title this time. I also adjusted the marker size so that the markers were a bit more prominent on the chart.

13. So, now that we have got geocoding that's not in an error state, what does the warning tell us? Click on the icon to see. This is what Spotfire reports in my case:

Spotfire is telling us that some of the values do not exactly match the names in the geocoding table, so the markers cannot be positioned on the map. Of course, this makes sense, as Spotfire cannot map the locations to their latitude and longitude if the locations do not exist in the geocoding table.

Unfortunately, there's not much more we can do with geocoding the city data—as we mentioned previously, the names of the cities are rather dirty in the original data and so they don't match the cities in the geocoding table. We could look at other columns in the data—it does appear that neighborhood is better coded in the Airbnb data, but I discovered that the Spotfire geocoding tables don't go to the level of neighborhood, so it's better to stick with geocoding by zip code at this stage.

For me, even though this attempt was unsuccessful, this was still a useful exercise. Exploring the geocoding options was very interesting. As always, every day is a day of learning!

After I wrote this part of this chapter, I did have a brainwave and was ultimately successful after using some advanced Spotfire functionality—I will cover how performed this and show you through the working solution after introducing the topic of feature layers.

Feature layers

Feature layers use **shapefiles** to represent features such as countries, rivers, and cities as vector-based polygons, lines, or points. Shapefiles are embedded as binary objects in a geocoding table, where they are linked to topological information such as map coordinates. The polygons, lines, and points can be filled with color. They behave similar to markers on a map, allowing you to select a state outline, for example.

Some of Spotfire's geocoding tables contain geometries that represent the various areas coded within them. They should be the first port of call when adding geometries to a map chart.

There are also many free online sources for downloading shapefiles. If an existing shapefile doesn't meet your needs, it is also possible to manipulate and create new shapefiles using a variety of free and paid software.

By way of a simple example, let's add a feature layer to the hourly temperature data that we first saw in Chapter 8, *The World is Your Visualization*. As you may recall, we used the data to create a heat map. This time, we will represent the data on a map chart. We'll do this by adding a feature layer and then using Spotfire's column-matching feature to color the features by average temperature.

Reopen the `Hourly temperatures` file and follow along:

1. Create a new map chart using the standard map and open the visualization properties dialog. The map chart won't place the markers in the correct place, but don't worry about that for now.
2. Select the **Layers** page.
3. Using the **Add** dropdown, choose **Feature Layer**, then **USA**, then **USA States**:

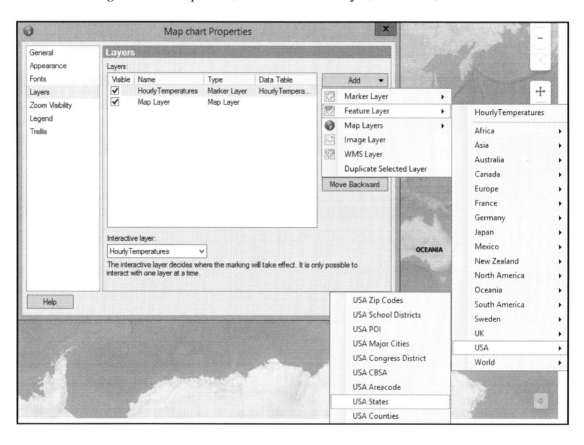

4. Now, visit the **Geocoding** page and choose **Feature by**: **State**:

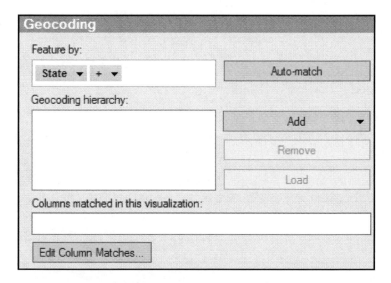

5. Next, visit the **Colors** page and set the color columns to **Avg(Temperature C)** from the **HourlyTemperatures** data table. Make sure that you choose the **HourlyTemperatures** data table before selecting the **Temperature** column:

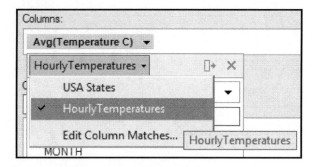

Of course, you could choose the degrees Fahrenheit column if you wish! Now, choose a suitable color scheme or design your own.

As a side note, you can always save a color scheme as a document color scheme or a library item or file so that you can reuse the color scheme again in other visualizations. You can also apply a default color scheme to a column (by right-clicking on the column in the data panel and choosing **Column Properties**, then entering the name of the scheme in the **DefaultContiniuousColorScheme** or **DefaultCategoricalColorScheme** property).

6. For now, hide the `HourlyTemperatures` layer from the map chart. Do this by deselecting it from the **Layers** page in the visualization properties, or from the **Layers** control on the chart.

You should now have a map of the United States with each state outlined, selectable, and colored by the average temperature for that state, which will look like the following screenshot:

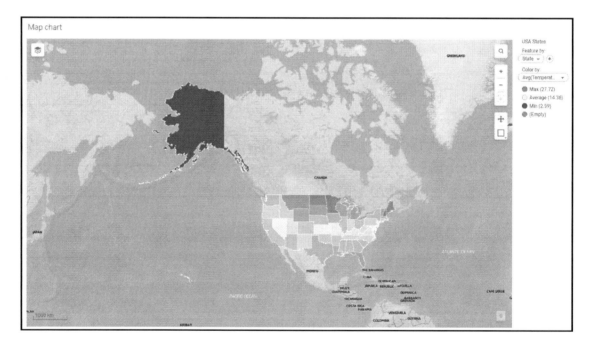

If the example didn't work, it means that the column-matching failed. We can check the column-matching and make sure it's correct—we can also improve the robustness of the column-matching by using Spotfire's built-in expressions. Let's check the column matches:

1. Return to the **Feature Layer Settings** for the **USA States**.
2. Navigate to the **Data** property page and scroll down to the **Data table matching** section. In my case, the match between USA States.State and Hourly Temperatures.STATE has been automatically created:

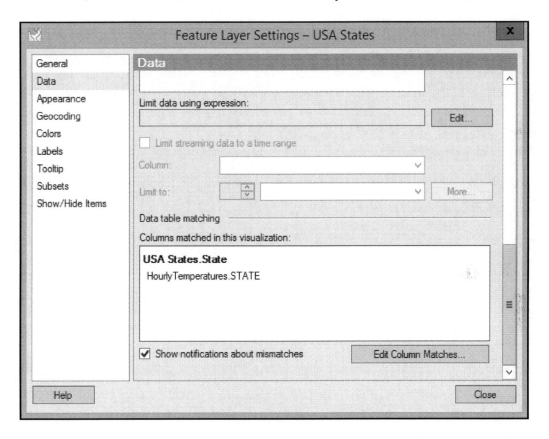

3. Click **Edit Column Matches....**

4. If the column-match is shown, edit it. If not, create a new column match. The settings we need are shown here:

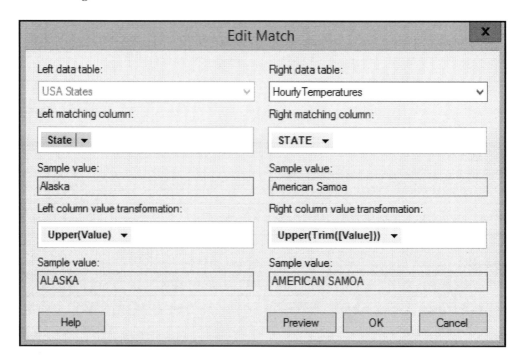

5. Once you've confirmed these settings, click **OK** to close the dialog, close all remaining dialogs, and return to the map chart. Note—in order to apply both upper and trim to the `HourlyTemperatures STATE` column, you'll need to right-click on the expression and choose **Custom Expression....**

As per the earlier geocoding example, where we were attempting to geocode by **City**, applying transformation functions to the columns gives the matches the best chance of working correctly.

You can, of course, further develop this example if you like. For instance, you could use the map chart to create details visualizations, like you can with any other Spotfire visualization.

For more resources for custom shapefiles and geocoding tables, take a look here:
`https://community.tibco.com/wiki/where-find-geographic-data-sour ces-spotfire`
Alternatively, you can look here:
`http://bit.ly/2Ui08Qh`

Using a data function to assist with geocoding

Now that I have introduced feature layers in Spotfire, I 'd like to move on to an advanced topic and show you how you can use a feature layer and the power of Spotfire's built-in statistical engine, combined with open source code released by TIBCO, to solve the issue with geocoding the Airbnb data.

Recall that the last time we looked at the Airbnb data in the previous example, geocoding by the `city` column wasn't successful. We couldn't use the `neighborhood` column either, because Spotfire's default geocoding tables don't support coding by neighborhood.

However, we can fix this! We will be using a published Spotfire data function that is able to determine which markers (when positioned by latitude and longitude) fall within a polygon on a map chart. If we load a shapefile containing neighborhoods, we can use the Points in Polygons data function to identify which markers belong in which neighborhood. We can then aggregate the data by neighborhood and show a single marker on the map for each neighborhood. This is a real example of how, using a bit of ingenuity, we can solve a problem with real-world data. It highlights the power and flexibility of Spotfire.

Follow along with me—there are quite a few steps, so I'll condense them as much as I can. In an effort to be succinct, I won't show screenshots for absolutely every step. Before we start, there are a few prerequisites. You won't be able to complete the example in the Spotfire web clients, but web player users can take advantage of everything you do here.

Please visit this page:

`https://mapcruzin.com/free-download-neighborhood-boundary-shapefiles.htm`

Alternatively, you can look here:

```
http://bit.ly/2Uk5J8Q
```

Download the appropriate shapefile for the city that you have loaded the Airbnb data for. I am continuing with New York City. Once you have downloaded the file, please unzip it into a folder of your choice.

Now, download the Points in Polygons Spotfire data function from here:

```
https://community.tibco.com/modules/points-polygons-data-function-tibco-
spotfire
```

Alternatively, you can download it from here:

```
http://bit.ly/2UExUip
```

Unzip that, too. You'll need to register on the TIBCO Community site in order to download the data function if you've not already done so.

The registration link is as follows:

```
http://bit.ly/2I60JhM
```

This example uses open source R packages in the data function. The data function uses Spotfire's own R engine—**TIBCO Enterprise Runtime for R (TERR)**. We need to add the packages to the TERR engine. Follow along with these steps to add the packages:

1. From the **Tools** menu, choose **TERR Tools**.
2. Switch to the **Package Management** tab.
3. Click the **Load** button to load the list of packages available to TERR.
4. Locate the `sp` package and install it.
5. Locate the `wkb` package and install it.
6. Spotfire will install both packages and the lattice package, which is a dependency.
7. Once you have installed the packages, the **TERR Tools** dialog should look like this:

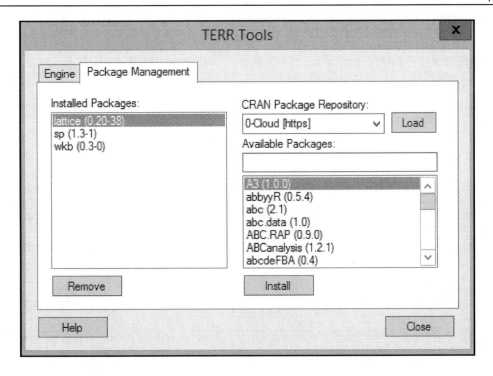

8. Close the dialog.

We are ready to begin adding the data function and do the geocoding! Follow along with me:

1. Open the Airbnb file again and duplicate an existing map chart.
2. Load the shapefile—you can add the shapefile as a new file to the existing analysis—in my case, the full name of the file is `ZillowNeighborhoods-NY.shp`. Spotfire is able to natively import shapefiles.
3. If you like, you can add a table plot showing the shapefile—you can see that the `Geometry` column contains shapes for each of the neighborhoods.
4. Add a new feature layer to the map chart, choosing the `neighborhoods` data table.

5. If you zoom in to show New York City, you should see something such as this:

6. Now, we need to register the data function in the `analysis` file. From the **Tools** menu, select **Register data functions....**

7. Next, let's import the data function code. Click the **Import** button and pick the `sfd` file that you downloaded earlier as part of the bundle from the TIBCO Community site. The `sfd` file defines the data function. The full filename is as follows:

```
[TERR] Points in Polygons for Longitude-Latitude
Coordinates_v1.0.sfd
```

8. For your interest, take a look around the dialog—of particular note are the **Script** box, **Input Parameters**, and **Output Parameters**—I recommend that you study

these. Here is the dialog with the script box shown:

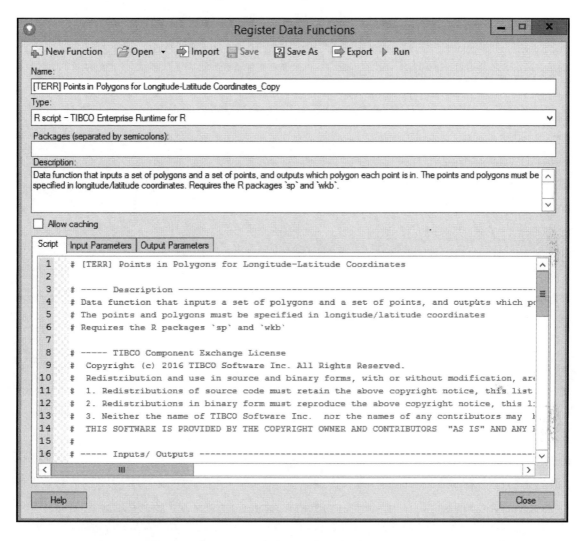

9. To register the data function, click the **Run** button.
10. Now, we need to connect the data function's input and output parameters to the data in the Spotfire analysis. For the input parameters, we need to tell the data function which columns contain the geometries and the unique identifier in the table. We also need to define which columns in the main data table contain the latitudes and longitudes of the points. There is a single output parameter of type column. We need to add the column to the main data table—it will identify which neighborhood each of the points belongs to.

11. I'll talk you through the process of connecting up one of the inputs in detail, and then just define what the others should be. Let's start with the **Geometry** input. Make sure it's selected in the **Input Parameters** tab.

12. For the input handler, choose **Column** and then select the **ZillowNeighborhoods-NY** data table, and make sure the **Geometry** column is selected:

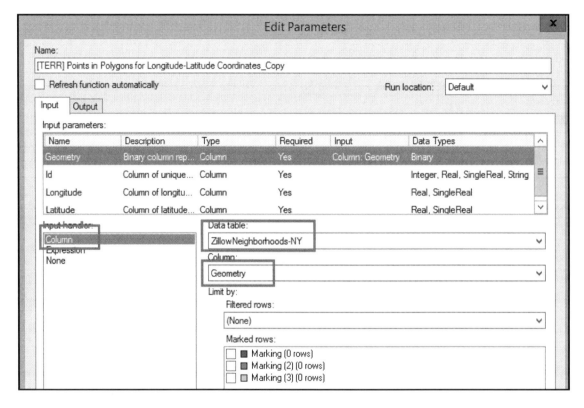

13. Now set the ID input to the REGIONID column in the **ZillowNeighborhoods-NY** data table in the same way.

14. The **Longitude** and **Latitude** columns should be selected from the Airbnb listings (main) data table for the **Longitude** and **Latitude** input parameters respectively.

15. Let's move to the output parameters tab and set the output parameter. You should map the ID output parameter as a **Columns** output handler and select the listings data table. The dialog should look like this:

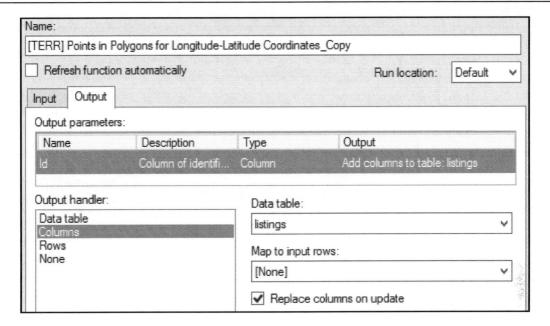

16. Click **OK**. This will have the effect of registering the data function and running it for the first time.
17. Close the register data functions dialog.
18. If anything goes wrong with running the data function, a pop-up warning will appear, like this:

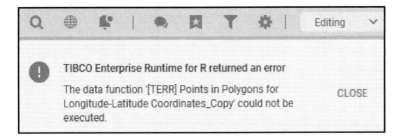

19. If you do get an error, you can click it in order to get more details. Hopefully, everything will work out **OK**. If you get stuck, you can always post a question on the TIBCO Community!

 You can edit an existing data function by selecting **Data function properties** from the **Data** menu in Spotfire.

Let's take a break here and discuss what we've just done. We have registered a data function in Spotfire. It uses a predefined snippet of R code that performs the function of determining which markers on the map fall within each of the geometries stored in the shapefile that we downloaded. You can check this out by adding a table visualization and showing the neighborhood and **Id(2)** columns from the listings table. Here are the first few rows from my data:

2 columns from listings	
neighbourhood	Id (2)
Brooklyn	193406.00
Manhattan	270842.00
Brooklyn	199001.00
Harlem	195267.00
Clinton Hill	273766.00
East Harlem	270828.00
Midtown East	274627.00

The **Id (2)** column represents the neighborhood IDs from the shapefile table. It's called **Id (2)** because there is already an ID column in the listings data.

You can think of the data function as doing the equivalent of an **Add Columns** operation, or join, but, this time, instead of joining on column values, we are joining using a geometry column.

So, how do we geocode on the new column that we have just added? Let's perform the following steps:

1. Edit the listings layer properties and show the **Positioning** page.
2. Make sure that **Geocoding** is selected and then choose the **Id (2)** column for geocoding.
3. You'll notice a red warning symbol—this tells us that no geocoding tables have been specified, so go ahead and add the **ZillowNeighborhoods-NY** data table:

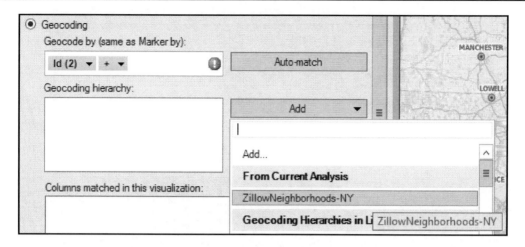

4. There are no column matches shown by default, so edit the column matches. Add a match between the **Id (2)** column in the listings data table and **REGIONID** in the geometries table:

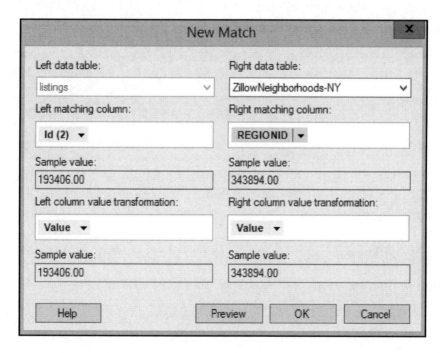

5. Close all the dialogs and return to the map chart. We 're done! Your map chart should look something like this:

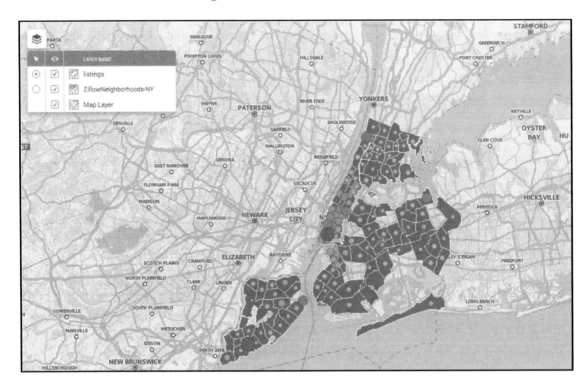

Notice how the markers are nicely placed in the center of each of the neighborhoods. It's also interesting to see how the price of the properties varies by neighborhood. In fact, I think it shows a better view of the data than the individual points—the individual points are somewhat lost in the noise, and there isn't much variability among them.

Adding Web Map Service data to a map chart

Web Map Service (**WMS**) is an Open Geospatial Consortium protocol for delivering geo-referenced map services over the internet.

WMS services cover all manner of geographical information (for example, geological information, weather data, and much more). The WMS data can be overlaid on a standard Spotfire map chart. TIBCO provides URLs to and information about some sample WMS URLs on the TIBCO Community:

`https://community.tibco.com/wiki/wms-sources-tibco-spotfire`

Alternatively, you can click here:

`http://bit.ly/2YR3J6J`

There are lots and lots of other services out there!

> One way to find publicly available WMS services is to search the internet with this query: `'Your data search''supported Interfaces:' wms`, for example: `'View footprint in:''supported Interfaces:' wms`.

When you find a WMS server of interest, you'll need the WMS URL so that you can paste it into a Spotfire map chart WMS layer. Not all the WMS links you find will work, however. Sometimes, the server will be down or no longer available.

Most WMS streams have multiple layers of information. Spotfire will show you the available layers, and you can choose which ones to include in your map. It's important to understand that you are streaming GIS data into your map chart from an external server, and you are dependent on the availability of this server and also on the form the WMS information takes. Also, just to state: you cannot interact with WMS layers like you can with a feature or marker layer.

Let's work through an example to see how WMS data works in a Spotfire map chart:

1. Open the hourly temperature example (or indeed any other example file, as we won't be using the data in the file itself).
2. Create a new map chart and remove all the layers except the background map layer.

3. Add a WMS layer using the **Add** dropdown in the **Layers** property page. Spotfire will show the following dialog:

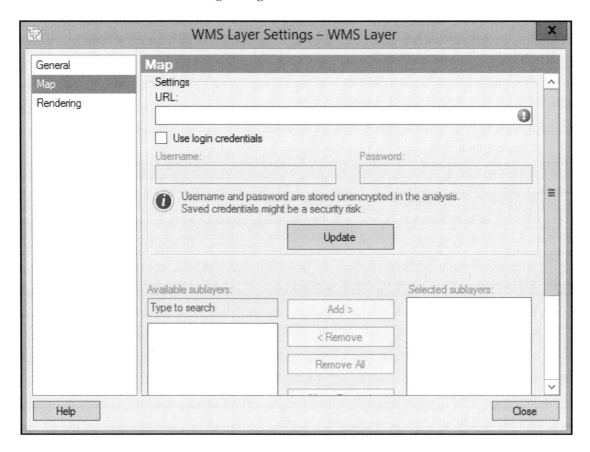

4. For an example WMS URL, I found this website:
   https://www.weather.gov/gis/WebServices
   Or you can click here:
   http://bit.ly/2Kb8VyU

5. I navigated through to the **Base Reflectivity Radar** service under **Current Weather**.

6. From there, I copied the URL for the WMS service. For reference, its URL is http://idpgis.ncep.noaa.gov/arcgis/services/NWS_Observations/radar_base_reflectivity/MapServer/WMSServer?request=GetCapabilities&service=WMS:

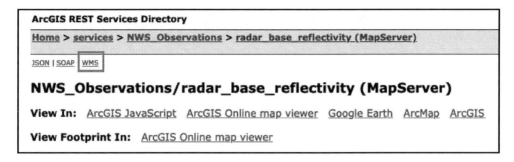

7. I 'm not expecting you to type that in!
8. Now, paste the link of the web service into the URL box in the dialog.
9. Click the **Update** button.
10. Assuming the link is valid and you are connected to the internet, Spotfire will retrieve a collection of sublayers from the WMS server. Here's how the dialog should look if everything has worked **OK**:

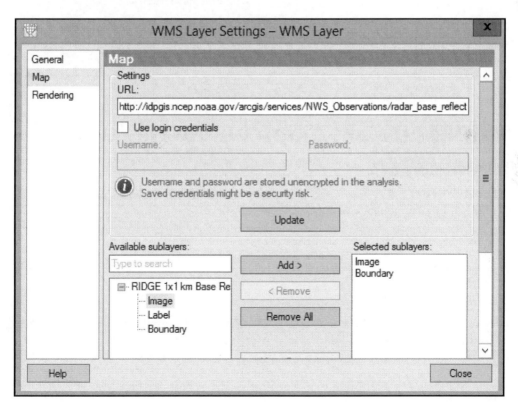

11. While still in the **WMS Layer Settings**, select **General**, and rename the layer appropriately something such as `Weather Radar WMS`.

The result is a WMS layer you can turn on and off with the layers control:

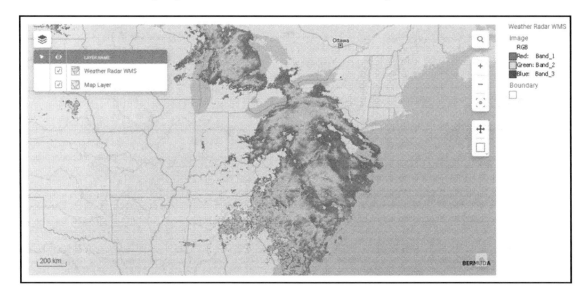

Creating custom maps using Tile Map Service layers

Tile Map Services (TMS) provide custom tile images that Spotfire can place on a map chart. You can get a nice list of suitable TMSes from here:

`https://community.tibco.com/wiki/geoanalytics-resources`

Alternatively, you can get the list from here:

`http://bit.ly/2OPwxry`

TMS tiles could be differently formatted maps, topography, satellite imagery, and much more. For the example in this section, we will add satellite information to a map chart using an API from `https://www.mapbox.com/`.

In order to follow along exactly with the example, please sign up for a free account:

`https://www.mapbox.com/`

Once you have signed up for an account at `https://www.mapbox.com/`, get your access token and store it somewhere safe.

Of course, you don't have to follow along exactly with the example—choose any other TMS that you like! In fact, there are totally free satellite image tiles shown on the page on the TIBCO Community.

Here's how to create a sample TMS layer:

1. Create a new map chart and remove all the layers from it.
2. Add a new TMS layer (hint—it's under **Map Layers** in the **Add** menu)
3. Copy the URL for the satellite TMS from the geoanalytics resources page from the TIBCO Community:

 I found that I had to copy the text of the URL from the page, rather than the underlying URL.

Satellite
TMS URL: https://api.mapbox.com/v4/mapbox.satellite/{z}/{x}/{y}.png?access_token=
{YOUR_ACCESS_TOKEN}
Copyright: © MapBox, Data © OpenStreetMap contributors, © Digital Globe

4. Now paste your access key into the relevant part of the URL—remove the curly braces from {YOUR_ACCESS_TOKEN}.

5. It's good practice to enter the copyright text and link, so I recommend you do so.

6. The dialog should look similar to this:

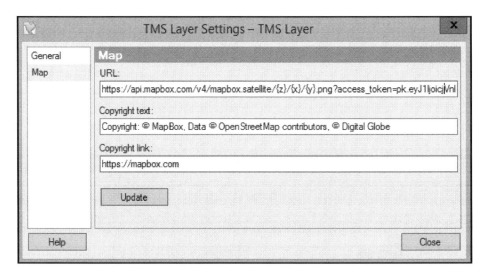

7. Click **Update** and close any dialogs to return to the map chart.

8. You should end up with something that looks like this:

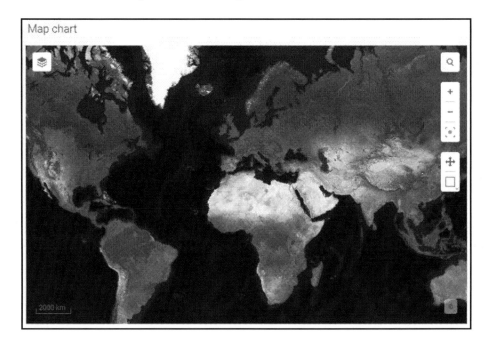

Cool! So, we've seen how we can add custom map tiles to a Spotfire map chart. Once we've done this, we can use the rest of the power of the map chart for analytics, just as if we were using the standard Spotfire maps.

Here's an example showing the average temperature in degrees Celsius in a marker layer:

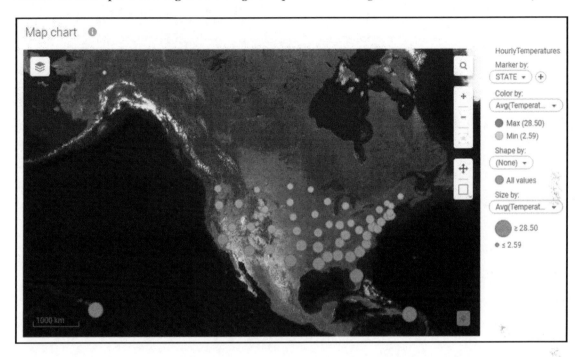

Using the map chart for non-geographic spatial analysis

The map chart can be used for any form of spatial analysis. For a simple application, all you need is a base image and some coordinate data. Think of the base image as the map layer and the coordinate data as a marker layer. With the right software, you could create relevant shapefiles and use them as a feature layer. Then, users can click on features to select data and interact with the rest of their data.

The base image could be a process diagram, a semiconductor wafer, an immunoassay plate, or the layout of an airport terminal.

You can plot markers on an image in appropriate locations on the image to indicate (for example) process stage timings, semiconductor wafer failures, immunoassay well results, or traffic through the airport terminal. The markers can be numbers, colors, or even mini pie charts.

There are a number of stages to creating a spatial visualization with markers:

1. Create or obtain a suitable image.
2. Map out the image's coordinate space so that you know where to place markers. This stage takes a little trial and error.
3. Link the coordinates you define in stage two with some relevant data.

The default coordinate space for your image is its dimensions in pixels, so this gives you the maximum x and y coordinates. You can quickly build x and y reference axes using a spreadsheet and then load the coordinates with the image to help you map out the points of interest.

First of all, I will show you a pre-built example that uses features only, and then we'll create another from scratch with markers to illustrate two possible use cases.

Mapping an airport

The TIBCO Community hosts a really complete example of mapping the San Francisco Airport in Spotfire. I am not going to repeat the step-by-step instructions here, but if you want to follow them, please visit the following link:

```
https://community.tibco.com/wiki/custom-spotfire-maps-sfo-airport
```

Or you can visit here:

```
http://bit.ly/2OTfg0S
```

This example covers creating the shapefiles and adding the background images. Features are used to select data in a dashboard that corresponds to visitor ratings in the airport.

The sample Spotfire analysis file is available to download from the Community from the previous link, or you can even use it interactively on TIBCO Cloud by following this link:

```
http://bit.ly/2UlxKNt
```

Here's a sample screenshot of the interactive analysis:

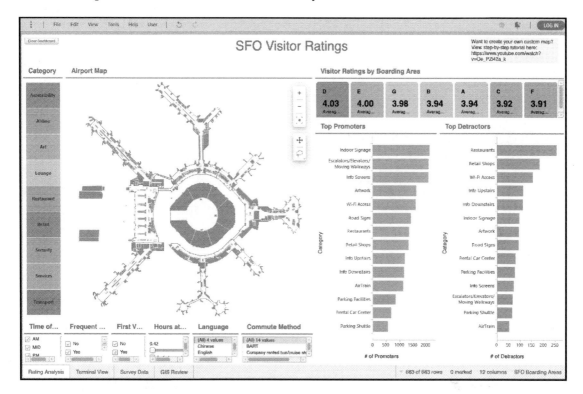

You can click on various categories or even regions of the map to hone in on the data that corresponds to the different areas within the airport.

Process mapping using a map chart

Consider a fictitious workflow for a website change process. The process map can be created using **Microsoft Visio**, or any suitable workflow software, and then saved as an image file. We can also create some fictitious process time data for this workflow, and we'll be using this data in this example. The files for the example (contained in WebPageChangeProcess.zip) are available here:

https://community.tibco.com/wiki/tibco-spotfire-primer-sample-data

They are also available here:

http://bit.ly/2Vhfy3K

Here is the sample process map, before any markers have been added to it:

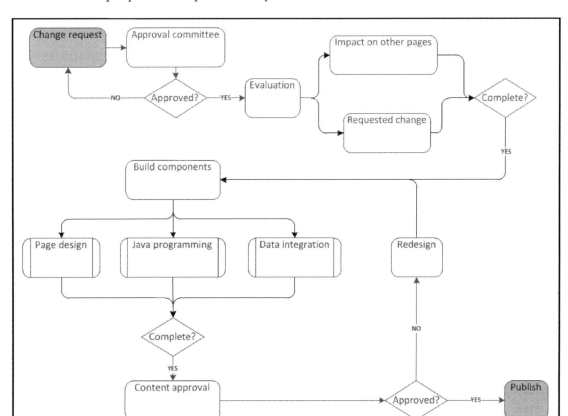

We'll be placing markers on each process step and using coloring to indicate whether a step is taking longer than it should.

Let's get all this into Spotfire as follows:

1. Create a new map chart, select the **Layers** property, and remove any layers created by Spotfire, including the base map.
2. While still on the **Layers** property, use the **Add** dropdown to add a new **Image Layer**. When the **Image Layer Settings** window opens, simply browse to the image you want to import, which is ChangeProcess.png in our case.

3. Now set the image's coordinate reference to **None**:

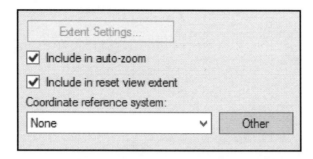

4. Close the dialog, select the map chart's **Appearance** property, and set the **Coordinate reference system** to **None**.

You must make sure that both the map chart and the image layer's coordinate reference systems are set to **None**; otherwise, the example won't work!

You should now see the process image, but to make it useful we need to add a marker layer. The first step is to map out the coordinates. One way of doing this is to create a file that shows the x and y coordinates in a marker layer. We can then determine the coordinates that are required for the markers in the process map. I've actually done this for you and provided the file, complete with coordinates. It's called `WebPageChangeProcess.xls`, but if you want to find out how I did this, then follow these steps:

1. Open up the `WebPageChangeProcess.csv` file in your favourite CSV editor (I used Microsoft Excel) and add columns for x and y.

2. Add the `coordinateMatrix.xlsx` dataset to the analysis file, and then add this as a marker layer to the map chart. Make sure that the coordinate reference system of the layer is set to **None**. Create the following settings:

Positioning	Coordinate columns set to x and y
Size by	None
Shape	A cross
Label by	Custom expression: `Concatenate([x] & "," & [y])` and **Show labels for:All**
Marker by	[Marker]

3. This is what you should end up with:

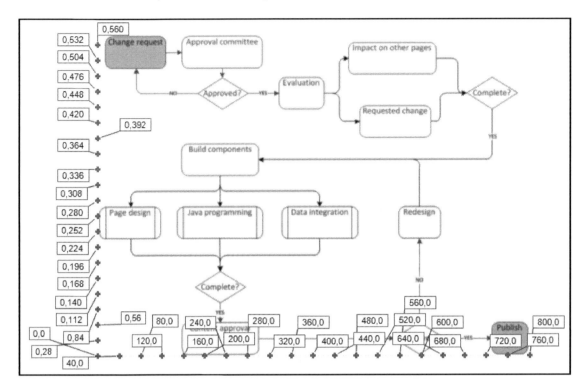

4. Now, we can trace across and up the visualization to find suitable coordinates for placing a marker in each of the process steps. For example, the **Approval Committee** box would best suit a marker at 232, 532.

5. Find coordinates that place markers in each of the process steps and add them to the file as you go.

6. Once you've completed this process, save the file.

Now, we have created a file that contains the process steps, how long they take, their target times, and suitable coordinates for x and y. The final stage in creating the interactive spatial visualization is the plotting of the data. We can do this by following these steps:

1. Load the data file we created in the previous section, or load the pre-built file, `WebPageProcess.xls`, into the analysis file.

2. Now, add two calculated columns to the table:
   Total Elapsed Time: `Sum([Elapsed Time])`
   Percentage of Elapsed Time: `[Elapsed Time] / [Total Elapsed Time]`

> Take a look at the data table using a table plot—notice that the **Total Elapsed Time** column gives a single value for the entire dataset, but the **Percent of Elapsed Time** column gives a different value for each row—this is because the **Total Elapsed Time** column uses the **Sum** aggregation method. It operates on the entire dataset. The **Percent of Elapsed Time** column operates on the data one row at a time since it does not use any aggregation methods.

3. Format the `Percent Elapsed Time` column as **Percentage**, with zero decimals by right-clicking on the column in the data panel, then clicking (**Column Properties** | **Formatting**).

4. Open the map chart's visualization properties, select the **Layers** property, and add the data table as a new marker layer, remembering to set the coordinate reference system to **None**.

5. Add the following settings to the new layer:

Positioning	Coordinate columns set to x and y.
Colors	`Percent of Elapsed Time`, no aggregation; **Color mode: Segments**, with three segments (0%-10%, 10%-20%, and 20%-33%). **Important**: you must use absolute values to set these segments and you must enter the percentages as `.1`, `.2` and `.33`.
Size by	None, but use the **Marker size:** slider to fit the markers to the image.
Shape	A square.
Marker by	`Activity`.

We have now superimposed a marker layer on the process flow image. Using the markers, we can see which steps are taking the most time. Here's what you should end up with:

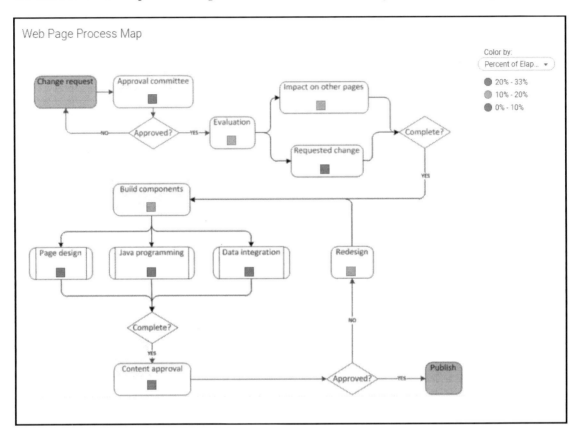

As an exercise, we can produce a complete example that draws upon the lessons we've learned in this book so far by adding a drop-down control to enable a user to choose which metric to show in the process map and to create details visualizations that respond to marking on the map. The broad steps are as follows:

1. Create calculated columns for `Total Process Time` and `Percent of Process Time`.

2. Create a drop-down control to allow the user to choose whether to color by **Percent of Elapsed Time** or **Percent of Process Time** (see `Chapter 3`, *Impactful Dashboards!*).

3. Adjust the map chart coloring so it colors by the user-selected metric.
4. Add two bar charts that are dependent on marking in the map chart to show the actual versus target and percentage elapsed time versus percentage process time.

You should end up with something such as this:

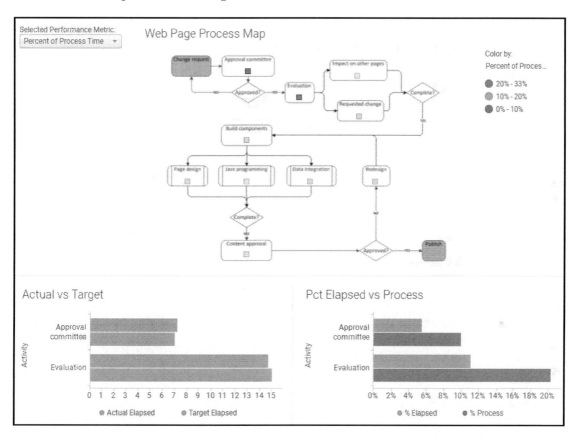

This is the sort of analysis a Lean Six Sigma practitioner or anyone interested in process improvement might perform. The beauty of the Spotfire map chart is that as long as the process flow stays the same, it can be quickly analyzed against different data points and metrics.

TIBCO GeoAnalytics

TIBCO GeoAnalytics is a cloud-based suite of tools for creating location-based applications in Spotfire and other tools. It comprises a JavaScript library for developing web-based applications, REST APIs, and a web application for geocoding and assessing, as well as visually improving geo-referenced data.

Covering this topic in detail is outside the scope of the book, but for more information, please visit the following:
```
https://community.tibco.com/wiki/tibco-spotfire-location-analyti
cs-mapping-geoanalytics-and-spatial-statistics
```
Or you can click here:
```
http://bit.ly/2FQkQgi
```

Summary

In this chapter, we have taken a close look at the Spotfire map chart, which allows you to plot your data in a spatial context and create interactive marker layers and feature layers, as well as reference maps, WMSes, TMSes, and image layers.

You have learned how to create a background map layer, how to use automatic geocoding to accurately position locations from your data on a map, how to incorporate and use a feature layer, how to add WMS data to a map chart, how to use custom tiles for the map background, and how to use the map chart for non-geographic spatial analysis.

Additionally, we have explored the usage of TIBCO Enterprise Runtime for R. We used a TERR data function to assist with geocoding some data.

There isn't room in this book to cover absolutely everything you can do with a map chart, so I would recommend visiting this page for a gallery showing the art of the possible:
```
https://community.tibco.com/wiki/gallery-tibco-spotfire-geoanaly
tics-mapping-and-spatial-statistics
```
Alternatively, you can click here:
```
http://bit.ly/2UEyTiq
```

Now that we covered the analytics capabilities of Spotfire, I'd like to move back to data. The next chapter discusses Spotfire data connectors and information links. It also covers big data and working with in-database data.

3
Section 3: Databases, Scripting, and Scaling Spotfire

This section will teach you how to load data from databases and how to design information links. It discusses in-database and in-memory analytics and how to combine them. It also covers scripting and how to extend Spotfire, and it details how to scale your Spotfire infrastructure and how to keep data up to date in analysis files. This section will broaden your horizons and make you think about the art of the possible with Spotfire.

In this section, the following chapters will be covered:

- Chapter 10, *Information Links and Data Connectors*
- Chapter 11, *Scripting, Advanced Analytics, and Extensions*
- Chapter 12, *Scaling the Infrastructure; Keeping Data up to Date*
- Chapter 13, *Beyond the Horizon*

10
Information Links and Data Connectors

So far in this book, we have loaded data from flat files—Excel spreadsheets, CSV files, Spotfire Binary Data Format files, and more. Obviously, the real world has many more data sources than flat files! The majority of data you will come across will be stored in a database, warehouse, data lake, or big data system. Spotfire connects to all of these and more!

In this chapter, we'll be covering Spotfire's information links and data connectors. Information links allow you to build abstraction layers over databases; connectors allow you to connect directly to databases and other data sources.

Along the way, we'll be discussing in-database versus in-memory data and analytics, data on demand, and streaming (live) data.

This chapter covers the following topics:

- In-memory versus in-database analytics
- Information links
- Database connectors
- Streaming data
- Spotfire integrations

In-memory versus in-database analytics

Spotfire supports **in-memory** and **in-database** analytics. So far in this book, we have only been using in-memory data and analytics. Spotfire's in-memory data engine is highly optimized for working with small, medium, and large datasets, but eventually, your computer is likely to run out of memory if you have very large datasets. People often ask me: how large is a very large dataset? Or how much data can Spotfire work with in-memory? For me, this is one of the most difficult questions to answer!

It really depends on how many rows and how many columns of data you are working with. I generally find that the Spotfire in-memory data engine can handle hundreds of millions of rows of data with tens of columns, or hundreds of thousands of rows with thousands of columns. If a dataset is bigger than that, then I recommend using in-database analytics or data on demand. Both of these concepts are detailed in this chapter.

When you load data into Spotfire's in-memory data engine, an entire copy of the data is loaded into the memory of your computer (or web server). The in-memory data engine is designed specifically for analytics—it compresses data, removes redundant columns, and swaps data to disk if memory runs low. The in-memory data engine can aggregate data at any level and can also show the raw data or details of individual rows. Using the in-memory data engine gives you the ability to use Spotfire's rich set of expressions that you'll have seen in `Chapter 7`, *Source Data is Never Enough*.

In-database analytics pushes the analytic power to the underlying database system. Spotfire can, via its connectors, query databases to get the information it needs to draw visualizations on extremely large datasets.

Imagine a bar chart showing global sales of all product categories for an extremely large consumer products company. You could try to load all that data into Spotfire, but I doubt it would work. Imagine the sheer volume of data—all the transactions for every store that sold every product. The transactional data could run into the billions or even trillions of rows. The load time would be significant and the IT infrastructure to support the transfer of all that data would be impractical.

A much better solution would be to execute a query against the database that just returns the information that Spotfire needs to draw the bar chart—it could be a query that returns quantities sold grouped by product categories over time. Then, all Spotfire needs to hold in-memory is the result of that query, which is what is shown on the bar chart. The resultant dataset is only a few hundred or thousand rows. Large database systems, particularly those that are so-called **big data** solutions, are highly optimized to return query results quickly on such large datasets.

Let's take it one step further in our hypothetical scenario. Now that the bar chart is shown, how do you drill into that data with details visualizations? Consider that the bar chart just shows what's going on in the data. You're highly likely to want to know why something is happening, which you would do by looking at the raw data in some way. Fortunately, Spotfire makes this pretty easy too. It uses a concept called **data on demand**. Data on demand is used to retrieve data from a database based on something changing in Spotfire. It can be configured to retrieve details of marked rows, filtered rows, or of fixed values, values stored in document properties, or details from a custom expression.

Data on demand can be used to perform another in-database analytics query or it can retrieve the raw row values into memory.

Information links

Information links are Spotfire's database abstraction method. They handle authentication, querying, and joining databases. You can create parameters that prompt users when loading data, or that allow programmatic control of data loading.

> To define or manage information links and their associated components, access Spotfire's information designer from the **Data** menu in an Analyst client.

Information links support joins between multiple tables, even across databases. You can also call stored procedures, enter custom SQL, or use information links to update database tables.

Information links only support in-memory data. They do not support in-database analytics.

Lastly, information links and their associated data sources are stored in the Spotfire library, so any users that use the information links must have access to the requisite folders in the library. This is extremely useful, since an administrator can tightly control which users/groups have access to the various information links.

There isn't room in this book to cover information links and information designer in full, but a short explanation of the various components that are used follows.

Data sources

Data sources connect to the underlying database. They connect via Java Database Connectivity (JDBC). When building information links, you'll need to start with a data source. When you create a new data source, you'll need to define the driver for the database and a connection URL. If you don't know how to define the connection URL, you will need to consult the database administrator or other relevant documentation for the database in question. You will also need a username and password for the database, or you could allow user authentication so that any end user will need to enter their username and password when using an information link that depends on the data source.

You can always create a default information model by browsing the database model in the data source, right-clicking on a database table, and choosing **Create Default Information Model...**:

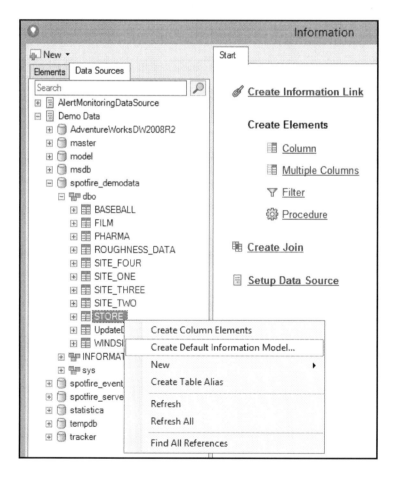

This will create a simple, default information link and underlying column elements from the database table. You can then modify or customize the information link that's been created.

Column

Columns reference the columns in a database table. You should make sure that columns are grouped nicely into folders so that you can find them easily for future information links. The default information model creates folders automatically for you. There's no need to create multiple copies of any column.

Joins

If you need to select columns from multiple tables, you'll need to define the relationship between those tables by defining and saving the necessary join elements. When you create a new join, Spotfire will expect you to select two column elements, one from each of the tables you wish to relate. Then, you will have to decide what type of join is appropriate: an inner join (return rows only where both columns match) or an outer join (return all rows from one table, including nulls, and only the matching rows from the other).

If the tables are related uniquely through more than one pair of columns, make sure that you define all the pairs necessary to define the relation. Once you've finished, save the join to a suitable folder and give it a logical name you will understand later.

Filters

You can use filter elements to predefine a filter on the data that is returned by an information link. Filter elements are defined similarly to column elements, except you include a filter expression. You then add the filter as an element to an information link.

Procedures

Procedures are code that are defined in the source database and run there. You will find procedures in the data source schema represented as cogwheel icons. Once you define a procedure as an information element, it can be added to an information link's **Elements** section. Information links don't just return columns, and so, they can be used to trigger procedures in the source database, the results of which may or may not be the return of some data to Spotfire.

Information links

The information link is the object you will invoke to import data into an analysis. The information link contains SQL and brings together all the joins, filters, parameters, and so on.

Loading data from an information link

To load data from an information link, you must browse to the information link in the Spotfire library—here's a screenshot illustrating this process:

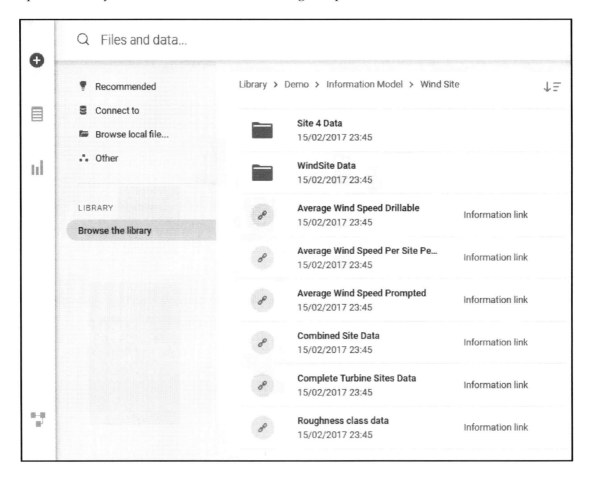

You can, of course, search for an information link using the search box shown in the preceding screenshot. Notice that one of the information links shown here will prompt for information from the user when loading the data. Prompts can be configured so that the distinct values are presented to the user so that they may choose which data to load.

Writing back to a database using an information link

It's possible to use information links to write data back to a database. There are a few ways to do this—for example, you can either call a stored procedure that performs the update for you, or you can enter custom SQL in the information link.

If you like, you can call the information link and specify its parameters by using **IronPython scripting**. IronPython scripting is covered in more detail in Chapter 11, *Scripting, Advanced Analytics, and Extensions*.

> For information on calling a stored procedure to update a database table, see this link:
> https://community.tibco.com/wiki/spotfire-write-back-using-stored-procedure.
>
> Alternatively, use this shortened link:
> http://bit.ly/2YYAmiR.

Using custom SQL to update a database is pretty straightforward if you are confident with SQL. Here are the outline steps:

1. Open an existing information link in information designer.
2. Click the **SQL...** button.

3. From there, click the **Pre-Updates** button to get to the SQL that's executed ahead of reading data:

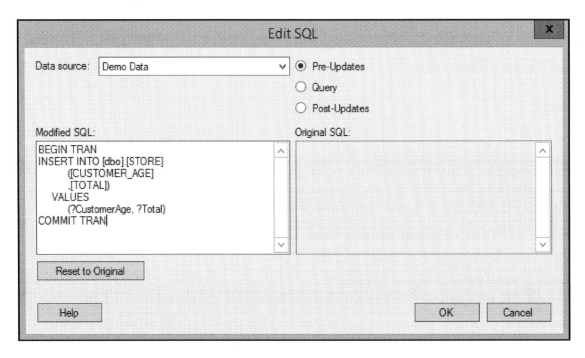

4. The SQL, which I entered here, is as follows:

```
BEGIN TRAN
INSERT INTO [dbo].[STORE]
          ([CUSTOMER_AGE]
          ,[TOTAL])
     VALUES
          (?CustomerAge, ?Total)
COMMIT TRAN
```

I am using Microsoft SQL Server here, so the syntax may be different if you are using a different database system to me.

It's pretty simple—it just inserts a new row into a database table. The question marks represent parameters. These are substituted with actual values when Spotfire reads data from the information link:

1. Click **OK** on the dialog, then expand the **Parameters** section of the information link. You'll see something that looks like this:

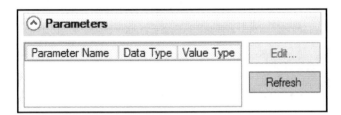

2. There's nothing there at the moment, so click **Refresh**.
3. In my case, I have two parameters, so they show up like this:

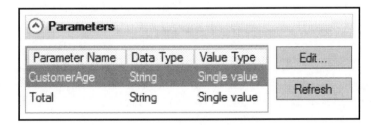

4. Both of these parameters are defined as float type values in the database table, so I should change them to **Real** type as this is the corresponding type in Spotfire:

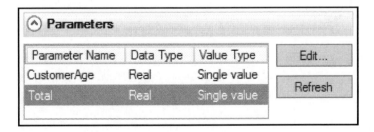

5. Now, we can test that the information link works as expected by clicking **Open Data** on the dialog.

6. Spotfire will prompt for the values of CustomerAge and Total (I am just showing the prompt for CustomerAge here):

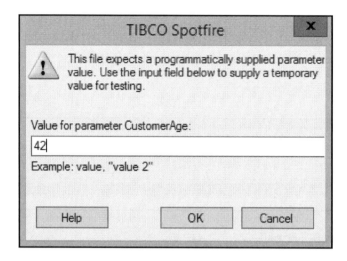

7. Finally, Spotfire will retrieve data from the information link.

8. The normal paradigm for using information links to write back to a database is to insert or update data in a database and then retrieve the updated data as a data table, all in a single, atomic operation.

You can call the information link and pass parameters using IronPython—see the link to the TIBCO Community that was given previously for how to do this. The principle is the same, regardless of whether you are calling a stored procedure or some custom SQL, as defined in this example.

Data connectors

Spotfire connectors allow you to connect easily to and analyze data from relational databases, cubes, OData sources, Hadoop systems, and other big data repositories. Using connectors, you can connect to a data source, view its structure, and select which data you'd like to analyze in Spotfire.

There's a great page that I recommend you read about the TIBCO Community:
`https://community.tibco.com/wiki/tibco-spotfire-data-access`.

Alternatively, use this shortened link:
`http://bit.ly/2I8sE0w`.

The page gives an up-to-date list of all the connectors that are available. There's also a really nice FAQ section linked from the page. I recommend you take a look at this page—of particular note is that some connectors support much more than their advertised data source—for example, the Microsoft SQL Server connector works with Azure SQL databases or warehouses.

At the time of writing, only two connectors are configurable in the Spotfire web clients—Google Analytics and Salesforce. However, if you configure an analysis using one of the other connectors, Web Player users will be able to use any data or connections configured, so long as they have access to the data source, or you save the credentials with the connection, or use a credentials profile. This process of saving the credentials or using a credentials profile will be detailed in an example later in this chapter.

> Please be aware that the connectors package must be installed on your Spotfire server and that you must have any dependent drivers installed on your computer. If your analysis uses connectors and is deployed to the web, the Web Player server(s) will also need the same drivers installed.

Loading data from a connector

The process of using connectors is broadly similar, regardless of the type of data source you are connecting to, so this example will use SQL Server for illustration. You'll obviously need to adapt to your individual scenario, but please follow along with me as I connect to an example database and retrieve some data. Along the way, we will look at in-database data and on-demand data loading:

    1. In Spotfire, click the + button, open the add data flyout, and then navigate to **Connect to**:

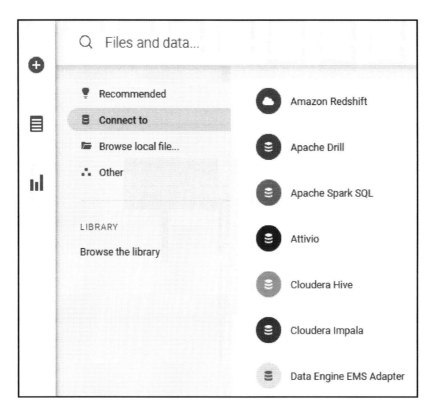

2. You should see the list of installed connectors. If you don't, it means that the connectors are not installed in your client—please make sure that they have been deployed to your Spotfire Server.
3. Scroll down to the connector for your chosen source system—in my case, it's **Microsoft SQL Server**. Click the name of the connector.
4. A new flyout will open, so click **NEW CONNECTION**:

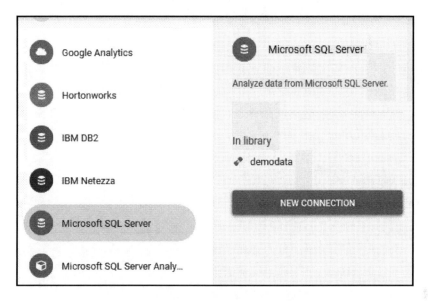

Note that I have an existing connection defined in the library on my server.

5. A dialog will open, which will allow you to define the connection parameters, so enter the requisite values to connect to your data source. Click **Connect** (or similar—each connector will be slightly different here):

6. Now, choose the database to open and click **OK**.
7. If all has gone according to plan, you should end up with a dialog that shows you the views in the connection. Mine looks like this:

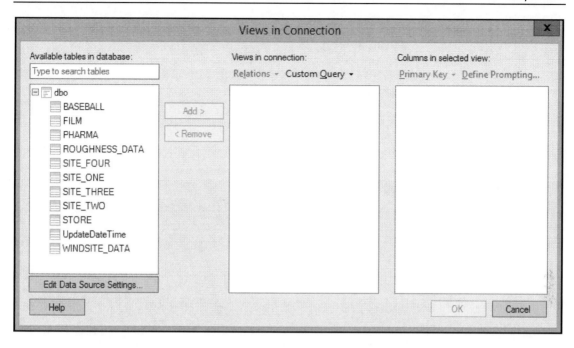

8. From here, it's a simple matter of clicking on some tables and bringing them into the **Views in connection** and **Columns in selected view**. Here's what my dialog looks like when I brought some tables and columns across and set a **Primary Key**:

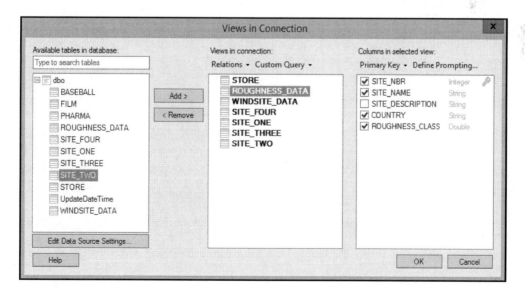

The **Primary Key** is a column that uniquely identifies every row in the data; that is, all the values within the column are guaranteed to be distinct.

Defining a **Primary Key** is useful for making sure that bookmarks can apply marking, even if the data has been refreshed since the bookmark was created.

You can also, if you choose, add related data tables or even enter a custom query.

9. Once you have defined which tables will be brought into your analysis, click **OK**.

10. Spotfire will then present you with a list of all the data tables that will be opened. By default, some connectors will keep the data in-database, so the tables will show as being **External**:

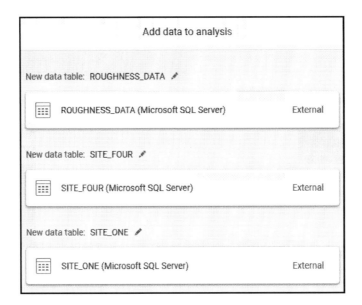

11. Of course, you can change this on a per-table basis so that the data is loaded into memory in Spotfire. For this example, we are going to keep the data external, so explore the settings if you like, but I recommend that you don't change any of them at the moment.

12. Click **OK** at the bottom of the list of the tables.

13. Great! The data is now ready for use with Spotfire. Note that I didn't say that the data has been loaded, because it hasn't! You can think of the metadata being loaded, but no actual data being present in Spotfire.

14. To illustrate that the data is ready, I have created a bar chart that shows average **WIND_SPEED per Date**, trellised by SITE_NUMBER:

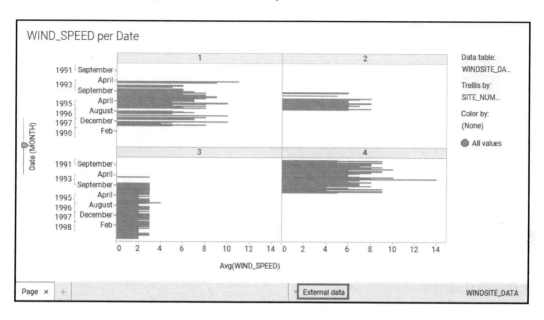

Notice that Spotfire tells us that the data is external (shown in the status bar). You can prove this by trying to export the data—choose **Export** from the **File** menu. All the options to export the data to a file are grayed out. This is because the data is not loaded into Spotfire's data engine and is therefore not available for export.

When defining the views in the connection, you can also automatically bring in related tables and perform a join on those tables. Here's an example screenshot that shows this:

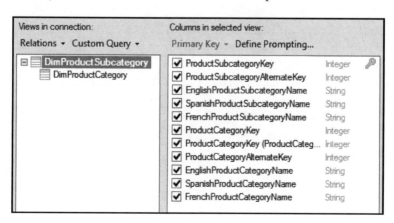

Any join that's defined here is a virtual join—that is, it's not executed until it's needed (if using in-database data). This significantly reduces the amount of data transfer from the database than might otherwise be required.

Using data on demand to retrieve raw data

If you want to perform detailed analysis on your data, you probably need to load subsets of it into memory. The process of setting up data on demand sounds a lot more complicated than it is! Follow along with your own data as I continue to work with the wind site data that I have at hand:

1. Let's begin by navigating through the process of adding new data and selecting the existing connection in the analysis:

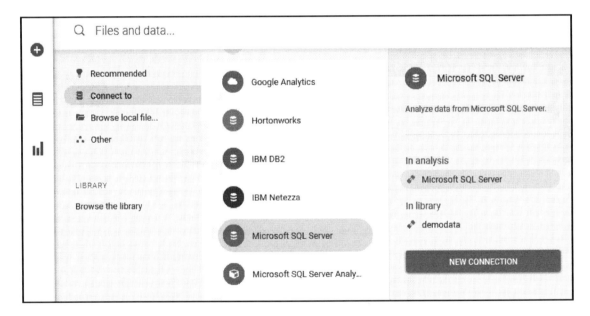

Of course, there's no need to define a new connection—we can reuse the existing one.

2. I'm going to add a second copy of the WINDSITE_DATA table to my analysis. This is done simply by adding the table to the views in connection—Spotfire automatically gives the table the suffix (2):

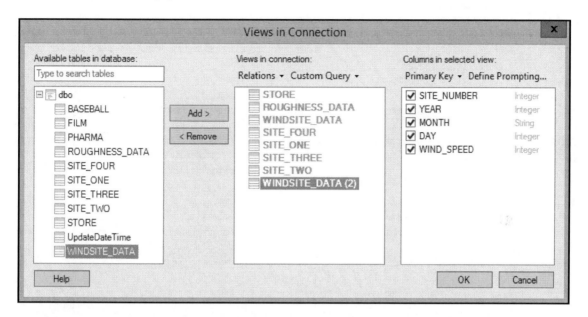

Of course, you could add another, different table that you know you're going to load on demand, but you must be sure to set up a relation between it and the original, external table.

3. Click **OK** on the dialog. This time, we must choose settings other than the default. Drop down the settings and then the sub-settings for the import, and choose **On-demand**:

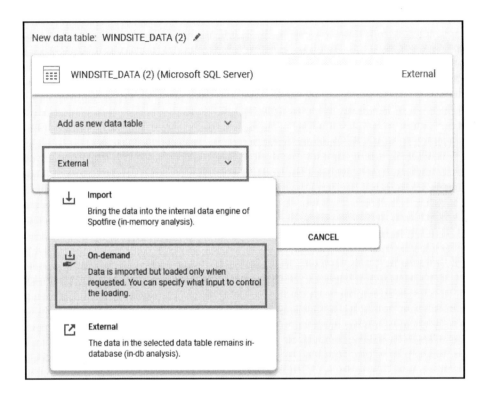

4. Spotfire will now show a warning symbol—this is because it knows the data is to be loaded on demand, but no settings have been defined for the **On-demand** loading. In order to define these settings, click the cogwheel:

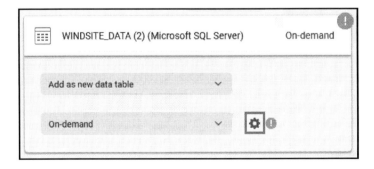

5. The **On-demand** settings dialog will open. You'll be working with different data to me, so you'll need to define different settings, but in my case, I must define inputs for SITE_NUMBER, YEAR, MONTH, and DAY. Here's how I have defined SITE_NUMBER:

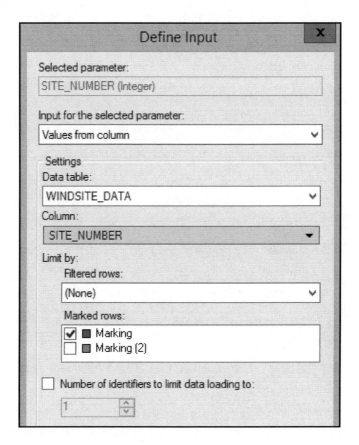

Notice how there is quite a range of settings here—it's possible to define the input as values or a range, or values/a range from properties, and so on.

6. For the YEAR, MONTH, and DAY columns, I must specify a range—this will make the data-on-demand query more efficient than if I were to use the individual column values:

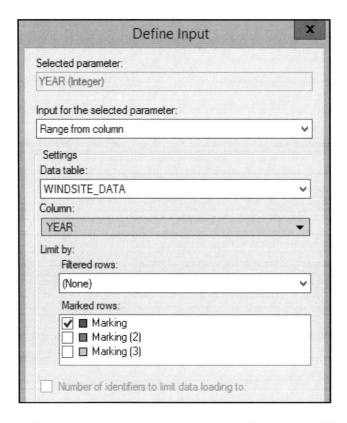

7. Define any further inputs. In my case, the final dialog looks like this. Notice how I have checked the **Load automatically** and **Allow caching** options:

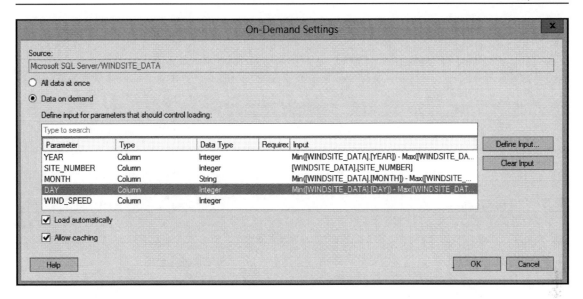

8. Click **OK** on the dialog and **OK** to finish setting up the on-demand data table.

9. Finally, to prove that the data is being loaded on demand, let's create a table plot that shows the second table. If we select that visualization, we can see that we have **0 of 0 rows** shown—the table plot is empty and so is the underlying data table in Spotfire:

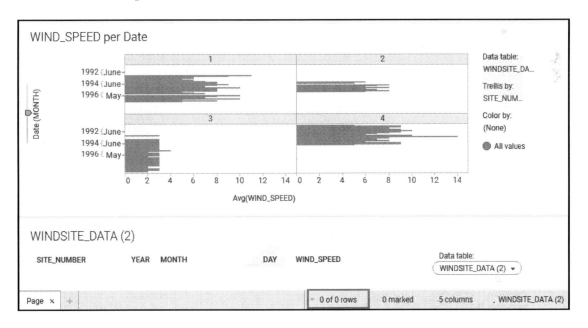

Notice that we have NOT created a details visualization. We could have done so, but then we would have had to relate the new (in-memory) data table with the external table, before marking and details visualizations would have worked properly. Of course, you can do this as an exercise if you wish, but it's not necessary in this case, as the table plot is automatically a details visualization because it is displaying data that has been loaded on demand by virtue of the data that is marked in the bar chart.

10. To test that loading data is working correctly, we can mark some data in the bar chart and return to the table plot, selecting it in order to make it the active visualization:

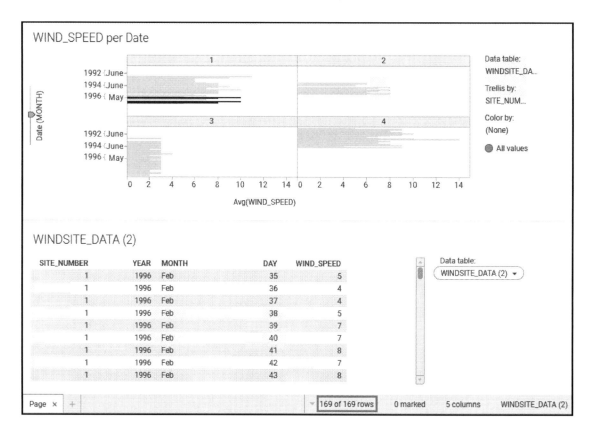

Now, it's clear that the data is being loaded into memory, but only the data that corresponds to the marking. You can confirm this by attempting to export data to a file like as before. This time, data is available from the second data table as the data is available in Spotfire's in-memory data engine.

Troubleshooting data on demand

Let's look at what happens if data on demand goes wrong. What if we configure it incorrectly? If I configure the YEAR, MONTH, and DAY columns to use individual values instead of a range and then mark a sizable chunk of data in the bar chart, no data will be shown in the table plot and Spotfire will show a warning. If I click on the warning, Spotfire gives the following details:

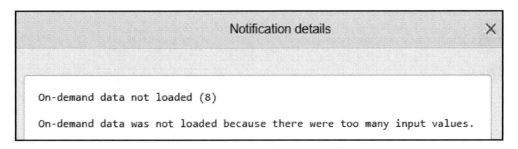

This tells me that I have too many input values to the query in the database. This is because there are too many values in the marked data to be passed to the on-demand query. Using min and max (that is, for specifying a range) is a much more efficient query than selecting data for the individual values and is entirely suitable in this case as I am showing a range of dates on the categorical axis of the bar chart.

If I further experiment with marking ranges on the bar chart, a different warning is displayed—here are the details in this case:

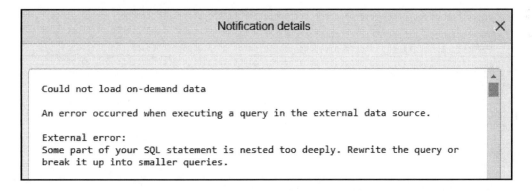

If I scroll down in the **Notification details** window, I can see the details of the query that has been submitted to the database:

Anyone can see that this query is completely impractical, and it's no wonder the database has thrown its hands up in horror!

This notification is a useful troubleshooting guide. I recommend that you use it when data on demand doesn't work as you expect.

In the first example error with data on demand, Spotfire already knows it's not going to be able to send the query to the database engine. In the second example, it thinks it can try, so it does send the query, but the database does not execute the query because it's too deeply nested.

This section was designed to be a warning—although it's easy enough to configure data on demand, it's also easy to get it wrong and to produce something that doesn't work in the real world. As I've stated elsewhere in this book, it's always important to test that everything works as it should, especially in nonideal or unexpected situations.

Custom expressions with in-database data

You can use custom expressions with in-database data. In fact, they are very useful. However, there are some limitations. The full suite of expression functions is not immediately available when working with external data, but there are some things you can do to mitigate this.

When Spotfire is showing external data in a visualization, the connector in use will translate Spotfire's internal data query into a query that the underlying data source understands. Connectors reveal their capabilities to Spotfire, so Spotfire understands those capabilities. The capabilities are also shown to you, the analyst, in the custom expression editor. Here's an example of the function help box in the expression editor when using external data in Microsoft SQL Server:

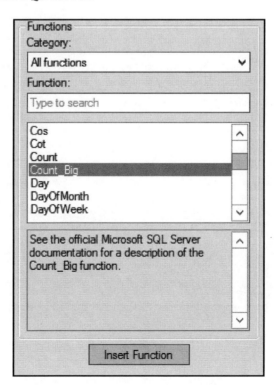

Notice how Spotfire suggests consulting the official SQL Server documentation for a description of the `Count_Big` function. Spotfire is just allowing us to use all (appropriate) SQL Server functions in the custom expression.

Naturally, this means that a lot of the custom expression functions that you are used to using in Spotfire (as discussed in `Chapter 7`, *Source Data is Never Enough*) are not available—at least, not at first sight.

So, how could we use some of the more powerful Spotfire functions when working with external data? For example, would we be able to use the OVER functions?

We can use the OVER functions, but only as custom expressions for visualizations, with a neat little trick! The OVER functions are not shown in the function help, but if we dig a bit deeper, we can use them by way of post-aggregation expressions.

Remember the THEN keyword? Again, this was introduced in `Chapter 7`, *Source Data is Never Enough*. It allows us to write post-aggregation expressions. We can use these to enable the powerful Spotfire expression language when working with external data. For example, this expression calculates the average, year-on-year difference with the wind site data:

```
Avg([WIND_SPEED])
THEN [Value] - First([Value]) OVER (NavigatePeriod([Axis.X],"Year",-1))
```

See how it works? The first line of the expression executes in the database itself. The database will return the average wind speed. The second line performs the Spotfire OVER function. What you don't see is the WHERE or GROUP BY clauses from the SQL expression that goes to the database. We can let Spotfire worry about that!

If we think a bit more deeply about what's going on here, we can envisage that Spotfire visualizes a small in-memory data table that represents the results of the original query in the underlying database. This means that we can perform our own custom expressions over the top of that data table.

To reiterate, you can use post-aggregation expressions when working with in-database data, but only within visualization expressions. You cannot use this method within calculated columns.

Of course, this is a pretty advanced topic, but I was certainly intrigued when I found out about the capabilities of post-aggregation expressions for this purpose.

Important points to note with in-database (external) data

There are some important points to be aware of with external data. I'll list the main ones briefly here for quick reference:

- The recommendations engine does not operate on external data, so you'll need to build all your visualizations manually.
- You cannot send external data to a data function—it is far better to use data on demand and use that as a data source for a data function.
- Filters are not created by default—you can create them on individual columns by clicking on the filter icon on a column in the data panel and creating the filter.
- If you are using a table plot to show external data, you MUST define a primary key on the data table. This is because Spotfire needs to have a unique identifier on the data in order to be able to identify the rows in the data source.
- You can't use box plots with external data.
- You can't use Spotfire's transformations on external data—there's no data loaded in Spotfire for the transformations to operate on.
- You can only use the data source's functions for calculated column expressions. You cannot use Spotfire's expression functions.

I recommend that you browse the Spotfire online help if you need more information on these points. It is very comprehensive.

Connection credentials for Web Player users and Automation Services jobs

This section is extremely important! If you connect to a data source using the methods we've outlined so far in this chapter and save your analysis to the Spotfire library, Web Player users will need to enter their database credentials to log in—they'll be presented with a dialog that looks similar to this:

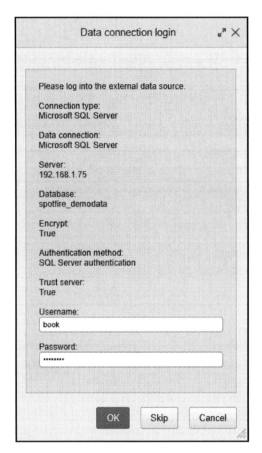

If this is what you require or what you intended, then all is well. However, if you don't want end users of your analysis to need to enter their database credentials, then you must perform some additional steps.

In addition, Automation Services jobs (see Chapter 6, *The Big Wide World of Spotfire*) that use your analysis will not work with the default settings.

You have two options—you can use a preconfigured credentials profile, or you can save the credentials with the connection data source. I do not recommend the latter as the username and password are stored unencrypted with the analysis file. Anyone with access to the file and the ability to download it could discover the username and password stored in the analysis file.

 If you need to use a credentials profile, then enabling this must be done by a server administrator. In addition, enabling credentials profiles will mean that all connections that use a particular connector on a Web Player or Automation Services instance MUST use credentials profiles. If you need different methods of logging in to the same connector within your Spotfire Web/Automation Services infrastructure, then I recommend creating multiple Web Player and Automation Services instances and configuring each of them independently to support the desired authentication methods.

We will now access the credentials settings for the connection and cover both options:

1. From the **Data** menu, choose **Data connection properties**.
2. Click **Settings....**
3. You should see a dialog that looks like this:

4. Now, navigate to the **Data Source** tab:

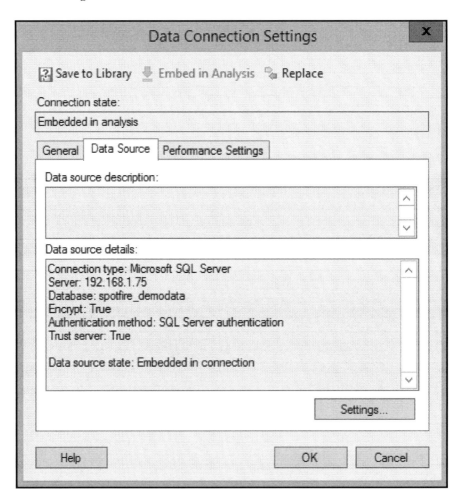

5. Click **Settings**:

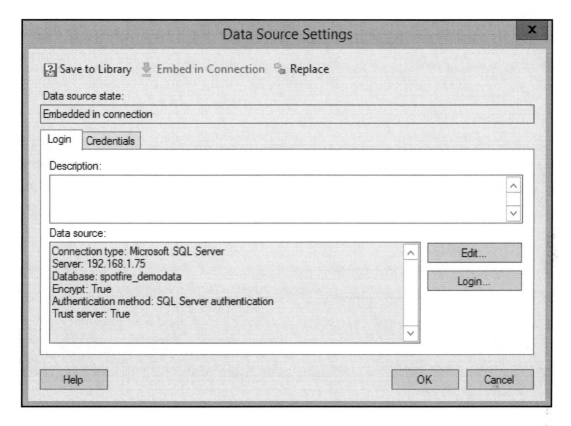

6. Navigate to the **Credentials** tab:

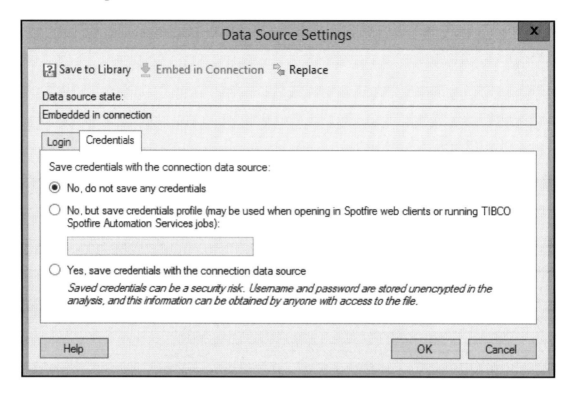

Let's study this dialog for a moment—notice how the default is to not save any credentials with the connection data source. The other two options are to use a credentials profile or to save the credentials with the connection data source.

Saving the credentials with the connection data source is the simpler of the two options for removing the need for Web Player users to enter their credentials and will allow Automation Services jobs to work. However, I don't recommend this option in general as the username and password are stored unencrypted within the analysis. This is fine if you are working in an organization where the data source is behind a firewall and does not contain confidential data, but it probably isn't in most other cases.

To set up a credentials profile, you'll need a Spotfire server administrator's help. I've detailed the steps here, so enlist an administrator now or go and see them with a copy of this book! If you are a server administrator, follow along with me as I configure my own server:

 This section uses Spotfire's command-line configuration tool. It's extremely powerful—if you've not used it before, then this section is a good example of how to get started with it and how to perform an important configuration change.

1. First of all, log in to the Spotfire server machine and open a command prompt. Change the directory to
   `\tomcat\webapps\spotfire\tools\spotfireconfigtool`:

```
                                    Administrator: C:\Windows\system32\cmd.exe

 Directory of C:\tibco\tss\10.3.0\tomcat\webapps\spotfire\tools\spotfireconfigtool

10/04/2019  10:20    <DIR>          .
10/04/2019  10:20    <DIR>          ..
10/04/2019  09:20               240 config.bat
10/04/2019  09:20               380 config.sh
10/04/2019  10:20    <DIR>          lib
10/04/2019  09:20             1,843 log4j2-tools.xml
10/04/2019  10:20    <DIR>          logs
10/04/2019  09:20         1,323,070 TIB_sfire_server_license.pdf
10/04/2019  09:20               249 uiconfig.bat
10/04/2019  09:20               389 uiconfig.sh
               6 File(s)      1,326,171 bytes
               4 Dir(s)   6,551,236,608 bytes free

C:\tibco\tss\10.3.0\tomcat\webapps\spotfire\tools\spotfireconfigtool>_
```

 If the Spotfire config tool directory doesn't exist, that means you haven't extracted the config tool yet—there's a `.jar` file in the tools directory that you must run first—this unpacks the config tool for you. Also, the TIBCO official documentation suggests that the default installation directory for the config tool is `tomcat\bin`—in my experience, this has not been the case. Just be aware and adjust paths/folders appropriately.

2. Now, we'll need to export the default `Spotfire.Dxp.Worker.Host.exe.config` file by entering the following command:

```
config export-service-config -b
c:\tibco\tss\10.version.x\tomcat\webapps\spotfire\WEB-
INF\bootstrap.xml --capability=WEB_PLAYER --deployment-
area=MyDeploymentArea
```

3. Obviously, please replace any file paths or names to deployment areas with those relevant to your environment. Of particular note is the location of the bootstrap file. This file provides bootstrap configuration information to the Spotfire Server and is created at the time of installation of the Spotfire Server.

 If you have multiple Web Player configurations, then be sure to add this option to the command line: `--config-name=MyConfig`.

4. You'll be prompted to enter the Spotfire config tool password. This password would have been set at the time of installation of the Spotfire Server. Once the command has completed, a number of files should be created in a folder called `config\root`:

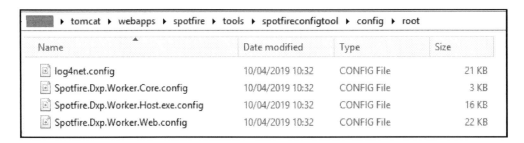

5. For security reasons, let's just verify that any configuration files distributed to Web Player nodes will be encrypted—check that the `<cryptography encryptConfigurationSections="true" ..../>` flag is set in the `Spotfire.Dxp.Worker.Core.config` file. It should be enabled by default:

```
24    </Spotfire.Dxp.Services.Settings>
25
26    <!-- Settings for the node service application. -->
27    <Spotfire.Dxp.Worker.Host>
28        <!-- protectSectionEncryptionProvider: The name of the
            algorithm to use when encrypting sections of the
            configuration files. -->
29        <!--    See
            https://msdn.microsoft.com/en-us/library/68ze1hb2.aspx
            for more information. -->
30        <cryptography encryptConfigurationSections="true"
            protectSectionEncryptionProvider=
            "DataProtectionConfigurationProvider" />
31    </Spotfire.Dxp.Worker.Host>
32
33 </configuration>
```

6. Now, let's update the `Spotfire.Dxp.Worker.Host.exe.config` file. Search for `Spotfire.Dxp.Web.Properties.Settings` and the `DataAdapterCredentials` section. Insert the following block into the `setting/value/credentials` section:

```
<entry profile="myprofile">
    <username>user</username>
    <password>password</password>
</entry>
```

7. Once we have done this, we need to enable the `WebConfig` method for the adapter/connector in use. We need to search for the `WebAuthenticationMode` section of the file. In my case, I am using the `SqlServer` connector, so I have updated my file to look like this:

```
275    <setting name="WebAuthenticationMode" serializeAs=
       "Xml">
276      <value>
277        <adapters>
278          <adapter name="Spotfire.SqlServerAdapter" mode=
             "WebConfig"/>
279          <adapter name="Spotfire.TeradataAdapter" mode=
             "Prompt"/>
```

8. We've finished editing configuration files, so let's save the file.

9. Now, we can reimport the updated configuration. Return to the command prompt and enter the following config command:

```
config import-service-config -b
c:\tibco\tss\10.version.x\tomcat\webapps\spotfire\WEB-
INF\bootstrap.xml --config-name=SqlServerWebConfig --delete-
directory
```

Specifying the `-delete-directory` option deletes the XML configuration files after the configuration has been imported. This is a useful security step as it ensures that the files are not left lying around on the filing system containing unencrypted passwords.

10. Now, we need to update the configuration of a Web Player service to use the new configuration. Open a web browser and visit the Spotfire administration console. The administration console was first introduced in `Chapter 6`, *The Big Wide World of Spotfire*.

11. Navigate to **Nodes & Services** and select the Web Player instance we'd like to configure:

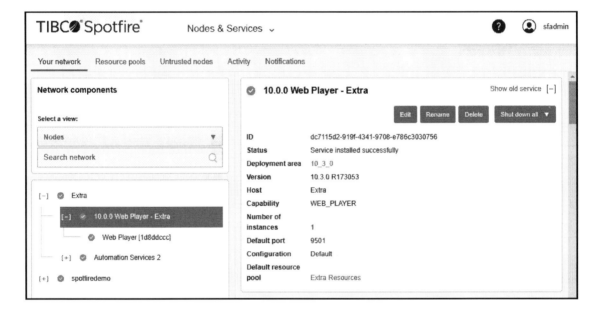

12. Edit the service instance and change the configuration to the new one that we just created:

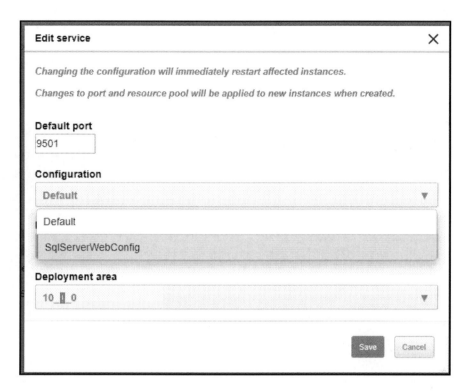

13. Save the configuration.

 Saving the configuration will restart the service instance, which will disrupt any active user sessions!

Now that the server administration job is done, we can return to Spotfire and start to use the credentials profile that's just been set up:

1. If you closed the **Data Source Settings** dialog, reopen it and find the **Credentials** tab once more.

2. Now, we need to specify the name of the credentials profile that was created by the administrator. In my case, it was `myprofile`:

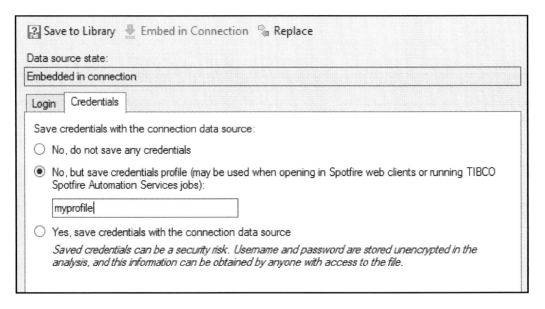

3. Click **OK** on the dialog and all other open dialogs to return to the analysis.

4. Finally, we can save the analysis to the Spotfire library and test it. I don't need to show you how to save an analysis to the library again, so just go ahead and test it!

To summarize this section, we have seen how credentials are used when working with data connectors in Spotfire Web Player. We (or the server administrator) set up a credentials profile, which is a secure way of managing credentials with connectors. Then, we used the credentials profile in our data connection and saved it to the Spotfire library.

Saving connections to the Spotfire library

Did you notice when working with it, that the **Data Connection Settings** dialog has a button to save the connection to the library? Being able to save the connection to the library is an incredibly useful and powerful feature. Just think about it—you can define the connection and save it in the library. Then, another Spotfire user can find the connection and use it in their own analysis.

Even better, a Spotfire Business Author or Cloud user can then use that connection to author their analysis on the web, without having to define the connection. Recall that most connectors cannot be configured using Business Author or Cloud web clients, so if you save a connection to the library and make it available, then you can surface all kinds of data for free-form analysis of users of the web clients.

To illustrate, I have just saved the connection from the last example into my Spotfire library. I have created a new analysis on the web and now I can browse to the connection and use the data within it:

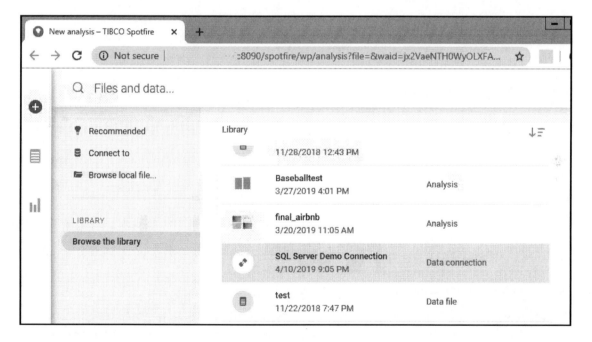

Clicking on the connection allows me to choose how I would like to work with each of the tables in the connection—whether I want to import the data or keep it external, if I want to exclude a table, and much more:

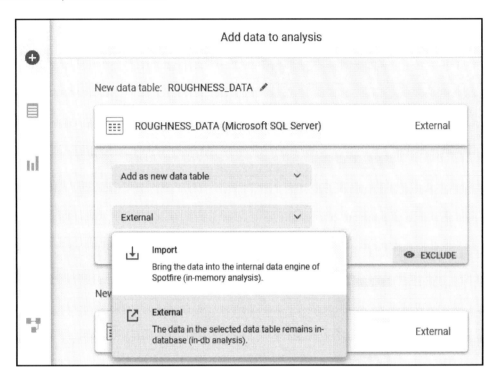

Streaming data

In a lot of cases, static data that's already been generated is analyzed too late. If you're looking at oil well production from yesterday and you notice that a machine broke down partway through the day, it's already too late. If you are monitoring mobile phone outages and can only see what happened last week, it's too late to do anything about the thousands of inconvenienced customers.

The combination of Spotfire and Spotfire Data Streams allows for a real-time visualization of data flowing through any process or system. In order to take advantage of streaming data in Spotfire, you will also need the Spotfire Data Streams software package.

Streaming data works with many (though not all) standard Spotfire visualizations and, provided that you create the necessary data relations, you can perform marking and filtering seamlessly between static (historical) and live data.

Unfortunately, the technology doesn't exist where I can put a live streaming demo into a printed book yet, so I suggest that you take a look on YouTube, here:

`https://www.youtube.com/watch?v=Byv-Nf6TC-o.`

Or, use the following shortened link:
`http://bit.ly/2U5Y2yj.`

Alternatively, just search for Spotfire Data Streams!

Streaming data is very easy to set up in Spotfire—it's enabled by use of a special data connector. All you need to do is choose the **TIBCO Spotfire Data Streams** connector when adding a new data table:

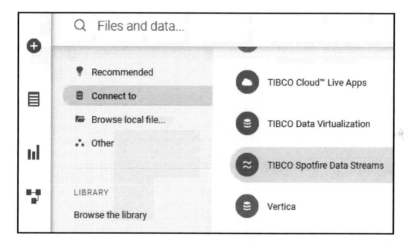

Then, connect to your Spotfire Data Streams instance and bring in the tables you want to visualize.

 When working with streaming data in Spotfire, the data will always be external. By now, you should be aware of what you can and cannot do with external data, and how working with it differs from in-memory data.

Spotfire Data Streams is a separate product available from TIBCO. It also ships with Live Datamart, the underlying database technology for streaming data.

Spotfire Data Streams is a data workflow tool that was specifically designed for real-time data streams. It can evaluate the results of statistical models, look backwards in data, and alert users when an event occurs. It is low-latency and highly scalable. Here's an example screenshot showing the part of a streaming workflow being developed in the tool:

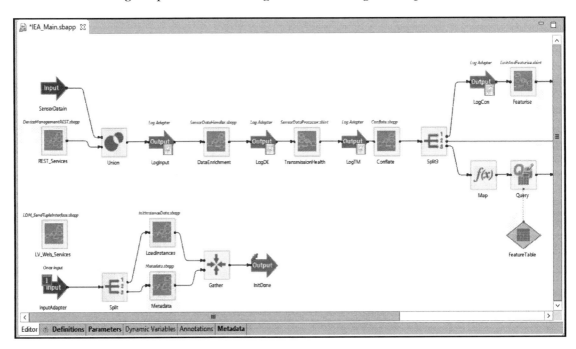

The example workflow is designed for working with equipment with sensors attached. It is part of a solution that takes data from sensors and runs a statistical model on the data, looking for unusual events. It generates alerts when sensor values begin to trend in ways that indicate that a potential failure is imminent. This solution, combined with Spotfire, gives users the ability to monitor equipment to understand why it fails when it fails. Users can then adjust the statistical model and monitor and improve the accuracy of the model over time.

Spotfire Data Streams is also marketed as TIBCO StreamBase. StreamBase and Spotfire Data Streams are being used for many different purposes within all sorts of industries. Examples of uses are fraud detection, predictive maintenance, manufacturing, and IoT.

I find that the most frequently asked question about Spotfire Data Streams is as follows:

> *"Do I need the Spotfire Data Streams product in order to work with streaming data in Spotfire? Can't I just connect Spotfire to another streaming technology?"*

The answer is, yes, you definitely do need Spotfire Data Streams. Spotfire cannot connect directly to other streaming technologies—this is because the Data Streams connector was written specifically for the TIBCO Spotfire Data Streams product. You can use the TIBCO Spotfire Data Streams product to connect to other streaming technologies as a piece of middleware in order to work with the other technologies.

Finally, one other point to note is that, like other external or in-database technologies, the Spotfire custom expressions can only use the functions provided by the underlying system—in this case, Live Datamart.

 Live Datamart is a data mart that's highly optimized for streaming data—for example, it has SQL functions to select time slices in data. It is designed for fast insert and fast query performance with low latency.

Since Spotfire uses Live Datamart, the expression functions provided by Live Datamart are available for use within Spotfire. You cannot use Spotfire's custom expression functions with Live Datamart.

Summary

In this chapter, you have learned about the main differences between working with in-memory and in-database (external) data and how to combine the two strategies by using data on demand. You understood how to use Spotfire's information links and database connectors and how to get started with streaming (live) data.

We covered in-memory versus in-database data in some detail. There's a need for both methods when working with data in Spotfire. This chapter discussed when and where you might need either strategy and explained the main differences between them. Custom expressions were shown, along with some useful tips for using post aggregation expressions with external systems to enable the use of OVER functions. We also covered data on demand, which is a great way to combine the advantages of in-database and in-memory analytics into a single solution.

We spent some time looking at credentials for data connectors and how to configure them securely for web-based users and Automation Services.

Finally, streaming data was covered, along with a brief introduction to TIBCO Spotfire Data Streams and TIBCO StreamBase. There are lots of resources on the internet for these products, so I recommend that you dig further if you want to know more.

The next chapter covers scripting, advanced analytics, and extensions. It covers how to work with IronPython, JavaScript, Python, TIBCO Enterprise Runtime for R (TERR), and more. It also covers how to extend Spotfire.

11
Scripting, Advanced Analytics, and Extensions

Now comes one of my favorite aspects of Spotfire. Its extensibility! One of the main advantages of Spotfire is that it's highly extensible and customizable. It can also be easily embedded into other applications.

This is a huge topic that could fill an entire book on its own, so think of this chapter as an introduction to the capabilities and the art of the possible. I'll point out what you can do and the basics of how to do it, with references to various resources along the way. You'll get the most benefit out of this chapter if you are a software developer (or at least dabble with software development), or if you are a statistician familiar with R, Python, or similar.

By the end of this chapter, you should have enough information to get started with scripting using IronPython, JavaScript, or any of the statistical programming languages and environments that work with Spotfire. You'll also know where to go to get more information on all of these.

This chapter covers the following topics:

- Scripting in Spotfire – the why, how, and what
- IronPython scripting
- JavaScript scripting
- Spotfire's Developer Tools
- Script trust
- TIBCO Enterprise Runtime for R and open source R
- Python
- Statistica
- Extending Spotfire
- The JavaScript API
- Server APIs

Scripting in Spotfire – the why, how, and what

There are several different ways that you can work with scripting in Spotfire, as follows:

- Automate various actions by calling the Spotfire **application programming interface** (**API**) using IronPython
- Manipulate the Spotfire user interface or use fancy controls by using JavaScript in text areas
- Embed advanced statistical analysis scripts using TIBCO Enterprise Runtime for R or open source R or Python

We'll be covering the various different scripting languages and why you would use them, how you use them, and what they can do for you.

Automating actions using IronPython

Using IronPython in Spotfire is comparable to the use of VBA in Microsoft Excel, although you need to do everything yourself in Spotfire—you can't record a macro and then go and edit it afterwards.

Spotfire has a comprehensive API that is based on Microsoft's .NET technology. We can work with the API using IronPython, which is a version of the Python programming language with extensions that work with the .NET framework. If you don't already know, Python was named after the hugely funny and influential comedy group, Monty Python. It seems that computer scientists do have a sense of humor after all!

To write scripts that use the Spotfire API, you need some programming experience and you also need to know how to use Spotfire's library of properties and methods. However, there are lots of example scripts on the TIBCO Community that you can just copy and paste or adapt to your specific use case. Example scripts and tutorials can be found here:

`https://community.tibco.com/wiki/ironpython-scripting-tibco-spotfire.`

Alternatively, use this shortened link:

`http://bit.ly/2UBdeZq.`

The main use of IronPython scripts is to automate various actions in Spotfire. You may have a number of steps for configuring a visualization. You may wish to apply a custom sort order to a column, or retrieve some values from marked data. You might want to trigger an action when a user clicks on a KPI chart or graphical table row, or when they change a property control. You may also wish to call a web service, or write back some data to another system, all based on what the user is interacting with in Spotfire at the time. All these things and much more can be done with IronPython.

Documenting the Spotfire API is beyond the scope of this book, as is providing a full tutorial for IronPython. All the resources you need are accessible from the link that was given previously, including a link to the Spotfire API documentation.

The Spotfire API documentation is primarily designed for .NET developers who are developing extensions to Spotfire. If you start to go beyond the example scripts, you'll likely need to reference the API documentation at some point. After you've worked with some examples and followed the tutorials, you'll soon get the hang of how to work with the API in IronPython. It's basically a case of translating the API calls into IronPython or calling them in a way that works with IronPython.

Important notes:
You can only author scripts when using the Spotfire Analyst client.
You **must** be a member of the Script Author Spotfire security group in order to author scripts.
IronPython scripts that have been authored with Spotfire Analyst work on Spotfire Web Player (in most cases).
IronPython scripts do NOT work on Spotfire Cloud for security reasons.

IronPython scripts can be created in a few different ways—by editing them directly through the **Document Properties** dialog (from the **File** menu), or by attaching them to property controls or buttons.

Rather than providing a tutorial for IronPython, I thought it would be more helpful to follow through an example of adapting a script from the TIBCO Community—my aim is to get you started straight away. As you follow the example, you'll learn how to work with IronPython scripts and the Spotfire Analyst API—we'll go through some troubleshooting steps as part of that process.

The example script sets which columns are shown on a table plot when a user changes a property control. Let's adapt it to the Airbnb data that we last looked at in `Chapter 9`, *What's Your Location?*:

1. First of all, open the Airbnb example as per `Chapter 9`, *What's Your Location?*. This is a good example to work with because the data has a lot of columns in it.

2. Now let's visit the page on the TIBCO Community that contains the sample script we'll be using. Its URL is as follows:
   `https://community.tibco.com/wiki/example-script-modify-which-columns-are-shown-table-plot`.
   Alternatively, use this shortened link:
   `http://bit.ly/2G5ZiMU`.

3. If we read the article, we'll see that it covers setting up a property control so that when the user changes the property control, the script will execute and change the configuration of the table plot.
   Of course, the article uses different data to the Airbnb data, so we need to adapt the script to use Airbnb data rather than the data shown in the article.

4. Create a new page, then add a table plot and a text area to the page. You should end up with something that looks like this:

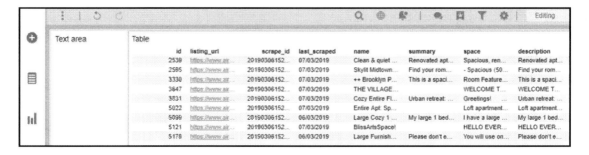

As a general principle, I prefer putting any controls at the top or left of a page. It's good user interface design practice, since most people work from left to right and, as such, it's much more intuitive to have your pages laid out like this.

5. Now, we need to add a drop-down control to the text area and configure it. Add a drop-down control to the text area and create a new document property of type **String**. Call it `SelectedMetrics`.

6. Configure the dropdown with `Fixed values` and enter the values that are shown here:

7. Now that we've configured the property control with its display names and values, we can attach a script to it, so go ahead and click the **Script...** button.

8. Select the option to **Execute the script selected below**:

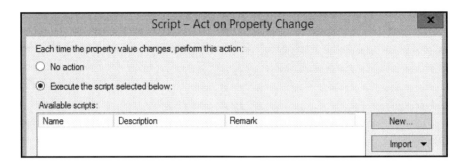

9. Click the **New...** button.

10. The IronPython editor window will open. Give the script a name. I suggest `SelectMetrics`.

11. Now, we can start editing the script itself. Revisit the TIBCO Community page and copy and paste the script text into the script editor window.

12. I'm sure that you now realize that we need to update the script to work with the Airbnb data, so let's scroll to the part of the script that sets up the columns:

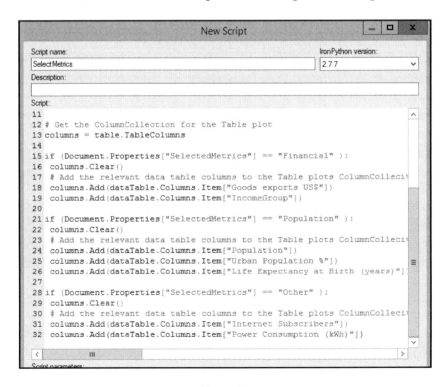

13. Let's look at the parts of the code that determine the current setting for the `SelectedMetrics` document property—it should be fairly obvious, but for avoidance of doubt, this is wherever you see something like this:

```
if (Document.Properties['SelectedMetrics'] ==
'Financial' ):
```

14. It's pretty easy to update the script for our example. In each of the three cases, update the `if` statements in the code for each of the three values we designed into the drop-down control: `Descriptions`, `Prices`, and `Beds and Bathrooms`. For example:

```
if (Document.Properties['SelectedMetrics'] == 'Descriptions' ):
```

15. The next bit of editing we need to do is update the code to set the correct columns in the table plot.

16. If we do `Descriptions` first, we need to update the code under the respective `if` statement to this:

```
columns.Add(dataTable.Columns.Item['listing_url'])
columns.Add(dataTable.Columns.Item['description'])
columns.Add(dataTable.Columns.Item['notes'])
columns.Add(dataTable.Columns.Item['summary'])
```

Important note: When working with IronPython, it's critically important to maintain indentation within code blocks. Any lines of code that are executed as part of an `if` statement must be indented under the `if` statement and must be at the same level. It's easy to get confused between space and tab characters, so I recommend that you choose a set number of spaces or always use tab characters when indenting code. It's unfortunate that the Community article uses spaces for indenting—I much prefer using tabs as I find it easier to be consistent when working with tab characters rather than spaces.

17. Now, we need to update the code for the other sets of columns. For `Prices`, I have chosen `listing_url`, `price`, `monthly_price`, `cleaning_fee`, and `security_deposit`.

18. For `Beds and Bathrooms`, let's use `listing_url`, `beds`, `bedrooms`, and `bathrooms`.

Important: All document property values and column names must be specified exactly as they are present in the Spotfire analysis file. The names of document properties, document property values, and column names are all case-sensitive. Getting these things wrong will mean that the script will not work properly.

A useful tip is to have a second copy of the analysis open at the same time as you are editing the script—that way, you can copy and paste column names, document property names and values, and so on, into your script code, without having to dismiss the script editor.

19. Before we complete the editing of the script, I strongly recommend that you do as I have, and replace all space characters with tabs—as mentioned in the tip earlier. This is pretty easy to do by highlighting the block of code under each `if` statement, holding *Shift*, and pressing the *Tab* key on your keyboard, then pressing *Tab* once more (without the *Shift* key) to indent the code correctly.

20. When you've finished coding, you should see something like this:

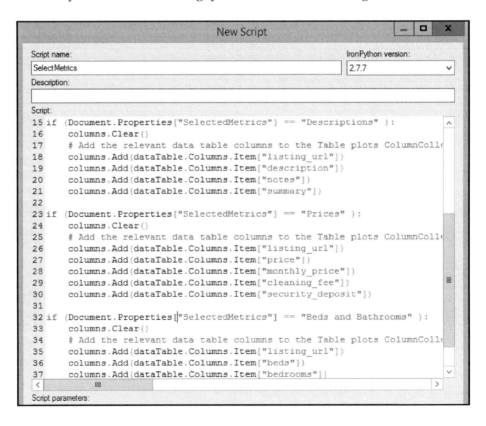

21. Before we can finish with the script entirely, we need to give it a reference to the table plot visualization on the page. We can do this by clicking the **Add...** button to add a new script parameter:

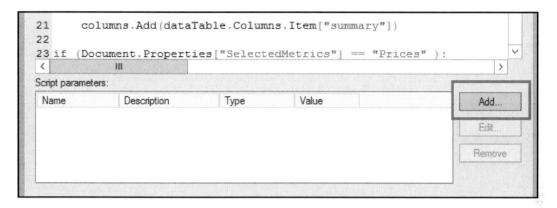

22. Enter the name of the parameter—this should be Tab as it matches what's used in the script.
23. Finally, make sure that the script is of type Visualization and that the table plot on your page is selected. You should end up with a dialog that looks like this:

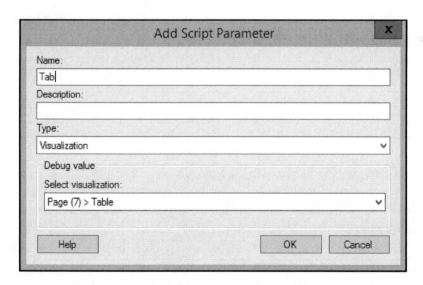

24. Note that this doesn't actually connect up your table plot to the script—at this stage, the parameter is only set up for debug usage.

25. Click **OK** on the parameter dialog.

26. We can now test our script! Click the **Run Script** button on the **Edit Script** dialog.

27. In my case, the script didn't run the first time. I wonder if you'll have the same problem. The error that was reported for me was that the **unindent doesn't match any outer indentation level**—that is, beyond the end of the script:

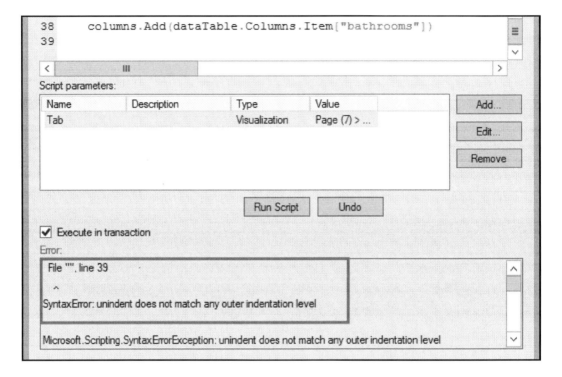

28. If we study `line 39` of the script, the line that apparently contains the error, we can see that the line appears empty. So, why is Spotfire complaining?

29. The error is probably caused by a stray space or tab character—either from editing the script to replace the space characters with tabs, or as a result of copying and pasting the script from the Community page.

30. Never fear—this is easy to correct—let's just remove the blank line and run the script again.

31. If we do this and don't see any error output, then all is well! Don't dismiss the script editor window just yet.

32. If you get stuck with this example, I recommend that you post a question on the TIBCO Community—someone should be able to assist you!

Before we can use the script in the analysis file, we need to connect it to the table plot visualization that we added to our analysis at the beginning of the example. Let's do this now by performing the following steps:

1. Click **OK** on the script editor window—we should now be back on the **Script - Act on Property Change** dialog.
2. We can configure the input for the parameter—this time, it's for real! Make sure that the table plot visualization is selected. The dialog should look like this:

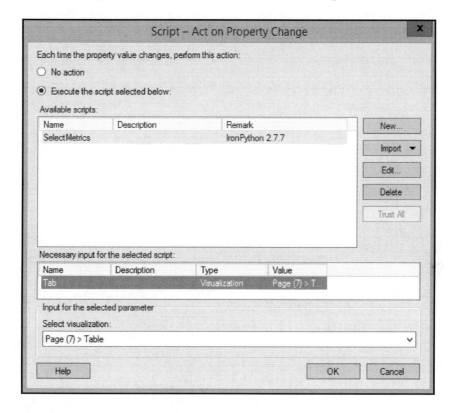

3. Click **OK** to set the parameter.
4. Click **OK** to dismiss the property control editor.
5. Click **Save** to save the text area.
6. Close the text area editor.
7. Now comes the exciting bit! We can test the script—try changing the drop-down control. The columns shown on the table plot should change according to the column selections we specified in the script.

8. Again, if your script doesn't work, have a go at troubleshooting it and if you're stuck, post a question on the TIBCO Community.

9. We're not quite done yet—I noticed that the `listing_url` column didn't work as I expected. Instead of nice, clickable URLs, I found that the URLs were just in plain text:

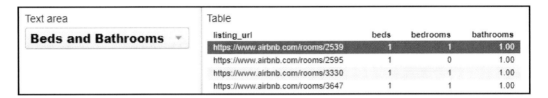

This is another of those examples where I think it's more useful to show you how to fix these kinds of issues, rather than just produce an exercise that always works perfectly.

The problem here is that the table plot doesn't know that the `listing_url` column should be rendered as a URL. It's not something we've touched on before, but columns in a table all have a **renderer**. The default renderer is text. You can also use a URL renderer, an image renderer, or even a custom table value renderer. If we look at the table plot columns and select the `listing_url` column, we can see that the renderer is `Text`:

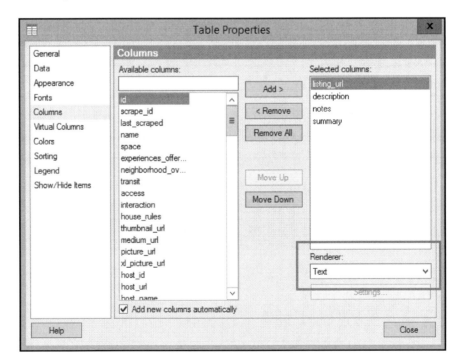

This isn't what we want. We could try setting the renderer to show a link (URL), but this would be pointless since the script removes all the columns from the table plot before adding the selected columns back to it. We need to edit the script to set the correct renderer for the `listing_url` column. In doing this, we can go and look at the API documentation to find out how to set the renderer for a column in the table plot. Follow along with me:

1. Open the documentation for the Spotfire Analyst API—it can be found here:
   `https://docs.tibco.com/pub/doc_remote/sfire_dev/area/doc/api/TIB_`
   `sfire-analyst_api/Index.aspx`.
   Alternatively, use this shortened link:
   `http://bit.ly/2IsT0cM`.

2. Click the search icon:

3. We know that we need to do something with a renderer, so let's search for
   `renderer`. The most helpful search result appears to be
   `TableColumnCollection.SetValueRenderer`:

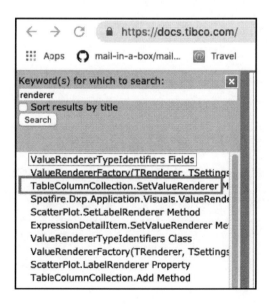

4. Let's click on the link. The `TableColumnCollection.SetValueRenderer` method documentation will be shown:

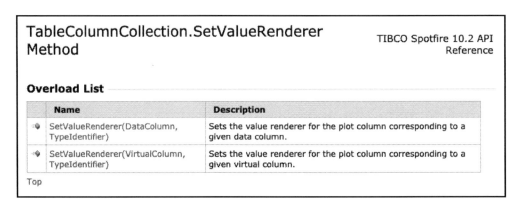

5. In order to use this method, we need to call it on the table plot object in the script and give it parameters of the correct type—a `DataColumn` and a value renderer `TypeIdentifier`. The `DataColumn` part is straightforward, but let's go and look at the `ValueRendererTypeIdentifiers Fields` documentation by clicking on it in the search result:

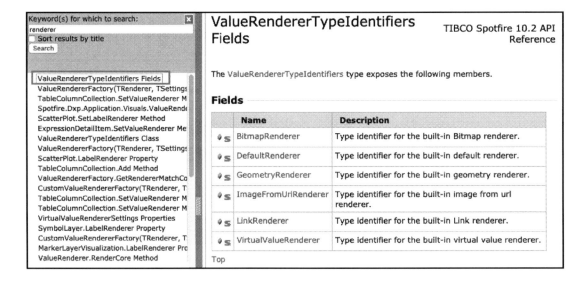

6. Let's use this information to set the renderer for the `listing_url` column.

We need to add a line of code to the end of the script. I've done the hard work and translated the documentation into IronPython for you. Let's go ahead and add the following line to the end of the script:

```
Tab.As[TablePlot]().TableColumns.SetValueRenderer(dataTable.Col
umns.Item['listing_url'],
ValueRendererTypeIdentifiers.LinkRenderer)
```

7. We'll dissect the script line later on in this example.
8. Let's try running the script. It doesn't work! The error we get is as follows:

```
NameError: name 'ValueRendererTypeIdentifiers' is not defined
```

9. This means that the scripting engine cannot find the class called `ValueRendererTypeIdentifiers`—in other words, it doesn't know what a `ValueRendererTypeIdentifier` is, so we need to tell it! This is done by adding an `import` statement to the beginning of the script.
10. To determine what we need to import, we need the documentation again. We must locate the `ValueRendererTypeIdentifiers` class in the documentation and study the Inheritance Hierarchy. Using the documentation, we can see where the `ValueRendererTypeIdentifiers` class exists in the hierarchy of the Spotfire API:

ValueRendererTypeIdentifiers Class
TIBCO Spotfire 10.2 API Reference

Defines the type identifiers for built-in value renderers.

Inheritance Hierarchy

System.Object
  Spotfire.Dxp.Framework.DocumentModel.TypeIdentifiers
    Spotfire.Dxp.Application.Visuals.ValueRenderers.ValueRendererTypeIdentifiers

Namespace: Spotfire.Dxp.Application.Visuals.ValueRenderers
Assembly: Spotfire.Dxp.Application (in Spotfire.Dxp.Application.dll) Version: 38.0.13322.5367
(38.0.13322.5367)

This translates to the following import statement:

```
from Spotfire.Dxp.Application.Visuals.ValueRenderers import
ValueRendererTypeIdentifiers
```

If we add the import statement and the line of code to the end of the script, it should now work!

Here's the result:

Looking good!

Before we conclude the example of an IronPython script, let's just dissect the line of script that we added to set the value renderer for the table column. For reference, the line was as follows:

```
Tab.As[TablePlot]().TableColumns.SetValueRenderer(dataTable.Columns.Item['l
isting_url'], ValueRendererTypeIdentifiers.LinkRenderer)
```

Each part of the line of code is shown in the following table:

`Tab`	This is a reference to the table plot—it is a generic Visual object at this stage, not an instance of a `TablePlot`.
`As[TablePlot]()`	This turns the generic Visual object into an instance of a `TablePlot`—without this part of the line, we could not call methods that are specific to the table plot.
`TableColumns`	Gets a reference to the `TableColumnCollection`—the collection of columns that belongs to the `TablePlot`.
`SetValueRenderer`	This is the method that we need to call on the `TableColumnCollection`.
`dataTable.Columns.Item['listing_url']`	Gets a reference to the `listing_url` column.
`ValueRendererTypeIdentifiers.LinkRenderer`	The type identifier for the link renderer.

By working through this IronPython example, you'll have learned quite a lot about developing IronPython scripts in Spotfire—you've seen how things can go wrong and how to go about troubleshooting the issues. You have also had a crash course in working with the Spotfire Analyst API documentation and how to translate the .NET documentation into IronPython.

Before we move off the subject of IronPython, I'd like to provide a few notes that will help you out:

- You can also attach IronPython scripts to buttons in text areas or as actions in KPI charts or graphical tables.
- You can access any IronPython scripts stored in a Spotfire analysis from the **Document Properties** dialog, which is accessible from the **File** menu.
- IronPython scripts are not magical! Nor are they mystical. A lot of people ask me if the fundamental operation of a Spotfire visualization can be modified by an IronPython script. For example: "Is it possible to use IronPython to modify a line chart to shade the area underneath a line?" The answer is "No." In general, an IronPython script cannot do anything you can't do in the Spotfire user interface. You should think of IronPython as a useful method for automating existing Spotfire functionality.

As an exercise, you could consider setting the table column widths programmatically. See if you can work out how to do it! Hint: each table column has a `Width` property. Try looking it up in the Spotfire API documentation.

Customizing the Spotfire user interface using JavaScript and HTML in text areas

One of the cool things about Spotfire is that its visualizations and text areas are all browser-based, even in Analyst clients. This means that you can customize aspects of the user interface, develop your own JavaScript controls, or manipulate property controls by showing/hiding them, and so on.

 The usage of JavaScript in text areas is totally distinct from the Spotfire JavaScript API. The JavaScript API is covered later on in this chapter.

You can also customize the HTML that's used in text areas—you can build table layouts, surround property controls with DIV elements, and more.

HTML in text areas is (by default) sanitized. This means that any HTML elements that could possibly lead to security holes in your Spotfire application are disabled. There's more information on HTML sanitation on this knowledge base page:

`https://support.tibco.com/s/article/Parse-Error-message-The-element-xxxxxx-is-not-supported-when-editing-HTML-of-the-Text-area`.

Alternatively, use this shortened link:

`http://bit.ly/2GhrzkB`.

The one important caveat with JavaScript in text areas is that there is no documented API for working with JavaScript inside Spotfire—this is deliberate. The HTML **document object model (DOM)** that's used in Spotfire is (necessarily) complicated and involved. It is liable to change with new versions of Spotfire, so the risk is that any manipulations you make to it may fail when you upgrade to a new version of Spotfire. In addition, modifying the DOM and working with it using JavaScript is not supported by TIBCO, so you are on your own!

Having said that, working with JavaScript is sometimes the only way to get a particular task done. If you're willing to experiment and to test your code with every new release of Spotfire, then you can achieve some amazing results!

 Many people confuse JavaScript with Java. They often refer to Java when they mean JavaScript—it's important to understand the distinction. Java is a fully specified software development framework with lots of packages available for developing rich desktop, mobile, and server applications (and more besides). JavaScript is a scripting language that's designed to run in a web browser or within node.js—a standalone JavaScript runtime. There are some syntax similarities between the languages, but they are essentially distinct and should not be confused.

JavaScript code must be used within text areas in your analysis file. If you develop a JavaScript script, you must use reference it in a text area on every page that you wish to take advantage of that script. However, you can write the script once and use it multiple times.

There's an excellent article on the TIBCO Community entitled Best Practices for Writing Custom JavaScript Code in Text Areas. Its URL is as follows:

```
https://community.tibco.com/wiki/best-practices-writing-custom-javascript-code-
text-areas.
```

Alternatively, you can find it by using this shortened link:

```
http://bit.ly/2Uf1k2e.
```

I recommend that you read the article as it will be kept up to date with the latest best-practice information.

Rather than detail a full example of a JavaScript script in the book, I would like to refer you to this page on the TIBCO Community:

```
https://community.tibco.com/wiki/how-include-your-own-instances-jquery-and-
jqueryui-text-areas.
```

Alternatively, you can refer to it using this shortened link:

```
http://bit.ly/2Z38aLT.
```

It's a really nice, practical example of how to begin to work with JavaScript in text areas. It also details a common issue—that of working with published scripts and JavaScript frameworks. The article focuses on jQuery and jQueryUI, two of the most useful (in my opinion) JavaScript frameworks out there. It discusses how to include these frameworks in your analysis and use them to create an accordion control—one that you can expand and contract—which is useful for hiding and showing various user interface elements in a text area.

Working a little bit with this example will be very helpful to you in understanding how to work with JavaScript and HTML in text areas, so follow along with me as we explore this example:

1. First of all, we need to download the sample Spotfire file from the page, unzip it, and load it into Spotfire.

2. When we load the file, we're presented with a dialog informing us that there are untrusted scripts in the file. These must be trusted in order to continue, so answer **Yes** to the prompt. Spotfire will show a list of JavaScript scripts:

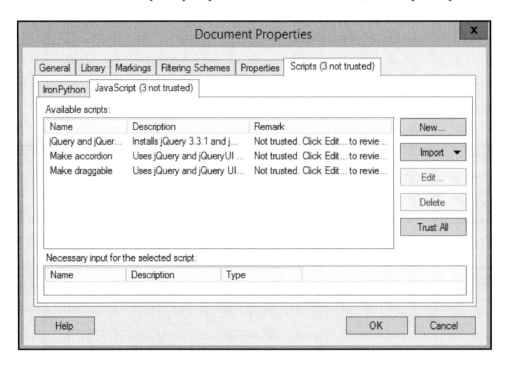

3. For now, we can just **Trust All** scripts, so let's click that button and then **OK** on the dialog.

 Script trust is an important security concern with scripts that are embedded in a Spotfire analysis file. In general, I do not recommend that you trust all the scripts in a file unless you know its source. Script trust is covered in full a bit later in this chapter.

4. A draggable DIV (grouped element in HTML) should be shown in the text area, along with an example accordion control:

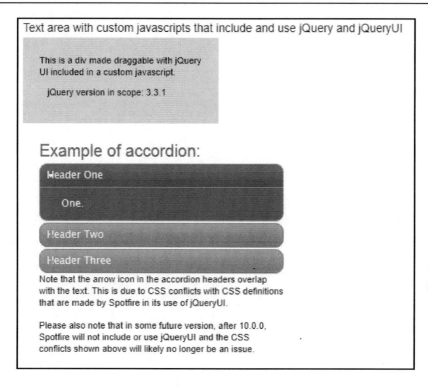

5. Note the warning about overlapping accordion headers—for me, that wasn't a problem as I was using Spotfire version 10.1.

6. Now, we can start to explore how JavaScript scripts are used in text areas. Right-click on the text area and select **Edit HTML**:

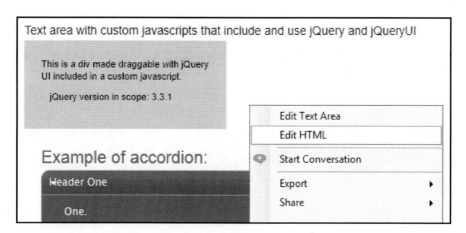

7. This will open the Spotfire HTML text area editor.

8. We can now study the HTML that is used to build the text area and the scripts that are used in the text area:

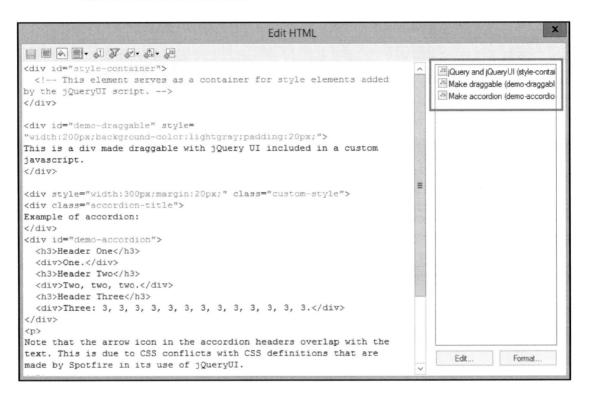

I have highlighted the scripts in the preceding screenshot.

There are three scripts in this example:

- `jQuery and jQuery UI`: This script installs jQuery and jQuery UI
- `Make draggable`: This makes the existing DIV element draggable (you can see it in the HTML code—it's called `demo-draggable`)
- `Make accordion`: This creates an accordion control and attaches it to the `demo-accordion` div in the HTML

We can edit any one of these scripts by clicking on the **Edit...** button and following these steps:

1. The **Insert JavaScript** dialog will be shown—in our case, it should look like this:

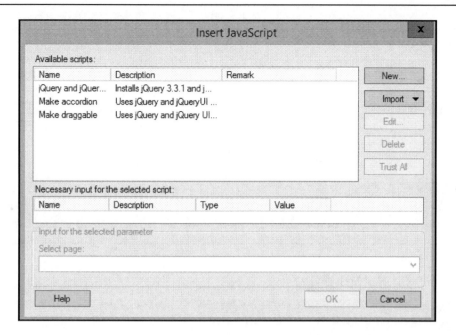

2. If we click on the `Make accordion` script, its input parameter will be shown. We can then click on the **id** parameter and note that the ID of the DIV for the accordion control is specified in the **Value** box:

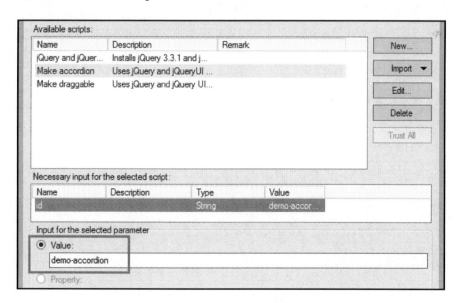

3. This is how we connect a JavaScript script to an element in the HTML code.

I'll leave it as an exercise for you to edit the various scripts and study their contents. Take a look at the jQuery and jQueryUI scripts—in there, you'll see that the entire (minified) source code of jQuery and jQueryUI have been pasted into the script.

Before we leave the topic of JavaScript in text areas, I'd like to cover an important aspect. You cannot choose Spotfire controls or visualizations as input values for parameters to JavaScript scripts directly. If you need to reference them in your script, you need to find the requisite elements in the HTML code—either in the HTML of the text area or the Spotfire document object model itself. We saw this when working with the accordion example previously.

The next section discusses the Developer Tools menu option in Spotfire, which is an extremely useful debugging tool when developing JavaScript scripts. It is also useful when developing JavaScript visualizations (covered in the final chapter of this book, Chapter 13, *Beyond the Horizon*).

If you do get stuck implementing this, or any of the other examples in this chapter, or get stuck with any aspect of the topics we've discussed, please post a question on the Community.

Spotfire Developer Tools

Spotfire Developer Tools is a really useful menu option that's disabled by default in Spotfire. If you're developing JavaScript in text areas or JavaScript visualizations, it's an essential tool.

We can enable this option in the following manner:

1. From the **Tools** menu, select **Options**.
2. Check the **Show development menu** option:

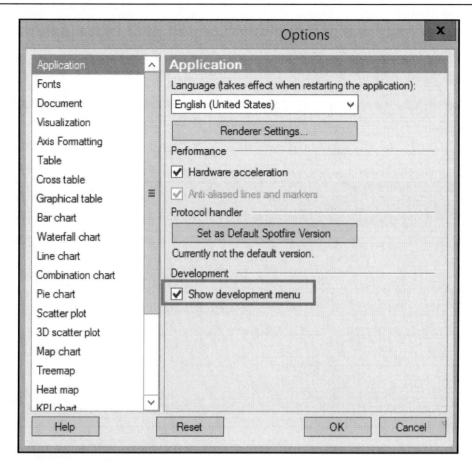

3. Click **OK** to dismiss the dialog.

Now, we can access the developer tools by choosing **Development** and then **Developer Tools...** from the **Tools** menu in Spotfire. This will open the Google Chrome developer console. Spotfire uses **Chromium Embedded Framework (CEF)** as its browser, so the tools here are exactly the same as you'd find in the Chrome web browser.

We can explore the developer tools really briefly:

1. Here's the initial display that's shown when we show the developer tools:

2. The first tab shows the HTML elements of the Spotfire DOM. You can browse the DOM by navigating its source in the box that shows the HTML source, or you can highlight different parts of the DOM in Spotfire by clicking the box with an arrow (highlighted):

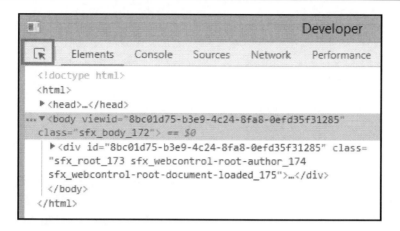

3. Once we have clicked the box, we can then return to Spotfire and hover over the part of the Spotfire document you'd like to inspect. Here, I've hovered over the DIV that represents the accordion control in the previous JavaScript example:

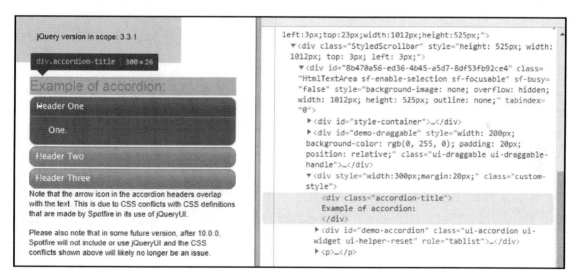

4. If we select the **Console** tab, we'll see any warnings or errors that get generated by any JavaScript running in Spotfire. We'll also see any console output that's generated by JavaScript Console.log statements. I've not shown a screenshot here as there are no errors or warnings being shown! If there were, we could click on a line of code in the console to navigate to the **Sources** tab.

5. We can use the **Sources** tab to inspect any JavaScript code that's causing an issue—from there, we can place breakpoints in the code or even modify it inline.

6. The **Network** tab is useful if your JavaScript calls out to anywhere on the web—you can monitor all requests from here.

I've covered the most often used tabs in the developer tools—I recommend that you view the inline help within the console if you need to know more.

There are two more options available in the **Developer** menu:

- **Reload browser**: This will reload Spotfire's browser. It's useful to make absolutely sure that any JavaScript code is reloaded and refreshed.
- **Copy URL to clipboard**: This copies the URL that the Spotfire Analyst client is serving to the CEF browser. This can be useful in certain cases since you can paste the URL into a Chrome browser window if you want to work with the HTML DOM outside of Spotfire. However, please be aware that working with it can sometimes cause problems with the Spotfire Analyst client.

The Spotfire developer tools are an essential part of working with JavaScript, custom HTML, and JavaScript visualizations in Spotfire.

Script trust

We briefly touched on script trust in the JavaScript example previously, so we'll now cover this in a little more detail.

If you load a Spotfire file that contains scripts that you have not previously trusted, then a warning will be shown, as we saw previously. You must then go and review the scripts and trust them in order to use them in your analysis. You can trust all the IronPython scripts and then all the JavaScript scripts in turn. However, I would strongly recommend that you review the scripts before you trust them implicitly.

The script trust mechanism is designed to protect you from harmful scripts that could, for example, reveal personal information, or compromise your organization's security in some way. IronPython scripts can be particularly dangerous as any IronPython script running on your machine has full access to it via the .NET framework. You have been warned!

Note that any scripts in an analysis will not work in web-based clients unless they have been trusted by a member of the Script Author security group.

TIBCO Enterprise Runtime for R and open source R

If we refer back to Chapter 9, *What's Your Location?*, recall that we used a **TIBCO Enterprise Runtime for R (TERR)** script to assist with geocoding.

TERR is TIBCO's own implementation of the open source R statistical programming language. It is designed for high performance and low latency, particularly when working with streaming data in TIBCO StreamBase and Spotfire Data Streams (see Chapter 10, *Information Links and Data Connectors*). A huge number of open source (CRAN) R packages are supported and available for use within TERR, and the list of packages that are compatible with TERR is growing all the time.

You can find out more about which packages are known to be compatible with TERR by visiting the home page of the TERR product documentation:

https://docs.tibco.com/products/tibco-enterprise-runtime-for-r.

Alternatively, use this shortened link:

http://bit.ly/2Z7LxWv.

The other advantages of TERR over open source R are that it ships with Spotfire Analyst, so you do not need to install anything extra to use it, and that it is supported by TIBCO. If you use open source R, you are at the mercy of the open source community when it comes to support. This isn't necessarily a bad thing, but it's nice to have official support.

You can't produce graphics directly with TERR, but you can create and display interactive JavaScript visualizations using various tips and tricks shown on the TIBCO Community. You can also create R graphics using the TERR RinR package—this allows you to call out to an open source R engine just for producing the graphics (or in the case that the open source R package is not supported in TERR).

For more information, please visit:

```
https://community.tibco.com/wiki/displaying-terr-graphics-tibco-
spotfire-using-jsviz
```

Or:

```
http://bit.ly/2IvdRMO
```

And:

```
https://www.tibco.com/blog/2015/07/23/spotfire-tips-tricks-addin
g-r-graphics-to-spotfire-case-study-dendrograms-2/
```

Or:

```
http://bit.ly/2UPvVYC
```

And:

```
https://support.tibco.com/s/article/Example-TERR-RinR-RGraph-dat
a-function-that-returns-a-column-of-R-qqnorm-graphs-in-a-
Spotfire-data-table
```

Or:

```
http://bit.ly/2GhAN0g
```

The first example shows how to use JsViz, a JavaScript visualization package in conjunction with TERR, to produce an interactive visualization. The second and third examples show using RinR to produce R graphics in Spotfire.

Of course, R scripting's main utility is for advanced analytics, predictive analytics, and machine learning. There are loads of resources on the TIBCO Community for how to do all of these and much more—the landing page for this topic is:

```
https://community.tibco.com/wiki/advanced-analytics-tibco-spotfire
```

Alternatively, use this shortened link:

```
http://bit.ly/2VGUbt4
```

We won't be covering an example of how to set up a Spotfire data function that calls out to TERR—this was demonstrated in Chapter 9, *What's Your Location?*.

One particular use of TERR is to create custom expression functions in Spotfire—you can register expression functions from the **Data Function Properties** menu item (available from the **Data** menu in Spotfire Analyst clients):

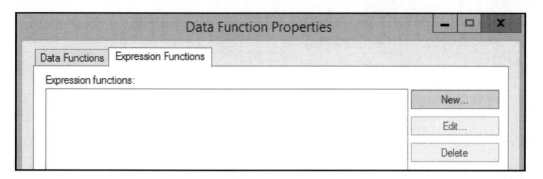

The inline help for this function shows a simple example of converting degrees Celsius into degrees Fahrenheit:

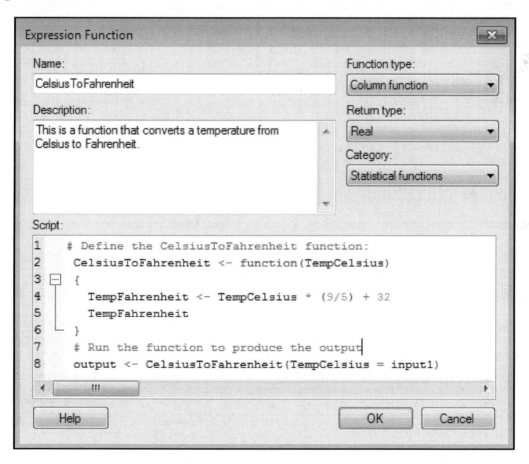

If we were to follow the example and create such a function, it would then be available for use within a custom expression in a visualization or a calculated column in a data table. We could use it like this:

```
CelsiusToFahrenheit([DegreesCelsius])
```

Here, `[DegreesCelsius]` is a column containing temperature values in degrees Celsius. Hopefully, you can see how the inputs map to the expression function with names such as `input1`, `input2`, and so on.

Spotfire can also work with Statistica, Python, Matlab, and SAS statistical functions. Open source R, Matlab, and SAS are enabled by using TIBCO Spotfire Statistics Services—part of the TIBCO Data Science suite. Statistica and Python are covered later in this chapter. The process for calling an open source R, Matlab, or SAS statistical function is pretty similar to that of using TERR.

Finally, a note about TERR and TIBCO Cloud Spotfire: TERR is enabled for use in TIBCO Cloud Spotfire, but the set of available packages is strictly limited to those that do not expose security holes.

Python in Spotfire

Python is hugely popular for advanced statistical analysis, machine learning, and predictive modeling. Until recently, it wasn't possible to use Python in Spotfire, but now it is, thanks to an extension that was developed by TIBCO. Using this extension, you can work with Python just as easily as you can with TERR or open source R.

You can find out more about the Python data function extension here:
`https://community.tibco.com/wiki/python-data-function-tibco-spotfire`

Alternatively, use this shortened link:
`http://bit.ly/2Gfk2l8`

In order to be able to use the Python data function, the extension must be deployed to your Spotfire server environment and then downloaded into your Spotfire Analyst client. Currently, it does not work with TIBCO Cloud Spotfire.

The process of setting up a Python data function is pretty similar to that of setting up a TERR data function, except that you need to target Spotfire at an installed Python engine. The documentation for the extension is comprehensive, so I suggest you start there if you're interested in working with Python in Spotfire.

Please do not confuse Python and IronPython—just like the potential for confusion between Java and JavaScript, you can easily get mixed up between Python and IronPython. It's important when working with these technologies in Spotfire to refer to them correctly. IronPython is for scripting inside Spotfire—for automating common tasks and interacting with the Spotfire API. Python is for advanced analytics and is used with the data function paradigm.

Statistica and Spotfire

TIBCO Statistica is a statistical programming environment. It has a graphical user interface for designing statistical workflows and many modules for performing statistical modeling tasks. You can learn more about Statistica by visiting this link:
`https://community.tibco.com/wiki/getting-started-tibco-statistica.`

Alternatively, use this shortened link:

`http://bit.ly/2URVAQa.`

Statistica integrates really well with Spotfire—in fact, there is a data function extension for Statistca, just as there is for Python. You can learn more about the extension here:
`https://community.tibco.com/wiki/tibco-statisticar-data-function-spotfire.`

Alternatively, the extension can be found here:

`http://bit.ly/2Ky0BcN.`

Just like the Python data function, the Statistica extension must be deployed to your Spotfire server. Also, like the Python data function, it will not work with TIBCO Cloud Spotfire.

Extending Spotfire

So far in this chapter, we have learnt about how we can script in Spotfire using various scripting and statistical programming languages and tools. It's also possible to extend the core capabilities of Spotfire by developing extensions in C# .NET using Microsoft Visual Studio.

For example, you could create a custom calculation method or a custom data function executor or a custom export tool. The complete list of extension types and some tutorials for creating them is here:

`https://community.tibco.com/wiki/tibco-spotfire-c-extensions-overview`.

Alternatively, find them using this shortened link:

`http://bit.ly/2VGJpCW`.

In order to develop an extension, you need to download the Spotfire Developer **software development kit (SDK)**. It is available from this web page:

`https://edelivery.tibco.com`.

You'll need to contact your TIBCO administrator within your enterprise to request an account. If you get stuck, I suggest emailing `support@tibco.com` with a request for access.

You'll also need a copy of Microsoft Visual Studio 2013 or higher—you can use the free Community edition, although the Pro

fessional editions are much more powerful!

If you set up your development envir

onment correctly in Visual Studio, it's possible to debug your extensions directly within Visual Studio—making use of breakpoints, variable watches, and much more.

There are some recent instructions for setting up Visual Studio for doing this and also so that it automatically builds any Spotfire packages, ready for deployment on your Spotfire server:

`https://docs.tibco.com/pub/sfire_dev/area/doc/html/GUID-625B17C7-3B83-4C4A-A562-83B4B010DCC8.html`.

Alternatively, use this shortened link to access the instructions:

`http://bit.ly/2GlCutT`.

The end result of developing a Spotfire extension is one or more deployable packages. These come in the form of `.spk` files. They must be deployed to a Spotfire server and then they can be downloaded into a Spotfire client—either an Analyst or a web-based client.

Spotfire extensions work with Spotfire Analyst clients or Spotfire web clients. However, they cannot be deployed to TIBCO Cloud Spotfire for security reasons.

The JavaScript API

The purpose of the JavaScript API is to allow Spotfire pages to be embedded in other web applications. Using this API, web applications can control Spotfire visualizations, filters, and markings. Web applications can also easily respond to events generated in Spotfire—for example, a web application could be configured to perform an action on some data that a user marks within a Spotfire visualization.

> Do not confuse the JavaScript API with the use of JavaScript in text areas in Spotfire. The JavaScript API is for embedding Spotfire analytics in other web applications; JavaScript in text areas is used for augmenting the Spotfire user interface.

Many of TIBCO's customers embed Spotfire in their externally facing web pages to present analytics and analytics applications to their own customers. In fact, it's possible to remove all Spotfire branding so that an end user doesn't even know that Spotfire is being used to deliver the analytics.

You can learn more about the JavaScript API by visiting this TIBCO Community page:
`https://community.tibco.com/wiki/tibco-spotfire-javascript-api-overview`.

Alternatively, visit the page using this shortened link:

`http://bit.ly/2ItsAI0.`

The JavaScript API does work with TIBCO Cloud Spotfire, but only with analysis files stored in public areas.

Spotfire Server APIs

The Spotfire server has APIs that assist with various tasks. It has an API for custom authentication and several web services for interacting with the Spotfire library, triggering scheduled updates (see `Chapter 12`, *Scaling the Infrastructure; Keeping Data up to Date*, for more on scheduled updates), managing users and groups, and much more.

You can learn more about the custom authentication API here:
`https://community.tibco.com/wiki/tibco-spotfirer-server-api-custom-authentication`.

Alternatively, learn about it using this shortened link:

`http://bit.ly/2P3LGWv.`

To read about the Spotfire Web Services API's please visit this page:
`https://community.tibco.com/wiki/tibco-spotfire-web-services-api-tutorials-and-examples`.

Alternatively, visit it using this shortened link:

`http://bit.ly/2FR9GYP`.

Summary

In this chapter, you've learnt how to get started with IronPython scripting and JavaScript scripts within Spotfire text areas. You've also learnt how advanced statistical analysis can be performed using technologies and platforms such as TIBCO Enterprise Runtime for R, open source R, Python, Statistica and others.

We've barely scratched the surface of what's truly possible with Spotfire's immense capabilities with scripting, extensions, embedding analytics in web applications, web services, and advanced statistical analysis. As I stated in the introduction, I could fill a whole book on this topic alone!

There were lots of links to content on the TIBCO Community—there's a huge wealth of information out there. I suggest that you go and explore the Community to its fullest extent. The content is of great quality and is increasing in quantity daily. It's kept up to date too, so I recommend that you use the links in this chapter to get started with perusing the online content.

The next chapter covers scaling the Spotfire infrastructure and keeping data up to date in analysis files. It's of interest to all skilled Spotfire Analysts as you need to know how to be able to serve your analyses to multiple users and how to keep data refreshed and up to date in those analyses.

12
Scaling the Infrastructure; Keeping Data up to Date

Chapter 6, *The Big Wide World of Spotfire*, gave an introduction to the Spotfire Server topology and its intelligent rules for routing and load sharing. Chapter 13, *Beyond the Horizon*, revisits this topic in more detail. As in Chapter 6, *The Big Wide World of Spotfire*, this chapter is primarily targeted toward the Spotfire administrator. However, if you are not an administrator, I still recommend that you read this chapter so that you have an understanding of the general concepts and can come back to this for future reference.

You will find comprehensive architecture and administration documents online (https://docs.tibco.com/).

In this chapter, we will cover the following topics:

- Context-aware load management with scheduling and routing
- Definitions of concepts used
- The Spotfire Server topology
- Scaling the Spotfire Server
- Spotfire Sites
- Web Player scaling
- Nodes, services, and resource pools
- Scheduling and routing, with explanations of the various rules
- Practical examples of routing rules

Context-aware load management with scheduling and routing

Spotfire's intelligent scheduling and routing server topology is (as far as I am aware) unique in the industry. It works with Web Player and makes the best use of the available server resources. Since it's specifically designed for Spotfire, it has context-aware load management. It knows which analysis a user is requesting and so it can route the user to the most appropriate Web Player instance. The most appropriate instance is determined by a set of rules that the server administrator defines.

Spotfire also shares memory and data between multiple users (if the analysis they are working with resides on the same Web Player instance), so it makes sense to share as much as possible and minimize the number of instances that have an analysis file loaded. Traditional load-balancing algorithms usually direct users to the least loaded server, or in a round-robin fashion. This is not always appropriate as it leads to multiple servers loading the same analysis files, consuming resources throughout the infrastructure. In fact, it can be a lot better to direct a user to a heavily loaded server that already has the analysis they require loaded in memory and being used by others.

By making intelligent choices about how users are routed to the various Web Player or Automation Services instances in your Spotfire infrastructure, you can ensure that Spotfire makes the most efficient use of available resources.

Finally, scheduling is a great way to make sure that data is kept up to date in a web-based analysis and immediately available to a user. A schedule refreshes data and keeps an analysis loaded in the Web Player's memory.

Some definitions

For quick reference in the future, here are some useful definitions. Each of these concepts are detailed in this chapter:

- **Node Manager**: A service that runs on a server machine that can host instances of Web Player or Automation Services
- **Instance**: An individual instance of a service of Web Player or Automation Services

- **Schedule**: A schedule for keeping an analysis preloaded and in the memory of a Web Player instance, and (optionally) keeping the data within the analysis up to date
- **Rule**: A routing rule that routes a user to a Web Player resource pool
- **Resource pool**: A group of one or more Web Player instances that can have users routed to them by way of rules

Server topology

In this section, now that we've had a brief explanation of scaling the Spotfire Server, we will be focusing on the Worker Service Tier. This is the part of the platform that contains the Spotfire Web Players, Automation Services, and Statistics Services:

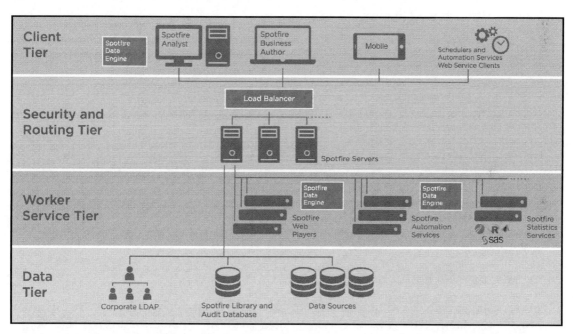

The Spotfire Web Player and Automation Services can be scaled to support as many users as you need. Spotfire makes really efficient use of resources in order to scale as effectively as possible using the available hardware. Spotfire's intelligent routing and scaling algorithms make it unique in the marketplace among business intelligence solutions. In fact, its competitors often recommend one web server per major application, but this is simply not necessary with Spotfire.

Web Player and Automation Services instances reside on Spotfire nodes. A node is set up by installing TIBCO Spotfire Node Manager on a server and targeting a Spotfire Server. Once that is done, all management of the node is performed via the Spotfire Server with the Administration Console. There's no need to visit the Node Manager machine at all, except for the usual tasks like applying operating system updates, or if you need to update the Node Manager software itself.

Scaling the Spotfire Server using clustering

The Spotfire Server (in the Security and Routing Tier in the diagram in the *Server topology* section) is a Java application that runs in Apache Tomcat. It's relatively lightweight and not very demanding of hardware resources.

Its main functions are as follows:

- User authentication
- User routing to Web Player instances
- Spotfire software package distribution (to clients) and deployment management
- Systems administration
- Spotfire library management—serving files and data

Clustering can be used to enable fault tolerance or to scale up the Spotfire Server to meet demand. Note that clustering is very different from scheduling and routing. Clustering applies to the Spotfire Server only and is done using a traditional load balancer. TIBCO supplies another product, ActiveSpaces, which is free to purchasers of the Spotfire Server. It enables the exchange of data between clustered Spotfire Servers.

Spotfire Sites

It's also possible to set up multiple Spotfire Servers that share a common database but are accessed individually. This concept is called "Sites" in Spotfire nomenclature. By setting up multiple sites, you can provide users with a server that is located locally to them. Users in each location are given a URL to log in to their closest Spotfire Server. This approach improves performance by minimizing latency due to distance. Nodes (running Web Player and Automation Services instances) are tied to each individual Site, which is worth remembering!

Another use for multiple Sites is to enable different authentication methods—for example, internal users may use Kerberos authentication, while external users (for example, customers or partners) would use username/password authentication. A single Spotfire Server can only be configured to use one authentication method.

 For more information on Sites, please visit Spotfire's online documentation at `https://docs.tibco.com`—search for the TIBCO Spotfire® Server and Environment Installation and Administration guide and then search for "Sites" within the documentation set.

Spotfire Web Player scaling

Please refer to `Chapter 6`, *The Big Wide World of Spotfire*, for a description of a scenario comparing traditional load balancing with Spotfire's intelligent routing schemes.

Scaling of the Web Player infrastructure is achieved by employing intelligent scheduling and routing rules. The rules route users to the most appropriate instance to service their requests. Scheduling and routing rules are configured via the scheduling and routing part of Spotfire's Administration Console (this is accessible via `http(s)://spotfireserver/spotfire`, where `spotfireserver` is the name of your Spotfire Server):

Note that **Scheduling & Routing** configuration is only available to users that are members of the scheduling and routing administrator user group or a general administrator (see `Chapter 6`, *The Big Wide World of Spotfire*, for details concerning the Administration Manager).

Nodes, services, and resource pools

Before we can set up scheduling and routing, it's useful to set up multiple nodes and instances, define some resource pools, and assign Web Player instances to these. The process is straightforward, but warrants a practical example as there are some potentially confusing aspects (installation of the Spotfire Server is out of scope for this book):

1. Run the Installation Kit for **TIBCO Spotfire Node Manager** (TSNM). It is supplied with the TIBCO Spotfire Server download (available from `https://edelivery.tibco.com`).

2. When installing TSNM, you will be asked some questions about the configuration. First of all is the **Node Manager Ports**. These are the ports that the Node Manager will be listening on—for registration from the Spotfire Server and for communication with the Spotfire Server when serving the Web Player or Automation Services:

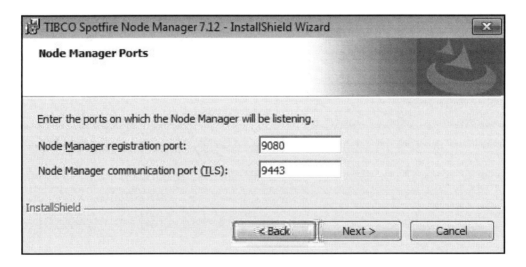

It doesn't matter (to Spotfire) what ports are chosen here—when registration occurs, the Node Manager service will tell the Spotfire Server which ports it is using. However, it is important to choose ports that are not already in use on the Node Manager Server machine and that are also open in the firewall! Spotfire provides its own certificate for TLS (secure) communication between the Node Manager and the Spotfire Server.

3. Next, you will be prompted to enter the name of the Spotfire Server. Strangely (I think!), you are requested to enter the name of the server, not a URL to it. However, that name MUST resolve to the Server, so make sure that you can "ping" it from the Node Manager Server. Also, you will need to specify the Server backend registration port and communication port. These were defined at the time the Spotfire Server was installed. Most administrators choose the defaults when the Server is installed:

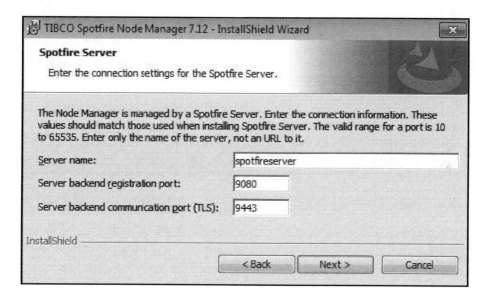

4. Next, select the names that the Node Manager Server is known by on the network. My Node Manager server is also called "Extra", but is not shown in this list. The names on the right-hand side of the dialog should all be resolvable from the Spotfire Server machine:

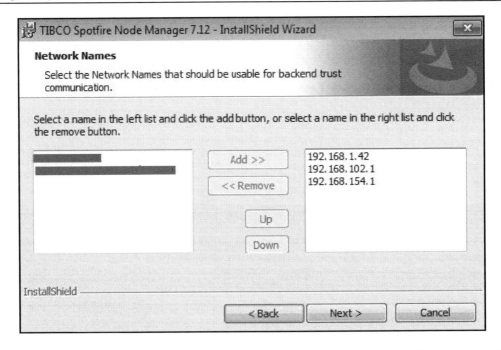

5. Finish the Node Manager installation and then be sure to start the service called **TIBCO Spotfire Node Manager** in the Windows Services applet.

6. Now, return to the Spotfire Administration Console and visit the **Nodes & Services** configuration pages. You should see a new flag on the **Notifications** tab:

7. You can go and check the **Notifications** tab if you like, but in this case, it's highly likely that there is a new node that needs to be trusted! So, visit the **Untrusted nodes** tab and trust that new node:

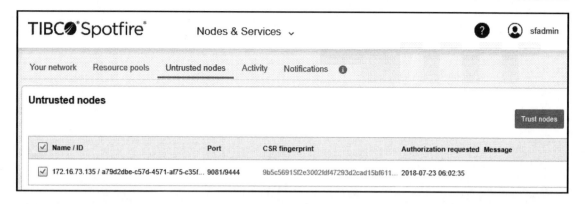

8. Once you have trusted the node, wait for a few seconds. If everything is ok, you shouldn't get a warning. If something goes wrong, I that recommend you go and check the Spotfire Server logs—it's usually possible to figure out what is happening by looking at the logs. The most likely scenarios for failure include the following:

   - Ports not open on the Node Manager Server machine
   - Problems resolving the Node Manager machine from the Spotfire Server machine

If you can't even see the new node in the **Untrusted nodes** tab, then something more serious is happening. It probably means that the ports for registration are not open on the Spotfire Server, or the Spotfire Server cannot be resolved from the Node Manager machine. Did you remember to start the Node Manager service? Did you specify the correct ports for connecting to the Spotfire Server?

There are some useful log files stored on the Node Manager Server—the default location is `C:\tibco\tsnm\[version]\nm\logs`.

In particular, check `startup.log` and `nm.log`.

9. Now, assuming everything appeared to go well from here, return to the **Your network** tab in the Administration Console. The new node should appear and have a green icon next to it to show that all is well. There won't be any services running on it yet (note the message saying `No services added`):

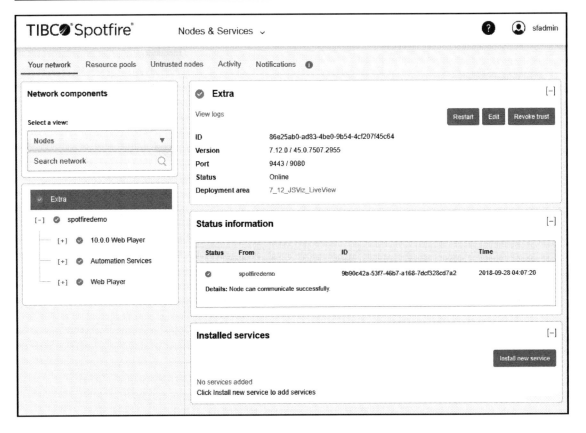

10. It's important to check that the node can communicate successfully. My example looks fine, so I can now proceed with installing a new service. For the purposes of this example, I'm going to install a Web Player service (but I could install an Automation Services instance too).

11. Click **Install new service**. I have set the configuration of the service as follows. Choose what works for your environment:

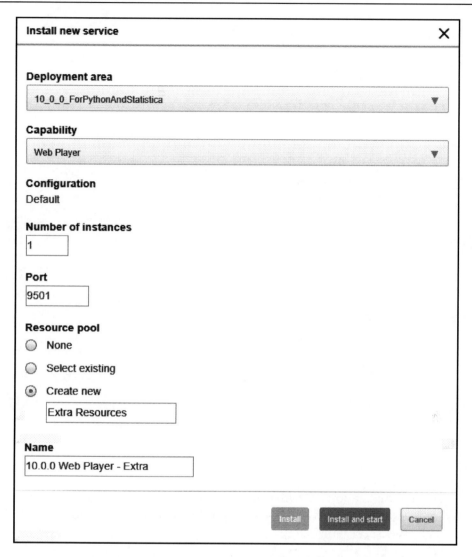

12. Note that I have created a new resource pool called **Extra Resources**. You will see how this is used later on. The port is used by the Web Player Service serve to the Spotfire Server. The port number that's used doesn't matter, but it must be open and not used by anything else on the machine. Click **Install and start**. After a delay, the web page should refresh to show that the service is up and running. If you want, you can view the log files on the Node Manager instance to monitor what's going on.

Installing and starting a new Web Player instance can take some time! The instance needs to start up and connect to the Spotfire Server. It will then download the deployment from the server and set everything up, before being ready for use.

13. Once the Web Player is up and running, you should see something like this:

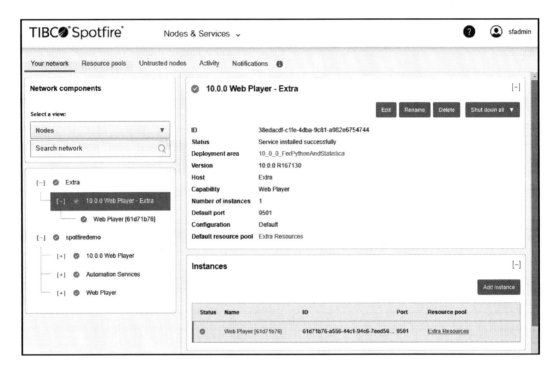

You'll see that, in my case, I have two nodes—one (`spotfiredemo`) has an Automation Services instance and a Web Player instance. The other (Extra) has a Web Player service instance.

 It is entirely possible to host multiple instances of Web Player or Automation Services instances within a single Node Manager. One reason to do this could be to use different deployments to serve multiple versions of Spotfire. Another could be to segregate users to their own Web Player instance that can be carefully managed in terms of its resources and users.

14. Finally, in my case, I need to assign the original Web Player instance on the `spotfiredemo` host to a resource pool. This gives me an opportunity to show you the **Resource pools** tab. Click the **Resource pools** tab:

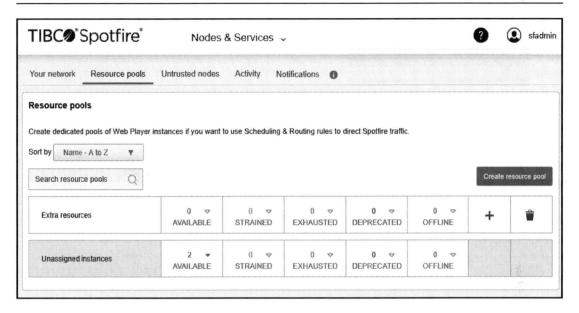

15. Click **Create resource pool**. Give the new resource pool a name and assign the instance to it:

16. Once you have created the resource pool, you should see something like this:

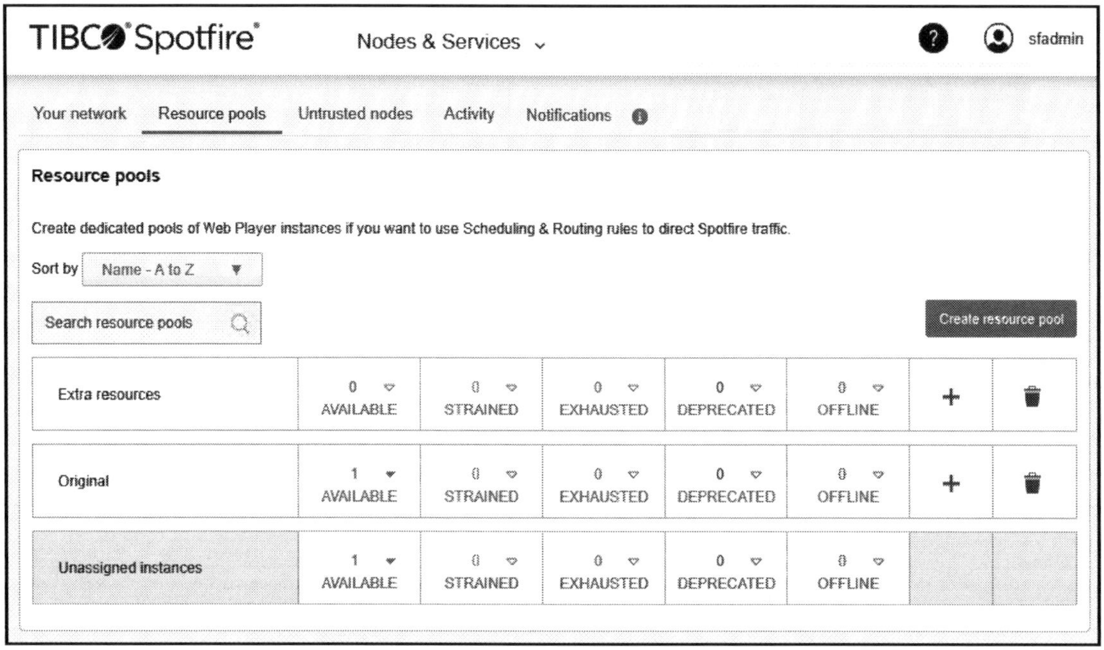

Spotfire Web Player scalability – Scheduling & Routing

Recall that the routing rules automatically route users to instances (via resource pools) in order to utilize the available resources in the most efficient manner. The routing rules are pretty simple, but in their simplicity, they deliver amazing value and results. First of all, I will briefly explain the rules and talk about how they should be applied for best effect. Secondly, I will provide some practical examples.

To access the **Scheduling & Routing** rules, use the **Scheduling & Routing** pages within the Administration Console. Here's the page on my system—blank, with no rules or schedules:

Before we discuss rules, let me just introduce Schedules. The purpose of Schedules is to keep analysis files loaded in the Web Player so that they are available immediately, with the latest data loaded and refreshed regularly. Schedules can even update an analysis while it's being used. Spotfire combines Schedules and Rules into a single concept, which at first might seem confusing. However, it's important to understand:

Rules: Determine which resource pool handles user requests for an analysis

Schedules: Determine when an analysis file is loaded into memory and how often the data is refreshed within it

It's pretty hard to overstate how useful Schedules are. They improve the loading times of analysis files significantly and make sure that data is kept up to date.

Routing rules – definitions

Rules are used to determine which resource pool handles a request for an analysis file.

File

A file rule is used to route an analysis file so that it is served from a specific resource pool or kept loaded and up-to-date. Some likely scenarios for using this rule are as follows:

- If an analysis file is large and consumes a lot of data, make sure that all users requesting the analysis file are directed to a single resource pool:
    - Data can be shared in memory and the running of the large analysis does not impact other analyses running within other resource pools
    - Minimise the number of times an analysis file is loaded on different resources (which would duplicate the overall resource usage)
- If an analysis file is to be used by a large number of users very regularly:
    - This is useful for an externally facing analysis file that is served across the internet.
    - To use the resources in a resource pool most efficiently, heavily load a web player instance to get as much usage out of it as possible. You only need to spin up new instances if the current instances become exhausted.

Group

A group rule routes all users in a user group to a resource pool. Likely scenarios for this are as follows:

- Business-critical users could be routed to a specific resource pool with plenty of resources and fail-over capability in order to keep the system responsive and available, no matter what
- Segregate executive and other users from each other—experimental users can't accidentally overload a resource pool intended for executive users that need guaranteed uptime
- Geographical routing—route users within a particular region to a resource pool that is geographically colocated with the users in the group

User

A user rule routes an individual types, this is probably the one that is lea user to a specific resource pool. Out of the three different rulest likely to be used. Maintaining groups is a lot easier than maintaining individual users and their individual routing rules. The scenarios for using a user rule are similar to the group rule, except that there is an additional overhead for managing the individual users.

I would recommend using group rules and managing group membership to allocate users to groups and therefore route them to the most appropriate resource pools, rather than using user rules.

Routing rules – practical examples

Having defined the rules, I believe it's helpful to examine some example scenarios and then choose which rule types to use, and then go and configure them!

Scenario 1 – manufacturing sensor data analysis

Manufacturing data, and particularly sensor data, typically contains large datasets with many rows and many columns. The data is also fast-changing, but only between the hours of 9 am and 6 pm during weekdays. Users only work with the data during the same (working) hours.

This scenario ideally matches a file-based rule. Typically, a rule would be set up to serve the analysis file and keep it loaded and up to date during working hours. Here's how to set up such a rule:

1. Click the **Create rule** button (while on the **Scheduling & Routing** overview page).

2. Make sure that the **FILE** type rule is selected and click **Next**:

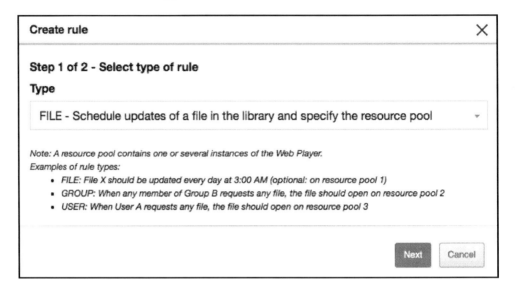

Don't worry about the way the rules are explained in the dialog here. I think it can be confusing and slightly overcomplicated, so let's keep it simple and carry on!

3. In the next dialog, start filling in the information. Choose a name for the rule that adequately describes it and choose the analysis file:

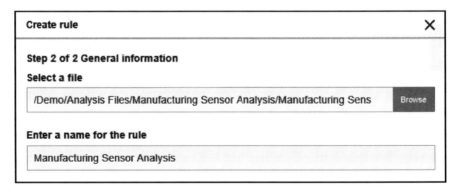

4. Now, choose the resource pool, number of instances, and priority. I am going to choose the **Extra Resources** pool:

Let's explain these options:

1. **Select resource pool**: The resource pool determines which resource pool will service requests for the analysis file.
2. **Number of instances**: This is used to restrict how many instances can load the file. In this case, there is only one available instance, but if there were more, Spotfire would allow the file to be loaded on multiple instances.
3. **Set a priority**: If there are multiple rules that match a particular scenario, which rule takes precedence? For now, we shall leave this set to 0.

5. Setting a schedule is the final part. In this case, we will set a custom schedule, so click the button to set a custom schedule:

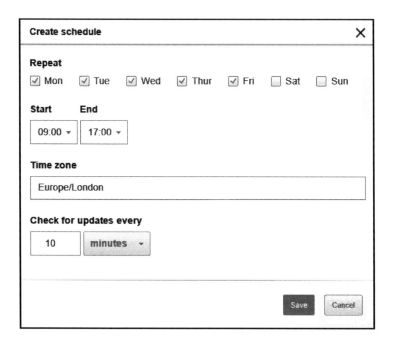

Important: It may appear that the schedule might mean that the rule is active during the times set in the dialog. However, that is not the case. The rule is **ALWAYS** active. The schedule only has any effect when the file is kept loaded in memory and is dependent on how often the data is updated.

You'll notice I have set the schedule for 9 am to 5 pm in the **Europe/London** time zone. It will check for updates every 10 minutes.

6. Save the schedule.
7. Save the rule.
8. Now, go back to the main page for **Scheduling & Routing**—if the file is scheduled to be loaded right now, it should show in **Files loading** or **Files successfully loaded** (at the top of the page). If not, you can easily check the checkbox next to the rule and click **Reload** to kick it off. It should happen in time anyway:

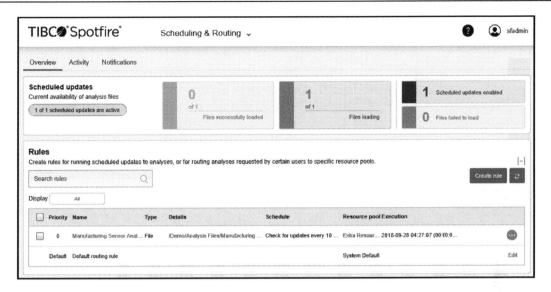

To summarize—I have created a rule and a schedule that routes all requests for the `Manufacturing Sensor Analysis` file to the **Extra resources** pool. The file will be kept loaded in memory so that it is instantly available and data will be refreshed (if new data is available) every 10 minutes.

Scenario 2 – separating critical functions and everyday operations

Imagine the following scenario—a utilities company relies on Spotfire for its critical functions. The sales executives are on the road all day and Spotfire is used as part of their selling process—they are comparing live energy prices and demand and using some compelling visualizations to impress potential customers. The amount of data being transferred and the volume of analysis is fairly low, but low latency is key, as is high availability.

Separately, the company also uses Spotfire for some pretty hefty number crunching and involved analytics by their operations department. They have many analysts that work with billions of rows of data. All of this is demanding on any IT infrastructure. The operations department is often experimenting with different ways of analyzing data but can afford for longer processing times than the sales executives. Due to the experimental nature of their work, they are tolerant if any large analysis that has been misconfigured (yes, it is possible to do this in Spotfire, but you have to try quite hard!) strains or exhausts their Web Player instances.

Neither the sales executives, nor the operations department, rely on a small number of files—they can be required to load any file from a large number stored within the Spotfire library.

A great way to satisfy the conflicting requirements of high availability with low latency on the one hand and demanding yet tolerant analytics users on the other is to use a group rule to send users to the most appropriate resource pool for them. In this and similar scenarios, I would recommend the following resource pools:

- A resource pool with several nodes and instances to serve the critical functions. Each node does not need to be very powerful or have lots of RAM. The analytics performed by the critical sales functions is lightweight and not demanding of resources, but high availability and low latency are key.
- A second resource pool with one or more very highly specified node machines. The analysis that's performed requires compute power and large memory resources, but failover is less important.

I will simulate this scenario using the infrastructure that I set up earlier in this chapter. Recall that I have two resource pools—original and extra. In this case, I am going to route all sales users to the original pool and all operations users to the extra pool. In a real-world scenario (for obvious reasons), both resource pools would be scaled up with extra nodes and instances as required, but the process is the same, regardless of the actual scale.

No schedule will be used as it's impossible to predict which analysis files will be required by which users. Indeed, with a group rule, it's not possible to specify a schedule.

The following are some prerequisites:

1. Set up a user group for the sales organization. I have done this via the Spotfire Administration Manager, but in most organizations, this would be done via LDAP or similar.
2. Set up a user group for the `Operations` organization.
3. Create a `Sales` user and an `Operations` user and assign them to their respective user groups.
4. Grant the appropriate licenses (software permissions) to the `Sales` and `Operations` groups.

Let's configure the **Group rule**:

1. Click the **Create rule** button
2. Choose a group **Type** of rule:

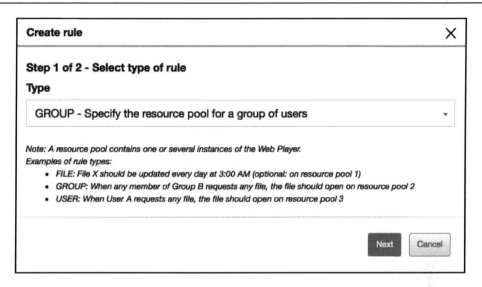

3. Click **Next**.
4. Name the rule, choose the user group, the resource pool, and the priority:

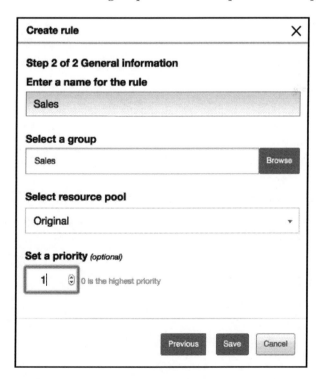

There are a couple of things worthy of note here.

5. There is no ability to specify a schedule for a group rule—this is because the group rule does not apply to a file. If you need to have a file preloaded in memory (optionally with the latest data), then the schedule must be set via a file-type rule.

6. The priority of the rule is set to 1. This means that a rule with priority 0 will override this rule in terms of the resource pool used—for example, if a file rule specifies that the file is always loaded on the **Extra resources** pool, then the file rule will take precedence.

7. Save the rule.

8. Create another group rule—this time, assign the operations users to the **Extra resources** pool.

9. Once done, my rules list looks like this (the rule for Scenario 1 is still present):

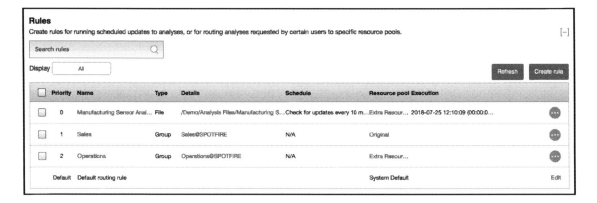

Verifying the example rules and schedules

Now that we have configured some example rules and schedules, it's useful to monitor them to see how they're being used and if they are working properly.

Checking the schedule

To check that a schedule is working properly, click on the **Activity** tab of the **Scheduling & Routing** page:

The check marks indicate that all is well! Here, I have expanded the first item on the list. You can see that, from here, I can view the diagnostics. Clicking this link takes me to the Web Player diagnostics view so that I can look at the logs or all the metrics on the performance and utilization of the instance.

Checking the routing rules for the scenarios

We can combine checking for the various scenarios into a single operation, since my examples all use the same infrastructure to illustrate these points.

The following are some prerequisites that I have taken:

1. I have logged in as a `Sales` user (Scenario 2) and opened the `Sales analysis file`.
2. I have simultaneously logged in as an `Operations` user (Scenario 2) and opened a file called `Large analysis file`.
3. Recall that we do not need to have a user opening the `Manufacturing Sensor Analysis` file since it is already opened by virtue of the fact that it is scheduled.

To check that the routing rules are working properly, visit the **Monitoring & Diagnostics** page of the Administration Console. From there, select the **Routing: Analyses** tab. In my case, this is the view, given the (combined) scenarios we described previously:

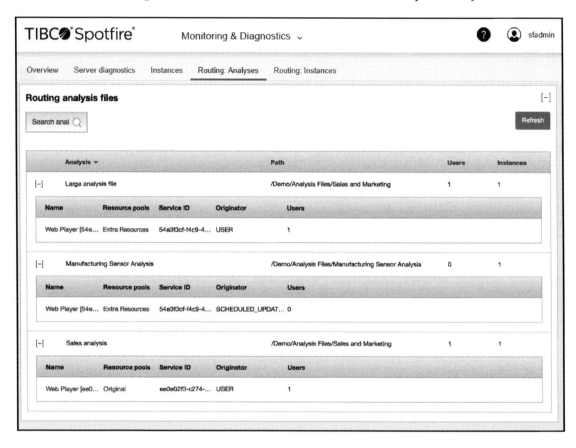

You can also view the current status via the **Routing: Instances** tab:

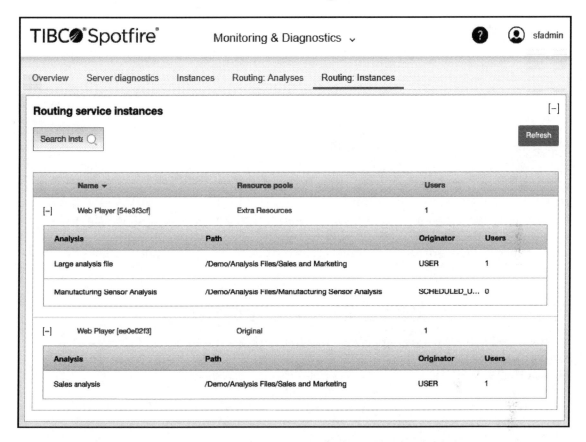

The `Manufacturing Sensor Analysis` file is opened on the **Extra Resources** resource pool (as intended—Scenario 1). The `Large analysis file` has also been loaded in the **Extra Resources** resource pool (Scenario 2). The `Sales analysis` file is open in the original resource pool.

Looking good!

Triggering an update from an external system

Spotfire has a web API for triggering updates. For more information and some sample code for how to call these updates, please visit this link on the TIBCO Community:

```
https://community.tibco.com/wiki/tibco-spotfire-web-services-api-tutorials-and-
examples
```

Alternatively, use this short URL to visit the Community:

```
http://bit.ly/2FR9GYP
```

Using this API, you can build a complete workflow, using Spotfire as an integral part of it. For example, an external system could run some critical process and update a database with results of that process. Then, the system would call the `UpdateAnalysisService` Web Service to make sure that an analysis has the latest data loaded and ready to use.

Notes on scheduling and routing

It's not possible to provide a set of scenarios that capture absolutely every eventuality, so the scenarios we have detailed thus far are just an introduction to the concepts of **Scheduling & Routing**. I do have a few notes that are worth sharing:

- Remember how useful scheduling is! It's a great way to ensure that data is kept up to date and is available immediately, without any loading wait times.
- You can only apply **Schedules to File** rules.
- I am not going to show a practical example of a user routing rule. User rules are very similar to group rules and I don't really recommend them, except in very special cases—it's far better to use group rules and administer the members of the groups rather than individual rules for individual users.
- The rule priorities will influence which instance serves a particular request.
- A file rule with a priority lower than a group rule will take lower precedence than the group rule. This can lead to undesirable results, like a file being loaded on multiple instances when this was not the intention. Look at the `Baseball` file here—I set up a group rule that uses the original resource pool and a file rule that uses the **Extra Resources** pool (with a schedule), and also loaded the file by logging in as a group member:

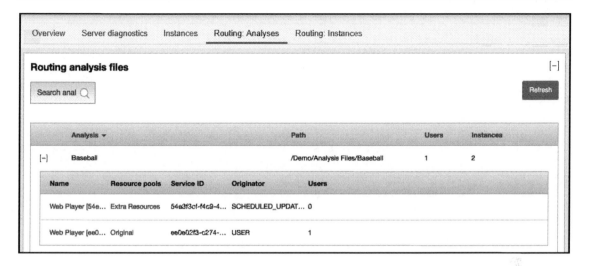

This defeats the whole purpose of Spotfire's routing rules—the intention is to minimize the number of instances that a single analysis file is open on. The correct way to configure this scenario would be to make sure that the file rule and group rule use the same resource pool.

- It's also possible to edit the default routing rule. This rule routes users when a request for an analysis file is not captured by any other rule. When editing this rule, you should select which resource pools should be used when no user-defined rules are matched.

Summary

This chapter was primarily concerned with scaling the Spotfire architecture to support the multiple needs of various organizations more efficiently.

We covered clustering of Spotfire Servers and the concept of Spotfire Sites. We introduced Node Managers, nodes, and services. Some time was spent explaining scheduling and routing and giving some example scenarios. I hope that the examples were useful and gave some insight into best practices for setting up an efficient and scalable Spotfire infrastructure.

Don't forget how useful scheduling is! It loads your data and keeps it up to date so it's instantly available. Use it!

The online documentation is always a good reference resource, so I recommend that you visit `https://docs.tibco.com/` if you want to know more about anything that was covered in this chapter.

The next chapter is the last in this book and it covers some advanced topics. It's designed to inspire you to take Spotfire to the next level!

13
Beyond the Horizon

This chapter details some key topics that you need to be aware of when working with **Spotfire** and taking your analysis journey to the next level. We'll start off by covering searching in Spotfire, then canvas styling and theming, followed by exporting (data and visualizations). We'll briefly touch on JavaScript visualizations—an excellent mechanism for creating custom visualizations in Spotfire. A pre-built extension for creating data-driven alerts will be discussed. We'll also cover some additional software products that can be useful for working with Spotfire.

Finally, a mention will be given to **TIBCO Cloud Enterprise**.

In this chapter, we will cover the following topics:

- Natural language search
- Canvas styling and theming
- Exporting from Spotfire
- JavaScript visualizations
- Alerting in Spotfire
- Additional software products – TIBCO Data Science, Data Virtualization, and more
- TIBCO Spotfire Cloud Enterprise

Natural language search

Spotfire X supports **natural language search**—you can use this feature to ask questions of your data or even to build visualizations or navigate the Spotfire user interface. You can type almost anything into the search box in Spotfire. Depending on what you type, it will do the following:

- Recommend visualizations or relationships in your data. For example, you could type `show me price`, or `what are my sales?`.
- Add data to markings. If we go back to the example of AirBnB data in `Chapter 9`, *What's Your Location?*, we could search for Queens—Spotfire will mine the data in all the columns and suggest that it should mark all rows for Queens.
- Navigate to visualizations that we've already created—just start typing the title of a visualization or a page, and Spotfire will present a range of options to you.
- Create a visualization. Just search for **Bar Chart**—Spotfire will allow you to create one with a single click.

I'm always finding new and interesting things with this search facility. I recommend that you experiment with it!

Canvas styling and theming

Spotfire can be styled and themed. You can access the features for doing this via the **Visualizations** menu, and then via the **Canvas styling** options. Best practices for styling and theming in Spotfire are documented here, along with some sample themed dashboards that you can download:

`https://community.tibco.com/wiki/visual-design-best-practices-tibco-spotfire`

Alternatively, you can click on this link:

`http://bit.ly/2XabKBW`

If you download one of these dashboards, you can easily import the theme into your own analysis. You can also import a theme from an analysis file that's stored in the Spotfire library.

As with any styling or theming options in any tool, it's possible to make some really poor choices and produce something that looks horrendous! So, go carefully, and use best-practice choices and combinations of colors and fonts, and so on.

Exporting from Spotfire

Spotfire has several export options. All are accessed by visiting the **Export** menu group, available from the **File** menu.

Visualization export

You can export as images to PNG or PDF files. Each image is exported as a single file.

Exporting data to a file or a library

Spotfire can export data to CSV, Excel, text, **Spotfire Binary Data Format (SBDF)**, **Spotfire Text Data Format (STDF)** or `ADO.NET (XML)` format files. It can export entire data tables, or rows limited by filtering or marking.

Microsoft Excel files generated by Spotfire do not support conditional coloring or formatting—only the raw data can be exported.

You can also export data to the Spotfire library—only SBDF is supported. Exporting SBDF to the library is a great way of sharing data that you've already transformed so that others can take advantage of the transformations.

In addition to data tables, you can export data from certain visualization types. Currently, the only visualizations that support data export are **cross tables** or **table plots**.

You cannot export data from external (in-database) data sources—at least, not without bringing some data into memory first (for example, by using data on demand).

PDF export

The **PDF export** option in Spotfire is extremely powerful and flexible.

You can choose which parts of an analysis file to export or produce a prepared report on. Here, you can see that I have chosen to export the current page—it's the map chart from the AirBnB example we worked with in `Chapter 9`, *What's Your Location?*:

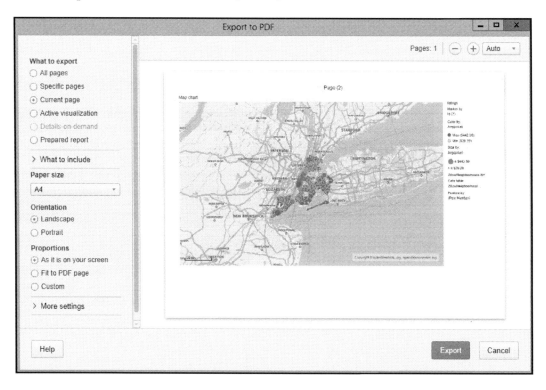

If you choose one of the standard Spotfire exports—to export all the pages, specific pages, the current page, or the active visualization—Spotfire will export what you see on your screen. However, if you design and use a prepared report, you'll have a lot more power and flexibility at your fingertips!

Producing a prepared report is akin to developing a report template in other tools. You have full control over exactly what is placed into the report. You can also specify that Spotfire will iterate over filtered values and produce multiple copies of selected visualizations—one per filter setting. In the following example (again, showing the AirBnB data), I have specified that the map chart should be generated twice—once for all bed-and-breakfast properties and once for all boutique hotels:

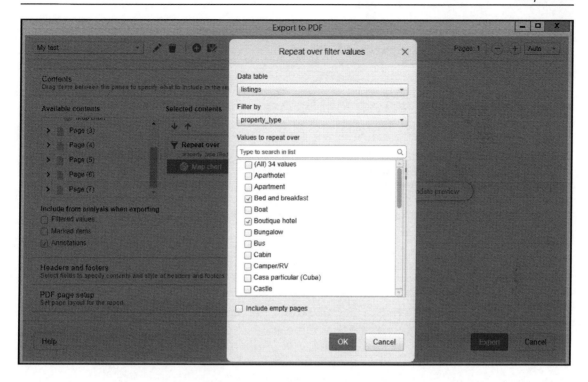

Once you've created a prepared report, it is then available for all users of the analysis. It's a great way to build consistent reports.

It's worth remembering that if you want to include dynamically generated text in your report, you should use text areas to hold this text—you might include calculated values within the text areas, for example.

Finally, if you want to export to PDF using Automation Services, you'll need to create a prepared report first. Here's an example Automation Services job:

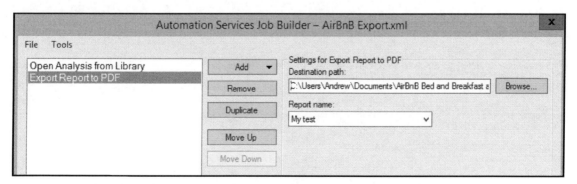

This section has covered how to work with exporting to PDF—both from the Spotfire user interface and also from automation services.

JavaScript visualizations

The suite of native Spotfire visualizations is extremely powerful and flexible, but what if you just *have* to have a particular visualization that's not supported by Spotfire? If that's the case, you can use the JSViz extension for Spotfire to develop JavaScript visualizations. The main page for this extension is here:

```
https://community.tibco.com/wiki/javascript-visualization-framework-jsviz-and-
tibco-spotfire
```

It can also be found here:

```
http://bit.ly/2XTtnXY
```

The extension is completely free of charge, but it's not officially supported by TIBCO. That being said, there are a lot of resources out there and lots of people are willing to help. JSViz, like any other extension, must be deployed to your Spotfire server and downloaded into your Spotfire client before it can be used. JSViz does work on Spotfire web (and in most cases, mobile) clients, but it does not work with TIBCO Spotfire Cloud.

JSViz comes with a full set of tutorials, a user manual, and some great examples—a donut chart, a Sankey chart, some Google gauges, and much more:

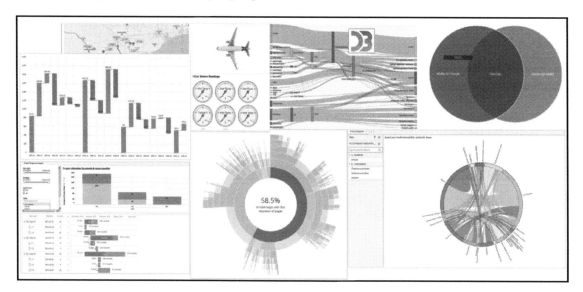

In order to get the best out of the JSViz extension, you'll need some experience of developing with JavaScript. Alternatively, you could develop a simple visualization in order to help you learn JavaScript—it's what I did!

I find that d3js is the JavaScript visualization framework that's best-suited for use within Spotfire—it's totally extensible and customizable—the only limits are your imagination and JavaScript skills.

 It's important to remember that d3js is a visualization framework. There are lots of examples on the d3js website, but d3js is not a suite of prebuilt visualizations. For pre-built visualizations, you could use HighCharts or similar. The disadvantage of a visualization library, such as HighCharts, is that these libraries are not as flexible or as extensible as d3js.

The way I recommend that you develop a JavaScript visualization is to follow these steps:

1. Search `https://d3js.org/` for an existing example that matches your needs as closely as possible
2. Refer to an existing example JSViz—I recommend the donut chart example—in order to see how a JSViz visualization is developed
3. Get the d3js example displaying inside JSViz without connecting it to Spotfire data—most d3js examples have a set of minimal data supplied with them that demonstrates the concepts
4. Set up the visualization to use Spotfire data—this is a matter of setting up any data tables as input to the visualization and then translating the **JSON (JavaScript Object Notation)** that JSViz supplies into the same format the example visualization expects
5. Tweak or adjust the visualization to meet your needs
6. Implement any additional functionality, such as marking, so that you can mark data in the JavaScript visualization and use the result of any marking operation in the rest of Spotfire

 Visualizationst hat are developed in JSViz support limiting data by filtering or marking (if you set them up correctly). However, by default, they do not support sending marked rows back to Spotfire. If you want to mark data in the JavaScript visualization, you will need to implement this yourself. It's normally the last thing I do, as not all visualizations need to support marking.

Most JavaScript visualizations produce **Scalable Vector Graphics** (**SVG**) objects—these are rendered directly by Spotfire's web browser. In order to implement marking, you'll need to compute the intersections between the marking rectangle that the user draws (by clicking and dragging the mouse) and the SVG objects that are produced by your visualization. The row identifiers of any SVG objects that intersect are sent back to Spotfire, which then marks the data.

 The developer tools are of particular help when developing JavaScript visualizations. The developer tools are detailed in `Chapter 11`, *Scripting, Advanced Analytics, and Extensions*.

Finally, it's also possible to create a configured JSViz extension. If your organization uses a particular JavaScript visualization a lot, then you can develop an extension that packages that visualization so that Spotfire analysts can just include it in their analysis.

Alerting in Spotfire

TIBCO has released an alerting extension for Spotfire—this tool provides conditional alerting on any data. It will send alerts by email or by triggering some custom **IronPython** code (for example, to send an SMS message or call a web service) if preconfigured conditions occur in your data.

The tool has a number of rule types. The one that's used most often is a simple threshold rule, which is configured from an existing visualization. It also supports the IronPython or Spotfire data function (TERR, R, Python, and so on) rules.

When an alert has been configured, end users of the analysis file can subscribe or unsubscribe to/from the alert. The subscription tool is available for Spotfire Analyst and Spotfire web clients.

 You can find out more about the alerting extension here:
`https://community.tibco.com/wiki/spotfire-alerting-extension`
Alternatively, it can be found here:
`http://bit.ly/2IoFTKo`

The alerting extension does not work with TIBCO Cloud Spotfire.

The extension is available at an additional cost—the community page details how to get in touch with someone at TIBCO who can provide more information.

TIBCO Data Virtualization

I already mentioned **TIBCO Data Virtualization** in Chapter 7, *Source Data is Never Enough*. It's an extremely useful tool for using with Spotfire—if you need to perform involved manipulation of data or work with slow data sources, if Spotfire doesn't support your underlying data source, or if you need to separate your Analytics data model from your underlying transactional data, then TIBCO Data Virtualization is a great choice!

Data Virtualization doesn't create a copy of the data. It exposes a virtual database to clients, such as Spotfire. Clients can then query the virtual data model and take advantage of Data Virtualization's intelligent querying, joining, and caching algorithms.

Spotfire has a native Data Virtualization connector.

You can find out more about TIBCO Data Virtualization at this link:
https://www.tibco.com/products/data-virtualization
Alternatively, you can find out more here:
http://bit.ly/2VRpmC8

TIBCO Data Science

TIBCO Data Science capabilities have grown enormously recently. Spotfire has always supported advanced data science through its ability to call out to TERR, R, Matlab, or SAS, but now TIBCO has **Statistica** and its own **Data Science Team Studio** products.

TIBCO Data Science is a unified platform that combines the capabilities of Statistica, Team Studio (formerly Alpine Data), Spotfire Statistics Services, and TERR.

Team Studio, formerly known as Spotfire Data Science (and Alpine Data Labs), is a collaborative web-based user interface that allows data scientists and citizen data scientists to create machine learning and data preparation pipelines. You can use the drag-and-drop interface and/or seamlessly integrate code via a Jupyter notebook node. You can also use Slack-like collaboration features to accelerate data science projects. Team Studio is particularly targeted toward in-database analysis. Its algorithms are optimized to push computations into any analytical source. When you execute data preparation and machine learning pipelines, the system's distributed execution engine can send computations to Apache Hadoop, Apache Spark, or databases. This capability allows you to run algorithms at scale without moving the data or optimizing algorithms based on database logic.

Statistica provides a rich desktop-based user interface that allows you to create sophisticated advanced analytic workflows using 16,000 functions. You can also seamlessly integrate Python, R, and other nodes within the pipelines. If you recall from `Chapter 11`, *Scripting, Advanced Analytics, and Extensions*, you can call Statistica workflows from Spotfire and show any results in your analysis.

Spotfire Statistics Services is a server environment for running statistical functions—it can call out to TERR, open-source R, Matlab, and SAS. It's primarily designed for use with Spotfire.

TIBCO Enterprise Runtime for R (TERR) is a high-performance, enterprise-quality statistical engine for providing statistical modeling and predictive analytic capabilities. It was covered in `Chapters 9`, *What's Your Location?*, and `Chapter 11`, *Scripting, Advanced Analytics, and Extensions*.

You can learn more about the TIBCO Data Science platform here:
`https://www.tibco.com/products/data-science`
Alternatively, you can click here:
`http://bit.ly/2ZesmKN`

KNIME and Spotfire

A lot of Spotfire customers use a combination of **Konstanz Information Miner (KNIME)** and Spotfire to do their advanced data analysis. There is more information available on KNIME here:

`https://www.knime.com/`

KNIME is a workflow tool for data science. It is free, open source software, but the server edition is paid for. KNIME and Spotfire are nicely integrated—you can call a KNIME workflow as a data function using a Spotfire extension that you can purchase from **EPAM** (a TIBCO partner). TIBCO also provides (via a KNIME update site) Spotfire-specific nodes for KNIME that read and write SBDF files or read data from Spotfire information links.

For more information on the integration between Spotfire and KNIME, please click on this link:
`https://community.tibco.com/wiki/knime`
Alternatively, you can click here:
`http://bit.ly/2v4UAtz`

TIBCO StreamBase and Spotfire Data Streams

We have already covered **Spotfire Data Streams** in Chapter 10, *Information Links and Data Connectors*. Spotfire Data Streams and StreamBase are essentially the same product. Spotfire Data Streams is specifically targeted for use with Spotfire for showing streaming (live) data in Spotfire. The combination of StreamBase and TERR is particularly powerful—since TERR is designed for low-latency and high-performance model scoring, in many cases, a TERR model can be executed on every data tuple flowing through a StreamBase workflow. That model could score transactions flowing through financial systems to evaluate the risk of fraud, or it could react to equipment sensor readings to predict the likelihood of imminent failure of the equipment. There are many other use cases, but they are too numerous to mention here!

Spotfire and Data Streams work really well together. Think of the sequence of analyzing your data and then building an operational model that you continuously monitor and refine over time:

1. Read your data into Spotfire.
2. Use Spotfire Analytics to determine *what* is happening.
3. Use Spotfire's visualizations, details visualizations, filtering, marking, and so on, to figure out *why* something is happening.
4. Build or refine an existing model in TERR to model the behavior (here, a data scientist may be useful!).
5. Use the model in StreamBase to score operational data.
6. Use Spotfire to monitor the results of the model—how accurate is it at predicting the future?
7. Use Spotfire to send modeling parameters to StreamBase to adjust the model.
8. Repeat the preceding steps to iteratively refine your process over time and get better results!

Iteratively understanding your data and processes, and monitoring and refining your model is the key to success in any real-world data-streaming application with statistical modeling. The more you learn and the better your model, the more value you'll get from it!

You can read more about StreamBase here:
https://www.tibco.com/products/tibco-streambase
Alternatively, you can click here:
http://bit.ly/2VPk4qK

TIBCO Spotfire Cloud Enterprise

During this book, I have referred to the Spotfire server. In a lot of cases, the Spotfire server will be installed on-premises, that is, as part of your own enterprise's internal IT infrastructure. TIBCO Cloud Spotfire is a multi-tenant **Software as Service (SaaS)** offering. TIBCO Spotfire Cloud Enterprise is a private **Platform as a Service (PaaS)** offering. It just happens to be managed by TIBCO and hosted on a cloud provider.

If you are using TIBCO Spotfire Cloud Enterprise, then none of the security-based limitations of TIBCO Cloud Spotfire apply. For example, extensions can be deployed to a Cloud Enterprise server, and you can run IronPython scripts on web player instances.

You can read more here:
https://community.tibco.com/wiki/tibco-spotfire-cloud-enterprise
Alternatively, you can click here:
http://bit.ly/2Iku2gD

Summary

This chapter has covered (in brief) some additional concepts. We looked at searching, styling, exporting, JavaScript visualizations, and alerting. Then, we moved on to cover some additional software products that are useful with Spotfire. Finally, we discussed TIBCO Cloud Enterprise.

Now that you've read this book, I hope you've been inspired to try Spotfire if you've not already got your hands on it. If you're a seasoned user, then I hope you've learned a lot as you've delved into these chapters in detail. I can certainly say that I have learned a huge amount about Spotfire while I was writing this book, despite my 10 or so years of experience with it! Spotfire is such a broad and deep product that it just begs to be explored further all the time.

I wish you luck on your analytical journey. Post questions on the TIBCO Community or look me up via LinkedIn if you get stuck with any of the examples, or if you want to know more!

Other Books You May Enjoy

If you enjoyed this book, you may be interested in these other books by Packt:

Big Data Analytics with Hadoop 3
Sridhar Alla

ISBN: 978-1-78862-884-6

- Explore the new features of Hadoop 3 along with HDFS, YARN, and MapReduce
- Get well-versed with the analytical capabilities of Hadoop ecosystem using practical examples
- Integrate Hadoop with R and Python for more efficient big data processing
- Learn to use Hadoop with Apache Spark and Apache Flink for real-time data analytics
- Set up a Hadoop cluster on AWS cloud
- Perform big data analytics on AWS using Elastic Map Reduce

Cloud Analytics with Google Cloud Platform
Sanket Thodge

ISBN: 978-1-78883-968-6

- Explore the basics of cloud analytics and the major cloud solutions
- Learn how organizations are using cloud analytics to improve the ROI
- Explore the design considerations while adopting cloud services
- Work with the ingestion and storage tools of GCP such as Cloud Pub/Sub
- Process your data with tools such as Cloud Dataproc, BigQuery, etc
- Over 70 GCP tools to build an analytics engine for cloud analytics
- Implement machine learning and other AI techniques on GCP

Leave a review - let other readers know what you think

Please share your thoughts on this book with others by leaving a review on the site that you bought it from. If you purchased the book from Amazon, please leave us an honest review on this book's Amazon page. This is vital so that other potential readers can see and use your unbiased opinion to make purchasing decisions, we can understand what our customers think about our products, and our authors can see your feedback on the title that they have worked with Packt to create. It will only take a few minutes of your time, but is valuable to other potential customers, our authors, and Packt. Thank you!

Index

Made in the USA
San Bernardino, CA
29 May 2019